The Verdun Regiment – Into the Furnace

Verdun! It is above all a battle of infantry. Dug in, under fire, asphyxiated. It's also a battle of devoted anonymous men, the sacrificed who have no story, but who've stopped cannons with their chests. The slow and relentless fight, distressingly bleak, in the mud, among the shell holes, through blankets of poison gas. That is what we had to endure on the right and left banks of the Meuse.

> Sergeant André L'Huilllier, 151st Infantry Regiment

The Verdun Regiment – Into the Furnace

The 151st Infantry Regiment in the Battle of Verdun 1916

Johnathan Bracken

Pen & Sword
MILITARY

First published in Great Britain in 2018 by
Pen & Sword Military
an imprint of
Pen & Sword Books Ltd
47 Church Street
Barnsley
South Yorkshire
S70 2AS

Copyright (c) Johnathan Bracken 2018

ISBN 978 1 52671 029 1

The right of Johnathan Bracken to be identified as Author of this Work has been asserted by him in accordance with the Copyright, Designs and Patents Act 1988.

A CIP catalogue record for this book is
available from the British Library

All rights reserved. No part of this book may be reproduced or transmitted in any form or by any means, electronic or mechanical including photocopying, recording or by any information storage and retrieval system, without permission from the Publisher in writing.

Typeset in INDIA by Geniies IT & Services Private Limited.

Printed and bound in Great Britain by TJ International Ltd, Padstow, Cornwall

Pen & Sword Books Ltd incorporates the imprints of Pen & Sword Archaeology, Atlas, Aviation, Battleground, Discovery, Family History, History, Maritime, Military, Naval, Politics, Railways, Select, Social History, Transport, True Crime, and Claymore Press, Frontline Books, Leo Cooper, Praetorian Press, Remember When, Seaforth Publishing and Wharncliffe.

For a complete list of Pen & Sword titles please contact
PEN & SWORD BOOKS LIMITED
47 Church Street, Barnsley, South Yorkshire, S70 2AS, England
E-mail: enquiries@pen-and-sword.co.uk
Website: www.pen-and-sword.co.uk

Contents

List of Abbreviations — vii
Maps — viii
Preface — xvii
Timeline of Engagements of the 151st Infantry Regiment — xxi
Introduction — xxii

Chapter 1	To Arms	1
Chapter 2	1914: To the Hilt	8
Chapter 3	The 'D' System: French Trench Networks	27
Chapter 4	1915: The Killing Year	34
Chapter 5	Opening Operations at Verdun	76
Chapter 6	Into the Furnace	81
Chapter 7	Shellography	116
Chapter 8	A Life of Battle	122
Chapter 9	The Infernal Machine	164
Chapter 10	Closing Operations at Verdun (May–December 1916)	196
Chapter 11	From the Somme to the Armistice: 1916–18	201
Conclusion	What Men Call Victory	232
Appendix I	Orders of Battle	241
Appendix II	Organization of the 151st Infantry Regiment	242
Notes		243
Select Bibliography		260
Index		263

*Dedicated to the memory of all those
who fought and suffered in the Great War*

List of Abbreviations

AC	Army Corps
Co.	Company
MG Co.	Machine-Gun Company
FAR	Field Artillery Regiment
IB	Infantry Brigade
ID	Infantry Division
IR	Infantry Regiment
LIB	Light Infantry Battalion

Maps

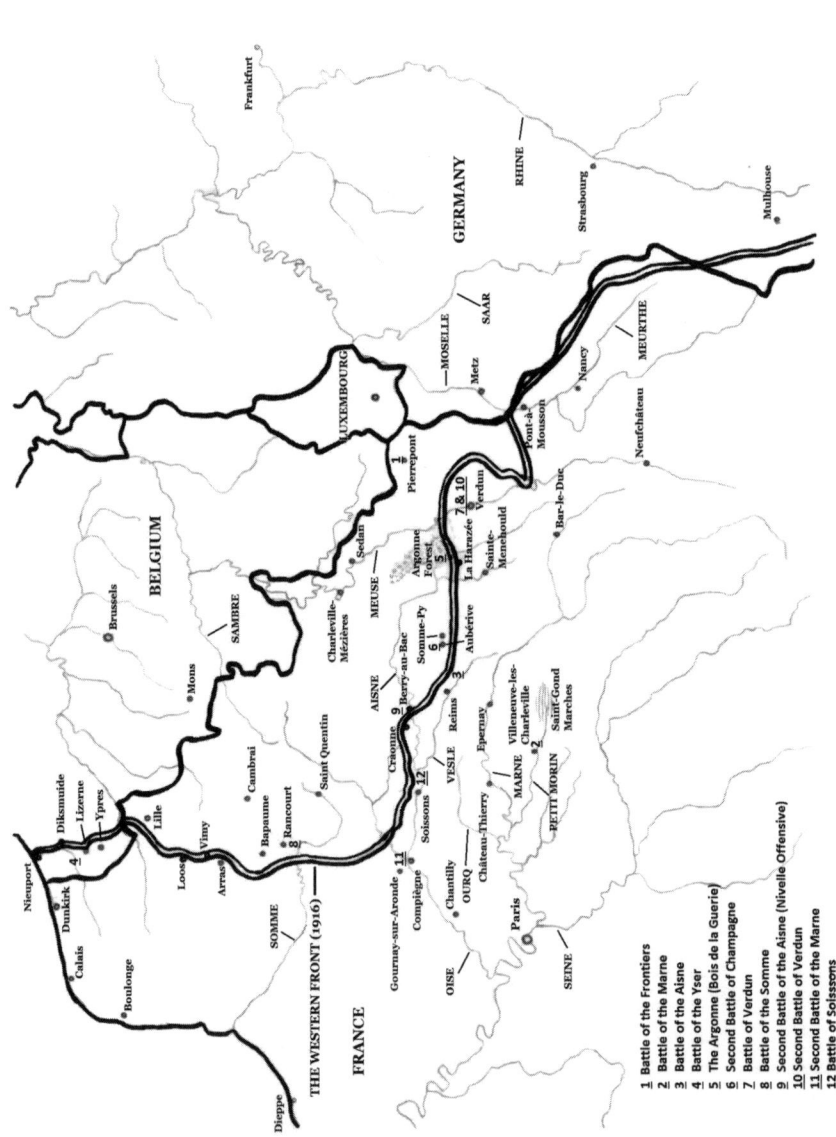

Map 1: The Western Front, 1916. Numeral place-markers indicate the major battles in which the 151 IR was engaged between 1914 and 1918.

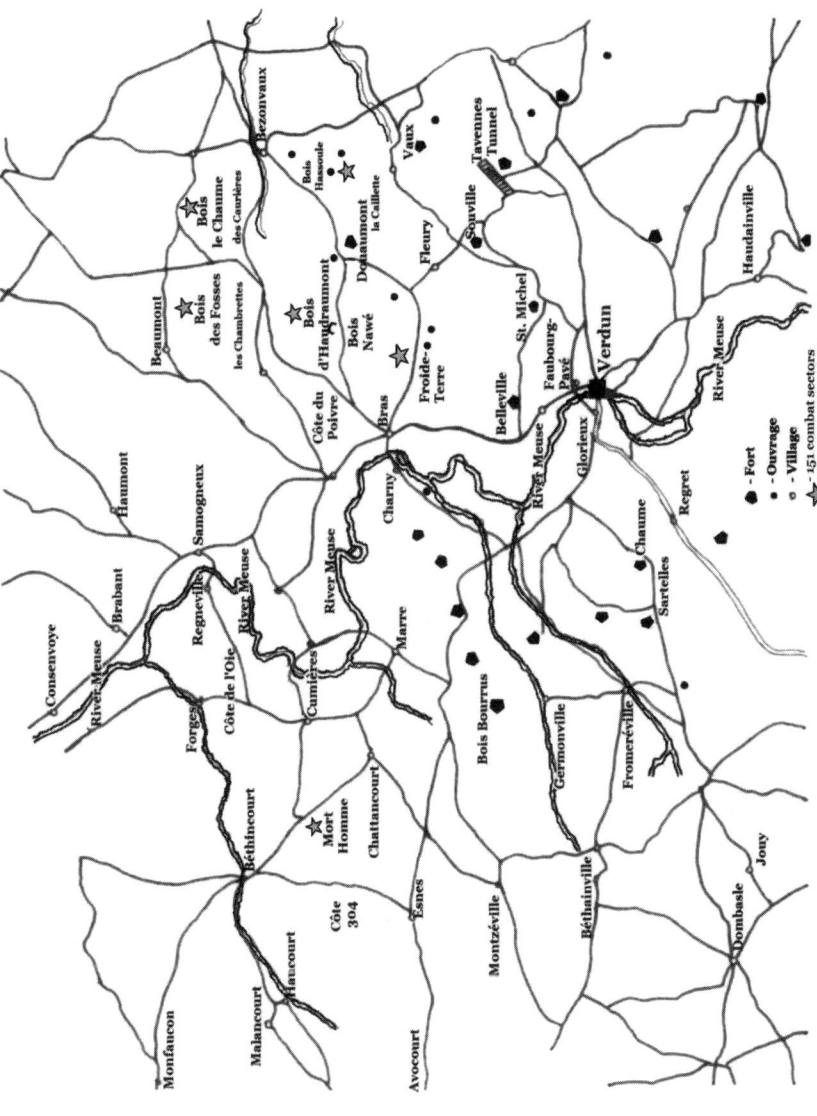

Map 2: The Verdun Fortified Region, 1916. Stars indicate the combat sectors of the 151 IR both in the Battle of Verdun in 1916 and the Second Battle of Verdun in 1917.

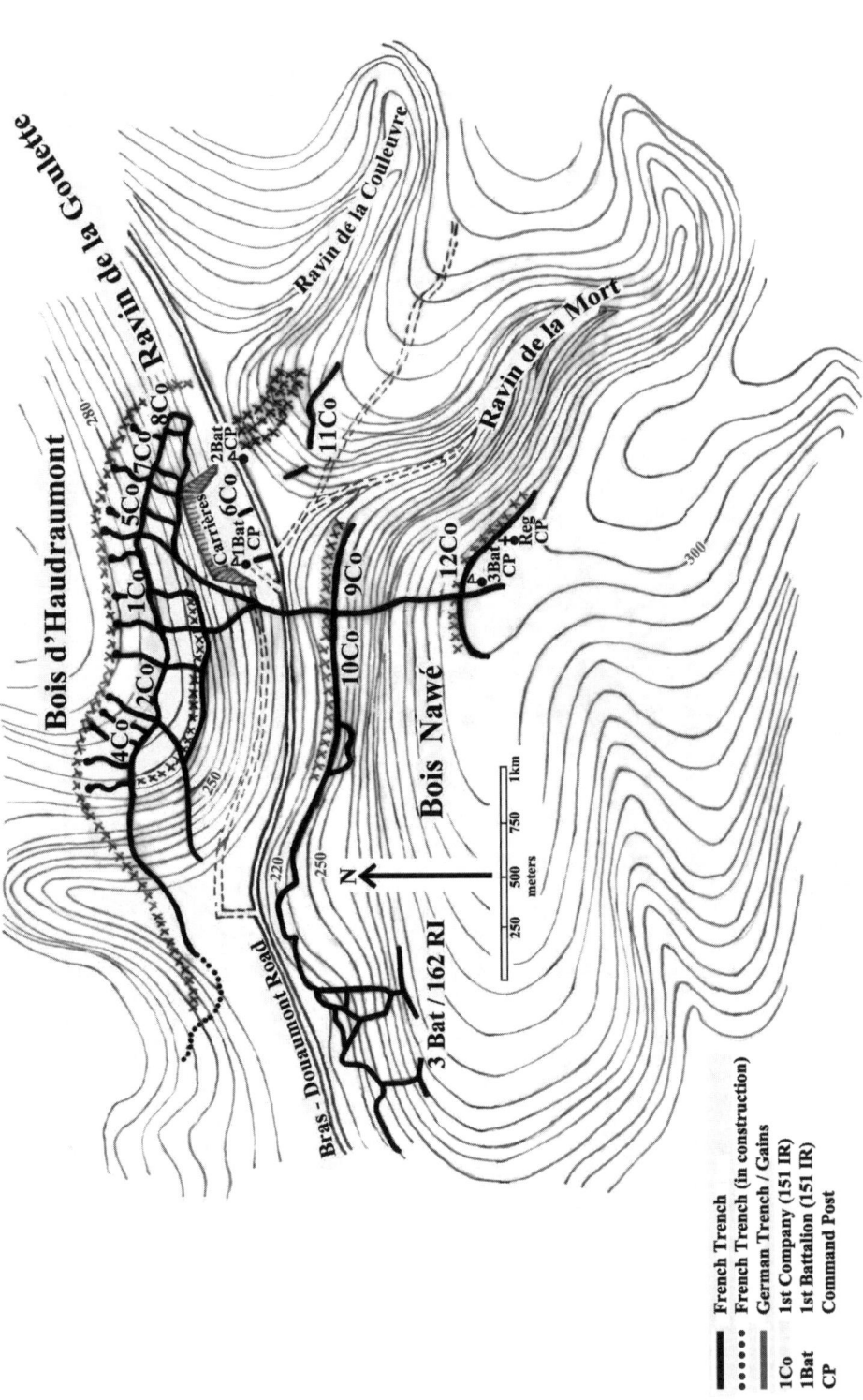

Map 3: Bois d'Haudraumont sector, end of March 1916. The entrenchments that the 151 IR completed during its three-week rotation in the sector are shown. (1:5,000 scale)

Maps xi

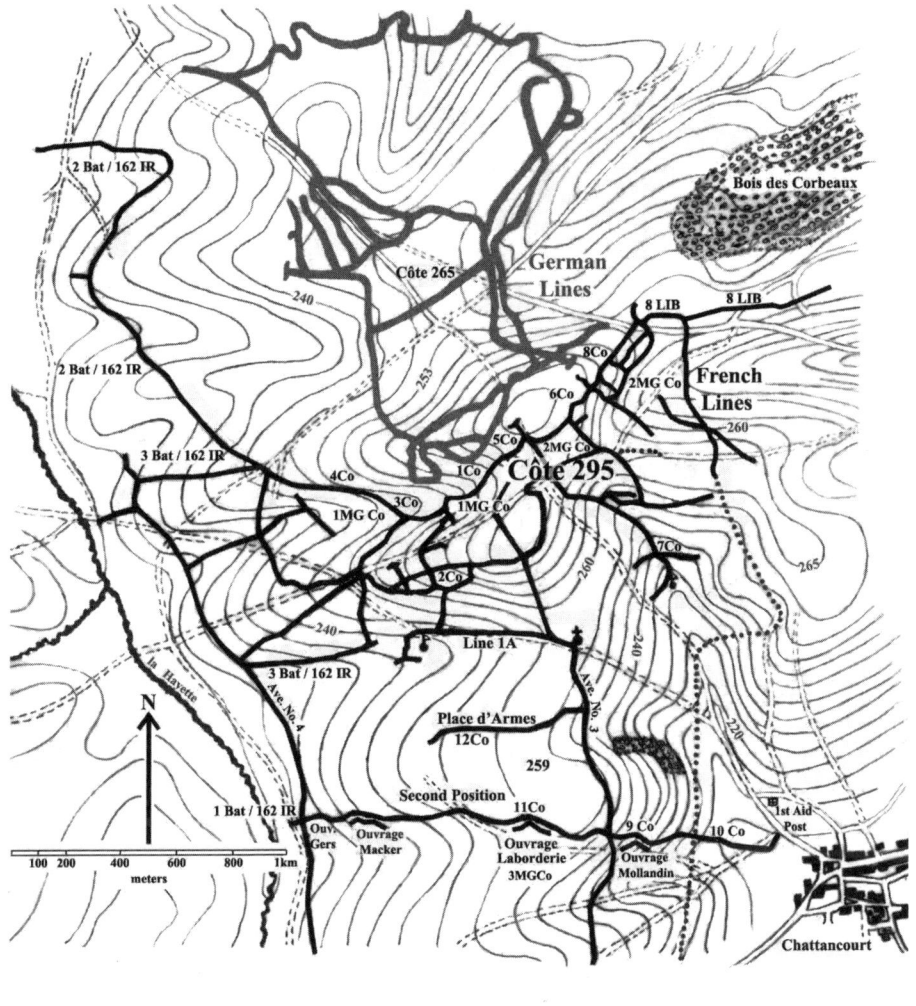

▬▬▬	French Trench
••••••	French Trench (in construction)
▬▬▬	German Trench / Gains
1Co	1st Company (151 IR)
1Bat	1st Battalion (151 IR)
CP	Command Post

Map 4: Mort Homme sector, showing the situation on the morning of 9 April 1916. The 1 Battalion is in line on the left, 2 Battalion in line on the right, and 3 Battalion in support. (1:10,000 scale)

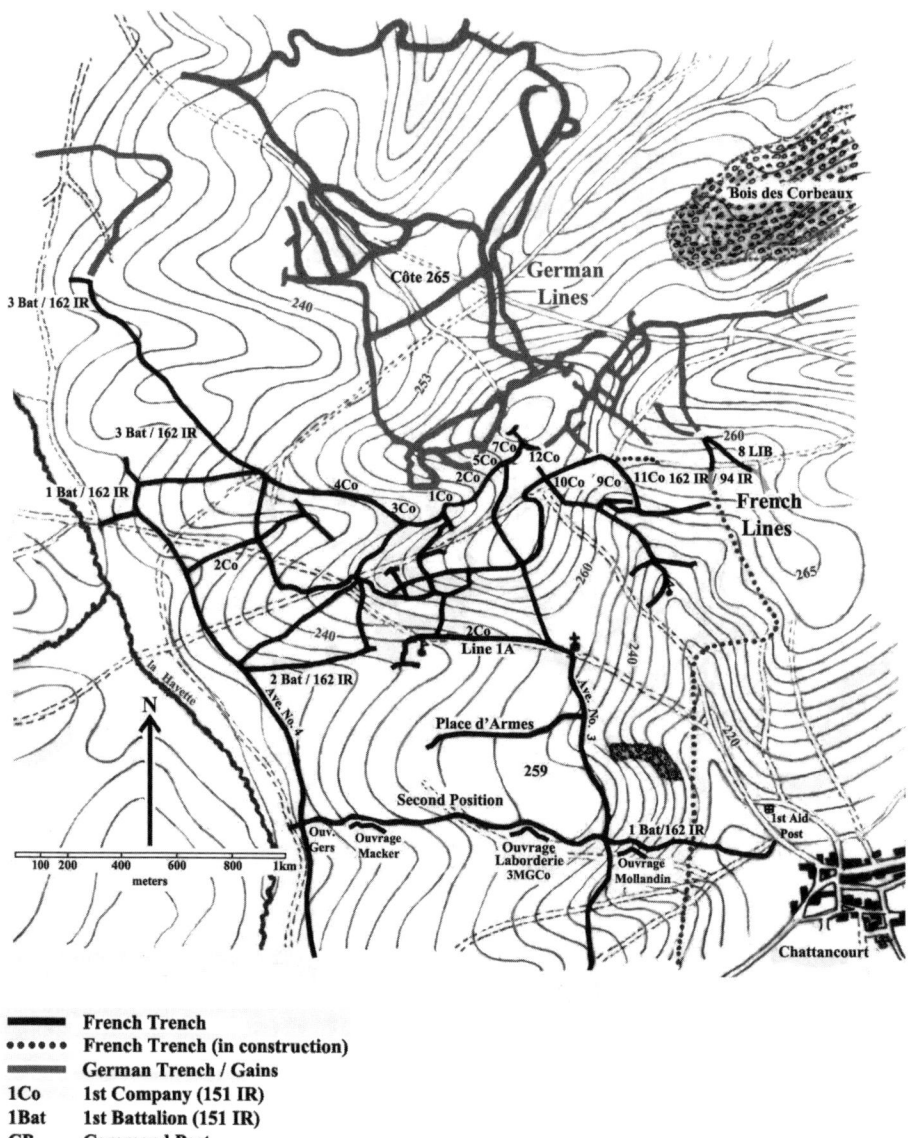

- ▬▬ **French Trench**
- ••••• **French Trench (in construction)**
- ▬▬ **German Trench / Gains**
- 1Co   **1st Company (151 IR)**
- 1Bat   **1st Battalion (151 IR)**
- CP   **Command Post**

Map 5: Mort Homme sector, showing the situation on the evening of 9 April 1916, showing German gains made by the end of day. The 1 Battalion remains in line on the left while 3 Battalion has counter-attacked on the right to plug the gaps opened by the decimation of 2 Battalion. (1:10,000 scale)

Maps xiii

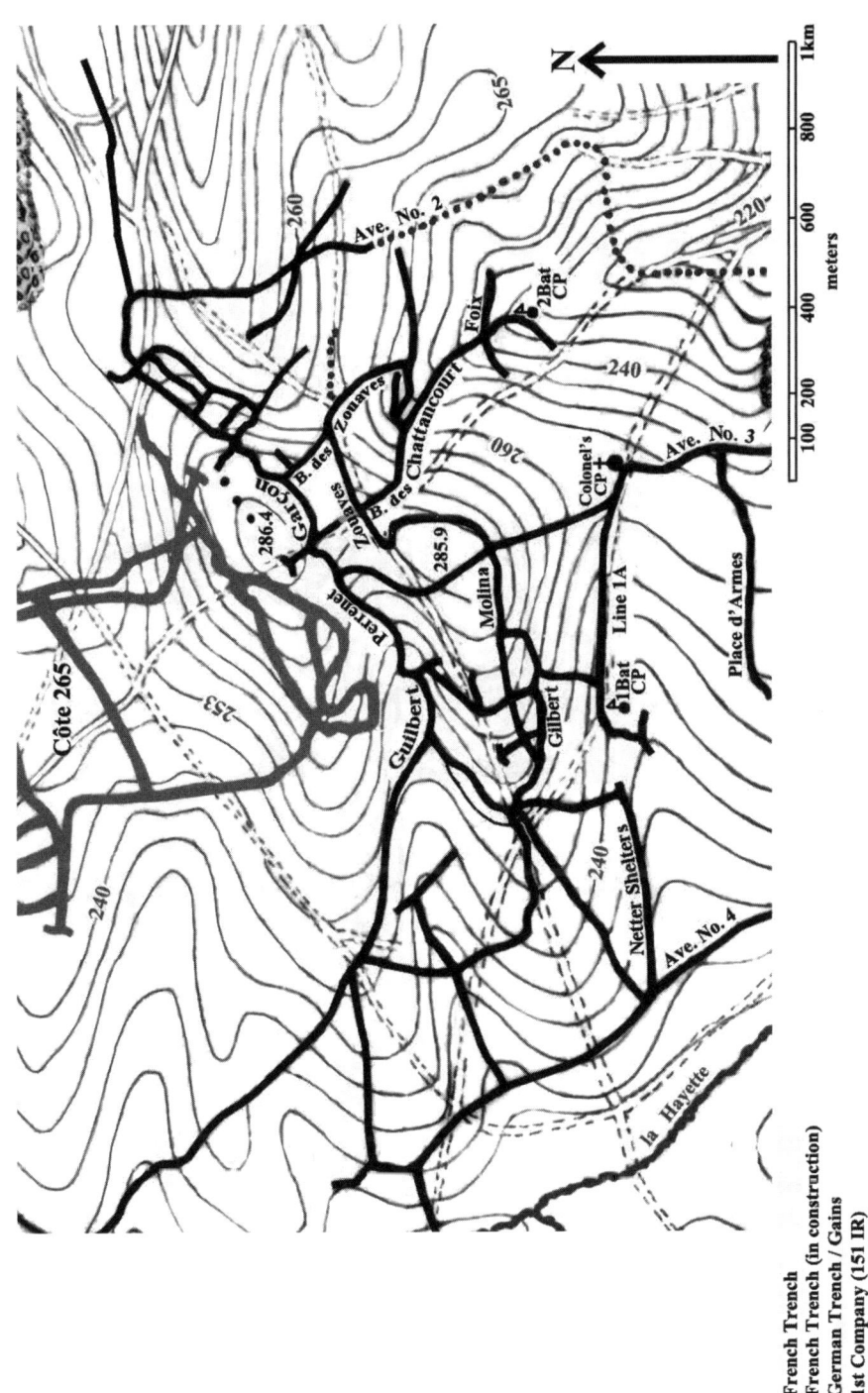

Map 6: Summit of Mort Homme, showing the entrenchments on 9 April 1916. (1:10,000 scale)

Map 7: Mort Homme sector, showing the situation on the morning of 20 May 1916. The 1 Battalion is in line on the right, 3 Battalion is in support, and 2 Battalion is at rest at Jouy-en-Argonne. (1:10,000 scale)

Maps   xv

■■■■■   French Trench
•••••   French Trench (in construction)
▬▬▬▬▬   German Trench / Gains
1Co   1st Company (151 IR)
1Bat   1st Battalion (151 IR)
CP   Command Post

Map 8: Mort Homme sector, showing the situation on the evening of 20 May 1916, showing German gains made by the end of day. With the annihilation of 1 Battalion, the 3 Battalion is deployed in line and in support. The 2 Battalion will go into line on the night of 20–1 May to relieve 3 Battalion. Elements from multiple regiments have also been pushed up to reinforce the flagging French line. (1:10,000 scale)

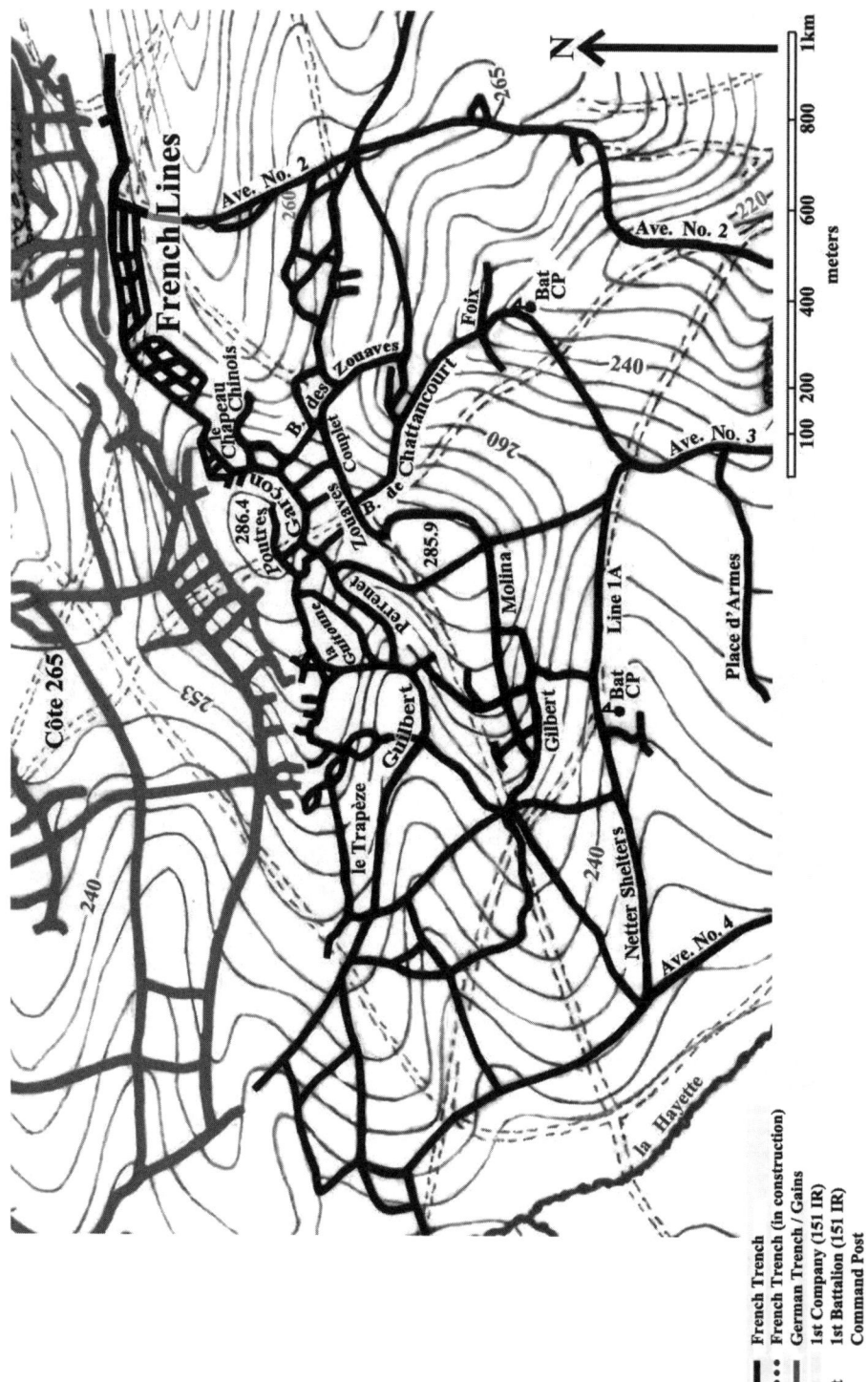

Map 9: Summit of Mort Homme, showing the entrenchments on 20 May 1916. (1:10,000 scale)

Preface

Despite holding the lion's share of the line, contributing the largest number of troops, and suffering higher losses than any other Allied nation on the Western Front, the story of the French army and the French soldier of the Great War continues to be little known to English-speaking audiences. Over 8.4 million Frenchmen were mobilized between 1914 and 1918, a figure that represents nearly half of the total male population. Over half would become casualties one way or another. By 1916, in seventeen months of fighting France lost roughly as many men killed as the United States has lost in all of its wars combined to date.

How is it that such sacrifice is not better remembered among anglophones? A good deal of this can be chalked up to the language barrier, as most of the body of literature on the subject remains in its native tongue. Anyone who wishes to delve deeper into the history of the French and their experience in the Great War must first surmount this obstacle. Perhaps the greater challenge though is the sheer scale. Like the other major powers, France mobilized millions of men between 1914 and 1918, and the size of these armies led to fighting that was unprecedented in its proportions. The immense scope of these events can be daunting to any person attempting to understand the human experience. What was it like to live through it, to be there on the ground, one of millions of regular people swept up in a phenomenon of breathtaking proportions?

In an effort to convey the French experience of the war, the approach here will be to focus on one of the defining battles, the Battle of Verdun in 1916, which came to symbolize the heroism, horror, and tragedy of the Great War. Verdun itself was vast in scale, involving hundreds of thousands of men fighting over dozens of square miles for nearly a year. It was truly a war within a war. To better assess and personalize this epic event, I will present a view of the battle from the perspective of a handful of soldiers who served together in the same army unit – the 151e Régiment d'Infanterie (or, the 151st Infantry Regiment). Fully three-quarters of the French army in 1916 was rotated into what the soldiers called 'the Furnace'. The 151 was one of hundreds of units sent to Verdun and, in many ways, its experience was no different to that of the many other units that fought and endured in this meat-grinder of a battle.

Yet the 151 – known colloquially as '*le Quinze-Un*', or the 'One-Fifty-One' – had a special connection to this place, which imbued it with greater meaning.

For the city of Verdun was its home garrison before the war. By extension, the 151 was the Verdun Regiment.[1] During the ten-month-long battle in 1916, the regiment was sent up to the fighting line three times. It was sent three times more in 1917 to capture ground the French had been unable to take back the year before. The suffering and privations the men of the 151 endured, the hardships they faced, and the sacrifices they made were not unique. What is unique, however, is the quantity and availability of first-hand accounts left by the participants. In conducting research for this book, I was able to amass the diaries and memoirs of six different individuals, all of whom were members of the regiment during its time at Verdun in 1916. Having so many eyewitnesses afforded a golden opportunity to both triangulate and corroborate accounts of the same people, places, and events. Importantly, they were written largely during the war, providing a contemporary view unadulterated by thoughts and feelings in the years after the war. Additionally, the body of testimonies comes from both officers and enlisted men, providing a rare glimpse into the lives of both those who gave orders and those who received them. Three of these accounts have been previously published: Second Lieutenant Roger Campana's memoirs, Second Lieutenant Raymond Jubert's autobiography, and Quartermaster Corporal Henri Laporte's diary. The other three remain unpublished in the holdings of the Service historique de la Défense at Vincennes: Second Lieutenant Roger Basteau's memoirs, Sergeant André L'Huillier's diaries, and Private Auguste Bordinat's memoirs.

I first encountered the memoirs of Campana and Jubert in the late Alistair Horne's *The Price of Glory: Verdun 1916* (New York: Penguin, 1991). Their vivid, moving accounts of the combat at Mort Homme helped to depict what Verdun was really like for those who did the fighting and dying. Horne's seminal work on the battle had a profound impact on my life. It was this book that catapulted me into the subject of the Great War and, more specifically, the life of the French poilu, the term used to refer to the average infantryman, the grunt. Literally it means 'hairy', in reference to his unshaven face. A better translation might be 'grizzled', as his rough appearance was a sign of the harsh realities of life at the front. Fashionable at the time, many men also sported long handlebar mustaches. In his shabby, mud-covered uniform, clad in a roughly cut sheepskin poncho for warmth, the poilu resembled more the ancient Gallic warrior than a modern soldier. And like Sampson from the Old Testament, this hair signified strength. The iconic images of these men and the compelling testimonies they left behind drew me to them and inflamed a passion to understand what they had seen and done.

Over the years, I have visited the Verdun battlefield on numerous occasions, walking the wooded hills and ravines, exploring the underground forts and forgotten dugouts, and sleeping in the innumerable shell holes that still pock that tortured landscape. Everywhere there remain the vestiges of the great battle:

crumbling concrete shelters, unexploded artillery shells and grenades, deteriorated rifle barrels, twisted barbed wire, perforated iron sheeting, rusted mess-kits and canteens. Lying everywhere on top of and just under the surface of the soil are rusting shell fragments by the millions. Most poignant of all, there are the human remains, bones, and fragments of bones I have routinely discovered there. Verdun remains a place of profound sadness. It hangs in the air like a heavy pall. Even today, the now forested slopes of Mort Homme hold a sense of foreboding. At night it is unsettlingly quiet, in stark contrast to the deafening noise that resounded there 100 years ago. Coming back from a trip there in October 2016, my touring companion remarked that he was struck by the tomb-like silence at Mort Homme. After wandering through the spooky pine forests, we noted that we'd not heard a single bird singing on the summit.

What follows is a humble attempt to capture the experience of a small group of poilus in the Battle of Verdun. The narrative will largely be driven by the testimonies of these men, so that they can tell their story using their own words. These will be used in combination with the official *Journal des Marches et Opérations* (*JMOs*) – the daily campaign journals of the 151st Infantry Regiment and the 42nd Infantry Division to which it was assigned – to provide context and to tell the larger story of the 151st Infantry Regiment. Following a brief background of the regiment and an introduction to the principal eyewitnesses, the actions of the regiment in the first two years of the war will be covered. As most of the principal eyewitnesses joined the regiment in 1915, justice will be done by exploring what they experienced before going to Verdun. The book will then delve into the role of the 151 at Verdun in 1916 and the parts these men played. Concluding chapters will cover the regiment's actions after Verdun and, ultimately, the impact the Furnace had on the lives of those who were thrown into it.

A few notes about the sources, phraseology, and translations appearing in the book. To a large extent, the chronology, place-names, statistics, and material details relating to events recounted in this book come from the aforementioned *JMOs*. It should be assumed that unless a different source is cited in the endnotes, the information comes from the *JMOs*. The other primary source materials are the regimental and the divisional records of the 151st Regiment and 42nd Division, which are held at the Service historique de la Défense de l'Armée de Terre at Vincennes. These are referred to in the book as the regimental records or reports and divisional records or reports. As is to be expected, dates and times cited in the eyewitness accounts sometimes differ from the *JMOs* and as far as possible, these have been reconciled.

Military units have been translated into the English equivalent. The designation between (active army) line infantry and reserve infantry has been dropped, much as the formal distinction itself had been by army commanders beginning in

1915. Therefore, the *151e Régiment d'Infanterie de Ligne* and the *351e Régiment d'Infanterie de Réserve* are expressed as 151st Infantry Regiment and 351st Infantry Regiment (151 IR and 351 IR), the *16e Battalion Chasseurs à Pied* is the 16th Light Infantry Battalion (16 LIB), etc. The same holds true for military ranks, though where no equivalent exists, the original French rank has been retained. Mainly, commandant (a rank typically conferring battalion leader), aspirant (an officer candidate), and adjudant (the highest grade of non-commissioned officer). When referring to specific place-names and geographic features such as a woods, hill, ravine or farm the original French has been left in place (e.g., Bois de la Gruerie, Côte 295, Ravin Sec, Ferme de Choléra). Similarly, certain French nomenclature for entrenchment features like *boyau(x)* ('communication trench(es)'), *parallels de départure* ('jumping-off trenches'), and *ouvrage* ('fortress') are left intact, particularly when referring to a named position (e.g., Tranchée Guilbert, Boyau de Chattancourt, Ouvrage Laborderie). Where there are variances in the spelling of place-names, I have selected the most common (e.g., Haudraumont rather than Haudromont or Haudremont). Unless otherwise specified, all translations are my own.

I would like to thank my commissioning editor at Pen & Sword, Rupert Harding, for all of his patient assistance and support in getting this book published. I am very appreciative of the Le Roy family for their generosity and friendship, especially Ellen Le Roy for providing a transcription of the memoirs of her great-grandfather, Charles Auguste Bordinat. My thanks to the cordial staff at Service historique de la Défense de l'Armée de Terre at Vincennes for the good work they do every day. I owe a debt of gratitude to my friends Andrew Yamato and Jenny Shyr for their wise counsel during this process, as well as Robert Healey, Jr for his help in cataloguing research information with me at Service historique de la Défense. Finally, I wish to thank my mother, Mary Jo, and my family for all their love and support during this project and over the many years.

Timeline of Engagements of the 151st Infantry Regiment

1914

22 August–5 September: Battle of the Frontiers
6–11 September: Battle of the Marne
12–30 September: Battle of the Aisne
23 October–11 November: Battle of the Yser

1915

17 January–17 July: The Argonne
25 September–8 October: Second Battle of Champagne

1916

10 March–24 May: Battle of Verdun
20 September–7 November: Battle of the Somme

1917

16 April–3 May: Nivelle Offensive
18 July–13 September: Second Battle of Verdun

1918

9 June–6 August: Second Battle of the Marne
28–31 August: Battle of Soissons

Introduction

Snow was falling heavily on the late-winter night of 9 March 1916 as the 151st Infantry Regiment trudged into the ancient fortress city of Verdun. The regiment had just completed the final leg of a gruelling forced march over deep-rutted roads made slippery by thick mud. Much of Verdun was now in ruins with a series of fires blazing away in the streets. Now and then, massive artillery shells fired from long-range German guns plummeted out of the dark sky and burst through the roofs and walls of the densely packed buildings and homes. A few miles to the north of Verdun along the heights of the River Meuse a mighty battle was raging. The sound of hundreds of cannon discharging and thousands of artillery shells detonating filled the air with a deep and incessant thundering, and illuminated the horizon with a continually flickering reddish glow.

As the exhausted men settled into their temporary billets in the town for a few hours of much-needed sleep, a call went out summoning all officers to the Hôtel de Ville. A grave sense of foreboding prevailed among the pensive gathering as their senior commander, General Deville, strode into the room appearing weary and agitated. Standing stiffly before them, he began tugging nervously on his greying goatee as he addressed the audience, his voice hoarse and cracking as he spoke:

> 'Gentlemen, Verdun is threatened. You are at Verdun and you are the Verdun Brigade. I won't hide the truth from you; we've been taken by surprise . . . I won't hide the mistakes from you; we must fix them . . . The situation was desperate; it's not yet stabilized. The sector that we're taking up? Chaos . . . The life which awaits us there? Battle . . . The trenches? They don't exist . . . No barbed-wire, no defensive entanglements, certainly no shelters . . . nothing . . . nothing! . . . Gentleman, don't ask me for supplies: I don't have any . . . Reinforcements: I don't have any to give you . . . Good luck, gentlemen!'[1]

And with that, General Deville abruptly departed the room leaving his audience in stunned silence. After conferring with Deville, Lieutenant Colonel Moisson, the commander of the 151, did not spare his words in addressing his subordinates.

'Your's is a mission of sacrifice. The post of honour is here, this is right where they intend to attack. You'll suffer losses every day, for they'll be harassing our positions. And on the day that they choose, they will wipe you out right down to the last man, and it is your duty to fall where you stand.'[2]

Their prospects were grim and the stakes couldn't be higher: quite literally the survival of France. Even before the Battle of Verdun eternalized itself as a symbol of French national identity, it already possessed an inherent and powerful meaning for the 151: Verdun was the regiment's hometown. For some this was not just figurative. At least twenty soldiers who had fought and died while serving in the 151 before this moment in time were born and raised in the city of Verdun itself, and still more were from the nearby villages of Belleville, Bethincourt, Forges, Esnes, Ornes, and others. This might have been a world war but for '*le Quinze-Un*', it was also a personal fight on home turf.

The 151st Infantry Regiment was first formed during the reign of Napoléon Bonaparte in the last great European conflict a century before. The *151e Régiment d'Infanterie de Ligne* was constituted on 2 January 1813. It would go on to distinguish itself in multiple battles and earned the first inscriptions on its regimental colours for its actions at the battles of Weissig and Wurschen in 1813. With the fall of Bonaparte and return of the Bourbon monarchy, the regiment was dissolved on 24 August 1814. The 151 would be re-formed during the Third Republic on 1 October 1887 and assigned to its first garrison at Belfort, where it remained for a decade. On 15 April 1898, the regiment would be relocated to the fortified city of Verdun in order to form, along with the 162nd Infantry Regiment, the 84th Brigade (the Verdun Brigade) of the 42nd Division. The 151 occupied the Miribel Barracks situated in Faubourg-Pavé. It was from these barracks that in the summer of 1914 the 151 would march off to a war unlike any other in the course of human history.[3]

By the time it marched back into Verdun on that cold night in March 1916, the 151 had already been through its share of horrible battles in some of the most violent sectors on the Western Front. The regiment received its baptism of fire in the Battle of the Frontiers in August 1914. After undergoing a series of gruelling forced marches during the Great Retreat, it participated in the Allied counter-attack at the Battle of the Marne and then the Battle of the Aisne in September. In October, the 151 was transferred to Belgium as part of the 'Race to the Sea' where it fought in multiple battles beside the North Sea and along the Yser Canal. With little time allocated for rest, in January 1915 the unit moved back to France where it engaged in six months of unrelenting combat in the Argonne Forest. Finally, it took part in the bloody check that was the Second Battle of Champagne that autumn. But the ordeal it was about to be sent into on the heights north of Verdun was quite unlike any the soldiers of the regiment had yet endured. As Private J. Ayon stated plainly: 'As soon as I saw the battlefield, even though I had already spent fourteen months at the front, I thought: if you haven't seen Verdun, you haven't seen anything of war.'[4] Over the course of March, April, and May 1916, the 151 would spend fifty days under fire in some of the most brutal combat in the history of war. The first rotation on the right bank of the Meuse in the Haudraumont sector dragged on for twenty days. After only a week of rest, the regiment was sent back to the Verdun front at the beginning of April. This time it was sent to the left bank to occupy the infamous Mort Homme ('Dead Man' hill), where it endured nine days under attack. Three weeks later, it returned to Mort Homme to suffer another twenty days. Not to be forgotten is that the 151 was sent back to Verdun three more times in 1917, for a total of six rotations and more than eleven weeks in the Furnace. The casualty figures were atrocious and the regiment only managed to remain combat effective (to use the modern parlance) in '16 and '17 through the arrival of replacements troops to fill the gaps in the ranks.

Casualty figures do not in and of themselves make Verdun the 'worst' battle of the war for either the French army as a whole, nor for the 151 in particular. In the case of the former, that dubious honour fell to the Battle of the Frontiers in August 1914, which resulted in the death or injury of 140,00 Frenchmen over 4 days, including 27,000 killed on 22 August alone.[5] The deadliest battle for the 151 was the Second Battle of Champagne, when 1,400 men fell between the 25 and 27 September 1915. Yet the toll of destruction cannot simply be measured in the numbers of killed and maimed. For Verdun destroyed men spiritually too. Those who survived those weeks in hell were forever changed by the experience. Certain conditions were unique to Verdun. The length and intensity of the artillery barrages, together with the sheer explosive power of the types of shells used, utterly destroyed the landscape along with the French positions. Trenches were flattened, concrete shelters pulverized, forests annihilated, entire villages wiped off the face of the planet. For miles on end, the surface of the earth was turned into the surface of the moon, where double and triple craters were the result of a land turned upside down. Verdun became infamous for its lack of trenches, of shelters, of military material, and organizational support. Strictly speaking, this was not always true. For certain periods and at certain places, entrenchments did exist, which were supported by the rings of underground forts that continued to function despite the exterior pounding inflicted by bombardments. Yet the sense of abandonment among the French soldiers was perhaps at no other place so keenly felt. Many expressed openly that they believed they'd been condemned to death when they were sent to Verdun. Sergeant Paul Dubrulle spoke for countless combatants of Verdun when he exclaimed: 'We are lost! They have thrown us into the furnace, without rations, almost without ammunition. We were the last resources; they have sacrificed us . . .'.⁶ The renowned historian Ian Ousby wrote in his work *Road to Verdun*:

> Nowhere, even in the First World War, did infantrymen feel so helplessly, so infuriatingly remote from the gunners supporting them. Nowhere, perhaps, did infantrymen feel so complete a sense of isolation as they did at Verdun. They felt, quite simply, the solitude of men who occupied positions of acute discomfort and danger, for hour after hour and for day after day, with only (in Maurice Genevoix's phrase) *mort de près*: death close at hand.⁷

When the great French novelist Jules Romains wrote his novel *Verdun* (the sixteenth installment of the multi-volume series *Men of Good Will*), he largely based his fictional telling of the battle on the memoirs of an officer from the 151, Second Lieutenant Roger Campana. In Romains' novel a fictitious officer of the regiment, after surviving the first rotation at Haudraumont, reflected on the true impact of his experience.

> These last nineteen days at Verdun have stunned me like a knock-out blow. Looking back on it all, I'm inclined to think that until then I might have managed to come through unscathed, and that's saying a good deal! . . . But now something's been broken that can never be replaced . . . I feel it in my bones . . . I confess that if you asked me, I should be hard put to it to say why. Except for the three days I have just told you of, I saw nothing and endured nothing that I hadn't already more or less seen and endured. I'm not sure I haven't even been through worse times. Of course, we were longer in the line than usual. But, all that aside, it's no use trying to find logical explanations of what one feels living that kind of subhuman existence . . . trying to reduce things to their proper proportion.
>
> What was it that so particularly demoralized me during that period? Not just going three days without food. No, I think it was the general condition of the sector we had been given to hold, the awful look of those scratches in the ground which they had the nerve to call trenches . . . the sordidness of everything, the absence of all organization, of all thought for the future; and the hasty digging we had to put in, under shell-fire, to some sort of reality into the second- and third-line positions which those slackers of the Fortified Zone had had six months, a year, to get ready, and with the added terror of bombardment – digging, that came on top of everything else, the exhausting job of mounting sentry, constant alarms, working parties . . .

> You've no idea how one comes to value, to rely on the organized routine, the human element, in a sector, especially when one has got used to it over a long period, when one has got into the way, each time one goes up to the line, of finding the little habits, the trivial round of duties, which one had left behind at the end of one's last tour . . . The place can at least be lived in, even if the sky is raining shells. But that valley of Haudraumont was hideous; no man could have lived there . . .[8]

The 151's service did not end at Verdun in 1916. It would go on to fight in the great Franco-British attack on the Somme in the autumn. In 1917 it would be thrown into the spring offensive, before being called upon to fight at Verdun again in the late summer. After a severely trying period, it would end the year training units of the newly arrived but inexperienced American army. With the return to open warfare in the spring of 1918, a new phase of near constant combat began which would only end with the Armistice in November. But more than any other battle, Verdun came to symbolize and define the tenacity and fortitude of the French soldier of the Great War, his courage, his devotion, his ability to endure in the face of hardship and horror. Who were these very ordinary people who seemed to perform near-superhuman efforts?

Chapter 1

To Arms

Background of the Regiment

The regiment that marched off to war in August 1914 reflected the pre-war composition of the unit, with the men originating from the areas from which it had traditionally drawn its recruits.[1] Roughly a quarter came from the departments of Meuse and Meurthe-et-Moselle in Lorraine and another quarter from le Nord and Pas de Calais in Northern France. Other large portions of troops came from the departments of la Somme and Aisne in Picardy, along with the 18th, 19th, and 20th Arrondissements of Paris. While conscription for new recruits continued to be done locally, war-time changes in how these men were distributed as replacements led to shifts in the geographical origins of the troop body. The process of *brassage* ultimately had a diversifying effect within formations.[2] Indeed, because of its high level of combat activity, this process was accelerated within the 151.

The shift began in the spring and summer of 1915 with the arrival of the first strong contingents of Southerners, Bretons, and men from Champagne. As the numbers of men recruited from Lorraine fell, the numbers of those coming from other regions conversely rose. When seen from the perspective of the war as a whole, around 70 per cent of the regiment was composed of men from the northern and eastern regions of France: Brittany, Normandy, Picardy, Île de France, Champagne, Ardennes, and Lorraine. Even within these regions there were concentrations. For example, 17 per cent hailed from the Departments of le Nord and Pas de Calais, with an equal percentage from the Departments of Finstère, Morbihan and Côtes-du-Nord. This in turn meant that 40 per cent of the regiment's ranks were made up of men whose home departments were either occupied by the enemy or on the front lines. Other regions were also well represented, with 17 per cent originating from the various departments in Southern France (i.e., Provence, Occitane, Auvergne, Rhône-Alpes, Aquitaine) and almost 10 per cent from the city of Paris. By the end of the war, every department of France was represented in the ranks to one degree or another, with particularly strong contingents from southern regions and from Brittany. There was even a handful of foreign-born soldiers from Algeria, Martinique, Belgium, Italy, Mexico, Poland, Russia, and Switzerland.[3]

Wherever these men originally hailed from, most were not professional soldiers in the true sense of the word but citizen-soldiers in the spirit of revolutionary

Jean-Jacques Rousseau.⁴ Before being drafted, the majority were peasants who worked in agriculture and husbandry: farmers, ploughmen, cowmen, shepherds, stable boys, and the like. Another solid block were factory and transport workers. The rest were shopkeepers, office clerks, civil servants, and various liberal professionals, and also students or professors. They varied in age, from as young as 18 to as old as their late 40s, though most were between their mid-20s and mid-30s.⁵ This cross section of French society was reflected in the ranks of the 151.

The Principal Eyewitnesses

Even as his men shot down the German troops rushing headlong towards their position, Raymond Jubert couldn't help but admire the courage of his enemy. And in truth, it seemed that his deep sense of compassion extended even to those on the other side as he watched their massacre unfold. Raymond Armand Alexis Jubert was born to Ernest and Nathalie in Charleville (a district of Mézières in the Ardennes Department) on 5 November 1889. The blonde-haired, blue-eyed Raymond came from a long line of industrialists who had been based in the Issoudin region since the seventeenth century. He also had a younger brother, Maurice, six years his junior. Jubert received a thorough Catholic education at the Institution de Saint-Rémy in Charleville. As was common for the French living in the regions bordering Germany, his education and upbringing was infused with underlying principles of patriotism and nationalism. From an early age, Jubert demonstrated exceptional literary and writing abilities. A poem composed by Jubert at the age of 14 entitled 'Salus, Patriae, suprema Lex' illustrates the young writer's influences:

> I hear the voice that controls my destiny,
> And while over there the wind of misfortune,
> Passes over the suffering country and extinguishes it
> A thought fills my heart.
>
> . . .
>
> The future is open, the people to conquer
> The country to save and Christ to defend
> For France and for God to suffer all and to die.⁶

At the age of 16, he began editing the Catholic periodical *Ames fervents* under a pseudonym, becoming familiar with notable literary figures of the time. He also started attending lectures and speaking at recruiting conferences for La Jeunesse Catholique. Beyond writing, Jubert had a penchant for travel, and each year for ten years he spent holidays with his family in the French countryside, the mountains, the sea, and abroad. He enjoyed being physically active as well, dedicating time to fencing and horse riding. Jubert's interest in letters drew him away from the industrial career of his father and led him towards the law, a path that also exempted him from mandatory military service. Receiving his licence to practise in 1910 from the Paris Law Faculty, he registered with Bar of Reims in 1913. On the eve of war he completed a thesis on the political ideas of Alphonse de Lamartine, the subject in many ways an obvious one. The renowned writer, poet, and politician was a devout Catholic who was a key figure in the founding of the Second Republic and the continuation of the Tricolour as the flag of France. Lamartine was also instrumental in leading efforts to abolish slavery and the death penalty.

Like many people in France at the time, the outbreak of hostilities came as a surprise to Jubert who was on holiday in Charleville at the time. On 25 August 1914, when the severity of the defeat in the Battle of the Frontiers became clear, he and his brother hopped on the last refugee train out of Charleville. For the next few months, Jubert would remain a refugee in Paris with the rest of his family. But he was not content to just sit idly by while so many others were doing their part. The day after Christmas 1914, he went to the 8th Arrondissement town hall and voluntarily enlisted 'for the duration' of the war, where he was assigned to the 91st Infantry (originally garrisoned in Mézières).[7] And so it was that a 25-year-old lawyer, entirely ignorant of all things soldiering, found himself a private in the French army. In a matter of months, he had not only completed his training but had been judged apt enough to be named aspirant on 15 April 1915. Five days later he was transferred to the 151, reporting to the regimental depot (relocated from Verdun to Quimper in September) for several days before being sent up to the front lines in the Argonne Forest.

When the fiery Corsican, Roger Campana, first arrived at the front, he proudly donned the bright blue dress cap worn by cadets at the prestigious Saint-Cyr military academy. His choice of headware was conspicuously out of place here. When an experienced front-line officer asked teasingly if he was going to the grand ball, the proud second lieutenant retorted he was going to face *les balles* ('bullets'). Gunfire and its effects would soon kill off his naivity, but his zeal would remain inextinguishable. Louis Charles 'Roger' Campana was born on 21 September 1893 in Bordeaux to François and Joséphine. Little is known about his childhood. He also had a deep love of country. His uncle had been wounded in the Franco-Prussian War at Gravelotte and his 18-year-old father enlisted to avenge him, a theme that ran through Campana's life. Indeed, he admitted that he and his friends were all indoctrinated in the 'cult of Revenge', which taught a reverence for the provinces of Alsace and Lorraine stolen away by the Germans. As young as 13, Campana proclaimed to his parents his intention to attend the Ecole Spéciale Militaire de

Saint-Cyr, France's elite military academy. And so, though he was a member of the class of 1914 scheduled to be called up in the autumn, in July 1914 the 20-year-old Campana was busy preparing for the rigorous oral examination for Saint-Cyr.[8] He remained diligent to the task at hand, confining himself to a depressing study room despite the stifling summer heat. But for him, the stakes were as high as the temperature. He had already passed the exam the year before with a high score. All that had stood between him and his dream of becoming a 'Cyrard' was the highly weighted physical performance test. On the poor advice of a friend who'd already passed the physical trials, Campana took a stimulant potion beforehand. Unfortunately for him, by the time it was his turn to perform, the effects of the stimulant had not only worn off but had given him a debilitating lethargy. He made it through most of the exercises well enough but when he arrived at the vertical rope climb, despite all his efforts he found himself entirely depleted of strength and unable to pull himself up. When the training officer mocked Campana, his Corsican blood boiled over and casting the rope in the officer's direction, he told the man to go to hell. The outburst earned him a big fat zero. And so a year later and a good deal humbler, Campana found himself in the same position. Pushing himself to focus and work hard, he found motivation in a wall painting done by a former candidate depicting a Cyrard in parade uniform. He imagined himself wearing the uniform, including the 'celestial' blue *caso* shako with its distinctive red and white feathered plumes fluttering in the breeze as he promenaded through the streets of Bordeaux at Christmas time.

Fate would intervene and before the exam date arrived, the general mobilization was called and the exams were suspended. Since Campana was on-track to pass, he was pressed into service and underwent basic training in the 144th Infantry Regiment, and together with the other Saint-Cyr candidates from Bordeaux, was assigned to a separate platoon of breveted *elèves-caporaux* ('corporal-candidates').[9] Time seemed to drag by for him in and with each passing week, his impatience to get into the fight grew. Seeing the flood of wounded arriving in Bordeaux to recuperate from their injuries only added to his anxious desire to be sent to the front in the naive fear that he would miss the war entirely. In November Campana was promoted to sergeant and then passed the platoon leader exam. Shortly thereafter he was breveted to second lieutenant. With the turn of the new year, Campana and his fellow Cyrards from Bordeaux were sent to join the 151. There were thirteen of them in all: Denevault, Marc Laguens, Dartiguelongue, Rogier, Feix, Richard, Chedal-Bornu, Cruège, Camusat de Riancey, Lamothe de Mondion, Canredon, and Arthaud de la Ferrière.[10] In six months, half of them would be dead. By the end of the war, only Campana would still be alive.

Gardening was simple work but Auguste Bordinat derived a sense of comfort from it. He enjoyed being outdoors and the calming methodicism of planting and pruning appealed to him. When it was his turn to go to the trenches, he did so without a longing for personal glory or malice towards the enemy. The former gardener made it his mission to just make it back home to his wife – and later, to his baby girl. Charles 'Auguste' Bordinat was born on 16 May 1887 in Menetou-Râtel, a small village outside of Sancerre in the Cher Department. He was the seventh of eleven children. When Auguste was only 6 years old, his mother passed away and his father gave him to the Child-Care Services of Bourges, along with his sister Stéphanie and his brother Paul. At 8, 6, and 4 years of age, they were the youngest of the eleven children and were consequently unable to work and help support the family income. Yet deliverance for the Bordinat orphans would not be long in coming. One day a lady by the last name of Tassain travelled to Bourges in search of a young girl to adopt who could help around the house and be raised alongside her own daughter. Upon arriving at the Child-Care Services centre, Madame Tassain found poor Stéphanie crying in the corner, and asked if she would like to come home with her. Stéphanie wanted this very much but protested that she didn't want to leave her little brothers behind. Not wishing to separate the abandoned siblings from each other, the kind-hearted Tassain agreed to take all three children.

Bordinat spent the rest of his early childhood in Farges. At the age of 13, he left to earn his living doing farm work. He laboured for five years when, having reached 18 years of age, he volunteered for military service in Bordeaux two years prior to the mandatory call-up date for the class of 1907 cohort. After completing his term of service in the army, Bordinat moved to Paris to join his brothers. The oldest, Paulin, was a road worker in the city of Paris who had married and bought a house in Saint-Gemme. It was there that Bordinat would meet his future wife, Eugénie. But city life didn't seem to suit Bordinat, and after a short time, he decided to leave Paris and return to the country. After marrying in October of 1912, the newly wed couple travelled to Châteauneuf-en-Thymerais (Eure-et-Loire), where Auguste found work as a gardener. The couple next moved to the Château de Comteville, near Dreux, where they were employed as caretakers. Not long after their arrival, Auguste was hired to work at the Mézières Mill in Mézières-en-Drouais.

In 1914, at the age of 27, Bordinat reported before the military medical board at Dreux. He was deemed fit for service and sent to join the 134th Infantry Regiment at Mâcon in February 1915. Once there he received another physical inspection but was this time judged unfit for active service and assigned to auxiliary service in the 58th Territorial Infantry Regiment. In April, he was sent to Fort Varois where he was assigned to the agricultural company to assist farmers in managing crops. From there he was billeted for the summer and autumn with a townswoman in Revigny whose husband had been mobilized in 1914. At the end of October he went before an inspection committee at Bar-le-Duc which informed he would be transferred to an active combat formation – the army needed more bodies at the front. And so at the end of November he was directed to the depot of the 27th Infantry Regiment at Dijon. Once there, his obligation was temporarily deferred and he was put to work in a mill instead. But Bordinat's luck could only last so long. In March 1916, he was sent back to the 27th Infantry depot awaiting assignment. On 5 May, Bordinat was told he and a small group of similar men had been assigned to the 151 as replacements and the next day they were sent up to Bar-le-Duc to await posting.

When André L'Huillier headed up for this first time to the front, he was marching back home. As a young boy, his father would take him hunting for small game in the forest near his hometown of Sainte Menehould. A few years later, he was gunning down men in the same woods. André Eugene L'Huillier was born on 8 July 1896 at Somme-Py (Marne), the son of Justin and Pauline. He had dark hair and gentle blue eyes, and as a child moved to Sainte-Menehould with his parents, where he attended school. At the age of 15 his father passed away, leaving his mother to raise him and his sister, Marcelle, alone. His mother made up for the lack of a parent by taking her children travelling around Europe each year during the summer holidays. In August 1913, he made a grand tour of England, Belgium, Holland, Luxembourg, the Rhineland in Germany, Switzerland, and Northern Italy. Fluent in English and German, L'Huillier recorded in a journal his thoughts on geography, his trips to cities and museums, and the customary clothing of the people. During this time, he was also active in the Union Sportive Ménéhildienne, a military club offering instruction and training on riflery, including the handling and firing of the standard French army service rifle, the Model 1886/93 'Lebel' 8mm. The following year, as the war clouds gathered, the 18-year-old L'Huillier was studying at the Université de Goettingen in Lower Saxony, Germany. Before war broke out, he returned to Sainte Menehould. As a member of the class of 1916, his period of mandatory military service was still two years off, at least on paper. Like Jubert and thousands of others, he felt obligated to serve his country and was fearful he might miss out on his generation's war.[11]

It was only natural that the curious and inquisitive L'Huillier began recording his experiences in black moleskin notebooks, 'what I saw, what I did'.[12] In the dramatic years to come, these would serve as a living journal of not only the life of the author but of the 151 at large. After months of waiting, L'Huillier acquired his mother's permission to enlist. As Sainte Menehould was in the zone of the armies, the eager volunteer reported to the recruitment office in Chalons-sur-Marne, where he was judged fit for service. From there L'Huillier was sent to Paris' 5th Arrondissement town hall on 18 November 1914 and signed his volunteer papers. When asked which regiment he wished to be assigned to, L'Huillier responded that he wanted to join the 151 from Verdun since he already had two school friends in the unit. As the depots of the northern and eastern regiments which had withdrawn to the interior were having difficulties supplying the men at the front with military clothing, he was told to purchase a good pair of boots, corduroy trousers, a knitted wool jumper, socks, and other small items for reimbursement at a later date. Because of his education, at Quimper he was placed in the corporal candidates platoon and assigned to a training company under Captain Le Moing. Coincidentally Le Moing and his wife were an acquaintances of L'Huillier's mother, a connection that engendered a cordiality between the officer and the young volunteer over the coming months. After suffering from a bout of strep throat and scarlet fever, he would rejoin his training company in early January. His pre-war military and weapons experience helped L'Huillier make up for the lost time. Earning high scores in target practice, physical exercises, and written exams, he was promoted to corporal in February and assumed command of his first squad, which included former reservists old enough to be his father. After several more months of training, on 15 June 1915 L'Huillier departed Quimper for the front with a strong detachment of reinforcements, all exuberant as they marched along arrayed in their new Horizon Blue uniforms.

Of the other eyewitnesses who provide a window into the experiences of the 151, less is known about their lives before the war. Like so many other youths of his generation, Henri Laporte was swept up in the inescapable tide of war. Born in Étréaupont (Aisne) in 1895, Laporte studied Industrial Science and Technology, and eventually joined the railway administration before the war. In August 1914, he was 19 and witnessed the Great Retreat while living with his family in Hirson (Aisne), a few kilometres from the Belgian border. He was called to service at Montreuil-sous-Bois, where he had taken refuge with his mother and two sisters on 27 November 1914, as part of the class of 1915. After several months of training at the depot at Quimper, Henri Laporte was sent up to the front to join the 151 on 10 April 1915. He could never have imagined the levels of horror he would find there. Still less is known about others whose written words serve as a testimony of the 151 and the war, mainly owing to a lack of information available in the public domain. There was Roger Basteau, another Cyrard like Campana who was given command of a platoon even though he admitted he had no idea how actually to perform his job. Marcel Olivier was a mathematics student who became oblivious to incoming artillery fire when he was engaged in solving a maths problem. Edouard Moisson was the commander of the regiment for some of its greatest battles, and was held in such esteem by his subordinates that they nicknamed him 'Papa Victory'. Many others too numerous to mention here appear as only passing figures, shadows shifting briefly across the wall. But each of them had their own hopes, desires, joys, and fears. Each had people in their lives whom they loved and who loved them. And each played a part in the story of the Verdun Regiment.

Chapter 2

1914: To the Hilt

Battle of the Frontiers

The beaming sun shone down on the long lines of deployed troops who, sweltering in their long blue greatcoats and red trousers, tramped up clouds of dust as they rushed about in sharp response to whistle and bugle calls. It was July 1914 and with tensions over the looming war at a peak, the units of the 42 ID were in the midst of conducting manoeuvres at the Verdun training grounds before anxious crowds of Meusians. Preparations were well underway for the 151's departure to Camp Chalôns for its regularly scheduled annual manoeuvres. While en route on 28 July the units of the division received orders to proceed immediately back to their garrisons. The 151 returned to Miribel Barracks at Verdun and placed itself in a state of war readiness. As a unit belonging to one of the Covering Corps, the 151 did not have to rely on the general mobilization to be at full strength. Consequently, it was able to deploy immediately from its garrison with a full complement of 57 officers and 3,090 men. On 31 July the regiment marched out the gates of Miribel, its regimental colours and band out front, and moved southeast towards the frontier. The next evening, the men were told that the general mobilization has been decreed for the next day. The 151 was assigned as the division's advanced guard and would post itself in the small villages of Pintheville, Marchéville, and St Hilaire situated between Sainte Menehould and Metz on the Woëvre Plain. It would remain there for two weeks, and busied itself with constructing a line of defensive entrenchments.

With the advance of the German 5th Army into France through the Ardennes Forest, the 42 ID was sent to check its movement. Over several days the division cautiously moved northeast probing for the enemy, with the 151 IR at the head of its column, entrenching in place and establishing a line of resistance whenever it made a long halt. By 21 August the regiment had reached Gondrecourt, where it received word that enemy forces had been spotted in Joudreville and the nearby environs. The 3 Battalion was ordered to to attack these locations, supported by divisional artillery, coordinating its movement with the 19 LIB. At the end of the day it had yet to make contact with the enemy, though it did connect with the chasseur battalion, which had reformed near Higny after having repulsed the enemy but suffering significant losses in doing so. The 151 would pull back to Domprix to billet for the evening and was instructed to be ready to depart at 4.00 am the next morning.

The regiment's baptism of fire would come on 22 August, the climax of the Battle of the Frontiers. As was the case with most of the great battles of the war, the Battle of the Frontiers was not itself a single engagement at one place or time but a series of battles between 7 August and 5 September, each of which involved tens of thousands of troops along a broad front. The engagement within the greater battle that the 151 fought in would be called the Battle of the Ardennes, involving the French 3rd and 4th Armies and the German 4th and 5th Armies, some 740,000 combatants in total. On an even smaller scale, the particular engagement the regiment particiapted in would be called the Battle of Pierrepont or the Battle of Baslieux. On the morning of 22 August the 42 ID begins its march north with the 151 acting again as advanced guard, accompanied by a company of engineers, a group from divisional artillery, and a squadron of divisional cavalry. Its itinerary was Saint-Supplet, Han-devant-Pierrepont, and Doncourt. The regiment advanced in column over the dusty roads with 1 Battalion in the lead followed by 2 and 3 Battalions, while 2 Company and the machine-gun platoon acting as flank guard. Intelligence from cavalry scouts indicated that no enemy force could be detected within a 10km radius of the march route. Reaching the village of Pierrepont, the lead elements of the 151 crossed the narrow River Crusnes and halted at the top of Côte 329 (1km to the north of Pierrepont), while the 2 Company pushed up to the entrance to Doncourt. It was from there that a body of enemy troops was observed between the Bois de Tappe and Bois de Doncourt, a kilometre to the north of the village. But the 151 had also been spotted. Suddenly the 1 Battalion came under fire from German artillery located on Lartimont Ridge as well as small-arms fire from the Bois de Doncourt.

No accounts from soldiers of the 151 can be found for their first engagement of the war. The sad fact was that so few of the soldiers who participated in the battles of 1914 lived into 1915, let alone until the end of the war, to record their experiences in a format that entered the public realm. There are a few eyewitnesses serving in other units that can serve as a testimony, though. Sergeant Paul Dubrulle, for example, described the sensation of coming under shell-fire for the first time, an experience that many in the 151 were undergoing.

> When a shell bursts a few metres away, there's a terrible jolt and then an indescribable chaos of smoke, earth, stones, branches, and – too often, alas! – limbs, flesh, a rain of blood. Immediately a frightful concert breaks out, the wounded screaming as if their souls were spilling out of them. For a few seconds you are overwhelmed by extreme terror and then, very soon afterward, a blessed relief. The crisis has passed, you can breathe again for a few moments, you come back to life.[1]

Following the prescriptions of the pre-war tactical theory of *attaque à l'outrance* (attack to the hilt), Colonel Louis Georges Deville immediately ordered the regiment into an all-out frontal attack. The 1 Battalion was ordered to occupy the Bois de Tappe and the Grand Bois de Doncourt to the north of Doncourt. The 3 Battalion was to move up on 1 Battalion's right to the eastern edge of the Bois de Goëmont to the southeast of Doncourt, where enemy troops had been spotted. Shortly after that, the 2 Battalion was sent up to Bois de Goëmont. But to reach the objectives, the battalions would have to cover nearly 2km of open ground, advancing across a wide, gently undulating plain that separated them from the enemy. They had no scouts out front and no artillery support. The men – heavily laden with all their full marching order and strikingly arrayed in their conspicuous greatcoats and trousers – went to the port arms and marched forward into battle. A veritable storm of shells, especially shrapnel, now came raining down on the companies as more German batteries to the north and east went into action. The fire produced an instant din of shrieking and hissing shells, intermingled with the sound of dozens of shrapnel balls, like some invisible hive of angry hornets. Bullets by the hundreds whined and cracked all around. Men began falling, throwing out their arms with a shout or spinning around like tops before collapsing in a heap. The enemy's fire was wreaking havoc and yet not a single enemy soldier could yet be seen. The companies advanced by platoons in bounds, the men charging forward a distance at the signal from an officer or NCO, then dropping down flat again, then rising back up to make another dash. With each bound, there were fewer troops in the ranks to continue on.

Though the companies managed to reach the woods, they suffered heavy losses doing so. Everything was chaos, noise, smoke, fire, blood. With the air filled with flying metal, many company officers remained standing as they endeavoured to encourage their men. The action was courageous as it was naive. With their sabres and bright red kepis, they only served to offer themselves as conspicuous targets. In minutes, the regiment's officer cadre was decimated. At the Bois de Tappe and Grand Bois de Doncourt, the now leaderless remains of 1 and 2 Companies fell back onto the village of Doncourt, where they rallied and then repulsed a German counter-attack. After sustaining heavy casualties reaching and holding the Bois de Goëmont, the companies of the 2 Battalion in their turn retreated in disorder to Doncourt as well, where they joined up with the 1 and 2 Companies. Elements of the 12 DI – having suffered the same fate in the Bois de Tappe – mixed in with the 151. There, the men were ordered to construct make-shift barricades at the entrances to the village. The rest of the day, in the face of intense artillery fire, the walled-in defenders held a defensive line stretching from Doncourt to Côte 329 to the southern border of the Bois de Grandchamp. In Doncourt, shells smashed into roofs, shattering tiles and collapsing walls. Dust mixed with the smoke of burning homes. Out in the open fields, the men could do nothing but hug the ground as bullets whined and snapped overhead, and shell fragments and shrapnel whizzed past like flying meat cleavers. Falling back on their training, the terrified riflemen threw their packs in front and scraped out shallow rifle pits in a desperate attempt to escape the gunfire. Captain Alphonse Grasset was in a very similar position a short distance away from where the 151 was engaged and described a comparable scene:

> The wounded offered a truly impressive sight. Sometimes they would stand up bloody and horrible-looking, amidst bursts of gunfire. They ran aimlessly around, arms stretched out before them, eyes staring at the ground, turning round and round until, hit by fresh bullets, they would stop and fall heavily.
>
> Heart-rending cries, agonising appeals and horrible groans were intermingled with the sinister howling of projectiles. Furious contortions told of strong and youthful bodies refusing to give up life.
>
> One man was trying to replace his bloody, dangling hand to his shattered wrist. Another ran from the line holding the bowels falling out of his belly and through his tattered clothes. Before long a bullet struck him down.
>
> We had no support from our artillery! And yet, there were guns in our division and in the army corps, besides those destroyed on the road. Where were they? Why didn't they arrive? We were alone. I was wondering, in my anxiety, whether we were going to lose all our men on the spot.[2]

This scene was being repeated all along the 151's battle front, which stretched over 2km from Bois des Tappe and Grand Bois de Doncourt to Bois de Goëmont and Bois de Grand Champ. In many places, the enemy could not be seen, concealed in the woods or sheltering behinds folds in the ground. In other spots, the opposing forces were nearer each other and could make out the silhouettes of the enemy. Here and there along the line, German forces tried to press their advantage and counter-attacked to drive back the French. The 8 Company of the 151 was thus annihilated before the enemy force was repulsed with heavy losses by the machine guns of the neighbouring 25 LIB and the 162 IR. As daylight faded, the firing began to die down with darkness bringing merciful relief. In the evening, the 151 received orders to break off contact with the enemy and to retrace its steps, crossing back over the Crusne and bivouacking to the north of Han-devant-Pierrepont.

The casualties for the day were truly horrifying, not just for the 151 but the French army as a whole. The 22 August 1914 would earn the regrettable title of the bloodiest single day in the whole of French military history. On the first day of major combat in the Great War, 27,000 French soldiers were killed; 40,000 more were wounded. In a matter of hours on its first day of action, the 151 had lost 800 soldiers, over a quarter of its effectives. Losses were particularly concentrated in 2 Battalion, where 8 Company was reduced to only twelve soldiers. Moreover, twenty officers had been killed or injured, a serious blow to unit leadership. One of them was Second Lieutenant and Saint-Cyr candidate George Le Balle, who had just celebrated his 21st birthday. Le Balle had been shot in the leg just before the major fighting erupted. Though he had apparently applied a tourniquet, he soon died from loss of blood. His final letter was found close to his body:

> My dear parents and much-loved little sisters,
> When you receive this note, your dear boy will be no more. While on patrol with six men, a bullet was fired a few metres away from me, which severed the artery in my thigh. So, abandoned, I have lived for another 24 hours and have been in God's embrace, where I will find you again sooner or later. So don't cry too much but pray for me.
> My last thoughts will be of you and of God! Kissing you for the last time, very long and tenderly.
> Your dear boy and kid brother saying, see you again in eternity.
> –Geo.

The 151 had suffered a severe shock on 22 August and it was not alone. All along the line, French and British forces were recoiling from the massive collision. In what would be referred to as the Great Retreat, French and British forces now steadily withdrew south and west into the interior of France as German forces pressed down from Belgium and the Franco-German border. Over the course of the next several days the 151 would conduct what would amount to a fighting withdrawal in a series of delaying actions. At Duzey, the Bois de Warphemont, Rouvrois, Pillon, and Bois Saint-Médard, the 151 alternately counter-attacked, retreated, and heroically resisted enemy infantry and artillery assaults to buy time for other units to fall back and for the wounded to be evacuated. In this stubborn resistance another 150 fell. By 25 August, the regiment had lost a third of its men and nearly half of its officer cadre. The next day, the 151 was finally ordered to break contact. The men had already been fighting, digging, and marching for five days without let up. But now they would have to carry out a long, brutal forced march south through an oppressive heat and suffocating dust. Along the way, they would pass over the heights of the Meuse north of Verdun and crossing over the River Meuse at Bras. By the time they'd reached their billets at Béthelainville in the evening of

26 August, the men had marched 45km. The next day, they would go another 20km west to Varennes and Cheppy.

Here the 151 received the first of many replacement troops to come. It was a detachment of reinforcements sent from the 351 IR depot at St Quentin (the reserve sister regiment of the 151), lead by battalion leader Commandant Monphous. The detachment comprised 9 officers and 927 reservists. The reduced companies of the regiment were subsequently reconstituted and the regiment's total effectives boosted back up to 3,250 officers and men. The regiment was given two days of rest before it was shuttled west to an area where the situation remained more dire. On the afternoon of 29 August, a counter-march back to the Verdun train station was made, which lasted all day and well into the night. In the early morning hours of the 30th, the battalions were loaded onto three cattle car trains and subsequently sent westward in the direction of Reims. There they would join with the other units of the 42nd Division, now detached from the VI Army Corps and under the command of General Grossetti. The division's mission was to conduct another fighting withdrawal, this time to protect the retreating elements of the 4th Army in the area south of Rethel near the River Retourne. The 151 was sent above Reims to form a defensive line to the northeast of Boult-sur-Suippes (Marne) at Ferme de l'Esperance. On the afternoon of 1 September, enemy forces made contact, and an orderly withdrawal commenced, moving by the southwest and south. Corporal Charles Salomon was a 25-year-old reservist who'd arrived with the 151 and been assigned to 8 Company as part of the large detachment dispatched from the depot of the 351. Until the war had arrived, Salomon had aspired to become a priest, but now he was swept up in the largest military conflagration in human history. 'From now on billeting will be more uncommon . . . We make contact with the enemy. Long and often indecisive fighting begins, fighting in the day and the night where no respite is given to the adversaries.'

On 3 September, an exhausting forced march was conducted in stifling heat 30km south to Champillon and Magenta, followed by another 30km the next day to reach Beaunay and Loisy-en-Brie. Chaos and congestion reigned as the roads become crowded with troop columns, artillery convoys, and flocks of pathetic refugees. The men entered into a state of mental bewilderment, dazed to the point of being almost comatose. They were short of food and supplies and, most of all, sleep. They were averaging only a few hours of sleep a day; the rest of the time was spent marching day and night. Every cell in their bodies seemed to scream out for rest. Infantrymen slept while they marched, their feet shuffling forward in an automatic, unconscious motion. Cavalry and artillery men, atop their mounts, slept slouched in their saddles and their horses plodded slowly along. When they were afforded a break, they collapsed in the ditches on the side of the road and immediately fell into a deep sleep, undisturbed by noise, commotion, or passing rains. To get back on their feet required a monumental effort. In nine days, the

151 had marched some 220km, 60 of those on just 3 and 4 September, all on the meagerest of rations and minimal sleep. A note in the 151 *JMO* mentions that the reinforcement of reservists who had arrived a week previously had already been greatly diminished as many men had dropped out of the ranks as stragglers due to physical exhaustion, heat stroke or illness.

On 5 September, the regiment continued to move south acting as the flank guard for the division. By the end of the day, its 1 Battalion occupied Chapton and the eastern edge of the Bois du Bout-de-la-Ville, while its 2 Battalion was on the left at the Bois de Saint Gond. To the north, the 3 Battalion was holding Villeneuve-lès-Charleville and Bois de la Branle. Since arriving in the Marne, the regiment had suffered only light casualties in skirmishing with enemy advanced elements, with fifty or so killed, wounded, or missing. But all signs pointed to a major battle to come the next day and the men were told to sleep on their arms in preparation. The French and British armies had been on retreat for two weeks. Now the troops – debilitated from hunger, dehydration, exposure, and fatigue – were ordered to turn-about and stand firm. In his Order of the Day, the imperturbable French Chief of Staff, General Joseph Joffre laid out the situation in stark terms:

> Now, as the battle is joined on which the safety of the country depends, everyone must be reminded that this is no longer the time for looking back. Every effort must be made to attack and throw back the enemy. A unit which finds it impossible to advance must, regardless of cost, hold its ground and be killed on the spot rather than fall back. In the present circumstances no failure will be tolerated.

Battle of the Marne

Like the Frontiers, the First Battle of the Marne encompassed a series of battles all unfolding at the same time over the course of days and along a massive front, stretching nearly the entire length of northeast France, and involving some 2 million combatants. Within the encompassing First Marne, the 151 would be engaged in what would be referred to as the Battle of the Saint-Gond Marshes, on the left flank of the newly formed 9th Army (under General Foch), which Joffre had formed to help plug the widening gap between the 4th and 5th Armies at the centre of the French line. While 5th Army was already on the offensive, moving northwards into the gap in the German line created when the German II Army Corps withdrew to the River Ourcq, the situation was very different on 9th Army's front. Here the German 2nd Army had already crossed the small river Petit Morin and the opposing sides collided with each other. What ensued was a bloody slugfest between the opposing sides, like two heavy weight prized fighters laying into each other, each trying to deliver a knockout blow.

The mission of the 42 ID on 6 September was to attack in the general direction of Vauchamps and Janvilliers, taking and holding the Petit Morin. The 84th Brigade was to progress to left front between the line of ridges of Villeneuve, Pommerose, and the line of Lachy, Charleville, with the 151 IR constituting the marching wing and the 16 LIB in reserve. Its right flank would be guarded by the 162 IR while five groups of artillery, in position to the north and west of Villeneuve-lès-Charleville, would guard the left. The first objectives for the 151 IR and 16 LIB were the ridge between Charleville and Les Culots, then the Pommerose Ridge (3km north of Charleville) and Corfélix. Prior to the attack, the 151 had advanced their positions further north, such that at dawn the companies of 2 Battalion were holding the advanced posts between the Culots, Charleville, and the Bois du Bout-de-la-Ville, isolated from the neighbouring corps on either side. The 1 Battalion was waiting in open columns in a small wood above the small quarry north of Villeneuve and sheltered from view, while the 3 Battalion was in position at Villeneuve and along the road that ran through Bois de la Branle that connected Villeneuve to Soizy-aux-Bois. The orders were for the 151 to begin its attack only after the 20 ID had sufficiently progressed on the left. Until then, there was nothing to do but wait.

The fighting was already underway when, at 7.30 am, German forces of the 2 Guard Reserve Division (likely the 78 Infantry Regiment) appeared along the Charmotte and Pommerose Ridges to the north. Immediately the 2 Battalion opened fire, its companies moving into the attack. As they did, they came under a violent enfilade fire from German machine guns in Corfélix and soon the entire 2 Battalion was forced to withdraw to the south. Once it reached the Villeneuve–Soizy Road, 5 Company rallied and, alone, attempted to establish a line of defence. As it did so, the company came under fire from French 75mm batteries, forcing it to retreat to the Bois du Bout-de-la-Ville. While this drama was unfolding, the 1 Battalion had come under fire from German riflemen and machine guns to its right, as enemy infantry surged out of the Bois de la Branle to the east. The companies attempted to face the attacking force but rapidly suffered heavy losses, and were themselves obliged to fall back first to Villeneuve and then to a ridge further south. Waves of German troops bore down on Villeneuve and Charleville but just as quickly, the tables were turned as the recovering companies of the 151 poured a withering fire on the enemy and stopped his movement. The companies of 2 Battalion had now largely reformed in the Bois du Bout-de-la-Ville, having been rallied in person by Commandant Pascal. The 3 Battalion was ordered to go to the support of 2 Battalion. With the line temporarily re-stabilized, orders came down to all three battalions: hold the line of Charleville–Villeneuve *no matter the cost*. After repulsing another German push on Charleville and Villeneuve, the 151 counter-attacked. The renowned author

Maurice Genevoix, a lieutenant serving in the 106 IR, led his platoon into an attack not unlike the one carried out by the 151 in front of Charleville:

> With a strange detachment I watch the lines of our men blue and red against the ground, advancing and advancing apparently without movement. About me the wheat bows down beneath a heavy, languid breeze, and with a certain feverishness I repeat to myself again and again: 'I am in it now! This is war and I am in it!' and I am astonished to see that all the things about me retain their ordinary appearance, to hear the snapping of rifles which is no more than the snapping of rifles. For, on the other hand, it almost seems as if my body had undergone some change, that it is no longer the same, that I experience different sensations with different organs.
>
> . . .
>
> We commence to advance. The movement is admirably executed, with the same regularity and deliberation as if we were on manoeuvres. Little by little there arises in me an exhilaration which raises me above myself. I feel that all these men are part of myself – these men who, at a gesture from me push forward despite the bullets shrilling towards us seeking chests, faces; the living flesh for billets.
>
> We lie down for cover, we rise with a jump; we run as fast as our legs will carry us straight for the hidden Boches – we long to see those Boches so that we can get at them more surely and chase them far from these fields ruined and trampled by their hordes.
>
> We are completely exposed and under fire. The bullets sing no longer; they pass invisible with a nasty, spiteful hiss. They are no longer at play but in deadly earnest.
>
> Clac! Clac! Two bullets have struck immediately to my left. The noise at once surprises and slightly amazes me; these bullets seem less dangerous when they sing and whistle. Clac! Clac! Stones, pieces of dried earth, spurts of dust fly into the air; we have been seen and they have got the range of us. Forward! I am leading, seeking a ditch, a slope, a fold in the earth wherein to shelter my men after the first rush – even the hedge of a field, or anything which will render them less visible to the Boches will do. A movement of my right arm shortens the line by half. I hear the tramp of feet, the rustle of the stubble lying in our course. And while we are running forward the detachment in support fires rapidly but steadily. Then when I raise my cap, that detachment in its turn charges at the double, whilst all around me my men's rifles come into play and speak unceasingly.

> Forward! To remain still would cost us more dearly now than the most furious assault. Forward! The men are falling rapidly, stopped dead in full course, some crashing prone without a word, others halting and staring stupidly, while feeling with their hand for their wound. And they say: 'They got me,' or, 'I got mine!' Often it is no more than a single expressive word. Almost all of them, even those whose wounds are slight, turn pale at the shock. The impression is borne in upon me that one thought alone is in all their minds; to get away very quickly, never mind where, so long as it be somewhere free from this eternal hissing of the bullets.[3]

For the remainder of the day there followed a confusing mix of orders and counter-orders, advances and retreats over green-leafed beet and potato fields north of the disputed villages. For his part, Corporal Salomon saw what he could only perceive as gross negligence by a certain reserve officer, who needlessly imperilled their men by ordering them into exposed positions for no gain, even as 'the shells come down like hail'. As daylight faded, an uneasy calm settled over the trampled fields strewn with the dead and dying. The situation on 9th Army's front was stalemate. On the right flank, German forces had pushed back French forces, manoeuvring around the Saint-Gond Marshes and crossing the River Somme, while on the left flank the German advance had been stopped in its tracks. In the night, the surrounding villages of the Marne, set alight by shellfire, blazed away like giant funeral pyres to the slain. Lieutenant Maurice Genevoix described what it sounded like on the battlefield at night after the fighting was done.

> And before us, the dark shadow that seems to groan with all the wounds that bled and were not dressed. Faint voices, weary from crying out: 'What have I done to get killed in this war?' 'Mother, oh mother!' 'Jeanne, my little Jeanne! Oh, say that you can hear me, my Jeanne!' 'I'm thirsty! I'm thirsty! I'm thirsty! I'm thirsty!' The cries appall us, they cut us to the quick. 'I don't want to die here, oh God!' 'Stretcher-bearers! Stretcher-bearers!' 'Bastards! Is there no one with any pity?' A German (he can't have been more than 20 metres away) intones, '*Kamerad Franzose! Kamerad! Kamerad Franzose!*' And lower down, pleading: '*Hilfe! Hilfe!*' His voice bends, breaks and quavers like a crying child. Then his screeching grows and all night long he was like a dog howling to the moon. It was a dreadful night.[4]

The next morning the back and forth fighting resume, a confused series of movements, ebbing and flowing across the fields and in the woods. French elements, composed of a complete mashup of units, made local counter-attacks, were repulsed, then recovered, then counter-attacked again. Though it was not yet discernible to the troops on the ground, on 7 September the tide of battle, indeed of the war up to that point, began to turn. The French 5th Army continued to push forward, wheeling on its right with the 20 ID as a pivot. The success of the 20 ID's advance allowed for units to be siphoned off as reinforcements to bolster the badly mauled 42 ID. A general counter-offensive began in the late afternoon. Rather than a simultaneous push by the entire division, a series of almost sporadic movements occurred on the regiment and battalion level. In a repeat of the disastrous episode the day before, just as 2 Battalion advanced from Villeneuve it once again came under fire from French artillery. And as before, Commandant Pascal had again to rally his companies as they fall back to their starting position. Along the rest of the division's attack front, the other units fought tenaciously but faced an equally fierce resistance and only minor progress was made. The fighting seesawed back and forth until dark and another uneasy truce settled over the land. The stubborn resistance put up by the German forces began to let up the next day, when the 151 advanced 2km to Les Culots and the Bois de l'Homme-Blanc. Corporal Salomon, who had made coffee with some comrades in a ruined house behind the badly damaged but still-standing Villeneuve church, now crossed a battlefield strewn with the bodies of both sides. 'The dead we come across were kneeling, head resting on the arm in a position taken against the artillery fire, but facing to the rear. Other comrades in different regiments have seen the same thing elsewhere. French dead, on the other hand, are always facing toward the enemy.'

In the chaos of these critical days, no official accounting of casualties for the 151 on 6 and 7 September seems to have been kept. The official post-war regimental history records the losses for the regiment for the 6–8 September alone as 600 men and officers with most these concentrated on 6 and 7 September. Given the number of stragglers and evacuated even before the fighting, it would be reasonable to assert that the regiment had lost a quarter of its effectives killed or wounded by 8 September. To relieve the pressure at the 9th Army's centre, the 42 ID was pulled off the line to serve as mobile reserve force. On the morning of 9 September, the units of the 42 ID were relieved by elements of the X Army Corps and headed 7km southeast to Lachy. As the units of the 42 ID converged together from the various points of the front, they marched off in columns of four towards Linthes, 12km to the east. By all accounts, the spectacle of the division moving in perfect order off the field of battle behind the general's pennant made for an impressive sight.

The 151 and other units of the division began an easterly advance towards the Moulin de Connantre and Euvy. The progression was made methodically from copse to copse, slowed by the capture of German stragglers along with hundreds of enemy wounded. Nonetheless, the 151 had covered about 20km on the 9th. The advance resumed the next day, the units turning northeast. By now the Germans were in full retreat and the French assault fell largely on air. By 11.00 am, the 151 had covered 7km until it caught up with the rear guard of the German XII Reserve Corps. Despite encountering resistance, the division pushed on towards Villeseneux and Soudron, with the officers of the 151 guiding their units using compasses read by the light of the moon. It was an eerie landscape with hundreds of bodies strewn across the fields from earlier fighting. The 151 continued to take in German prisoners and weaponry, advancing more than 30km on 10 September. In the darkness of the woods, individuals and small groups of men became lost and separated from their units, or mixed with other formations.

With the German army in retreat, French commanders pushed hard to try and catch up and deliver a knockout blow. But the troops were utterly spent after nearly a month of marching and fighting. Their uniforms were in rags. Their bright-red trousers had faded to a pale brick, the dark blue of their greatcoats dulled in vibrancy. Companies were reduced to two-thirds or even half the normal number of effectives. Officers were in shorter supply than artillery shells, the latter which now had to be carefully rationed out. The roads, choked with columns of artillery and infantry, were in a deplorable state. German commanders were desperate to salvage what had nearly been a victory, while Allied commanders believed they saw the end in sight. And so the troops were asked to dig deep within themselves and find the strength to push on. Over the course of the next few days, the 42 ID marched another 50km to Chalons-sur-Marne, Juvigny, Bouy, and reaching Mourmelon-le-Grand on 14 September, where at last there was a pause in the marching and a chance to restock and resupply.

There, the Germans started to dig in, taking advantage of the terrain to occupy the high ground and other defensively advantageous positions, and resistance grew stronger. The 151 took up positions south of the village of Aubérive-sur-Suippes along the ancient Roman road leading off towards Reims to the west. The first signs of trench warfare now appeared. After several probing attacks on the enemy lines with little success, the 151 was ordered to entrench and erect accessory defences, replete with *boyaux* ('entrails', which the interminable, winding communication trenches resembled), rest shelters, and latrines to the rear. Hygiene had already proved to be an issue early on and orders came down for additional latrines to be dug with strict instructions for the men to use these exclusively to relieve themselves. There was also the issue of the unburied dead, who were lying out in the open between the opposing lines, and orders went out that any bodies close to the regiment's lines should be buried. As if to mark the transition in the nature of the fighting, Colonel Deville was promoted and given command of the 84th Brigade, with Commandant Monphous taking over as the 151's new commander. In his departing words, Deville expressed his reluctance at leaving the regiment he had commanded since November 1912 and his admiration for the spirit and aptitude all the officers, NCOs, and soldiers had always shown, even in the most difficult of circumstances.

French commanders continued to search for an opportunity to punch through the increasingly calcifying enemy lines and turn the flank. The ever-increasing entrenchments, though rudimentary in nature, were already proving lethally effective at stopping infantry attacks. The 151 was shifted 30km west towards the outskirts of Reims, where it was thrown into the assault on 24 and 25 September against entrenched enemy positions at Petit Sillery and surroundings. Only minimal progress could be made and at great cost in what is referred to as the Battle of the Aisne. After 5 days of fighting the regiment lost more than 400 killed or wounded before the attacks were called off. The 151 was significantly understrength by now. A divisional report from 7 October registered only 22 officers and 1,828 men being present for duty. Despite its weakened state, the unit had many more trials to undergo.

Battle of the Yser

It was clear that this part of the front was in deadlock, with two parallel lines of trenches facing each other. But the Race to the Sea was in motion as Allied and German armies attempted to outflank each other, first through Picardy, then Artois, and finally Flanders in Belgium. On 16 October the regiment was informed that it was being transferred out of its sector together with the rest of the division. Soon word came down that it was heading far to the north, where the front met the sea: Dunkirk. There, Allied commanders had hurriedly patched together a mixed force composed of the remnants of the Belgian army together with British regulars, French rifle-marines and even a division of older territorials. The 42nd Division was being sent by train to bolster this force. Upon arriving at Dunkirk on 20 October, a welcome surprise was waiting for them in the form of reinforcements sent from the regimental depot; 16 sergeants, 50 corporals, and 500 privates, as well as a handful of junior officers. Some of these were new recruits of the class of 1914 who'd been called up early and incorporated after only a few short weeks of training. Now they were about to be thrown into the maelstrom of combat. For its first mission, the 42 ID was to conduct an attack through the urban areas that stretched along the North Sea, in conjunction with a general attack by the Belgian army further inland. The 151 would be the lead assault element for the attack, making it quite literally the extreme left flank of the Allied forces at the very end of the Western Front.

At 6.00 am on 23 October, the 151 commenced its attack from its starting positions at Saint-Idesbald and Zeepanne. Four hours later, it had progressed 10km to Nieuwpoort. Rain was now pouring down as the 151 pushed on to Crombez Pavilion and from there to Westende. Though the regiment was supposed to cross over the River Yser using the bridges in Nieuwpoort, these were under intense German artillery fire. Making matters worse, columns of Belgian troops along with numerous automobile convoys jammed the roadways and reduced the advance to a crawl. Consequently, it was necessary to rely on narrow pontoon footbridges constructed by the engineers to get across the river, and this could only be done in small groups all the while under fire from artillery. It would take an hour just for 3 Battalion to complete the crossing. During the operation one of the footbridges ruptured and, taken together with the difficulty of advancing over the sand, the movement became considerably delayed. The 2 and 3 Battalions managed to take the first objectives and passed over the old Belgian trenches. But they stopped short of Westende, which was under bombardment by enemy artillery, and pulled back to occupy the Belgian trenches for the night.

The night was pitch black as relentless rain transformed the ground into a swamp. Throughout that dark night, German forces launched multiple counter-attacks. On two separate occasions, 10 Company was encircled but managed to fight off the attackers. The firing lasted until dawn and was so prolonged and intense that the two left companies of the 3 Battalion ran out of ammunition. Commandant Monphous sent 8 Company up as reinforcement, yet before it reached the trench it was assaulted by a force twice its size rushing forward from only twenty-five paces away. Now caught unprotected out in the open, the company frantically rushed to reach the refuge of the neighbouring company's trench. The German attackers arrived right on the heels of the fleeing company, capturing a half-platoon before opening a withering enfilade fire on the entire battalion, forcing it to withdraw a few hundred metres to the rear. By noon, instead of continuing the offensive on Westende, the entire 84th Brigade found itself set back on the defensive, and having to reorganize its positions during the day. Already the 151 had lost more than 300 men with nothing but deadlock to show for it. So, in the early morning of 25 October, the regiment began to be pulled off the line, to be shifted southeast to link up with Belgian forces near Ramskapelle. Before 3 Battalion could be relieved German infantry supported by artillery attacks again. Without adequate support, the battalion fell back to the far bank of the Yser where it hastily dug some rudimentary entrenchments. As high tide came in, the water level of the Yser rose and quickly flooded the battalion's shallow trenches. There was no choice but to hunker down in the freezing salt water. The 151 needed to buy the Belgian engineers the necessary time to carry out King Albert's torturous order to open the sluices and flood the plain.

Before the 151 could move off to conduct its new assignment, it had to wait for the floodwaters to rise in front of it. For next few days it would hold onto a line of trenches near Booitshoeke, intermixed with Belgian units. Under fire the whole time, it would repulse a series of enemy attacks throughout the day and night of 29 and 30 October. With Commandant Pascal wounded, command of 2 Battalion had been given to a mere lieutenant. As Belgian units to the left started to give way, 3 Battalion was thrown into the attack to retake Ramskapelle, supported to its right by 2 Battalion and to its left by a mixed force of zouaves, tirailleurs, chasseurs, and Belgian troops. On the last day of October, a detachment of reinforcements consisting of 220 men and a handful of officers was distributed among the companies. Even with them, the 151 had only 2,060 men. The regiment was then shifted again to participate in yet another assault, this time on Diksmuide, 12km to the southeast. Before it was relieved, the 151 suffered yet another blow to its officer cadre: its commander, Commandant Monphous, was seriously wounded by shell fragments. Commandant de Bontin temporarily took over, while Captain Clémendot assumed command of 1 Battalion. From 2 to 5 November, the 151 carried out a series of attacks on Diksmuide and neighbouring farms. Advancing across a muddy morass only nominal progress could be made in the face of a deluge of fire coming from the German entrenchments. Because of the meagreness of its entrenchments, the battalions suffered significant losses as they sat powerless and practically unprotected under the deluge of German small arms and artillery fire.

Since 25 October, the 151 has suffered an additional 370 casualties with little to show for it. The sickening futility of bayonet charges against an entrenched enemy equipped with machine guns and heavy artillery had become an inescapable reality. But that did not deter French commanders from believing a breakthrough was still possible. The 42 ID was ordered to once again shift further southeast to the northern outskirts of Ypres. On 7 November, the 151 relieved a unit of territorials at Lizerne and Steenstraet on the left and right banks of the Yser Canal. Two days later, the 151 attacked Bikschote, where again only minor advances could be made. To try to get closer to the Germans, the men were instructed to start digging *boyaux* towards the enemy lines. The men worked throughout the night and the next day, all the while under constant artillery fire from the front and flank. But orders demanded that they hold onto their meagre gains no matter the cost and, wherever possible, to keep pushing forward. Throughout the night of 9–10 November, a heavy barrage by German artillery targeted the regiment's trenches and this continued until just before dawn. By then, a thick fog had developed, greatly reducing visibility. The shelling stopped abruptly and immediately thereafter, emerging through the heavy mist and fog, was a skirmish line of German troops practically on top of the 151's first-line trench. Right behind it was a large mass of German infantry.

Rifles erupted in a blaze and a desperate fight ensued. In a matter of seconds, 7 and 10 Companies were slaughtered in their trenches. By the time the regiment's machine guns opened fire, German troops were only 20m away. The 1 MG Platoon was surrounded and captured. The gunners of 2 MG Platoon had just enough time to spike their own guns before they were all shot down as they attempted to flee. The 3 MG Platoon fought on bravely until all the gunners were killed in position. A savage hand-to-hand fight ensued using fists, rifle butts, and bayonets. Even the officers resorted to using their pistols and sabres. Second Lieutenant Couplet, commanding 8 Company, ceremoniously broke his sabre rather than surrender it. Initially captured by the enemy, he took advantage of the chaos and managed to make his escape soon after. During this time, the other officers and their men remained in their trenches and continued to resist the enemy despite the overwhelming odds. Eventually the German attack was broken up and what was left of the regiment regrouped on the left bank of the Yser Canal before reorganizing its positions. At nightfall, the 151 was sent to the rear to reorganize under Commandant de Bontin's orders, where the magnitude of the catastrophe became clear. The 10 November would represent one of the greatest single-day losses for the 151 in the entire war. Of the 1,905 men that were last reported in ranks, over 1,000 had been killed, wounded, or were captured. Out of an already inadequate cadre of twenty-four officers, only eleven now remained. The other units of the division suffered equally horrendous losses. The next day the 151 was reconstituted into a single battalion of three companies temporarily under Captain Clémendot's orders.

End of Year Situation for the Regiment

After a rapid reorganization in the rear, the demoralized fragments of the 151 were sent back up to occupy the first- and second-line trenches above the Steenstraet bridge. Overnight the weather had turned foul, with strong winds and heavy rains lashing down on the depressing scene. The trenches quickly assumed a deplorable state as they flooded with icy, muddy water a foot or more in depth. In some places, the men stood waist deep in it. The following day, the regimental roll had its lowest number of soldiers reporting for duty than on any other day of the war, a paltry 684. For the next week, the men were put to work on erecting a belt of wire entanglements and digging out new trench networks between the Yser Canal and the hamlets of Lizerne and Bernardplaats. Owing to a lack of sufficient reserves, the men had to stay in the lines under extremely trying conditions. All the while, German artillery kept up a bombardment on the French lines as the cold rain continued to fall. The men, utterly exhausted, were forced to sleep (or try to sleep) standing upright in their inundated trenches. Unaccounted for in the casualty reports were the numbers of men evacuated due to illness and trench foot, whose feet were literally rotting off. For some, the limits of endurance had been reached, even among the professional officers. On 14 November, Commandant de Bontin relinquished command of the regiment and was evacuated to the rear due to physical and mental exhaustion. Having endured months of seeing so many of his young soldiers killed and maimed, the commander had reached the end of his tether. For a few days, a battalion commander from the 162 IR, Commandant Edouard Moisson, would temporarily take over. Moisson would play a major role in the 151 in the years ahead but for the time being his first post would last only a few days before he handed command over to Colonel Edouard Dillemann. A career officer at 52 years of age, Dillemann had been serving as the regimental commander of the 106 IR since 1913 before coming to the 151.

Within a few days, reinforcements began to arrive from the 151's depot. Strong detachments consisting of over 150 NCOs and nearly a 1,000 men (two-thirds of whom were fresh recruits of the class of 1914). Even with these replacements, the unit remained well below its theoretical complement and this situation continued until the new year. By then, a continuous line of trenches stretching some 440 miles from the North Sea to the Swiss border had solidified as the Western Front. With winter in full swing, the 42nd Division was finally given a reprieve from major operations. Instead, it would receive an initiation into the daily trench routine, the battalions being rotated between the various lines trenches and their billets in villages immediately behind. When up in the trenches, the men spent the days and nights working on fortifying the lines, providing security parties for the engineers as they erected more wire entanglements, and occasionally carrying out reconnaissance patrols. The conditions in the lines were horrendous, the trenches filled with 1 to 2ft of standing water. After a month in the Lizerne–Bernardplaats sector – the 151 was shifted 10km southeast to the outskirts of Ypres, in the area of Zillebeke–Verbrande Molen. Though the Battle of Ypres had officially ended two weeks before, this did not mean that the sector had gone quiet. Local raids continued be conducted with deadly results, and another 170 of the regiment's ranks were killed or injured.

Yet, the losses would be largely offset by large numbers of reinforcements arriving in mid-December. These detachments marked the first occasion when the regiment received replacements sent from the depots of other units, the 147 and 148 IR, originally based in the Ardennes. Additional reinforcements arrived in the following days, 1,200 in all. Christmas 1914 was passed in the trenches much like any other cold, miserable day in the Ypres sector, albeit that the loneliness and longing for home were amplified. On Christmas Eve night, 7 Company was sent out on patrol to reconnoitre ground in preparation for an upcoming raid. Its progress was impeded by a thick maze of abatis, along with scores of bodies of the

German dead. Despite what may have occurred in other areas of the front, there's no evidence to suggest that there was any sort of fraternization with the enemy in the 151's sub-sector. While it is possible that some of the men engaged in a back and forth exchange of Christmas caroling as some reports recorded in other units, such pleasantries were unlikely given the number of men in the 151 whose home regions had been invaded and occupied. Whatever the case, Christmas Day was made happy if only by dint of there being no gunfire.

The 151's days in Belgium had come to a close along with the year 1914. On 29 December, the men were informed they would be relieved of their positions the following night and would depart the sector for good. The regiment's contributions from October to December had won it great renowned and established its reputation as a hard-fighting unit. Consequently, the 151 would receive its first battle honours since 1813 with the inscription of 'L'Yser' on the regiment's national colours. On New Year's Eve, the entire 42nd Division set off in column heading towards the Belgian–French border, with the 151 assigned billets in the French border town of Wemaers-Cappel. Before crossing back to French soil, and seemingly as a way to put a final stamp on 1914, an execution of a quarter-master sergeant would be carried out by firing squad. The 34-year-old former clog-maker was a husband and father of two children from Chauny (Aisne). Though he believed his family had been evacuated, he had received no news of them since the war began. When his company returned to the trenches, the sergeant was found intoxicated at a cafe in Ypres while having the company's pay on him. Sent before a war council, he was found guilty of abandoning his post in the face of the enemy with the sentence of '*Fusillé pour l'exemple*'. And so at dawn on 31 December, the regiment was formed up to watch the execution. After being subjected to the ceremonial shaming rituals of cutting away his coat buttons and tearing off his rank stripes, the sergeant was tied to a post, blindfolded and made to kneel. With the firing squad formed up and ready, the adjudant in command raised his sabre, and shouted the order 'Fire!' A salvo of rifle shots rang out, the man slumped down. A sergeant then approached, placed his revolver above the man's head, and delivered the *coup de grâce*. The sergeant had likely been suffering from acute anxiety and depression caused by the unknown fate of his family. But these were desperate times and the French authorities dealt with these with desperate measures. No mercy could be shown to those judged as shirking their duty. So the husband and father of two was executed to set an example for others.[5]

The year 1914 had seen fighting on a scale and intensity never experienced before in the annals of war. As with the French army as a whole, the regiment had suffered titanic losses. The casualty rate among officers was particularly high. In its first 3 months of fighting, the 151 IR has suffered roughly 4,000 casualties, equating to a casualty rate of 125 per cent if the theoretical strength of 3,250 is used. By far, it was the deadliest period of the war for the 151 and the French army as a whole. These losses were offset by the flow of replacements circulating into the regiment, which allowed it to remain operational (or to use modern parlance, combat effective). After the initial boost of reservists from the 351 IR – older men who'd served in the 151 during their active-duty service prior to the war – the majority of the reinforcements who arrived were 'recuperated' troops who'd been wounded or fell ill but judged fit enough to return to active service. Only about a fifth of the replacements were 'young soldiers', new recruits from the class of 1914 who started to be incorporated at the end of the year. The new arrivals were in turn themselves chewed up in the relentless fighting, and by year's end the regiment's ranks were considerably thinned.

Apart from a need in men, there were also great shortages in uniforms and equipment. Request after request was filed by regimental command, demanding restock in either worn out or missing articles of clothing and equipment. The men needed new trousers in subdued tones to replace their worn out and faded red ones. They were in desperate need of boots, socks, blankets, knitted woollens, entrenchment tools, wire-cutters, and more. But perhaps most pressing of all was that the troops needed rest, both physical and mental, from the severe strains impressed upon them. They had spent weeks in soupy mud and flooded trenches, while being constantly under fire, carrying out or repulsing incessant attacks, and performing Herculean tasks. Now with the approach of the holidays and a new year, the regiment was promised a much-needed week's rest off the line. At the start of 1915, it would leave the flooded fields of Flanders for good. But the cruel, grinding nature of the war ensured they wouldn't have long to recuperate. The 151 would soon be sent to another sector where the intensity of the fighting could not be cooled even by the cold, foul weather of the first winter of the war.

Chapter 3

The 'D' System: French Trench Networks

The men and officers of the 151 had first been introduced to what life in the trenches would be like in the flooded plains of Flanders. They became more accustomed to the experience over the winter of 1914–15. Gradually through the early spring and into the summer of 1915, the line of entrenchments along the length of the Western Front solidified and grew into a dense network of defensive entrenchments that varied between half a mile to several miles in depth on each side. The distance between the opposing first lines likewise varied from sector to sector. They could be as far as 1,000m apart but generally were much closer, between 100 and 400m. In some sectors the lines were closer still, only a few metres apart in places. As early as January 1915, under Joffre's orders, the French army laid down a pattern of 'active' and 'passive' zones along the length of the front, with the former offering covering fire for the latter. In theory, under this system the active zones were composed of strongpoints covering front and flanks together with protected secondary positions for counter-attack troops. The passive zones, only lightly manned, were heavily wired and covered by the strongpoints.

By the summer of 1915, three defensive lines – first line, second or support line, and reserve – had become the norm, each separated by several hundred metres. And each of these lines consisted not just of a single trench facing parallel to the enemy's but a confusing network of siege works. There were parallels (also known as firing trenches) and cover trenches situated a short distance behind them. Salients, reentrants, retrenchments, redoubts, outposts, observatories, saps, dugouts, underground galleries, ammo and supply dumps, and all connected by *boyaux*. At the end of 1915, French commanders estimated that for each mile of front, there were 20 miles of trenches. By the following year, this number was thought to have increased to 30 miles of trenches per mile of front, as the trench networks grew into veritable labyrinths. By 1916, in the more active sectors the number of defensive lines increased to four or five.

While the British and the Germans adopted a rigid system of fire bays and traverses, the French approach was less formulaic, often consisting of simple zig-zags without much complexity in design. The condition of the average French trench often shocked visiting British personnel. Even as late as the spring of 1916, Lieutenant Henri Desagneaux of the 359th Reserve Infantry Regiment was struck by the lack of organization in the preparation of defensive works:

> I am in charge of the wooden defence works at Lattes, Cugnes, and Rappont. These works were begun by the 121st Light Infantry Battalion, continued by the 120th and taken over by the 359th Infantry. I come to the following staggering conclusion: there is no overall plan for these works, everyone is building as he pleases. The 121st had their plan, the 120th didn't like it and modified what had been done, whilst the 359th has another conception of the defence works.
>
> Here is an example of such organization: the 121st was building machine-gun shelters at ground level; the 120th abandoned these to construct others beside them below ground. The light infantry dug trenches 90 centimeters wide with framework of interwoven branches built over them; in our regiment, the soldiers are digging them 1.2 meters wide with ready-built frames. We cannot therefore continue the works as it was . . . When we leave, our successors will undoubtedly have their own method of work and that's how after twenty months of war, nothing is done.[1]

Fire steps were constructed along the side facing the enemy to allow soldiers to observe enemy activity and fire on attacking troops. Observation and sniping was done through reinforced observation posts or concealed loopholes dug into the parapet. In front of the first-line trenches, advanced listening posts were dug and connected to the main trench line by a narrow sap. The connecting line might be subterranean but just as often they were not, and indeed many of these small advanced posts were nothing more than reinforced shell holes. Separating these look-outs from the enemy were belts of barbed wire entanglements erected to hinder enemy attacks and infiltrations. The extent of the entanglements constructed depended on the intensity of fighting, the propensity and intensity of artillery shelling, the proximity to the enemy lines, and the industriousness of the unit currently occupying the line. As the months went on, the thin belts grew in depth, consisting of a messy bramble of barbed wire affixed to stakes and rising to 4ft or more off the ground, and mixed with low-lying ground snares, strips of metallic trellis, expandable coils of wire, and freestanding obstacles like the ancient *chevaux de frise.* It was not uncommon for a belt of entanglements to expand to 10 or 15m in depth, and these themselves were doubled or tripled by adjoining belts. Only the occasional narrow passage cut periodically through allowed for the passage of patrols and work parties.

Fires were seldom allowed in the trenches, and were outright forbidden in the first line, as the smoke and fire only served to mark one's positions for enemy artillery, machine-gun, or sniper fire. The more fortunate or resourceful might have a small, charcoal-burning brazier to huddle up to in cold weather, often improvised from a salvaged metal drum. But often nothing of the sort was available. Practically no provision was made for the soldier's personal sanitation, and any such facilities in the trenches were rudimentary at best. Latrines were nearly always inadequate in both their preparation and number. Normally located in the support line, the typical latrine consisted of a shallow trench over which the man would squat to relieve himself. The more luxurious might feature a wood beam laid horizontally across a pit on which to sit and a wattle screen for privacy. Soldiers on duty in the first line though would simply relieve themselves in a quiet corner of the trench or an abandoned sap. Second Lieutenant Roger Campana of the 151 RI told of an exception to the rule while serving in Champagne in October 1915. A certain fastidious staff-officer seemed to believe his personal mission was to ensure that the first-line trenches was run more like a rear area barracks. In a moment of levity, Campana made the mistake of joking with the commandant that they had been sent up to the trenches with rifles and not brooms, a quip that brought down a scolding lecture about the proper construction of latrines. The staff officer even insisted that a design of his own creation be constructed, which the men took to calling 'staff listening posts'. And while the latrines might have achieved the degree of privacy intended, the safety provided by the commodes was less convincing.

> Several hours ago we received a volley of 'toadies' [mortar shells] . . . I suddenly saw bolting from the regulation latrine Private Vermeulen, holding in one hand his breeches halfway up around his knees while his shirt remained pulled up in the most indecent fashion, exposing his naked belly. He was spattered from head to toe with a mix of excrement and earth (but mostly excrement) and trembling with fear:
> 'Oh! Lieutenant!' he stammered, 'it wasn't quite my time yet, it seems. This damn toady came straight down at me and I barely had time to finish my business when it fell right in the middle of the latrine! Fortunately for me it made a fougasse, otherwise it would have blew me to pieces! A real geyser of shit, I tell ya! . . . All the merchandise came right down on my head and back, and there was a lot since the pit was almost full.'
> –'That's a system of drainage the commandant hadn't foreseen. Don't come over here, you really stink!'
> –'Maybe we should put on our gas-masks?' one his comrades proposed laughing.[2]

In order to reinforce the trenches and prevent cave-ins from the effects of rainfall, soil pressure, and shell-fire, the walls of the trenches were revetted. The French employed a multitude of methods and materials to this end, all defined by the characteristically inconsistent, non-uniform, yet resourceful measures of the French army in this war. Overall organization and supply – coupled with the aforementioned misguided mindset of senior commanders – remained inconsistent throughout much of the war and units taking up the line often had to improvise as best they could using whatever supplies and natural resources were on hand. As late as March 1916, material shortages were still a common occurrence.

> [L]et's say no more about the generals who succeeded each other in this sector, and their commanding general who should have known all about it – a part of the front, stabilized for more than a year, hadn't a panel of sheet metal or simple plank of wood to protect the soldiers from a downpour between two shifts of guard duty or two work details.[3]

By and large, French soldiers were left to fend for themselves and make do as best they could with the resources they could find or make on their own. Yet, it is this resourcefulness that marks one of the greatest virtues of the French soldier well worth mentioning here. In this environment, a system of work developed out of exigency on its own outside of official channels. It was system that became the governing force over all trench construction and indeed the French army as a whole: *le Système 'D'*. The *'D'* was an abbreviation for the verb *débrouiller*, 'to slog through'. Perhaps one could include with this the additional meanings of coping, of improvising, of making do. At its heart was a blend of spirit of resourcefulness and endurance:

> The 'Slogging Through System' is to make something out of nothing, to seize opportunity and luck when it presents itself, to use the circumstances, the terrain, the men, and all that falls under one's hand to attain the objective. The *'D'* System solves all problems by improvised means: it's the French system. The Boche had worked for years to create a formidable war machine . . . But when the storm which was to annihilate us was unleashed, who ended up being astonished? It was the Boche, for little Tom Thumb had fought fiercely. The Boche . . . has not yet understood that all the strength of the little Frenchman is in the *'D'* System.[4]

While their industrious enemy was building with planks and heavy timbers, and liberally pouring concrete for the construction of their entrenchments, French soldiers were reverting to their knowledge sourced from working the land. As a consequence, French trenches were defined by a primitive-looking hotchpotch of construction materials and techniques that looked like something more from the Stone Age than a modern entrenchment. To brace the walls, felled timber or pruned branches were used to form a variety of revetments, all ancient in design and use. Commonly they were interwoven into segments of panelling called wattles or wattling, or assembled into open-ended baskets called gabions, which were filled with earth once placed in position. When supplies were available, sandbags were used, as well as chicken wire, metal trellis, corrugated tin, and wood planks. But more often than not, many French trenches had no revetment at all and the walls were left unsupported. Cave-ins were all too common, and often the material was not on hand to repair it. And what about shelter for the men living at the front? Once again, the '*D*' System was the law of the land. Gabriel Chevallier spoke about the resourcefulness of the poilu in the way in which his comrades constructed their shelters.

> What was particularly striking about these makeshift constructions was that the materials used were themselves just bits of scrap and rubbish: old pieces of wood, old weapons, old pots and pans. With no resources except their wits, the combatants had come up with this primitive solution. A few metal implements sufficed for all their needs and life thus returned to the most basic conditions, as if to the dawn of time.[5]

The first *abris* ('shelters') thrown up in the autumn of 1914 were woefully inadequate, typically consisting of some logs or branches laid over the top of the trench with a few shovelfuls of earth thrown on top. For French soldiers, life in the trenches in 1914 and 1915 meant existence without any real protection against the shells. As the war progressed, French commanders realized the importance of having adequate protection for the troops and improvements were made. But these were still modest and often insufficient for withstanding heavier shelling. The rudimentary nature of French shelters stood in great contrast to the well-built, subterranean bunkers of German army, which were provided with amenities unheard of on the French side.

Ultimately, the amount of protection afforded was determined first by the purpose of the post and the importance of its occupants, and last in the pecking order of importance was the poilu. Proximity to the enemy's lines also played a part, as the heavier fire-power was typically directed not against the first line (owing to the proximity to the enemy's own line) but the supporting positions. Moreover, as French military doctrine evolved, the first line came to be viewed as merely an impediment to slow down an enemy advance in the event of an attack. And so it was in the first line that shelters were often negligible to non-existent. At best, a few sticks or a section of corrugated tin would be laid across the top of the trench with a few shovelfuls of earth thrown on top. Commonly, a small niche would be scraped out of the trench wall under the parapet, large enough for one or two men to fit. For a door, a tent-canvas would be draped over the tiny burrow to help block the wind and rain. One soldier writing for the trench newspaper *Le Filon* clarified that anything more than one of these dirty little alcoves was considered: '[A] sumptuous luxury only known in dead sectors . . . Everywhere else, you crouch down in a niche in the side of the trench, shrinking back ridiculously, wrapped up in tent-canvas . . . to sleep'.

It was only in the covering and support trenches that more substantial dugouts were built. Referred to alternately as *cagnas*, *guitounes* or *gourbis* – all words borrowed from the Arabic language spoken in French Algeria and Morocco which translate as 'hovel' or 'shack'. Most French dugouts were small in size and intended to house only a squad or two and were built to withstand the impact of light to medium calibre shells, and a direct hit could easily cause the shelter to collapse. Universally, they were no more than dark, wet, stinking, lice-infested, rat-ridden, cramped rectangular pits dug several metres under the parapets. For those closer to the surface, logs or heavy planks were laid crosswise over the top and finished off with sandbags or loose earth. When available, vertical supports of timber were added but just as often they were not, much to the chagrin of the occupants. The floor and walls were left bare with only a thin layer of straw laid down for bedding, which quickly became soiled with mud, filth, and vermin. Virtually no other furnishing was provided aside from repurposed ammo crates which were used as tables and chairs. If there was an abandoned village nearby, there might be an opportunity to equip the place with simple furniture, though as the war progressed this occurred less and less frequently. After thirty-six months of front service, Louis Barthas returned to his regiment's depot in Brittany and exclaimed: 'It was the first time since I'd been at the front, since 1914, that I'd seen benches and tables put to use by poilus for eating their meals.'

With no bunks, the men slept on the floor, packed in together like sardines, using their haversacks and knapsacks as pillows. The only lighting came from candles and small kerosene lanterns but these were permitted only if the entrance was well hidden from the enemy's view. Any source of heating might come from a small brazier but more often even this was lacking. Later in the war, deeper dugouts were constructed down to 3 to 5m underground and reinforced above with sheet metal, iron rails, or logs. While offering better protection from shelling, these only reinforced the troglodyte existence of the men. Paul Cazin, serving in the 29th Infantry Regiment, offered a description of the archetypal dugout found in the second line:

You go down 8 to 10 steps. You now find yourself in a dark cubby-hole, rectangular, low ceilinged, with some straw on the ground (though not always) that acted to scent and contain the earth. Sometimes when the soil was chalky the shelter was cold and seeping wet. For walls, deeply planted supports allowed the rifles to be hung up as furnishments. When a shell fell close by, the shelter sounded like the inside of a drum. A little bit of earth would become dislodged from the timbered roof and fall on you. If the canons were silent, you were plunged into the silence of a cave. Wet, this hole, so very wet, and completely infested with lice.[6]

Conditions were only moderately better for line officers who were typically housed together in a command post occupied in shifts. As a slight improvement, the walls, floor and ceiling might be lined with logs or planks. Some basic furnishment may also have been procured by the more resourceful, including a seat, wooden bunk, and perhaps even a small stove. Lighting was again provided by candles, kerosene lanterns, and acetylene lamps. Of course the more senior the officer, the nicer the accommodations. But it's safe to say that regimental officers of all grades led a rustic life, though rustic perhaps puts too soft an edge on it. Platoon and company commanders suffered right alongside their men, coping with most of the same privations and hardships. At the start of 1915, a whole cadre of new, bright-eyed officers would soon arrive at the front and learn for themselves what life in the trenches had in store for them.

Chapter 4

1915: The Killing Year

In the Argonne

After welcoming the New Year at Wemaers-Cappel, the 151 was transported by rail to the suburbs of Amiens, 100km to the south. As it reorganized its skeletal companies, the first groups of reinforcements of the new year arrived from the relocated depot in Quimper. These were on average company size (about 200 men) in strength, which helped quickly to boost the regiment's numbers. Some were late arriving new recruits from the class of 1914, 19 and 20-year-olds who'd been hurriedly pressed into service in the autumn of 1914 after only a few weeks of training. However, until April 1915 and the arrival of the class of 1915, two-thirds of the replacements were either reservists transferred to active duty (the army found a better use for them) or veterans who'd been wounded in combat the previous summer or autumn and had been returned to front-line service.

On 11 January, the regiment received orders to make ready for immediate departure – the 42nd Division was needed back at the front. Shuttled overnight by rail to Villers-en-Argonne, Daucourt, and Ante (Marne), the battalions hurriedly undertook preparations for their return to the front line. Word came down that they were going up to the Argonne Forest, lying immediately to the north of Vienne-le-Château. The news was also that the 151 had been assigned to a new army corps, the XXXII, commanded by General Humbert, which would be composed of the 40 and 42 IDs. Though there were many experienced hands presently serving in the 151 who'd already been to 'the dance', as the saying went, for a portion of men their baptism of fire would come in the chaotic labyrinth of the Argonne, in a sector called Bois de la Gruerie. Not long into 1915, the name would be deformed into its new nickname, 'Bois de la *Tuerie*' – 'Slaughter Wood'. Unlike other sectors on the Western Front, the Argonne was an active sector for the duration of the war, and the greatest period of intensity lasted from the summer of 1914 to the summer of 1915. It wasn't simply the length of the operations, though. The fighting in the Argonne had a signature all of its own. Densely packed pines and birch trees, thick vegetation, and a confusing jumble of steep ravines worked to reduce visibility and enhance the sense of claustrophobia. The opposing trenches were very close to each other, between 25 and 50m, and in some places the lines actually connected, the two sides separated from each other by only a sandbag barricade. It constituted a radical change in landscape for the men, coming from the flat, featureless fields of Flanders. The combat in the Argonne would be relentless: sudden raids, artillery bombardments, and grenade attacks. The fighting was up close and personal. And underlying all of this, quite literally, a war of underground mines was being waged, each side detonating explosives under their foes' positions to gain the upper hand over one small portion of front. The positions themselves had innocuous sounding names – Dry Ravine, Lost-Children, White o' the Eye, Half-Moon, the Goose Foot, the Pig Tail. But these would take on a profound and lasting significance in the minds of those who fought there.

Only two weeks had passed since leaving the flooded trenches of Flanders when, on 15 January, the regiment was alerted that it would be going up to the front-line trenches the next day. Over the past week, additional detachments of replacements had arrived, some being incorporated directly in the trenches after the regiment had taken up its positions. By the 20 January, the total number of effectives would reach its peak at 46 officers and 2,732 men. Accompanying these timely reinforcements on the night of the 15th was a group of fresh-faced second lieutenants, thirteen of whom were candidates of Saint-Cyr – Roger Campana and his dozen comrades from Bordeaux. Campana was assigned to the 5th Company under the command Second Lieutenant de Sainte Croix. Another newly minted officer and Saint-Cyrien arriving separately from the Bordeaux contingent was 19-year-old Roger Basteau, who was assigned to 7 Company under Captain Carré. Immediately upon arriving at the front, Second Lieutenant Basteau felt like he had entered a different world and it was a rude shock to his system. This was a world of persistent cold, mud, filth, and rain. It seemed impossible to get warm, or to keep dry, or to remain clean. Even for the officers, there was little in the way of food and one of his first meals at the front consisted of canned lobster meat, a piece of Camembert cheese, some dry biscuits, and coffee, all served cold in driving rain. For the men it was cold soup and bread. In the dark early morning hours of 16 April, the fledgling officers were introduced to their platoons. Campana noted that his platoon was composed entirely of men from the north together with the various northeastern departments of France. The veterans in their ragged and dirty uniforms stood in stark contrast to the new officers in their crisp, light-blue greatcoats, and reflexively they looked upon their new commander with irony in their eyes. Were these boys – younger in age and inexperienced in the harsh realities of war – to be their leaders? For his part, Campana looked on them with admiration and his first impressions were good. Basteau was more forthright in his account of their reception: 'We knew nothing, or almost nothing, about how to do our job! Our arrival wasn't well received by the old NCOs who'd all gone through the '14 campaign. They have only the most minimal confidence in us young officers coming from the rear who've not yet received their baptism of fire.'[1]

Time was short and Campana and the others were afforded little time to get to know the men. This would have to happen in action. Soon 5th Company, together with the rest of the regiment, were loaded into trucks and driven 17km north to La Neuville-au-Pont. From there, 1 and 3 Battalions marched east to the little town of Florent-en-Argonne, while 2 Battalion proceeded 12km north to the even smaller hamlet of La Harazée. When not serving on the front line, these tiny rural villages would act as the 151's home for the next seven months. La Harazée in particular would be the ready reserve area to the trenches that lay a little more than a kilometre beyond it. As Campana approached the front line for the first time, he heard:

> A low rumbling, almost like a distant storm. Gradually, it increased in volume and turned into a strong rolling sort of noise that was like the sound of large wagons bouncing along a paved street. The detonations seemed to reverberate a hundred times over and over. Then the rolling sound grew louder, more resonant, more terrifying. Suddenly the whole scene came into view. Against the grey sky there were little white puffs that looked for all the world like snowflakes: they were shrapnel shell bursts.[2]

The column of heavily laden men advanced silently. As it passed through the ruined village of Vienne-le-Château, the sky grew darker as night began to fall. Around them, the ground had been gouged with shell holes. Further damage was visible from the stone walls of the village which had been knocked down by shellfire. On either side of the road were overturned caissons and splintered trees. A short way off, the narrow creek of la Biesme overflowed its banks and reflected the pale, fading light of dusk. As the sound of the cannonade grew louder, individual detonations of shells could be clearly distinguished, followed by quick stabs of light that lit up the sky in flickering flashes. To complete the dismal atmosphere, a heavy downpour commenced. Arriving at last at La Harazée chilled in their drenched clothes, 2 Battalion spent the night and the next day in the hamlet before customarily heading up to the lines on the evening of 17 January together with 1 Battalion. The regiment would occupy the subsector of Fontaine de la Madame, relieving the 120 and 147 IRs of the 4 ID. In liaison to their right would be the 162 IR, while to its left were units of the 40 ID. They entered the first *boyau* at the outskirts of La Harazée, plunging into the dark and narrow communication trenches that led to the second and first lines. Cold rain fell silently down. Occasionally, signal rockets shot up into the sky shedding a bloody light across the foreboding hills, while serrated saplings standing like giant quills cast evil-looking shifting shadows. Campana relates:

The floor of the trench consisted of a thick, sticky mud that made progress laborious. Stray bullets whistled overhead or bore into the trees around us with a sharp crack. Occasionally a shrapnel shell burst in the woods, the sound of the explosion reverberating between the steep ravines like a huge thunderclap. We are passed by stretcher-bearers heading back down the line carrying the dead on their litters. It sends a chill down the spine.[3]

After going some distance, the columns came to a halt. Word was passed down from man to man that the guide who was to lead them into their assigned positions had not arrived. They would have to wait. Hours passed as the men waited in silence in the chilly rain. At last the guide turned up and the column resumed its slow progress in the inky darkness, the men running into tree trunks felled by shell-fire and stumbling upon craters full of icy water. After what seemed like hours of trudging and bumbling along, they arrived in the first line. Campana and his platoon had relieved a platoon of the 147 IR and now occupied a section of trench covered with logs that were topped with a layer of earth. At last, Campana found himself in a front-line trench, no more than 30m from the enemy. After establishing liaison with the units on his right and left, Campana sat on the firing step and took in his surroundings. As he listened to the sound of a fire-fight blasting away nearby and the detonations of shells in the wooded ravines, Campana was beside himself with joy. This is precisely where he wanted to be, right in the thick of things, at the 'post of honour'. He was still uninitiated in the cruelties of war – his time would soon come.

The terrain in the 151's new sector was practically the polar opposite of the largely flat, open land around Ypres: a series of undulating hills and plateaus cut by steep ravines and covered in densely packed pines and undergrowth. Along the bottom of many of the ravines wound shallow streams, named after the natural fountains from which they sprang. Running down the centre of the 42 ID's sector was la Fontaine-aux-Charmes ('the Spring of Charmes'), which bifurcated at the level of the first line into the Fontaine-aux-Charmes to the west and the Fontaine de la Madame to the east. The situation that the 151 found itself in was tenuous. On the right, 1 Battalion was holding a shaky line atop a hill some 200m in elevation called Blanleuil (more traditionally, Blanlœil or Blanc-L'œil – 'White o' the Eye'), where a portion of the trenches were recently taken and currently held by Germans troops after violent close-quarter combat. Immediately to the northwest of Blanleuil and separated by a steep ravine was another hill of equal height called Enfants-Perdus ('Lost Children'). There, a company held a line of trenches isolated from the neighbouring positions. On the left, the companies of 2 Battalion held a similarly fragmented line, with one of them occupying a trench situated in the bottom of the Fontaine-aux-Charmes valley. Another position was on an adjacent hill known as la Sapinière, which was held by a single platoon clinging to its steep slopes. It too was isolated from those around it and could only be reached under cover of darkness.

In the wintry conditions the bottom of the trenches had been churned up into a quagmire of thick, sticky mud composed of heavy clay characteristic of the Argonne. The men sunk into it up to their shins, though in spots it was knee-deep. The cold was made all the worse by rain and snow. Added to the natural miseries were the man-made ones. German artillery was active and shrapnel shells frequently burst in the shredded canopy of the forest, while light and medium calibre high explosives smashed into the trees and struck down around the regiment's lines. All of this produced a tremendous racket, as each detonation reverberated throughout the steep ravines. The pale grey light of morning gradually revealed a mutilated forest of brown, black, and grey trees, slashed and splintered by artillery fire and bullets, which stood in stark relief against the white of the snow that blanketed the ground and clung to the butchered branches.

Already on its first day in the line there were casualties and the scribe for the 151's *JMO* recorded the year's first combat losses: three men killed and fourteen wounded by shell-fire. In fact, Campana himself had received a rude welcome to the front. While standing in his trench, he was struck in the right thigh by a small shell fragment, which fortunately was already spent and caused only bruising on his skin. Still sleep-deprived from the journey up the night before, he soon dozed back off only to be suddenly awoken by the detonation of a German 77 shell landing close by. There was another blast and a then another, even closer still. Raising himself up, Campana heard one of his men call out:

> 'Lieutenant,' Niquet, a little sergeant from the Class of '14, cried out, 'I really think that we are rep—'
>
> I didn't hear the end of his sentence. Suddenly I felt as though I had been punched square in my face and I fell back. I laid there for several moments completely stunned. When I came to, my nose, my mouth, my eyes were filled with dirt, and my ears rang with a continuous grinding sound, like a locomotive derailing. But all of this immediately dissipated before the horrible sight in front of me. I froze, terrified. Niquet lay at my feet, his head crushed, formless. His greatcoat was covered with mud and brains. Blood was splashed on it in spots.[4]

Campana realized he had been hit a second time, this time somewhat more seriously. Looking down he saw that his breeches had been torn in two spots. A shell fragment had penetrated his right thigh and blood began to seep from the wound. It didn't appear to be too bad to him, so he chose to remain at his post. Quickly bandaging his leg, he then set off with Second Lieutenant Sainte-Croix to tour their position. Peering through a loophole in the trench wall Campana could make out, stretched out on the slopes, grey and blue forms: the German and French dead from previous fighting now rotting between the lines. The air was filled with a strange cacophony of sound as stray bullets zipped high overhead like super charged bees, making a dull thud as they burrowed into the ground, whining loudly when ricocheting off something hard. Campana believed he had observed explosive bullets fired by the Germans smashing into the trees. It was a claim often asserted by French soldiers suspicious of the conduct of the German invaders, who'd already committed atrocities in 1914. Any nefarious new weapon introduced by the Germans – flamethrowers, poison gas, aerial bombings of civilian areas by zeppelins and planes – was perceived as the savage Boche up to his usual devious tricks. More likely in this case, Campana and his compatriots were simply witnessing the destructive ballistic effects of a normal bullet. Despite all the firing, the enemy had no intention of attacking, only of keeping up their harassing fire as the men huddled in the cold, shivering in their muddy holes. As the reality of trench warfare began to sink in, Campana betrayed his naivety when he wondered to himself: 'Where are the beautiful charges of former times, sounded by bugles and beaten by drums under a blue sky in the clear bright of day? Will these things return?'

The snow continued to fall throughout the afternoon and soon it was dark. During the night, combat patrols were sent out to make contact with the enemy. There was a certain rowdiness and chicanery to these activities, something that was reinforced by the occasional name-calling and derogatory exchanges between the troops on opposing sides. The patrols and small raids that had already become so common in the Argonne served no real strategic value other than to harass the enemy forces. And though there was an element of horseplay to it all, the consequences were serious indeed. Some patrols tossed crudely made bombs into German listening posts, high-tailing it back to friendly lines even before the resulting blasts had gone off. Others simply got lost in the woods, accomplishing little else but to provoke a lively fusillade from the opposing side, which triggered a response in kind from the jittery men in the French lines. By the end of their second day on the line, the 151 had lost another dozen men killed or wounded.

Two days had passed since Campana received his flesh wound. His thigh had now swollen up and a large red and purple bruise surrounded the wound, and every time he came down on his right leg, he felt a sharp shooting pain. But Campana refused to go to the first-aid post for fear of being evacuated to the rear after only just arriving at the front. To distract himself, he spent the day chatting to his men about their families and plans for the future. The conversation was accompanied by the noise of French 75 shells whistling loudly as they rushed overhead, exploding in the German trenches with a loud crash. But then just as quickly as it had begun, the barrage ceased and silence returned to the lines as night approached. The temperature dropped and the men huddled piteously together trying to use their combined body heat to keep warm. The frigid cold and the slobbering mud soon proved to be the real enemy. It was merciless and it took a toll just as much as the bullets and shell fragments.

> The sticky mud rose up to their knees in some places and up to their thighs in others. It is a sort of greenish-brown clay, really awful. The more you walk, the more you sank into it and if you remain in place, it's even worse. It feels like your feet are being gnawed at by a thousand ants or at times like they are covered in burning coals. They swell up from dropsy, they turn red, purple, brown, as if they were becoming gangrenous.
>
> Tonight three of my men have had their feet completely frost-bitten and were evacuated this morning. The leg-wraps impair the circulation of blood and it's impossible to take off your shoes, for if an attack is ordered at that moment, it would have to be made bare-foot in the snow.
>
> We don't think about death. The whistling bullets, the bursting shells, they don't frighten us. It's easy enough to ignore them. But this cold, this terrible cold! My feet felt like blocks of ice. Oh, I only wished to go on the attack. That would at least warm us up a bit.[5]

Campana's condition quickly deteriorated. Along with his infected wound, leg pains, and numb feet, a wracking migraine and then a burning fever overtook him, followed by bad congestion. Early the next morning he was finally evacuated, only returning to the regiment at the end of April. He had lasted only three days in the trenches, a true testimony to the everyday attrition of the Western Front.

A bloody routine set in of frequent shelling by artillery and bursts of gunfire, which then died down as quickly as they had erupted. Grenades and improvised bombs became the weapons of choice, bursting in the confined spaces and reaping gorey chaos on both sides, accompanied by the sounds of shrieks and yells of pain and fear. Small raids and counter-raids were short, bloody affairs that often resulted in nil gains. Occasionally though the enemy would catch a night watchman off guard, or successfully infiltrate and seize a part of a trench line. Then the enemy party would barricade themselves into the conquered section, stubbornly defending it with grenades, before eventually being overwhelmed by a superior counter-attack force. Increasingly, German *minenwerfers* ('mine-throwers') caused havoc as the French lines were continuously targeted with a sudden and accurate fire. These mortars shot a tubular metal projectile packed with powerful explosives in a high arc that proved devastating to entrenched positions. The bombs, the shape of which led to poilus calling them 'Stove-pipe' bombs, had a tendency to tumble clumsily end-over-end in their silent flight. Like the French army as whole, the 151 was insufficiently supplied with mortars any where near as accurate or powerful. Instead, they had to rely on the 'D' System. Utilizing what were called Cellerier mortars (named after the front-line soldier who came up with idea), unexploded 77mm shells were opened, emptied of their contents, mounted to wood sabots and by so doing repurposed as makeshift mortars. These crude weapons were the best many poilus could hope for, for the time being. But the Celleriers were no match for the powerful *minenwerfer*.

The 151 would only be relieved after spending an abnormally long two weeks in the trenches of Slaughter Wood. In that time, it had suffered over 350 killed and wounded, and hundreds more evacuated from illness or frostbite. A roll taken once the unit was off the line had only 44 officers and 1,990 men present for duty. This represents a snapshot in time. From then on, the total number of effectives would constantly fluctuate over the coming months as replacement troops arrived by the hundreds, counter-balanced by the loss of these same men from combat and illness. But on average the number would hover between 2,000 and 2,500.[6] The regiment's reprieve would be pitifully short. In the face of continued enemy attacks, the battalions were successively sent back up to the line after barely four days of rest.

Thereafter, a regular rotation to and from the trenches was established. Typically the battalions of the regiment would relieve each other in the first or second lines. When operational circumstances dictated, interior reliefs by companies within the lines were conducted. Generally, each rotation in the lines lasted five to seven days, followed by an equal amount of time off the line when circumstances permitted. When out of the trenches, the battalions were by and large billeted in the same villages of Florent, Croix-Gentin, or La Harazée (in ready reserve), set up in barns, makeshift shelters of sticks and earth, or in tents. In any case, they were rarely more than 8km from the front line, always within earshot of the gunfire. Up in the line, mostly their job was to dig, construct, haul supplies, and stand on watch. When not on duty, the men played cards, wrote and read letters, chatted, smoked, and tried to get some rest. This last was made difficult by constant fire-fights and bombardments, which disrupted any semblance of sleep cycles. When in the trenches, there was no question of washing and after a week in the line, the men were filthy. Much time was spent in the rear removing lice that infested their hair and clothing but usually to little avail. The men just had to get used to the constant biting and itching of the insidious vermin.

The fighting in the Argonne devolved into a series of bloody reprisals more like vendettas than military operations. It was a tit-for-tat tribal war over local objectives that barely registered on a map. Typical of one of these operations is an attack carried out on 17 February by 1 Battalion, under the 44-year-old Commandant Eugène Segonne. Segonne – a graduate of Saint-Cyr and winner of the Chevalier de la Légion d'honneur and the Croix de Guerre – had started the war as a captain on the regimental staff of the 151 before being transferred to lead the 8 LIB as a commandant in September 1914, a post that he held until he was wounded in November. After recuperating, Segonne was transferred back to the 151 on 18 January to take command of 1 Battalion. Now he was ordered to send his battalion to counter-attack in coordination with the 16 LIB to retake a portion of trenches on Blanleuil that had been lost to a German raid. To assist in the attack, three underground mines were dug by engineers at various points under the Blaneuil positions.

At 8.00 am, the mines were detonated and followed by a 10-minute bombardment of the new model 58mm mortars. At 8.10 am, the infantry jumped out of their trenches and raced up the slopes and 45 minutes later the objective was back in French hands and the gains consolidated. The reconquered positions were then subjected to a bombardment by the enemy of 77s and 105s as well as bursts of enfilading machine-gun fire. Not long after, a strong German counter-attack force was sent in and overwhelmed the defenders. Elements of the 151 sent back up the hill to attack again were quickly driven back. All in all, the operation cost the 151 nearly 160 men. More than 350 more had been killed or wounded in the supporting units. Among the dead was Commandant Segonne. The next day, 1 Battalion was ordered to attack Blanleuil again. Every single man who left the trench was immediately either killed or wounded, and the attacks were soon called off. The futile attacks of 17–18 February were the bloodiest days in the month of February, which ultimately claimed 440 casualties. A German retaliatory attack on the morning of 1 March – utilizing artillery, mortars, tear gas, and the explosion of two mines – significantly ratcheted up the violence. That attack cost the regiment 166 killed and 178 wounded and set off a series of back-and-forth attacks over the next several days. Scores of men were shot by rifle or machine-gun fire, struck by shrapnel balls, or mutilated by shell and grenade fragments. On average the 151 lost ten men a day during the month of March. But this number is deceiving, for as with any monthly period, the unit spent roughly two weeks off the line. In the actual two weeks of March it was in the trenches, some 575 men were killed or wounded. To add to the butcher's bill, were again hundreds more evacuated for sickness, frostbite and trench foot.

Ultimately replacing the the fallen Segonne was Commandant Edouard Jean Victor Moisson, the battalion leader from the 162 IR who'd briefly been posted to oversee the 151 after the black day of 10 November 1914. Moisson arrived to the 151 a week after Segonne's death, taking over as the commander of 1 Battalion in March. Born in Boulogne-sur-Mer (Pas de Calais), the black-haired, grey-eyed career officer and husband was 49 years old in 1915. As a young man he had attended Saint-Cyr and was promoted to Chevalier de Légion d'honneur in January 1914, while serving as a battalion leader in the 162 IR. Commandant Moisson had been wounded the previous September while serving in this regiment. As commander of 1 Battalion in the 151, his courage under fire and compassion for his men quickly earned him the respect and devotion of his his subordinates. When Colonel Dillemann would leave the regiment on 9 May to take command of the 80th Infantry Brigade, Moisson was promoted to lieutenant colonel and given command of the 151. Moisson, would make a habit of touring the front-line trenches and placing himself in exposed positions under fire. His infectious fighting spirit and caring disposition endeared him to the men of the 151 and earned him the nickname of 'Papa Victory' (one wonders if his second given name of 'Victor' might have played a part in this as well).

The 151 would manage to remain combat effective throughout this time only because of the periodic influx of replacement troops, which continued to arrive in company size detachments, like the turning of a massive human waterwheel. Throughout the spring of 1915, these were generally troops who had already been wounded or evacuated due to illness, but who had since recovered and were declared fit for front-line service. Others had been scoured from the rear services, men who were serving in auxiliary branches or who'd previously been declared unfit for service. A majority continued to come from the regiment's depot at Quimper, men from the areas the regiment had traditionally drawn: Meuse, Ardennes, Nord, Paris. But they also came from the depots of other regiments from Cantal, Charente, and Dordogne in the south, and the Loire-Inférieure in Brittany. Beginning in mid-April, the new recruits of the class of 1915 started arriving at the front and were incorporated into combat units.

Arriving at Florent with a large detachment of these *bleuets* ('rookies') on 20 April was Corporal Henri Laporte. Laporte was assigned to 8 Company, which was commanded by Lieutenant Couplet, the same officer who had broken his sabre and managed to escape capture when the regiment had been overwhelmed at Steenstraet the previous November. With one of his pals from basic training, Laporte picked out one of the huts made of sticks and earth to pass the night in. Its primitive appearance reminded him 'of a picture from one of the first pages of "The History of France"'. The next day he would make the long arduous march up to La Harazée, arriving in the early morning hours.

> The moon is still shining and presents a truly eerie sight. Almost all the homes have huge, gaping holes in their roofs. The place looks deserted. the silence is broken by the sound of cannon blasts. The column advances as quietly as possible. We are covered in dust and a bit tired from the

weight of the pack and rifle. At 9.00 am we take up our billets in partially destroyed houses and stables. This first exertion of getting us close to the lines has wiped us out and as soon as we put our packs on the ground and place our equipment, we fall asleep on the little bit of straw provided us.[7]

Back in the line, casualties among the officers had continued to rise. On 14 April, the 151 lost yet another battalion leader when Commandant Vaudescal (3 Battalion) was killed while carrying out a reconnaissance at Enfants-Perdus. The second commandant of the regiment to be killed in the Bois de la Gruerie, he would sadly not be the last. But it was among the junior line officers where there was the greatest need of replenishment. On 27 April, a shell landed in the trench Second Lieutenant Basteau was in, killing a corporal and two men, and projecting several small shell fragments into Basteau's face. He was evacuated but his injuries fortunately proved to be only flesh wounds and he was back in the trenches twelve days later. On the same day Basteau was sent off the line, Aspirant Raymond Jubert had arrived and was assigned to 2 Company. So too did the recuperated Second Lieutenant Campana, who was now assigned to 4 Company, commanded by Lieutenant Vincent. Out of curiosity, Campana decided to pay a visit to his former company (5th) to see his old comrades. He was disappointed to discover that none of the men he'd previously served with still remained, the combat on 17 February and 1 March having been particularly devastating. Included among the dead were four of his Saint-Cyr comrades-in-arms: Denevault, Marc Laguens, Dartiguelongue, and Rogier. But Campana was actually relieved to be back at the front. Passing up through the woods under shell-fire, he was soon back on the front line with his company in the trench known as the *Queue de Cochon* ('pig-tail'), a mere 10m from the enemy. And though the German troops were tenacious, the men of the 151 proved they could dish it out as well as they could take it and Campana, in particular, was a tough nut:

> We bring up two crates of grenades and I copiously provision the four men in the listening post, which is in an old boyau that is only separated from the Boche listening post by a barricade of sandbags . . . [The next morning] a note wrapped around a stone lands in the post. I unfolded it and read the following inscription . . . 'Frenchmen, you're done for, but we're fed up too. Don't throw any more bombs and we won't throw anymore.'
> I wrote under this inscription 'Cambronne's word' spoken in the evening at Waterloo, carefully refolded the paper, wrapped it back around the stone, and threw this new type of projectile back into the enemy trench. I then distributed to the four men near me 50 grenades and we

threw them without let up on the Boches to show them simply that we weren't done for nor were we fed up.⁸

Campana had already been initiated in the ways of war. Now it was Laporte's turn to enter the trenches for the first time. Entering the entrance to the *boyau*, they advanced in the greatest silence, talking and smoking being prohibited. As they moved up they passed by countless communication trenches that wound off in various directions into the dark night. From time to time there was a sound like a speeding siren, high and shrill, of stray bullets. Laporte and his comrades moved single-file into a deep *boyau* made pitch black inside by the overhead covering of logs. 'An order comes along in a hushed tone which we pass along: "Fix Bayonets". First moment of excitement. I ask the man next to me, a vet: "Are we going to attack?" "No," he tells me, "it's a precaution taken when going up into the first-lines."'⁹

His first night in the line, Laporte didn't sleep a wink. Laporte was struck by how close the lines were to each other, especially the advanced listening posts, which in some cases were only a few metres away from the enemy's. There was the occasional rifle shot exchanged by the opposing sentries and flares shot up into the sky from either side. On his second day, without warning, French 75s unleashed up a barrage, the shells grazing low overhead in an ear-splitting whistle before exploding in a roll of thunder on the German trenches opposite. Laporte's platoon was told to evacuate their trench in order to avoid being struck by any short-falling rounds. As they filed back into the *boyau* of the second line, the Germans inundated the trench they'd just left with bombs. The fire of the 75s doubled and Laporte and his comrades began hurling grenades into the German trenches.

> One of my comrades standing next to me is wounded by a bomb fragment. Another has his leg crushed into pulp. A third is horribly slashed open, his blood soaking the bottom of my greatcoat. We're all crouching down now, no longer standing to throw grenades. This demonstration lasts two long hours. I don't have a scratch on me. It was our baptism of fire. But my poor comrades are carried out by stretcher-bearers. These are the first I see get sent back and I begin to realize that this is what war is. Yet isn't this why we're here afterall, to defend our soil which the Germans have tread upon? We swear at this moment to avenge our comrades. Already one, who had only just arrived, has died.¹⁰

Moving back to the second line, Laporte was comforted to find the first shelters – simple rectangular holes large enough to hold five or six men, which were dug 2 or

3m down and covered over with logs. For the men on watch, small cavities were scratched into the trench wall, which afforded only a modicum of shelter from the elements. As Laporte and his comrades settled into one of these tiny shelters, a horrible smell began rising from the spot where he was seated. Dislodging bits of earth with his shovel to find the source, he was horrified to discover he'd been sitting on the rotting corpse of a German soldier. After completely unearthing the rotted remains, stretcher-bearers came to disinfect the spot with chlorine before removing the body in a tent canvas.

By the spring, life in Slaughter Wood had settled into a relentless pattern of surprise raids, brief fusillades of rifle and machine-gun fire, seemingly random attacks by grenades and bombs, and sudden storms of trench mortars and artillery shells, all of which provoked almost immediate retaliation in kind. In the front lines, the once-peaceful forest of pines and birch was now only a confusing jumble of jagged and smashed trees, inextricably interwoven with masses of wire entanglements of every description. Lying scattered about here and there were helmets, rusted rifles, pieces of equipment, and scraps of clothing, and the pathetic remains of bodies and pieces of bodies. As the weather warmed, the smell of rotting flesh wafted through the air, summoning an army of flies to descend upon the small corner of hell. And through all this destruction and death undulated the little brook known as the Spring of Charms, its cool water now polluted with poisonous chemicals and human carrion. Beginning in April, mine warfare started ramping up as both sides took turns at blowing each other up. The method of exploding underground mines beneath the positions of the opposing side was not new in this part of the front. The occasional use of mines to prepare the way for attacks had been experimented with as early as October 1914. Invariably, the goal was to blow up an advanced section of the line and then rush forward a group of men to occupy it to make the position untenable to the enemy and eventually connect it to one's own lines. Now, mines would become a weapon routinely deployed in the Bois de la Gruerie to assist in taking local positions.

Laporte got to experience first-hand what it was like when one of these frightening blasts went off.

> We were provisioned with grenades, and after having received the necessary instructions, we waited impatiently to see what would happen. Barely a quarter hour had elapsed when we felt the earth tremble and, as soon as it did, there was a frightful din. Two or three tons of earth, with dead bodies included, were projected high into the air. Shouts, curses, rifle shots. The 75s went into action too. The mine had been blown, tossing up the German trenches. All together we immediately pelted their trenches with a volley of grenades. We were so over-excited that, throwing aside

> all precaution, we stood on the fire-steps, exposing half our bodies to the enemy's shots. The sergeant-major who was our platoon leader yelled for us to get down, but we could no longer hear his shouts. We were enraged, and threw without let up the missiles that sewed death across from us. It was war: to protect yourself you must put your adversary out of the fight. Moreover, this was all reciprocal.[11]

Laporte quickly learned the ways of the front, mainly, how to stay alive. To deal with the Germans *minens*, they had adopted the 'shuttle' system: rushing this way and that in order to evade the projectiles as they plummeted to earth. A deadly game of hide-and-seek with the German bombs.

> After the engineers set off a mine, the Germans retaliate with *minens*. One of these lands a metre from us in the bottom of the trench. I have just enough time to leap to the side with my two neighbours. It causes more excitement than harm, as the trench takes the brunt of the blast. From all sides these 'stove-pipes' come raining down on us. Our sad trench is demolished once again. We're blinded by the dust and smoke. It takes a superhuman effort to not lose control of one's wits entirely. Death is on the look-out for us at every moment. Very close to me, one of my comrades is hideously torn to pieces . . . These macabre bundles are now routine sights for us, though each time our hearts ache. Everyone's faces are grave. What horror, this war.[12]

Not long after, while eating his soup, Laporte spots another mortar speeding down towards him.

> I only have time to make a quick jump to the side. A shock, an explosion, a shower of stones, a thick cloud of black smoke . . . that's all I remember. I had been thrown two metres away, though with no harm done except for a simple concussion. My rifle and my pack had been smashed. In the boyau, two of my comrades were stretched out lifeless.
> . . . Another big Minemm [*sic*] speeds straight at us. With two comrades, we have just enough time to take cover in the entrance of a shelter to a mine gallery. I'm closest to the trench. A violent explosion is produced above our heads, the gallery gives way and we are partially buried in the earth. At the same moment, I felt what was like a hammer blow on my waist. I struggled as best as I could to free myself and not to suffocate. My other comrades in the trench are too busy sheltering themselves from the falling projectiles to notice that three of us are buried.

> After a while, I managed to free myself completely. My face is bloodied from the cuts produced by the falling stones. My two other comrades who had entered the gallery first were killed under the collapse. My body half-dislocated, I crawl on my stomach as best I could toward the second-line... I went a dozen metres, but feeling that my strength would abandon me, sheltered myself as best as possible under a shelter. I then perceived immediately just above me the rumbling of a heavy bomb. It arrived in a thundering noise, exploding right on my makeshift shelter. Again everything collapsed on me and I remained under the rubble for about an hour. Impossible to move except for my right foot. I'm lucky when a calm settles back in and several engineers going down the boyau see my moving foot. They manage to free me and carry me to the first-aid post. There, after a brief cleaning-up to disinfect the wounds (especially on my head and face), I'm laid out on a stretcher and evacuated out of the first-aid post of La Harazée.[13]

Though Laporte's whole body was in terrible pain there were simply too many wounded at La Harazée needing care. After being examined by a doctor he was told he had no serious injuries other than being strongly concussed. After resting for three days, he left with his company as it was heading back to the rear, walking with the help of two comrades 9km back to Florent. In May, the mining increased. From 6 May to 15 June, the French alone exploded seventy-eight mines.[14] In the pages of the 151 *JMO* covering the month of May a total of twenty-one mine detonations were recorded, sixteen of which were set off by the Germans. At midnight on the night of the 16–17 May, Campana and his platoon got caught in one of several detonations under the first line at Blanleuil.

> It felt like the earth opened up to swallow us whole. Stones, huge masses of earth plummeted down everywhere, crushing my soldiers. I had thirty-five men before the explosion and only eighteen afterward. The majority had been buried under the debris. Buried alive! They had met the most horrible end possibly imaginable and among them was my orderly. The poor boy had been killed following me to the front. I cried hard over it. He was very attached to me. I used to let him sleep in my hovel and more than once I would wake up to find two blankets over me, mine and his, which he'd covered me with so that I wouldn't get cold. He was fine with just his greatcoat and if the temperature dropped too low, he'd go out into the trench to warm himself by walking up and down.
>
> ...

> And this poor boy had suffered the most awful of agonies. Covered over by several cubic metres of earth, he had slowly suffocated. We couldn't help him and we never found his body. It was one of the particularly painful moments of the war for me.[15]

The remaining eighteen men in Campana's platoon had all been banged up to one degree or another by the debris. Campana himself had been struck by a large stone on his right side, which produced a sizeable purple bruise. But their was no time to fret over such injuries, for the Germans had taken advantage of the destructive blasts to launch a raid of their own on the regiment's positions. For a few minutes, there was savage hand-to-hand fighting in the trenches.

> The next morning we picked up two dead bodies entwined together: a German and a Frenchman. The German, who'd been been horribly mutilated by the knife wielded by our man, used his last strength before dying to rip open the throat of our man with his bare teeth, and their stiff bodies looked like they were still locked in mortal combat.[16]

By the next day, Campana's right side had become more and more pained as a fever overtook him. But he refused to be evacuated, fearing that it would look suspicious if he let himself be evacuated so soon after the German raid without an obvious wound. And worse, he had only arrived just a few weeks before and he had come here to fight. He wouldn't allow for a repeat of his curtailed first tour. Only after his company was relieved the following night did Campana finally allow himself to be evacuated, having literally dragged himself back to La Harazée. It was soon revealed that his excruciating pain he was suffering was due to an appendicitis, likely caused by the blow he'd received from the large stone. He was sent to Toulouse where he was twice operated on in June. It was while recuperating in Bordeaux in July that Campana would learn the sad news of the death of his Saint-Cyr friends, Feix and Richard. Campana would have to endure another period away from his comrades suffering at the front, returning to the regiment again in October.

On the same day that Campana was recovering from his surgery in Toulouse, a group of reinforcements some 600 strong had just arrived at Sainte-Menehould. Among them was 18-year-old Corporal André L'Huillier, who after seven months of training in Quimper was making his homecoming. After posing for a portrait with two of his friends at a photography studio in town, L'Huillier and the other replacements marched north to Florent-en-Argonne, where he was assigned to 4 Company under Lieutenant Vincent. The next several days were spent conducting exercises and drills. To the north, the guns thundered away and only the hand-grenade and bomb-throwing exercises were of any interest to L'Huillier now that he was at the front. To relieve the stress and distract the men, a football match was also held between the 162 and the 151 (the 151 won 3–0, with L'Huillier scoring one of the goals). Just before going up to the trenches, the regimental band of the 162 IR would put on a concert for those who were about to face the guns. The tune of 'Le Rêve Passe' was made all the more impressive by the accompanying deep rumble of the guns and shelling. On 23 June he was sent up to La Harazée and then into the trenches.

Attack of 30 June

The month of June would see a steep escalation in the level of violence, as the Germans continued their development of new weapons and battlefield tactics. Both sides continued to shoot, shell, bomb, and blow each other up. The Argonne had become the proving ground for many of the German army's new weapons and battlefield tactics. On the night of 10 June, the Germans would release asphyxiating gas on the regiment's first line at Blanleuil. The delivery method was crude: the gas was contained in glass containers projected onto the French trenches, which shattered and released the gas. Thanks to the rudimentary gauze pads and protective goggles the regiment had received not long before, casualties remained light. But it was a harbinger of things to come. In the first six months of 1915, the XXXII Army Corps had lost 20,000 killed or wounded, and had 16,000 more evacuated from sickness.[17] For its part, the 151 had already suffered over 2,100 dead and wounded. Calculating this number into a percentage of loss is difficult given the constant flow of replacements into the regiment. Still, given that the peak total of effectives was on average around 2,700, this represents a combat attrition rate of over 75 per cent. Many of these casualties were able to recover from their injuries and subsequently returned to the regiment. Even still, on display was the appalling burn rate of everyday trench warfare in the Argonne without any major battles. What would real combat look like?

The terrifying answer would come on 30 June. A simple but brutally effective plan would be employed by German commanders. A small section of front would be selected as the target for an attack. A short but intense artillery bombardment conducted by the heaviest of weapons would then be unleashed, the effect of which was something akin to dropping one enormous bomb on the enemy positions. Then, a mixed force of grenadiers accompanied by engineers would infiltrate the destroyed positions, followed by groups of supporting infantry, machine-gunners and mortarmen. Slowly but steadily, the Germans made methodical advances, all the while avoiding the need for massive accumulations of men and materiel. At 2.30 am on 20 June, they loosed an intense barrage against a small section of front in the neighbouring Bagatelle sector, occupied by units of the 40 ID. For the assault, the Germans has assembled some of the heaviest calibre of guns yet seen in the Argonne – long-barrelled 100mm and 150mm cannon, powerful 210mm howitzers, and a great number of medium and heavy *minenwerfers*. And employed for the first time among the shrapnel and high-explosive ordinance were poison gas shells, a new and far more effective delivery method over the fixed canisters previously used in large-scale chemical weapon attacks. The fighting soon spread along the whole front, from Binarville to the Four-de-Paris. The French first-line trenches were totally destroyed and heavy losses inflicted. The attack was a great success and ten days later elements of the German 5th Army launched a general attack along the entire front of the French XXXII Corps using the same tactics. Included among the arsenal of heavy artillery, mortars, and poison gas, were flamethrowers and tens of thousands of the new model of stick grenade.

The 30 June represents one of the most severe trials of the war for the 151. In the early morning hours, what had been a normal exchange of mortar fire at Blanleuil suddenly exploded into a violent bombardment by German artillery and mortars. The storm of heavy *minens*, 150s and 210s – the heaviest calibre guns to date that the 151 had been subjected to – turned the forest into a hell of exploding metal, flying debris, and clouds of earth and smoke. On the morning of the attack, the 2 Battalion of the 151 was up in the line, the other two having been recently rotated to the rear areas for rest. Taking the brunt of the assault in the first-line trenches on Blanleuil were 5 and 8 Companies. The bombardment continued unabated for four hours as German rapid-firing revolver cannon and machine guns joined in, gouging off the tops of the parapets, collapsing the loopholes, and generally making it difficult and dangerous to watch for signs of the imminent attack. Breathing was already difficult in the smoke and dust-filled air just as poison gas was added to the nasty mix, obliging the men to tie on their gas pads and goggles. The day grew warm. Losses steadily mounted. The dead lay where they fell while streams of wounded descended down into the Ravin Sec to the first-aid post, where Doctor-Major Dalidet hurriedly applied dressings. In all the ravines a thick, suffocating smoke collected and darkened the sky. Hours passed like this. Then at 7.30 am, the enemy's fire lifted off the French first lines, and along the entire Bois de la Gruerie front, the German infantry attacked. Almost right away stick grenades started raining down into the 5 and 8 Companies trenches. As quickly as they could, the men snatched them and tossed them back out only moments before they exploded.

When the attack hit, Private Laporte was with four men from his platoon in the second line at the intersection with a *boyau* and cut off from the rest of the company. As the sound of the first German grenades began to burst all around them, they quickly threw up a makeshift barricade of backpacks and then using the supply they had by them, started tossing out grenades one after another. In the first line there was savage hand-to-hand fighting. Overwhelming the defenders, German troops soon began pushing towards the second line held by 6 and 7 Companies. German troops scampered down Blanleuil into Ravin Sec but a barrage of 75 shells cut them down. Second Lieutenant Basteau was in a trench with two platoons of 7 Company, close to the *Patte d'Oie* ('Goose-foot') at the bottom of Ravin Sec. This section of trench had overhead cover provided by logs covered with earth. But while it afforded modest protection it was at the same time unable to be properly defended. Close-quarter combat was raging all around them, the combatants fighting out in the open and in the trenches and *boyaux*, separated by narrow barricades of sandbags.

> The first wave of Germans pass over my covered trench without seeing us (we'd also been unable to fire on them) then, having been stopped by the machine-gun fire coming from the support-line, they fall back a little and pass back over our heads. A new wave arrived and finally overwhelms my trench, the enemy getting under the logs which we were unable to both fire out of or escape from. So the two platoons are separated: one is pushed back up Blanloeil; the other with me attempts to reach the Ouvrage de Marie-Therese, where the 162nd is barely managing to hang on. A gap is created between the two infantry regiments and it's into this hole that I stumble with fifteen men. Grenades burst, I'm wounded in both thighs. I get them quickly dressed at the first-aid post by Doctor Dalidet, allowing me to retake command of a detachment of men from the 151st and 162nd.[18]

While Basteau was running about with his men, Laporte and his comrades had now walled themselves into their small corner of trench using anything they could find. While some tossed grenades, others used their rifles to shoot down German troops who attempted to leap over the top of their trench. One of Laporte's comrades was struck in the chest by a shell fragment. Second Lieutenant de la Ferrière who was with them continued to empty his revolver over and over. Lying in dreadful pain beside Laporte was Sergeant Rolina, whose legs had been terribly shredded. With the enemy pressure too great, they had no choice but to abandon their poor comrade. For Laporte, it was a particularly agonizing moment, one which would haunt him for the rest of his life.

Back at Croix-Gentin, L'Huillier and the rest of 4 Company had been trying unsuccessfully to get some sleep in spite of the bombardment raging a short distance away. Suddenly a sergeant burst into their barracks and shouted: 'Everybody up, packs on, stack arms. We leave in a quarter hour.' – 'That's it,' quipped a Parisian street urchin, 'time to go to the dance.' The 1 Battalion had been called up to counter-attack against the enemy. L'Huillier was going into combat for the first time, a mere 12km from his home, in the same woods where as a child he would go hunting with his father. Approaching the front lines, at Four-de-Paris they came under machine-gun fire. Then at La Harazée, they were subjected to their first experience of being gassed. Fortuitously, 1 Battalion had received gas pads and goggles just two days before and was able to move through the gas clouds largely unaffected. On the road to Binarville and the glades that bordered the road, they suffered losses while waiting for further orders. They were out in the open with no cover and yet within view of the enemy. In the rush up to the front, they had left behind their entrenching tools. Now they dug desperately with their bare hands, clawing at the earth until their nails were torn and bloodied.

It was here that Jubert witnessed the death of his friend, Second Lieutenant Henri Richard (1 Company), a memory that seared itself into his consciousness. Richard – who happened to be L'Huillier's platoon leader – was a handsome 19-year-old with delicate features, wispy blond hair and clear blue eyes. He was also one of those who'd arrived with Campana in January. Nearly a year later, while coming off the line at Verdun, Aspirant Jubert would the relate the details of his death to Richard's still-grieving uncle, a NCO in another passing regiment. While pinned down under fire and struggling to scratch out some cover, Jubert heard someone call out that Richard was in need of a dressing bandage. Looking around him, he saw Richard lying a few steps away behind a mound with his head resting on a log. His sleeve torn by the bullet that had struck him, he reached out his pale arm towards the stretcher-bearers.

> He had his usual expression, the same soft eyes, and when he caught sight of me, he gave me the same smile I had come to know.
> 'Where are you hit, dear boy?
> 'Can you see, broken arm.
> 'That's Providence,' I said, 'just a few months of hospital.'
> He made a weary smile, closed his eyes, and lacked the strength to answer.
> 'Are you in pain?
> 'Yes, but only to leave you all.'
> When a bullet cracked down on the ground nearby, he suddenly stood up: 'Watch out, watch out for the machine gun that got me!' Then, as I did not seem to be moving far enough away, in a beeching voice he cried out my name. A few seconds later, as he was being carried off, a shell arrived and blew him away . . . thinking of him will always bring tears to my eyes.[19]

But the situation was critical elsewhere on the 42nd Division front too. The 1 Battalion was rushed up to the neighbouring sector of Bagatelle to the west of

Fontaine-Madame in support of the 8 LIB, where enemy forces had outflanked French works and completed a double-envelopment of the chasseurs of the 8 LIB. The fighting was savage, hand-to-hand, man against man. The next day Jubert would be evacuated, covered in blood, shot in the right arm and in the right foot, and with eleven grenade fragments in his legs. Jubert would survive his wounds, and after months of healing return to the regiment in October. Preliminary reports for the 151 had close to 300 killed, wounded or missing, mostly concentrated in 5 and 8 Companies. The front had been temporarily stabilized but the fighting resumed the next day with more German shelling and infantry attacks. Casualties climbed on both sides. Over the course of the day and late into the night, a series of murderous attacks and counter-attacks were carried out, as the dead piled up on the parapets. Basteau was among the injured, his second wound received in the Argonne. A shell had exploded close to his head, bursting his right eardrum while simultaneously projecting a shell fragment into his left hand. That evening he would be evacuated, joining Second Lieutenant de Riancey who'd been badly wounded in his arm.[20] In the middle of the night, 3 Battalion in its turn was thrown into the fight to launch a counter-attack on Bagatelle, but in the event, only minimal progress could be made. Grenade fights continued throughout the morning and afternoon of 2 July before a powerful enemy bombardment erupted again along the entire front.

Once again, after several hours the bombardment lifted and the enemy's infantry attacked. L'Huillier was in the midst of it. He had already received fragments from a mortar shell in his left thumb and chin when the Germans attacked. This first assault repulsed, they attacked again and again; seven times in all. L'Huillier's company also carried out two vigorous bayonet attacks that pushed the enemy back. Back in the second lines at Blanleuil and Ravin Sec, despite a deadly crossfire of enemy machine-gun fire, the fragments of 2 Battalion continued to put up a stubborn resistance behind their barricades of sandbags erected in the access *boyaux*. In the chaos, companies of the 151 were by now completely scattered throughout the woods, often intermixed with neighbouring units. Among the missing were the commanders of 1 and 3 Battalion, Commandants Dô and Remy. With Commandant Dô nowhere to be found, command of the regiment went to the sole remaining battalion leader, Commandant Adamy.[21] Gradually, the dispersed fractions of the 151 that could be wrangled up were reassembled and relieved. In the chaos of the shattered woods, some elements were stuck out under fire, sheltering as best they could among the shattered trees and growing number of shell holes. L'Huillier was out on a skirmish line when an incendiary bomb burst above him. Liquid flame showered down onto him, setting his capote alight. L'Huillier struggled to undo his equipment and then quickly tore off his capote.[22] He had already suffered burns on his entire lower half and one of his cheeks. Somehow he managed to get back to the first-aid post, before joining a group of walking wounded travelling back to Florent. The next evening he was transported to his old high school in Sainte-Menehould, since converted into a hospital operated by the Red Cross. There he was attended to by none other than his mother and sister in the same classroom he had taken German lessons as a student. Laporte had managed to survive as well. But after drinking out of desperation from a stream that reeked of dead bodies, he and a number of his friends fell ill. When his temperature rose to 105 degrees, Laporte was diagnosed as having contracted typhoid and evacuated to the rear. He would suffer from terrible migraines and body aches for weeks. But gradually he would recover his strength and like Campana and Jubert, Laporte would eventually rejoin the regiment that October.

Over the course of three days of uninterrupted fighting, the 151 had put up a valiant but ill-fated defence. Losses were extreme. Divisional rolls put the total number of effectives for the 151 before the eruption of battle on 30 June at 2,425. By 2 July, less than 25 officers and just over 1,400 were still present for duty. The rest of the 1,100 soldiers were killed, wounded, or captured. Among the dead and wounded were thirty of the regiment's officers, including Commandants Dô and Remy, both of whom would later be confirmed as killed in action. With their deaths, the total of battalion leaders lost since the start of the war was brought up to nine. Commandant Remy – who had been promoted to command 3 Battalion when Commandant Vaudescal was killed in April – had particularly distinguished himself in the fighting. Tenaciously resisting the flood of German attack troops, Remy had refused to surrender even when it was clear that capture or death appeared to be his only options. It took wounding him at close range to finally take him as prisoner. But before he could get out of danger, he was struck again, this time by a bullet in the head which killed him instantly. Some weeks later, Moisson would be presented with a translation of an article from the *Frankfurter Zeitung* (*Frankfurter Gazette*), dated 3 August 1915, in which was related the heroic struggle of the 151 at Bagatelle on 2 July. Special homage was paid to Commandant Remy, and the article reported that his German captors had rendered him posthumous honours in the rear, citing him as an example of heroism.

The battle in Slaughter Wood wasn't over. Since being relieved, combat had continued unabated and with a renewed German offensive on 13 July, the 151 was sent back into the fight. This time Lieutenant Colonel Moisson personally lead 2 Battalion into the assault to retake positions in the St. Hubert subsector, to the east of Fontaine-Madame. The hard fighting continued into Bastille Day on the 14th. Again and again, for two days and two nights, the companies of the 151 attempted to push forward against storms of gunfire. As the battle devolved into a fight within the *boyaux* carried out with hand grenades, the men dug in and erected sandbag barricades at each turn and intersection to reinforce their hard-won gains.

By the time the 151 was finally relieved on 17 July, another 500 men had been killed or wounded over the course of 5 days. When the regiment formed back up in Sainte-Menehould, just over 1,200 were left to answer the call. Yet it seemed just as quickly as the war ground human beings into pulp, new bodies were there ready to be fed into the machine. After the regiment was pulled off the line new reinforcements began to arrive, so that by August the new regulation number of effectives had been exceeded, with 65 officers and 2,950 men filling the ranks of the 151. This boost had a large effect on the demographic profile of the regiment.

The relentless, grinding nature of the fighting in the Argonne Forest proved one of the severest trials the regiment would undergo in the war. In total, the 151 *JMO* recorded over 4,200 killed, wounded, or missing in combat in the Argonne – a casualty rate of over 150 per cent. Divisional records would have this number even higher. With the regiment being fully wiped out, losses were only absorbed by the near constant flow of replacements. It could be argued that the Argonne is where the last vestiges of the regiment that had marched off to war in August 1914 had more or less met its end. With the exception of a shrinking core of officers and men, most of those who had fought with the 151 during the Frontiers, the Marne, and the Yser had either been killed or seriously wounded and unable to return to service. On 29 August, the regiment celebrated the first anniversary of its baptism of fire at Pierrepont and Doncourt. Concerts were played by the regimental band and the regiment was reviewed by the divisional commander, General Deville. All the officers and men who'd participated in the fighting that day were assembled and organized into the original companies they'd belonged. Standing proudly together were 16 officers and 303 men. Nine-tenths of the original members of the regiment of 1914 were gone. What would emerge from the crucible of the Argonne was a unit composed of both experienced veterans and new arrivals who quickly assimilated and contributed to the fighting traditions of *le Qunize-Un*. It was in Slaughter Wood where the regiment cemented its reputation as an elite unit. The 3rd Army commander, General Humbert, affirmed this status personally. Reviewing the regiment as it paraded past, he expressed his satisfaction with the excellent bearing of the men.

In the beginning of August, the 151 was again moved with the 42 ID to the Champagne region in anticipation of a new French offensive there in the autumn. The men didn't know this yet of course. All they knew was that compared with the Argonne, this part of the front was calm. The 151's mission for the time being was to complete a mind-boggling 25km of entrenchments in two months. Arriving at Camp Chalons at Mourmelon-le-Grand, the regiment was immediately put to work digging *boyaux* to interconnect the trenches in the Aubérive-sur-Suippes sector. It was back-breaking work that could only be done at night to avoid observation by the enemy. After weeks of digging, though, rumours about what was coming seemed to bear out. They were once again going on the attack. To reinforce this notion, interspersed within the mundane work of digging were periods of instruction, which incorporated specialist training for pioneers, sappers, telephonists, stretcher-bearers, trench mortar-men, grenadiers, and machine-gunners. They went through rigorous physical training too, including long marches in full kit weighing more than 60lb. The wisdom of assigning such physically demanding labour to the same units that would be carrying out an extended combat operation is questionable. Surely it would have been better to designate other support units to this task and dedicate additional instruction or even rest to the ones who were about to be called on to go into battle? Alas, for reasons unknown, this would not be the case and on 10 September (two weeks before the battle was to begin) the regiment was sent to take up their assigned positions with still more work to do. Their orders were to dig in front of the new first-line trench a *parallel de départ* ('departure parallel'), a jumping-off position from which they would leave on the day of the attack. All of this was meant to close the distance between the French and German lines and thereby lessen the amount of ground the troops would have to cover in their advance. But this meant working out in the open, on the far side of their own wire, several hundred metres out into no man's land. All the while, the enemy was sending up illumination flares, obliging the workers to throw themselves to the ground. Finally, as no provision had been made for shelters, the men were told they would need to dig their own. All of this was an enormous amount to complete and work continued uninterrupted day and night.

Second Champagne Offensive

The battalions of riflemen had become battalions of workers, who carried weapons of picks and shovels, sandbags and sticks. With the increase in activity in the French lines, the Germans soon opened up a harassing fire to disrupt the working parties, and over one four-day period, forty were killed and wounded. Day after day and night after night, the battalions laboured, right up to the final days before *jour-J* ('D-Day'), scheduled for 25 September. By now, the scale of the coming French assault was clear. The operation would be carried out by the Centre Group of Armies (under General de Castelnau), comprising the 2nd, 3rd, 4th, and 5th Armies. The 2nd and 4th Armies would be spearheading the assault along a 25km front, stretching from Aubérive on the left to Ville-sur-Tourbe on the right. The assault itself would be made across wide, undulating plains entirely barren aside from occasional thickets of pine trees and the clusters of small villages.

On 22 September the massive French preparatory bombardment began. A total of 1,300 field guns and 650 medium and heavy pieces had been gathered for the task. It was the most powerful concentration of firepower yet seen on the

Western Front and the longest-lasting uninterrupted barrage to date. It continued unabated for three days and nights, with roughly a million shells being fired before a single French soldier went over the attack. It was later calculated that one sector 100m wide and 1,500m in depth received 3,600 shells per hour. Among the deluge of shells, several large mines were be detonated under the German lines as well. Never before had such an accumulation of guns and materiel been seen. Never before had an operation of this scale been so minutely prepared. To lighten their load the men of the 151 were instructed to leave behind their packs. Each man carried with him his normal equipment with 160 rounds of ammo, one haversack of reserve rations and the other packed with grenades and a gas mask, while the blanket and tent canvas were rolled together and worn wrapped around the shoulder in bandolier fashion. For the first time since the summer of 1914, French soldiers were truly uniform in their appearance. All the men were now entirely clad in the new horizon-blue uniforms. They also donned the new Adrian steel helmet, which had been distributed to the combat formations in time for the opening day of the attack.

The 151 would be attacking from trenches southeast of the village of Aubérive, on the extreme left of the French army's attack front. One can only speculate if those in the ranks understood the significance of this place and the bitter irony it held. For it was here almost a year to the day that the 151 had dashed against the primitive German entrenchments in a vain attempt to end the war after six weeks of fighting. The attack plan for 25 September 1915 placed the 151 behind the 94 IR and the 8 and 16 LIBs, forming the 3rd, 4th, 5th and 6th waves of the attack. Detached from the 1 Battalion were 3 and 4 Companies, which were assigned as the division's right flank guard in the first wave. The division's first objectives were two of a series of interconnected strongholds, designated *Fortin* '414' and *Fortin* '413'. French commanders knew that taking the heavily fortified strongholds would be difficult, which is why they had instructed that the French lines be advanced to no more than 200m from the German first line. But this also telegraphed to the enemy exactly where the attack would fall, and the time it required to complete the *parallels de départ* afforded the enemy ample time to further strengthen his defences. Additional machine guns were provisioned and placed in well-concealed steel-armoured turrets, along with 77 mm cannon. The Germans had also increased the amount of their barbed wire entanglements, which were in many spots 50m in depth. Still, French commanders were confident that the artillery would destroy the machine-gun nests and clear away the wire belts in advance of the infantry attack.

On the eve of the attack, the weather turned foul. Storms moved in bringing wind and drenching rain, which greatly impeded artillery observation. Roads and trenches turned into a slippery slurry of chalky mud. Despite the gloomy weather, the spirit of the men remained high. Generals and privates alike were confident in a decisive victory that would at last break the deadlock and bring about an end to the dreadful war. One of them was L'Huillier, who'd returned to the 151 in August. He had recently been promoted to sergeant and had been given command of a squad in 3 Company. With his original birth town of Somme-Py less than 9km from their jumping-off positions, he saw the coming offensive as an opportunity to rescue his grandmother and aunt, who remained trapped behind German lines. The regiment's total number of effectives was lower now than its peak in the previous month owing to recent transfers together with casualties and sick cases suffered in the build up. Going into the offensive, the 151 reported 65 officers and 2,668 men on its rolls.[23] On the night of 24 September, in driving rain, the 151 departed Camp Chalons in order to reach its *parallels de départ* by 6.00 am. *L'Heure-H* ('zero-hour') was set for 9.15 am.

The guns continued to thunder away as the masses of men filtered slowly into their jumping-off positions. By 5.30 am on the 25th, the units of the 151 had reached their assigned *parallels de départ*, immediately behind the 94 IR and the 8 and 16 LIB. The 162 IR was on their left. As they waited impatiently for *L'Heure-H*, the French artillery's preparatory bombardment bolstered their spirits, especially since there was little response coming from the German side. This would be the great offensive they had all been waiting for, the last of the war. There was a sense of hope that the preparations being made would ensure a 'proper' battle, one in which victory would at last be had. A fine rain was falling yet spirits in the French trenches remained high. After seventy-five hours of continuous bombardment, everything before them appeared to be entirely smashed. All the trenches and access *boyaux* were packed full. The sight of thousands of men (130,000 in all) standing side by side instilled a fierce pride and brimming assurance. Regimental colours were unfurled to be carried over the top with the first wave. Some units even brought their bands up into the front lines to play the men off to the attack. That morning, the whole French army seemed to smell victory. A ration of brandy was passed around to the men, who took strong swigs to steady their nerves. Minutes before they were to go over the top, the cry of '*Baïonette au canon!*' was given by the company commanders and an almost giddy excitement rippled through the ranks as the men affixed their bayonets to their rifle muzzles.

Then, with two minutes remaining before going over the top, there was an ominous sign: the German artillery at last opened fire. So too did the machine guns, by the dozens. This could not be. These were all, or nearly all, supposed to have been entirely destroyed by the French artillery. A dreadful sinking feeling must have poured over the hearts of many. Sergeant L'Huillier was with 4 Company in the most advanced departure trench. Looking off to his left he could see the units of the 40 ID, followed by zouave and tirailleur formations, advancing towards their objectives while the 'Coffee Grinders' (poilu slang for machine guns from the sound they produced) started rattling away. But there was no more time to be a looker-on. The officers and NCOs who'd been intently staring at their wristwatches counted down the final seconds until 9.15 and then it was their turn to go. L'Huillier's platoon leader, Second Lieutenant Desnoyer, blew his whistle and cried out: '*En avant! A la baïonette!*' As one, the men climbed up on the parapet, holding their rifles low in one hand, and deployed into line. Overhead, French shells continued to pass as the artillery lengthened its fire.

Then the German machine guns opened up. In seconds, a deluge of bullets swept in and entire ranks of men were immediately mowed down. L'Huillier could distinguish at least six guns to the front and flanks that were sweeping their front, and quickly they created an extreme crossfire, a true killing zone. The first wave pressed on in spite of the mounting losses, the companies moving towards the gaps opened by their artillery in the most advanced wire entanglements and it seemed that they would arrive at their objective soon. Then disaster struck. After advancing less than 100m, the assault wave ran into a fully intact double belt of barbed wire. It had been strategically placed in a shallow hollow running parallel to the enemy front line and its location meant that it had gone nearly untouched by the preparatory bombardment. The entanglements were 50m deep and stood shoulder height, comprising barbed wire intermixed with metal trellis, with supplemental belts of ground wire set low off the ground to a depth of 15m. With the German first line less than 100m away, entire companies were literally mowed down by machine guns and 77 shells coming in from both front and flanks. The men collapsed in heaps. Those with wire-cutters desperately attempted to cut through the wire but were quickly riddled with bullets, their bodies caught and suspended upright by the wire. Any attempt to advance was utterly futile. There was nothing for the survivors to do but to lay down in front of the belt of wire and take cover as best they could, pressing themselves as low as possible into the earth, using the bodies of the dead as a human parapet. Hugging the ground to escape the metal storm of death, L'Huillier saw the Second Lieutenant (and Saint-Cyrien) Louis Chedal-Bornu struck in the side. An adjudant who crawled up and tried to bandage the platoon leader's wound was himself killed in the act. The commander of 3 Company, Captain Pernnet, already shot in the cheek, tried to order a retreat but was himself immediately shot again and killed.

> Anyone who's wounded and twists about in their pain, or who simply makes the slightest move, is machine-gunned. It being impossible to even budge, I abandon the notion of advancing. I stop my men, shouting to them 'Get down!' I hunker down in front of the barbed-wire entanglements, sheltering in a shallow shell-hole, face pressed into the

earth and arms stretched out . . . playing dead. My only hope is for our artillery to destroy the Boche stronghold and for the arrival of a second assault wave so that I can join up with them.[24]

The 3 and 4 Companies were decimated alongside the other units of the 42nd Division in the first wave.[25] The second assault wave (made up of the 9, 10, 5, and 6 Companies) followed in the wake of the first wave only to meet the same fate as their predecessors. The air was full of hundreds of swarming bullets and shell fragments, snapping and whistling past in their flight, bursting into the ground, smacking into bodies with a dull thud or loud crack as bone was broken. Occasionally there was the sound of a sharp metallic rap as rounds struck the helmets of those lying prone. The 1 Company was then ordered over the top on its own in an attempt to find a gap in the wire, the men only able to advance by crawling along the ground before they too became pinned down. Elsewhere along the French front the attack had been more successful. In those sectors, the artillery had effectively smashed the German first line defences and the assault waves were able to break through much of the German first line. French forces had taken Navarin Farm (over a 2km advance) along with the Buttes of Souain and Tahure (4km). Along with inflicting thousands of casualties on the enemy, nearly 14,000 Germans had been taken prisoner. Perhaps in part because of the advances being made on other parts of the front and the need to make progress against *Fortin* '414', two hours after the second wave had departed, 11, 12 and 2 Companies were sent in. In their turn, they too were stopped dead in front of the wire. German machine guns then directed their fire onto the top of the *parallels de départ*, making any exit or reentry practically impossible. The entire regiment was now trapped out in the open.

> Oh, these minutes, these hours I endured! Bullets whistling and passing around me, some tossing up the ground as they struck. It was raining too. One moment, with my hands stiff from the cold, I tried to shift my position a bit. Immediately a German machine gun pointing in my general direction sent over a hail of bullets. I'm hit in the neck and several bullets pass through my haversack.[26]

Pinned down all day long, L'Huillier faced a new threat as French artillery started firing again on the German positions and barbed wire, in an effort to help clear the way for checked companies. But this meant shelling close to the ground where L'Huillier and the other terror stricken survivors of the assault waves were sheltering. They were completely defenceless as French shells came screaming down around them. A shell fragment from one pierced L'Huillier's helmet, just missing his skull. Reciting the Lord's Prayer, he thought of his parents and a letter he'd received from his mother before going up to the lines, where she told him to not be afraid, that he was brave and that he'd make it through. He felt neither of these last things seemed true at this moment. Hours passed. As darkness fell, the companies of the 151, hopelessly intermixed with chasseurs from the 8 and 16 LIB, scrambled back to the *parallels de départ*. Miraculously, L'Huillier still found himself among the living and now took advantage of the rain and fog to slip away. To lighten his load, he carefully removed his blanket, haversacks, ammo, emptied his canteens, and then started crawling in the direction of where he thought the French lines were. '*Wer da*!' a voice cried out in German. Aghast, L'Huillier immediately understood his disastrous error and quickly made an about-face. As stealthily as he could, he slowly crawled back, moving from shell hole to shell hole, passing over the countless bodies of the dead. Each pull through the slippery mud a pull towards life and away from death. From time to time, enemy illumination flares shot up into the sky, casting a shifting light over the ghastly plain. After great efforts, L'Huillier at last arrived back at the French lines and shouting 'France, One-Fifty-One!' for identification, threw himself into the trench occupied by his regiment's pioneers. But his troubles weren't over. After rejoining the seventeen men remaining in his company, a 'Big Black' (150mm shell) suddenly arrived, bursting on the parapet of the trench and causing the wall to collapse on top of him. L'Huillier's cry for help was stifled by the chalky earth crushing down and slowly suffocating him. But his luck would hold out once more as several men managed to unearth him before the worst could happen. Spitting up blood from internal haemorrhaging, he was evacuated to the first-aid post and from there sent to a hospital in Bordeaux. L'Huillier would survive his injuries, eventually returning to the 151 in February 1916. He was also cited in the Orders of the Division for his conduct during the fighting, earning him the Croix de Guerre. But his dream of liberating his original hometown of Somme-Py had died on the field with his comrades.

In the Aubérive sector, whole lines of Frenchmen lay dead in front of the wire or macabrely suspended in the entanglements, machine-gun fire strafing back and forth, raking the bodies again and again. No mercy was shown by the victors. Casualty reports for 25 September were sketchy at best. In total, the 42nd Division had lost around 5,000 infantrymen, chasseurs, and engineers. In the 151 *JMO*, only 69 were confirmed as killed and 296 wounded, while 450 were reported as missing. Among them was the commander of 2 Battalion, Commandant Adamy, who was later confirmed as killed. The figures from the *JMO* are more than likely inaccurate and a tally taken by divisional staff on 27 September may be closer to the real number, with a confirmed 196 killed, 367 wounded, and 889 missing. The tragic reality was that the vast majority of these 'missing' were in fact lying dead out on the plain. The fact that divisional reports had only 725 riflemen present for duty two days later – a number that would only rise once new reinforcements were received and incorporated – is an indication of this grim reality. It seems fair therefore to put the regiment's losses at roughly 1,400 dead and wounded.

But the battle had only just begun and there was still killing and dying to be done. The division was to retake the offensive the next morning with the reorganized companies of the 151 leading the way. The operation seemed plagued from the outset. With the German strongholds appearing to still be relatively undamaged after a brief preparatory bombardment and certain units unable to get into position in time, the 9.00 am start time was postponed to noon. But the order to delay the attack was not transmitted in time to the 1 Battalion. Consequently, 2 Company went over the top at 9.00 am entirely unsupported and straight into their own artillery barrage, suffering heavy losses before quickly falling back. Then, the regiment's trenches were shelled by a battery of French 75s, and morale plummeted.

Nonetheless, at noon the remnants of 1, 2, 8, 10, 11, and 12 Companies dashed over the top again and formed into their skirmish lines. The units were immediately taken by a crossfire of machine-gun fire but still managed to reach the location of the German wire in a single rush, only to discover that it still remained largely intact, with some sections even showing signs of repair work carried out during the night. Two platoons of 11 Company did succeed in making it through the wire and established a foothold in a section of the German first line after a fierce fight with grenades. Due to intense gunfire they couldn't be reinforced, so they had to do their best to defensively organize the conquered position. Losses were once again heavy, especially among the platoon leaders. German artillery and machine guns pitilessly strafed the ground in front of their wire, shredding the bodies of the dead and wounded. That evening and continuing over the next several days, the 151 would make a number of other attempts to take *Fortin* '414', none of which would succeed. The only thing to change was the body count, as hundreds more were killed and maimed. On 28 September, only 13 company officers and 533 men were still present for duty in the line. When a detachment of 500 replacements arrived, there was little other choice but to incorporate them directly in the front lines rather than wait for the unit to be pulled off the line. The depressed survivors could do nothing but huddle in their original starting positions, which the Germans continuously shelled and machine-gunned. After orders arrived telling the men to fortify their departure positions, it simply confirmed the obvious, that the attacks were a complete failure. On 1 October, the 151 was relieved by elements of the 7 ID and headed back to Mormelon-le-Grand for a rapid reorganization, facilitated by the arrival of hundreds more replacements from the 151 depot.

Among them was Second Lieutenant Roger Campana, who was now assigned to 1 Company. Campana had spent the the summer and autumn recuperating from his appendicitis surgery at the 351 IR depot in Douarnenez (an annexed depot for the 151), where he was put in command of the company of recuperating soldiers who'd been wounded or invalided from sickness but judged fit enough to return to active service. There, he had imparted advice to the new soldiers who'd yet to go to the front. Campana hammered home that they should be brave but prudent. Most of all, they should listen to the vets, watch how they operate, and do what they do.

> Many young new recruits going into combat felt the need to boast in front of their comrades. They look through the loop-holes for too long and put their heads above the trench thinking they would earn the respect of the older soldiers. In reality, this achieved the opposite effect.
>
> When speaking about these young screwballs, the veterans who've already seen death close up so many times don't say: 'They're brave.' Quite the contrary they say 'Look at these greenhorns trying to impress us! When they've done six months of campaigning and the bullets have tanned their hides, they won't be such smartasses.' . . . And if they are a young NCO who commit this mistake, the men say: 'They don't know anything about war. In an attack, they'll get us all killed.'
>
> More often than not those who feel the need to play the hero are the same ones who hunker down real low when shells and bullets are actually passing by high overhead. They are braggarts ignorant of danger. True courage doesn't consist of making light of death during calm moments when it's nearly certain to not come, or even in exposing oneself unnecessarily to danger and getting killed for no purpose. To the contrary, it's in dispassionately sacrificing oneself without a second thought when the success of an operation requires it.
>
> . . .
>
> Courage does not exclude prudence and when you look around it's often those with the most prowess and who brag the most . . . who are often the most cowardly. They're conscious of their cowardice and try to compensate for it with bluffs. In a heavy bombardment you'll often find them at the bottom of a dugout . . . By contrast, you see the smallest soldiers – insignificant in appearance, timid, quiet, and looking more like little girls than men – who on the day of the assault are transformed in tigers or lions.[27]

After being given barely two days to rest, the regiment received orders to report back to the front. Boosted back up in strength to 25 officers and 2,070 men, the 151 would be participating in an attack in the sector neighbouring its first. As soon as it had relieved the 150 IR, the enemy began a heavy bombardment on their positions, which included a great quantity of poison gas shells. The trenches themselves were already badly damaged from the shelling and had collapsed in numerous places. Once again, the men were instructed to dig a departure trench at night in advance of the first line. On 6 October, the 151 IR would assault Bois 'H' and the western portion of Bois 372 in tandem with the 162 IR to its right. From the very beginning, things again got off badly. Overcrowding in the *boyaux* delayed one of the battalions of the 162 from arriving at its starting position in time for *l'Heure-H*. Even before going over the top that morning, the men sensed that the fire was not having the desired effect. Gone was the exuberant confidence from the first day of the offensive. In its place was a dark sense of foreboding. The initial advance was aided by thick fog but once the formations approached the enemy lines, they were spotted and the same nightmare seen in September unfolded again. The preparatory barrage had completely missed the German wire entanglements, while the German emplacements in Bois 372 also seemed untouched. On the right, the two battalions of the 162 were stopped dead in their tracks, as a deadly enfilade fire took the units of the 151 by the flank. Campana had missed the opening attack on 25 September but had learned what happened first-hand from the morose survivors. Now he would get a chance to see for himself the frightful butchery of battle on the desolate plains of Champagne.

> The moment has come: a signal from the Captain [Salaiin], a whistle-blow: 'En avant!' A bound of 10 metres is made in an unsettling silence, then suddenly a frightful fire of musketry, thousands of bullets whistle by and drill into bodies. Shouts of rage, groans, entire lines of blue greatcoats mowed down in place like wooden soldiers and a sudden stop in front of an impenetrable entanglement of barbed wire. 'Lie down!'
>
> We let the bursts of gunfire pass over our heads. Our artillery starts up again with a more powerful fire and the enemy machine guns stop firing. I look around me. Hundreds of men were lying down in skirmish lines in the plain. The captain gets up: 'Stand up and about face!' he cries. Only about 50 men rise, the others remain lying face down in the grass – they were all dead.
>
> The sight of all these lifeless bodies in their light blue greatcoats, never to rise again, made me shudder. We went back to our departure trench. Our lieutenant [Garriguès] was among the dead. A half-hour later we attack again but without success. Our Colonel [Moisson], the bravest of the brave, 'Papa Victory' as the men affectionately called him, came up to ask us to make a third try. Looking above the parapet, he immediately was struck in the head by a bullet. The morale of the soldiers was deeply affected. Still, three more times we threw ourselves

into the attack, only to break upon the cursed entanglements each time!

In the fifth assault, our captain was struck down by a shell fragment and I took command of what remained of the company. Commandant Brugère reassembled the battalion in the departure trench. The terrified survivors didn't want to leave the trench anymore and began to murmur amongst themselves. Their commander exhorted them in vain:

– 'Are you ready to make another go?'
– 'It's a massacre!' – 'We're going to get killed for nothing!'
– 'For nothing? No, for France! Come on, one last time!'
– 'Well you go first then!'
– 'First? Yes, certainly!'

The commandant takes his pipe, packs it calmly and then lights it. Taking ahold of his walking cane, he dashes forward crying: 'Forward, boys! This is for France!'

All the survivors dashed forward behind him. He went a dozen metres before collapsing as the bullets rained down like hail, dropping a number of soldiers. And for the sixth time I ordered in my turn what remained of the company back to the departure trench. An adjudant went up to the body of the Commandant, leaned down towards him to see if he was dead or simply wounded, but then collapsed on top of his body. A corporal who crawled up to do likewise suffered the same fate. Captain Le Boulanger took command of the battalion. We were the only officers remaining.

'Such disgraceful and idiotic carnage, I tell you. How do they expect us to take this stronghold when it's still defended by an entanglement 50 metres deep without the smallest breach and is protected by multiple machine guns. If we're ordered to attack a seventh time, the men will no longer follow us. The only thing it will serve to do is to get us killed like the Commandant.'[28]

Back in the 151's original *parallels de départ*, Campana was only just recovering from the emotional shock of what had transpired. He would record the immediate aftermath of the senseless assaults he and his men had been ordered to carry out.

Another regiment comes to fill our gaps and the departure trench is transformed into a first-line defensive one. But all afternoon the fusillade carries on. The enemy showed a disgraceful conduct: he amused himself for several hours turning our wounded and dead into paste. We listened to the German bullets ricochet off the ground, pierce into helmets and drill into the bodies with a dull thud. At 2.00 pm, we perceived over the sound of the explosions wailing, cries of agony, the groans of our wounded. At 5.00 pm, only the creeping of Mausers [German rifles] broke the silence. Between our lines, there were only the dead.

We imagine the anguish of our poor soldiers pinned down to the ground, suffering as they wait from one moment to the next for the bullet that will give them another wound or finish them off. Understanding that nothing could survive this awful nightmare, some found the strength to stand or to start crawling back toward us. But they didn't get far: the Germans watching them immediately gunned them down. When can we give them the same treatment and slaughter them without pity!

. . .

The morale of the men at this time is dreadful. At first, they were simply happy to learn that the fighting was over. Egoism trumping all, they were just happy to still be alive. That mattered most. But then the knowledge of having escaped death was taken for granted, so they began to occupy themselves with other thoughts. They criticize the operation, outraged by the results. A few headstrong ones knew how to adroitly sow discouragement, and that was especially easy now as the soldiers could see with their own eyes the hundreds of dead – their comrades just the evening before – lying between the lines, before the impenetrable thicket of metal entanglements. They believed they had been sacrificed for nothing and they were distraught by the notion that the thing could be repeated all over again.[29]

For his part, Campana laid the blame for the disaster squarely on the inadequacies of the artillery in failing to destroy the enemy's deep wire entanglements. He saw no reason to cast aspersions on senior commanders. Certainly he was correct on the point about the artillery. But it's difficult to not see the clear failing on the part of commanders to fully recognize the impossibility of the situation. When it was obvious that the wire had not been cut and that no progress could be made, what purpose did it serve to continue sending the men back into the attack again and again? It was the height of folly and madness. Losses for the regiment on 6 October as put down in the 151 *JMO* included at least 28 killed, 141 wounded, and 61 missing. Again, the records of the the 42 ID are perhaps more reliable: reports list 38 killed, 103 wounded, and 188 missing and likely dead. Whatever the exact casualty figure, the next day there were 400 fewer men on the unit rolls, including the battalion commander killed and the regimental commander wounded. After being kept in the line under fire for another five days, the 151 would return to Mourmelon where it was given a week's rest.

End of Year Situation for the Regiment

Even before seeing the pitiful massacre unfold on 6 October, Campana found himself becoming more and more a fatalist, convinced that his fate was already determined in advance. It was a way of coping with the constant brushes with death, the endless 'what ifs', and the agonizing uncertainty of what horrible fate the future held for him. It was a view that was only reinforced by his experiences in Champagne. Weeks passed since the terrible days of 25 September and 6 October, all the while the long rows of dead lay stretched out in front of the regiment's lines in plain sight. Campana made several attempts to find the body of his friend Second Lieutenant Chedal-Bornu, who L'Huillier had seen wounded on 25 September. Campana felt keenly the pain of uncertainty for those back home whose loved-one had been classified as 'missing'. At night he made several forays into no man's land, taking with him two reluctant stretcher-bearers to drag back as many bodies as they could on a tent canvas. It was ghastly and dangerous work:

> They must have been killed while trying to escape the bursts of gunfire, for the majority were lying stretched out on their chests like soldiers given the command to 'Lie prone'. Others though faced to the sky, knees pulled up into their chests, arms crossed, hands clutching tuffs of grass, indicating by their appearance how painful their suffering had been ... The enemy was not far off, we could hear his picks at work in his trench. We took the corpse closest to us. He was a big clean-shaven boy, his face as black as soot. We lifted him up with difficulty. It was as though the ground was a like a jealous lover, desperately clinging on to keep him. Hardly had we lifted him up than a horrible odor overwhelmed us. Wanting to hasten the dismal chore, we quickly placed another body in the tent-canvas, but the rifle that his hand was still grasping struck the barbed-wire. A shot rang out and though no one was hit, the alarm had been given and bullets started whistling past. We ran back to our trench, dragging the two cadavers behind us.[30]

The next night they brought in two more but on the second trip out, they were caught by an unexpected burst of gunfire, wounding one of the stretcher-bearers and pinning down the group for more than an hour. Lying among the heaps of putrefying dead, bullets drilling into the already shredded bodies with a dull thud, Campana was forced to press his face close against that of one of the dead. The image of the dead man's face – whose gaping mouth and half-open eyes seemed to be mocking Campana's predicament – would forever burn itself into his memory. Once the firing died down, Campana snipped off the ID tags from the wrists of the dead around before returning back to his trench. Ultimately the unrecoverable dead would be mourned en masse in a memorial service held on 1 November at the military cemetery at Mourmelon commemorating the lives lost from the 42 ID.

The Second Champagne Offensive would drag on until the end of October before being called off by General Joffre. The weather by now had become deplorable. It rained constantly, sometimes for days on end. The trenches flooded with a mixture of dirty white water and mud the consistency of porridge. The men themselves were plastered from head to toe in it. The walls of the trenches slowly collapsed in a soft slither and the Sisyphean task of shovelling mud and bailing out water commenced. Rain alternated with ice and snow squalls. Despite the cold, thousands of enormous rats – which grew to gargantuan proportions from feasting on the dead – scampered about everywhere. To amuse themselves and to keep warm, the men chased them around and did their best to bayonet them. The soup could only make it up to the front line after exhausting efforts by the resupply parties, but would typically be cold by the time it arrived. For shelter, the men slept in small dugouts, out of which water oozed from the bare walls. It wasn't uncommon for these to flood with a foot or more of water, just like the trenches above, and many nights were passed bailing out water with canvas buckets. Their clothes and blankets soaked through, getting some sleep was difficult if not impossible. Now and then some shells would arrive and kill or wound a few men.

Large groups of replacements filtered into the ranks to once again bring the unit back up to strength. Some were older men dragged out of support echelons and transferred to combat units but most were recuperated veterans who'd already seen action, had been wounded or fallen ill but had recovered. Those declared fit again to carry a pack and a gun were rotated back to the front. One was Corporal Laporte, who'd returned to the regiment on 15 October having recovered from his near fatal bout of typhoid. He was assigned again to the 8 Company, yet apart from his platoon commander and a small clutch of survivors, he found no other friends remaining from the company he knew in the Argonne. While Laporte had been fortunate to have escaped the offensive, he now had his first winter in the trenches to endure in the dreary plains of Champagne.

> A glacial wind blew all night. I'd received from my mother a wool balaclava. It was certainly welcome and helped to retain the heat under my helmet. But it was the feet that really suffered . . . I was seated for a little while along the fire-step and felt my trousers start to freeze and stiffen. So I made some efforts to try to stand. I managed to do this only with difficulty and walked a hundred paces to keep the ice from giving me frostbite. This had happened to one of my comrades who was then

evacuated because of it. You mustn't fall asleep, otherwise you'd suffer frostbite, or even death.³¹

And so the long days and nights of late autumn and then winter passed as the regiment took on a tedious rotation, with a week in the line wallowing in the mud followed by a week's rest back at the barracks in Mourmelon, and then back up to the line. In the trenches, the men once again resumed their role as labourers first and foremost, leaving the rifle to shoulder picks and shovels. Most of the work was done at night to avoid being targeted by the enemy whose first line was only 200m away. Long hours were spent toiling away in the dark, digging new connecting trenches or deepening and widening existing ones, bailing out water and mud, installing revetments or filling sandbags to help shore up the walls, and erecting their own thick belts of barbed wire entanglements in no man's land. It was exhausting work often lasting all night, made all the more difficult by the afflictions of sleep deprivation, damp, and cold. Even when they were off the line 'at rest', the men were kept busy with long periods of drill and exercise. Even Campana complained about the effects of these activities:

> Our rest ends tomorrow, but how can you call this 'rest' when we go off on exercises every day from 8.00 am to 10.00 am and again from 1.00 pm to 4.00 pm . . . When our men come out of the trenches they need to forget they're at war for a little while . . . to banish the obsessive vision of death which so haunts them. So why are we on manoeuvres morning and evening? Arms drill, platoon exercises, bayonet fencing – are these still of any use in the type of war we're waging now? In my view, these exercises only serve to exasperate the men. But orders are orders and we have to follow them.³²

The end of the year was a dark time for the French army as a whole. Still, the strength of the poilu came from their ability to endure and keep 'slogging through'. And the soldiers of the 151 – from simple soldier to senior officers – serve as an exemplary model of these qualities. To reward the improved discipline and martial spirit demonstrated by his new men, Campana arranged *Marraines de Guerre* – female war penpals who sometimes became something more – for the men from enemy occupied territories who were cut off from their families. The small joys of receiving correspondence and small gifts from the Marraines were of great emotional support. Trying to find any sign of positivity in their current situation was imperative. November changed into December and a new 151 emerged like the proverbial phoenix from the ashes of ruin that was 1915. However, at its centre there still remained a small core of officers, NCOs, and privates who had served in the regiment's ranks since early 1915 and carried on its qualities of courage, tenacity, and fortitude. As the year came to an end, the 151 held several formal parades and ceremonies, where they were reviewed by division and army corps generals. On the final day of 1915, Moisson – now recovered from the bullet wound he took to the head in September – reviewed the regiment, addressing his good wishes to the regiment as it continued to evolve into a new type of army. One made up not simply of riflemen but of specialists trained in the latest weaponry integrated with the latest tactical developments in large part modelled after those employed by the Germans. The culmination of this metamorphosis was on display during the New Year's Eve review.

> On 31st December the Colonel passed the regiment in review. It was superb. The battalions had formed up in the large sunny fields. Far away on the Moronvillers heights, we could see rising up in big black or grey plumes the smoke of the 210 and 150 shells. The regimental flag was at the centre of the festival. Our old colours testify to our many heroic fights as its glorious silk, ravaged by bullets, flapped proudly in the wind. It was in order to save this sacred object, the emblem, the country, that so many brave men will sleep forever in the fields of Pierrepont and the Marne, in the plains of Ypres, in the dark woods of the Argonne, and on the white soil of flea-ridden Champagne. And it is to save this still that these thousands of men are ready to sacrifice themselves in their turn in the battles to come.
>
> The parade was very beautiful. The magnificent regiment! The magnificent look! The magnificent soldiers! When you think of all these men fighting for months and months, when you think that they've endured all the hardships, all the sufferings that humans can endure, you say to yourself in watching them march with martial allure and heads held high: with such men we must and we will be victorious. And someday soon when we set off to boot the enemy out of France, we'll be proud to march at the head of such brave men and lead them on the path of glory. In this *prise d'armes* I've found my dear 151st again. It will accomplish marvellous things soon.[33]

The year 1915 proved itself to be a brutal ordeal for the 151, as it had been for the French army as a whole. The names of the places and towns where the unit served became etched into the memory of those who experienced the greatest of hardships. In total, the 151 suffered as many as 5,400 casualties in 12 months, effectively being wiped out twice. This number does not include the scores of men evacuated from illness, disease, frostbite and trench foot, or shell-shock.

Specialist Training and Refitting (1 January–24 February)

The start of the year 1916 would see the 151 continue its stay in the *Champagne pouilleuse*. The first two months would pass in the usual fashion when out of the trenches: going through the normal routine of exercises, instruction, formal ceremonies and reviews, and performing labour fatigues. On 3 January, the regiment marched to its new billets to the southeast of Mourmelon-le-Grand. The 1 and 3 Battalions were lodged at Les Grandes-Loges, 2 Battalion and regimental staff at Bouy. There, the regiment would spend three weeks undergoing a new programme of infantry instruction. It was a new initiative passed down to the armies for dissemination and incorporation into the combat tactics employed on the small-unit level. Based on existing skill sets, achievements, and aptitude the men were divided into groups designated for training as hand grenadiers, rifle machine-gunners, trench mortarmen, signallers, etc. Those riflemen not assigned to a specific weapons specialty became *voltigeurs* (perhaps best translated as 'skirmishers'), a term resurrected from the Napoleonic era to designate a well-trained foot soldier, especially in the use of multiple weapons. Building on the instruction and training of 1915, this was the latest evolution on the path to forging the new army Lieutenant Colonel Moisson had described on New Year's Eve.

Along with this advanced instruction was the ubiquitous regimen of foot-and-arms drill and physical conditioning which included long marches with full packs. Despite the tiresome schedule of life out of the trenches, it was certainly better than life in the trenches and the respite proved to be a much-needed tonic. As Second Lieutenant Campana declared:

> For ten days we haven't heard a single cannon shot. It's a complete mental rest for the men, and despite the numerous training manoeuvres, they are enchanted with their new life. In the immense barn where my platoon is billeted, I had shacks constructed of wattling and sapling branches so that the men are sheltered from the cold. And at the centre I've had a small theatre set up where every Sunday we stage performances. My poilus have decorated their billets very tastefully. They've woven garlands of ivy and mistletoe to festoon the interior of the barn and their new home has a very pleasant look.[34]

This time was interspersed with a handful of ceremonial events, held with the idea of bolstering morale and reinstilling *esprit de corps*. There were reviews by General Deville and General Gouraud (commanding 4th Army), awarding of the Croix de la Légion d'honneur, Croix de Guerre, and Medaille Militaire to individuals who'd distinguished themselves in the fighting the previous autumn, and a flag ceremony involving the regimental band which was attended by General Joffre himself. Such martial thrills provided a momentary break from the monotonous days of training and work that otherwise defined this intervening period.

On 24 January the entire regiment, including two companies of the combat train, took part in manoeuvres with the other units of the 42 ID at Camp Chalons. This was immediately followed by a labour assignment that continued for weeks. The entire regiment was put to work in the construction of a third line of resistance between Saint-Hilaire-au-Temple and Mont de Billy. For sixteen days in seven-hour shifts the men toiled, first erecting barbed wire entanglements and then excavating the initial trace of the trenches along the entire front of the new position. Despite the banality of the task, the soldiers-turned-navvies applied themselves diligently, even finishing ahead of schedule. After completing these defences, the regiment moved off to new billets in the outskirts of Chalons-sur-Marne, and then again to Pogny and Vésigneul-sur-Marne in the third week of February. Before heading out a sanitary inspection was carried out by a certain Doctor General. Campana told the story:

> This 'oak leaves' [in reference to the collar insignia worn by doctors in the medical service] enjoys a sad reputation, for he has a habit of distributing punishments in profusion during the course of his visits and it's with terror that we've learned of his arrival. When he showed up at the neighbouring company without warning, the soldiers immediately scattered like a flock of sparrows, rushing behind the pillars, burying themselves into the hay, hiding behind the carts.
>
> 'There's no one in this unit!' he yells at a NCO who wasn't able to get away in time. 'That's too bad considering that it seems to be set up in a pig pen, equipment hanging in every corner, as well as rifles.'
>
> Noticing some shoes sticking out of a barrel broken open and filled with hay: 'And they chuck their galoshes up against the barrels!' – pulling on the boots, which then give resistance. And for good reason as the boots were attached to a pair of legs. 'Why, there's a dead body hidden under the straw! This is abominable! Sergeant, turn over this barrel and put this dead man out in the open.'
>
> The NCO complied but what was exhumed was not a dead body but a soldier, all abashed but most certainly alive, who had improvised and dove into this strange hiding place thinking he'd escaped from the wrath of the Doctor General. Without warning he bursts into my billets just as my section was assembled for inspection, and as a result, no one had the time to get away:

'Your men are all provided with gas masks?' he asked me.

'Yes, sir.'

'Form them up at the attention in line of two ranks!' This was done immediately.

'Gas alert! Gas alert!' the general yelled. And no one moved.

'Well, why are you waiting to put on your masks? If this had really been a gas attack, you'd have all croaked already!'

'You maybe, you'll croak. But us, we'll just die!'

It was Private Coutant, an old gamekeeper and poacher from Sissonnne – whose wife and six children had been burnt alive by the Germans – that had so casually uttered the catastrophic remark before the absolutely stunned senior officer. After recomposing himself, he shouted:

'Firing squad! You'll be shot for daring to say such a thing! I'm going to immediately ask your colonel that you're shot tomorrow morning! Lieutenant, lead me to your colonel! This is unbelievable! This is unbelievable! There's no more discipline!'

I have to add that our valiant Papa Victory wouldn't allow himself to be intimidated by the enraged high-brass doc' and the brave Coutant would only be slapped with eight days in prison.[35]

The next week was spent with the men installing themselves in their new billets at Pogny and Vésigneul. The war had made its mark here, the homes having already been badly damaged by artillery fire during the fighting in 1914. Rejoining the regiment at its new cantonment was Sergeant L'Huillier. Having recovered from his injuries suffered in the attack on Aubérive the previous September, L'Huillier volunteered to return to the front. He was to join a detachment of reinforcements composed of 4 corporals and 108 men. After a long five-day train ride – which took him from the 151 depot in Quimper to Rennes, Chartres, Orleans, Troyes, Mailly – he at last arrived at the village of Pogny on 18 February. After being greeted by Lieutenant Colonel Moisson, L'Huillier was assigned to 3rd Platoon, 6th Company, 2nd Battalion, Lieutenant Cavallier in command.

He was happy to discover that a few old comrades from his days in the Argonne and Champagne still remained. What's more, L'Huillier learned that the battalion was commanded by his old commander and friend from his basic training, Commandant Le Moing. L'Huillier arrived in time for the resumption of the daily training schedule, with the days divided into periods of specialist instruction and officer education, combat exercises, courses on signalling, simulated gas attacks, and cleaning of equipment and weapons. The regiment like most other units in the French army was of the mind that any major action was still months away, and they were correct. The next big Allied offensive was planned for the spring.

There were moments of excitement to cut into the routine but by and large, there was only the tedium of life in the rear. This changed on the night of 20 February as French searchlights swept the sky in search of German zeppelins. Unbeknownst to the fascinated audience of poilus, these were harbingers of the terrible destruction to come. For these dirigibles had been sent out on coordinated bombing runs against high-value targets behind the front lines in preparation for the assault on Verdun the next morning. When the searchlights suddenly caught sight of one in their powerful beams, anti-aircraft guns opened up. Soon after the zeppelin was struck and ignited, causing the craft to come down in flames near Revigny. For a few days more, the men of the 151 would remain blissfully unaware of the living nightmare unfolding some 50 miles off to the east.

Chapter 5

Opening Operations at Verdun

Verdun is a place that has been quite literally soaked in blood for millennia. It was a site of legendary battles dating back to the time of the ancient Gauls and its strategic location on the River Meuse ensured it would play an important role in the control of what would become the nation of France. Standing before the Gate of St Paul, created as portal way through the ancient ramparts, is a monument inscribed with the dates Verdun has been under siege: 450, 485, 984, 1047, 1246, 1338, 1552, 1792, 1870, and of course 1916. There was also fighting there during the Second War and partisan *maquisards* were executed on the same ground that their fathers and uncles had fought on a generation before. Originally a Bronze Age stronghold, when the the Romans arrived they would name it *Verodunum*, meaning 'strong fort'. In the fifth century, as Attila the Hun invaded the Western Roman Empire, he failed in his attempt to seize the place. When Charlemagne's Frankish empire was divided in three – leading to the creation of what would become France and Germany – under the Treaty of Verdun of 843, the town became part of the Holy Roman Empire. In the siege of 923, it was split off from the Holy Roman Empire; Henry II took it back in 1552. Later, in 1648, the Peace of Westphalia that ended the European religious wars awarded Verdun to France.[1] Under Louis XIV a citadel was built in the centre of town by the renowned military engineer Vauban. The fortified city played a crucial role after the Franco-Prussian War of 1870 as a defensive line of protection against German threats along the eastern border.

After the Franco-Prussian War, Séré de Rivières orchestrated the construction of two lines of fortresses from Belfort to Épinal and from Verdun to Toul to serve as defensive screens against future German invasions. Verdun guarded the northern entrance to the plains of Champagne and, therefore, the approach to the French capital Paris. Extending between 2 and 8km from the seventeenth-century citadel, a double ring of twenty-eight forts and *ouvrages* were constructed around Verdun on the most advantageous elevations above the Meuse River valley and offering mutual fire support. Thus, when Verdun is referred to, what is really being spoken of is not just the town but the surrounding system of fortifications known officially as the Fortified Region of Verdun. Through the last two decades of the nineeenth century, many of the fortifications were modernized and made more resistant to artillery. This included adding cushions of sand and thick, steel-reinforced concrete tops, which were buried under the earth. As armament, 75mm and 155mm guns were placed in shell-proof turrets along with machine guns to protect the ditches around the forts. Reinforcement and additional armaments continued to be added in the years leading up to the Great War. All of these modifications allowed Verdun to resist the German invasion in 1914 – the forts withstanding even the massive 420mm Big Bertha artillery attacks – and Joffre used it as a pivot during the Battle of the Marne.[2]

Though the war had become deadlocked, the massive bloodletting of French forces in 1915 had clearly weakened France. The German Chief of Staff, General von Falkenhayn, believed that the French were getting close to breaking point. Although a breakthrough in the Western Front might no longer be possible, Falkenhayn believed that the French army could be defeated in one final knockout blow if a sufficient number of casualties were inflicted. His plan was to attack a position from which the French could not retreat for both strategic and symbolic reasons. At the same time the position was so important to French national pride, they would pay anything to keep it. That place was Verdun. In effect, Falkenhayn would intentionally create a meat grinder to destroy the French army. In explaining his plan to the Kaiser, Falkenhayn wrote: 'A mass breakthrough – which in any case is beyond our means – is unnecessary. Within our reach there are objectives for the retention of which the French General Staff would be compelled to throw in every man they have. If they do so the forces of France will bleed to death.'

The Germans would also benefit from a strategic advantage. Verdun was a salient that threatened the main German communication lines but conversely this also meant that it was surrounded on three sides. Communications from the French rear to the front were poor, as were supply lines, with only a single road connecting Verdun to important hubs such as Bar-le-Duc, 50km to the south. Though Verdun was surrounded by a ring of forts, many of these had had their cannon stripped away and troop garrisons reduced in strength so that they could be deployed in the field. Falkenhayn predicted that for every German soldier, more than twice as many Frenchmen would fall. Recent scholarship has pointed to Falkenhayn's plan of attrition as a post-war substitute invented by the general to cover over the lack of clear objectives – something akin to painting the bull's eye around the arrow. Crown Prince Wilhelm, the commander of the German 5th Army that was to carry out the attack, seemed to indicate as much in his accounting. He, along with a number of his contemporaries, believed the real objective was to break Verdun's defences and then take the city itself; effectively a breakthrough offensive after all.

Despite urgent demands from the French army chief-of-staff, General de Castelnau, the defensive positions and troop levels around Verdun remained wholly inadequate against the onslaught that was soon to come. General Joffre insisted on marshalling France's resources for the long-planned Franco-British joint offensive along the River Somme in the Picardy region to the northeast.

In January 1916, French airmen had detected German preparations for the Verdun offensive, and on 11 February, a French intelligence officer discovered a build-up of German troops on the right bank of the Meuse. Joffre at last permitted some hastily arranged efforts to reinforce the defences of Verdun and over the next ten days, thousands of men and dozens of guns were moved to Verdun to bolster the line. The attack was originally scheduled to begin on 12 February but due to heavy snow, rain, and fog, it was delayed for over a week, allowing the French precious time to rush up two more divisions of the French XXX Army Corps (72 ID and 51 ID) and make some moderate improvements to the defences. When the forecast showed a clearing in the weather, German commanders set the date of the attack for the next day.

At 7.15 on the morning of 21 February the assault was opened with a nine-hour artillery bombardment by 1,200 guns firing over a million shells on a front of 40km. From the Bois d'Avocourt on the left to Étain on the right, the ground exploded with a violence unsurpassed in war. Trenches and fortifications were flattened as entire forests began to disappear with trees shattered, uprooted, tossed into the air like matchsticks. The tactical plan called for a continual series of limited advances intended to draw the French reserves into the trap. Each of these advances was itself to be secured by an intense artillery bombardment, brief for surprise and making up for its short duration by the number of batteries and their rapidity of fire. By this means the objective would be taken and consolidated before the enemy could move up its reserves for counter-attack. The Germans were employing a new tactic with their artillery carrying out 'box barrages', where instead of targeting specific lines, entire zones were saturated. In just the first week alone, the French first line in the Bois des Caures – an area that was 1,000 by 500yd – would have 80,000 shells fired into it. There was a pause in the fire at midday, designed to lure the French artillery to open fire in anticipation of an infantry assault and thereby give away their positions. It worked, and the German artillery bombardment resumed, systematically destroying many of the remaining batteries and strongpoints. At 4.45 pm, the German 5th Army attacked with three army corps: the III, VII, and XVIII. In the vanguard were German storm troops and combat engineers armed with sacks of grenades and flamethrowers, whose mission it was to probe into the French lines in advance of the main body of the infantry force. They were the infiltration methods first tested and refined in the Argonne Forest.

One of the regiments facing the deluge of shells was the 151's old reserve regiment, the 351 IR, which occupied first-line positions in Brabant-sur-Meuse and in the Bois de Consenvoye. To their right in the Bois d'Haumont was the 362 IR, sister regiment to the 162 IR. By the end of the first day, German troops had penetrated the French lines in these woods. Significant gains were made elsewhere along the line as well. The following day the Germans capitalized on their gains, easily repelling French counterattacks. After putting up a heroic resistance, the 51 ID began to collapse. At Brabant the 351 fell back and retreated to Samogneux at the edge of the Bois des Caures. The next day, it counter-attacked without success as the remains of 51 ID slowly retreated to the Bois des Fosses. Even several days in, senior French commanders did not appreciate the seriousness of the attack, with General Joffre convinced it was a distraction for the real blow that was to land elsewhere. By the evening of 23 February, the Germans had overrun the French first line. They had advanced 5km, seizing the villages of Brabant, Wavrille, and Samogneux. They had also wrested control of the Bois des Caures after two light infantry battalions commanded by Colonel Émile Driant fought a valiant but doomed resistance. The XXX AC had begun to disintegrate, having lost over 26,000 men (60 per cent of its strength). Entire regiments had been wiped out and the handfuls of survivors started to withdraw from the second line of defence. Only the arrival of the XX AC on 24 February kept the French defence from collapsing and avoided a complete rout. That evening, de Castelnau pleaded with Joffre to send the 2nd Army (under General Phillipe Pétain) to the Verdun sector. By then the enemy had taken much of the French second line, capturing Beaumont, Louvement, Bois des Fosses, and Bois des Caurières. Disaster struck on 25 February, when the centrepiece of the Verdun fortifications, Fort Douaumont, fell almost without firing a shot. It had been taken by a handful of enterprising Germans soldiers who had slipped into the superstructure and captured the tiny garrison force sheltering inside. The enemy had also taken Vacherauville, Côte du Poivre, and the top portion of Bois d'Haudraumont. On this same day, Joffre consented to de Castelnau's wishes and General Pétain was appointed to be commander of the Fortified Region of Verdun and the 2nd Army was ordered into the fight. His orders were to hold the right bank of the Meuse at all costs and Pétain threw himself into the task despite a severe case of the pneumonia.

Meanwhile, contrary to Falkenhayn's expectations, his own forces had been suffering significant losses from day one. The small pockets of poilus who had survived the German artillery bombardments often put up a fierce resistance. As the Germans continued to advance south, they came within range of the powerful French artillery on the left bank of the Meuse, which quickly inflicted serious losses on the attack units. With the weather and the constant shelling, the ground turned into a sea of mud and the German guns became stuck. Their infantry continued to be pushed forward and often attacked in dense masses only to be ruthlessly cut down by the French long-range guns on the opposite bank. One of the areas that saw mass slaughter was the Ravin de la Dame, which was soon renamed Ravin de la Mort ('Death Ravine'). By 27 February, French resistance had begun to stiffen and the German advance slowed. When the village of Douaumont was finally captured on 2 March after a week of ferocious fighting, four German regiments had been practically destroyed there. On 8 March the Germans captured the defensive works surrounding Bois d'Hardaumont, but then over the course of ten consecutive days got bogged down in a series of bloody but inconclusive attacks on Fort Vaux and the village it was named after.

The French units being sacrificed were buying precious time for reinforcements and resupplies to be sent from the rear to shore up the French defence. With the railway line going through Verdun in peacetime already cut off since 1915 and under continual shelling, only a narrow gauge line known as *le Petit Meusien* was available to ferry supplies and munitions into Verdun. The bulk of men and materiel, however, was transported up along a narrow provincial road connecting Verdun and Bar-le-Duc. French officers organized a motorized supply chain on an unprecedented scale, transporting men and materiel to the front in a fleet of more than 3,000 trucks, which ran uninterrupted, night and day, for weeks. The narrow dirt road was eventually widened and hardened and became so critical to the French effort at Verdun that it earned the name *la Voie Sacrée* ('the Sacred Way'). As the battle progressed over weeks and months, it is estimated that each week an average of 90,000 men, 17,000 animals, and 11,000 trucks hauling 500,000 tons of materiel passed over the road in a constant stream of traffic day and night. To maintain the surface, a small army, some 8,000-strong, of older territorials and *Annamite* (Vietnamese) indigenous colonials was given the sole task of keeping the road in good state.[3]

With the Germans having failed to gain an immediate decision at Verdun, they realized that the British (and now to a lesser extent, the French) were moving forward with preparations for their massive offensive on the Somme. For the next four months, they would keep up the pressure at Verdun in order to disrupt the Allied plans and to try to break the French army. France would continue to pour men and materiel into the 'Furnace of Verdun' during the spring and summer in what effectively became a holding action for the Somme. With the German advance on the right bank stalling, Falkenhayn expanded the scope of his offensive to the left bank in order to take the heights there providing observatories and shelter for the devastating French artillery. On 6 March, two German corps (VI and X Reserve Corps) crossed the River Meuse at Brabant and prepared to mount attacks on the heights protecting the French guns. With their line under severe strain, the siphoning off of French forces from other areas of the front continued. Caught now in Verdun's inescapable pull of gravity was the 151. To the men, there was only one inevitable outcome – a fight to the finish.

Chapter 6

Into the Furnace

March to Verdun (25 February–9 March)

The German offensive on the positions north of Verdun had already been underway for four days when, on the night of 24 February, the 42 ID was alerted to be ready to march the next morning. Before dawn the next morning the 151 would begin its progressive approach to Verdun in what was referred to as *étapes*, or 'stages'. The regiment's first stops were at Soulanges, Ablancourt, and then Possesse. Given reports that the massive German cannonade could be heard as far as a hundred miles away in the Vosges mountains, it's certainly conceivable that the distant rumbling was audible from the 151's billets at Pogny and Vésigneul, only 50 miles away. None of the available eyewitness accounts mention hearing it either on the opening day of the offensive or in the immediate days that followed. The men would have been accustomed to the sound of the front and ever-present rumble of artillery. Whatever the case, the men learned about the German assault first from rumours recounted by the hundreds of troops who'd been recalled from furlough after 21 February. The anticipation in the ranks was palpable. While they knew the life that awaited them in the days ahead would be defined by the rigours of combat, there was an eagerness to get into the fight, to see the job done. Second Lieutenant Campana wrote:

> We're marching to Verdun! We were alerted in the night of the 24th–25th and in the morning of the 25th, we departed the pretty village of Pogny with the regimental band out in front. We're off to fight again, and the fighting will be particularly hot this time . . . [Yet] the thought of fighting to save our old garrison town is welcomed with an animated joy. The regiment moves off superbly. The morale of the men is excellent.[1]

Even later, despite there being some conception of what the experience would entail, to fight at Verdun would become a rite of passage. It was the very scale of it all, in every sense, that perhaps unconciously drew soldiers to want to see it for themselves, to be able to claim they played a part no matter how small. This was especially true for those who had not yet been there. In his novel *Verdun*, Jules Romains captured this feeling of being involved in something much greater than oneself. Despite the imminent threat of death or dismemberment, there remained an inescapable yet elusive draw for the men going into battle:

> From the moment the march started, the men were conscious of a feeling similar to that which they had experienced on leaving Pogny, and again when they had set out from Possesse, but this time raised to higher power: the feeling that they were being drawn into the orbit of a whirlpool.
>
> Over there, beyond the rolling landscape, brown, light green, dark green, dotted with great patches and stripes of shining white snow; beyond the billowing grasslands and winter woods, twenty or twenty-five miles off, lay a great flaming object, still invisible, but roaring away in the distance, a furnace set in the hollow of the hills and sucking into its blazing heart everything within range. They felt themselves being dragged to the centre of the attraction, shovelled into the vast and hungry maw. The thoughts that went on in the secret heart of any single man had very little importance when set against the cosmic activity in which he was called upon to play his part.[2]

The regiment was in full marching order, including a complete complement of 120 rounds of ammunition on each man – a load weighing over 60lb. It was an exhausting forced march, the first section of which spanned two days, as the regiment marched first to Soulanges before making a halt at Bassu. Here they encountered the field artillery unit assigned to the 42 ID, the 61 FAR, along with elements of the other units of the division, all moving toward Verdun. Retaking the march, the regiment passed Vanault-le-Chatel where it defiled past General Deville and then trudged on another six hours straight through the rain and cold before stopping for the night at Possesse. In two days time, the 151 had marched 60km. As the men, muddy and soaked to the bone, threw themselves down in the barns and outbuildings in town, endless convoys of trucks rumbled through the main street, heading in the direction of Verdun. The regiment would remain in Possesse for several days, passing the mornings and afternoons in exercises and regimental manoeuvres. On 28 February, the fall of Fort Douaumont was announced to the men who grew impatient to get into the fight. To bolster morale, the regimental band serenaded the troops and townspeople. When the band struck up '*Chant du Depart*', the men joined in and sang along.

Before departing Possesse, Campana was approached by one of his men, who'd come to him with a sad tale and an even sadder request. The soldier proceeded to tell him that he'd already been wounded three times since being mobilized in August 1914. He had left behind a wife and 3-year-old daughter in Paris. Surprised that the man had not been decorated in that time, the soldier explained that he had been sent before a War Council for desertion and received a deferred sentence of four years' public service. The reason for his desertion was complicated though. After being evacuated for receiving his first wound, a friend came to tell him that his wife had been cheating on him while he was away at the front. At first, he refused to believe it. But his suspicions became aroused during his convalescence furlough – his wife wasn't acting the same way towards him. Nonetheless, the soldier forced himself to chase away these dark thoughts, they were unbearable to think about, and he soon was sent back to the front. Disastrous news arrived later on when his neighbours wrote to inform him that his wife had run off with a civilian leaving his little girl behind. The news threw him into a panic and, without asking permission, he set off to Paris. After recovering his daughter and placing her in an asylum, he immediately returned to the front and rejoined his regiment. Nevertheless, the man had deserted and was sent before a War Council for the crime. But fate had worse in store for this unfortunate soul:

'I've been evacuated twice more and this past January, when I was at the depot I learned that my child was very ill. I returned as quickly as I could to Paris with permission this time, but I arrived too late . . . my little girl was dead . . . and now I have no one . . .'

He could no longer hold back his tears. His pain was hard to bear.

'I never believed a day would come where I'd be so unlucky. My wife was so good to me, so affectionate, she sobbed when I left for the first time.'

'Poor fellow!'

'Seeing that my child was dead, I wanted to kill myself but I thought at that time it was a cowardly act, because there were so many people who wanted to live and who are going to get killed at the front. Me, I don't want to live anymore, it's death I need. But I want to die with a purpose. So, Lieutenant, at present we're going off to fight. I've come to ask you – and this is the point of my visit – to give me a job when you need volunteers for attacks or raids. When I think of all the good fortune I've had and that it's all gone now, life is too painful for me. I want to die!'

'My poor friend, I will remember at the necessary times what you've asked of me today. But I must discourage you, you're young, you still have time to make a new life.'

'No, Lieutenant, never again!'

'Think on it perhaps, but each time you have a heavy heart, come confide in me your troubles, it might help calm your pain. In those moments, you'll find in me not your commander but a comrade, and you'll feel less alone.'

He left me and I shook his hand betraying more emotion than I wished. Poor devil, he suffered greatly. For him life had become too much to bear and only death is capable of curing those wounds.[3]

And death was surely waiting for them all in the days to come. The 151's Calvary would begin well before they arrived at the fearsome maw of battle. The regiment would first have to undergo a week of gruelling forced marches. On 3 March, the regiment left its billets at Possesse and as it did, the weather turned more foul, with pelting rain alternating with blinding snow. As the regiment passed through the Meuse villages they were greeted by the townspeople. Standing out in front of their ruined homes, they applauded and cheered as the men filed passed in a scene not witnessed since the early stages of the war in 1914. Though they may not have had an awareness of the dire operational situation unfolding at Verdun, the seriousness of events was not lost on these civilians, who seemed to understand the stakes. And here, filing past them were not just soldiers of France, but soldiers of the Verdun regiment, who were going to meet the foe in a battle that could well determine the outcome of the war.

Certainly, the warm reception by the locals helped to bolster the spirits of the men during the exhausting march, made all the more difficult by the weather that alternated between rain and snow, and the muddy, rutted roads that impeded their progress. Nonetheless, the regiment had covered 90km in a week. The 151 made stops at Noirlieu, Sivry-sur-Ante, and Daucourt before continuing onto its former billets in the Valmy Quarter of Sainte-Menehould, the regiment's cantonment during its service in the Argonne Forest the year before. L'Huillier was beside himself at the thought that he would have the chance to see his family before going into battle. As the regiment arrived at the southern entrance to Sainte-Menehould, it halted to realign its ranks. The men were brought to attention, ordered to shoulder arms, and then set off again in cadence. The band struck up a martial tune and the 151 marched into town and down the main streets in splendid order. All along the route, L'Huillier caught sight of his friends from before the war, as crowds cheered the men on. But the real surprise came when he spotted his own grandfather – a veteran of the Franco-Prussian War of 1870 – standing on his front doorstep. With permission given to leave the ranks, L'Huillier ran up to his grandfather and embraced him, both men overcome with emotion. Rejoining the ranks and proceeding towards the town centre he next saw his grandmother, followed shortly thereafter by his mother and aunt dressed smartly in their Red Cross nurses' uniforms.

After arriving in the Valmy Quarter, L'Huillier obtained permission to join his family for dinner with Sergeant-Major Pinchard, who had saved his life on 25 September 1915 when he had been buried by the blast of a 'Big Black' shell. It was a joyous occasion and an inexplicable comfort to be able to spend the night in his own home, in his own bed. The next day, when the regiment was given liberty for the day, L'Huillier brought several more of his NCO and officer friends back home to share a good bottle wine and some brioches. Enjoying one final night in his own bed, L'Huillier arose in the dark of the early morning of 6 March. Packing his haversack full of sweets and tinned food, he gave each of his family members a long embrace and set off to rejoin the regiment. A few hours later, the regiment was back on the march heading southeast to complete its next stage, which would take them circuitously to Verrières, Villers, and Passavant. It was another long, trying slog over roads made slippery by ankle-deep mud. By the time it reached Triaucourt it was already getting dark. After an hour's break, the footsore column set off again. Progress was made at a crawling pace through the muck and the cold, as the moon shone the way with its mournful light. Finally they reached Èvres and Bauzée-sur-Aire late in the night. At the end, the 151 had marched 40km in a single day, reportedly setting a new record for the regiment. As they had seen before, the villages they now occupied had already been ravaged by the fighting in 1914. Campana recorded:

> Sections of wall stood on both sides of the road and we felt like we were marching into a necropolis. Only the sound of our steps broke the silence. From this desolation a strange charm emanated, undefinable and mysterious.
>
> We were able to find some barns in which we passed the night but we were very cold. [The next] morning, it snowed heavily. I visited the village. It's as dismal during the day as it is beautiful at night. We find only stones, beams blackened by fire, rusty and twisted iron rods, shapeless debris, parts of tables, wardrobes or beds. The church is in a lamentable state, only its clock is still intact. All the stained glass is broken, the altar is demolished, the sculptures no longer remain save the Christ figure, miraculously spared and gazing with sorry eyes on this sad spectacle. 'Love one another', the inscription has once read.[4]

The men spent the night where ever they could find shelter – dirty barns, mice-infested shacks, squalid pigsties – left to fend for themselves as usual. With their clothes soaked and splattered in mud, most had a hard time getting sleep despite the fatigue. After being given a day to recuperate from the long march, the regiment left Bauzée and Èvres on 8 March to continue its journey to Verdun. A wicked blizzard of snow enveloped the column, the gusting wind biting at the faces of the men. To shield themselves, the men flipped up the collars of their greatcoats or pulled their scarves up over their faces. Hands were shoved into pockets or sheltered in the folds of their clothing. It was a wet, dark night as the battalions trudged into Jubécourt and

Ville-sur-Cousances, where they rested for a few hours. It was there that all the units of the 42 ID – the 151 along with the 162 and 94 IR, the 8 and 16 LIB, the Territorial Engineers Company 6/3, and the 61 FAR – assembled to move off as a division.

Late in the night of 8–9 March, the 151 received orders to leave its billets and move to Verdun. Lieutenant Colonel Moisson, with other senior officers and MG company commanders, headed off in advance of the regiment to reconnoitre its new sector. In Moisson's absence, Commandant Tisseraud (3 Battalion commander) took over. The regiment departed Ville-sur-Cousances at 5.00 am and marched towards Rampont, climbing and descending various ridges as it went until reaching the main Paris–Verdun road (today's D603). The further they advanced eastward towards the great battle, the road became increasingly crowded with convoys of trucks laden with munitions and supplies. For Verdun was developing into a great beast that needed to constantly fill its belly with bullets, shells, materiel . . . and men.

And as they shuffled along, the column would suddenly be overtaken by a line of trucks. Calls of 'To your right . . . to your right . . .' would rise up, the warning rippling up from the tail to head of the column. And the men would grumble as they begrudgingly complied, elbowing their right-hand neighbours off the road. Alternately, the head of the column would quietly make room for a throng of refugees. The two bodies of people moving in opposite directions passed each other in silence. Those men from the occupied districts of northern France found this to be particularly painful, as they saw in them the sufferings of their own families, whom they had been cut off from for years. Campana recorded: 'The road was crowded with trucks, wagons loaded with furniture, women, old folks, children. Dombasle and the neighbouring villages had been evacuated. The agonized faces of these poor people who fled their once happy homes was painful to see. [In turn] they looked upon us with pity as we passed them by.' And underlying it all was the deep bass rumbling of the distant bombardment.[5]

Night was falling as the regiment passed Blercourt, where the general congestion of vehicles, troop columns, and refugees worsened. Eventually there was no choice but to abandon the Paris–Verdun Road at Baleycourt, where they turned left onto a gravelled track that passed along the western edge of Bois des Sartelles, climbing steeply to the north. At the intersection of the Sivry-la-Perche road, the column turned right and continued along the top of the high ridge. On some distant heights they could already see the heaviest calibre shells exploding, accompanied by a deep rumbling of countless cannon discharges and shell bursts. To the left of the road, the regiment passed Fort Sartelles and then Fort Chaume. The men began to wonder how much longer their torture would last.

> Once we reached Fort Chaume, our fatigue got worse, which was the fault of the company commander at the head of the column. The terrain

undulated greatly and the men of the first company quickly descended the slopes without concern for those who followed behind them. The other company commanders, not wishing to lose contact, quickened the pace. The movement spread by degrees and amplified itself, so that the unlucky men of 12th Company often had to march at the double-time only to come to an abrupt stop, since the first company had descended the previous downhill quickly but would then climb the next uphill just as slowly. This accordion movement goes on for more than an hour and you can easily imagine the torture that the unfortunate men of the trailing companies had to endure, as they were obliged to run, stop suddenly, run again, and all while carrying a full load.[6]

For Campana this torment was only further exacerbated as he was once again suffering from an acute attack of intestinal pain. Despite the burning feeling in his belly, his fear of missing out on the big battle to come outweighed his discomfort and Campana maintained his place with his company. His efforts would soon pay off as the column now reached the final ridge overlooking the town of Verdun from the southwest which provided an unbroken view of the horizon.

> An incredible view spreads before our eyes. Extending along the horizon was a blood-red band of light, the redness and brightness of which gradually fading to a purple hue that seemed to take over the entire night sky. In the distance small purple lights flickered, went out, suddenly brightened again. There were easily a hundred of them: they were German shells being illuminated by fires below, as the homes of Verdun burned in the night.[7]

The image of the Furnace had now materialized, manifested by the thousands of cannon discharges and bursting shells, the parabolic rising and falling of illumination flares, and the flames of the burning villages and forests of the Meuse. Despite the onslaught on their senses, the men still had further to go before they could rest and try to get warm. Corporal Henri Laporte, in 8 Company, was one of those who'd been suffering through the long marches to Verdun. He recorded in his diary:

> After three days and three nights of forced marches through rain and snow, and stopping only to eat, we arrive [at Verdun]. The ground was frozen and slippery, the snow was still falling. The town is being bombarded. Shells were bursting and fires burned all around. Our last stage had been tough: we've marched without stop for twenty-four hours.[8]

Descending down the last height into the suburb of Glorieux, the regiment finally arrived in the city of Verdun between 10.00 and 11.00 pm. The town appeared to be deserted. The streets were filled with wooden beams, tiles, shards of glass. As they shuffled along on their weary legs, the men were tripped up by telephone wires that hung from the houses and snaked across the ground. Beds, cabinets, and arm chairs lay pell-mell among the rubble from which twisted iron rods jutted out here and there. From the breaches in the facades and smashed window frames, the sky appeared to become redder in colour as the glow of burning fires created a shifting, evil light. After winding their way through the ruined streets, the regiment filed into rue Saint-Saveur and was assigned lodgings where they spent their final evening before being sent up to the front lines. One battalion was billeted at the Hôtel de Ville, another at the Sainte-Catherine Hospital, and the third at the Congregation of Sainte-Catherine (Sainte-Catherine Church). The protection afforded by these buildings was dubious at best. Laporte recorded:

> [M]y company billets in a group of abandoned houses. We were lodged (the men of my half-section and myself) on the third floor, in a room with a ceiling that was gaping wide open, punctured in the centre by a falling shell. A moment later, some poilus from the section brought us some food stuffs (forgotten, certainly intentionally, by the inhabitants). We listen to the sound of a distant cannonade and the shell explosions in the neighbourhood, which now and then caused our little pigeon house to shake. We were tired from the long march and tremendous effort exerted. We soon fall asleep, undisturbed by the falling shells.[9]

The officers meanwhile would have to wait a little longer before getting their rest. Late that night, General Deville summoned all the officers from the units of the two brigades under his command to the Verdun Hôtel de Ville. There, he held a short briefing to address the role the division was to play in the dire period ahead. To those present, Deville seemed to be in an ill-temper. Standing stiffly before them, he began tugging nervously on his goatee as he addressed the solemn audience. Jubert remembered it this way:

> 'Gentlemen, Verdun is threatened. You are at Verdun and you are the Verdun Brigade. I won't hide the truth from you; we've been taken by surprise . . . I won't hide the mistakes from you; we must fix them . . . The situation was desperate; it's not yet stabilized. The sector that we're taking up? Chaos . . . The life which awaits us there? Battle . . . The trenches? They don't exist . . . Don't ask me for material: I don't have any . . . Reinforcements: I don't have any to provide . . .'[10]

Second Lieutenant Basteau remembered the address somewhat differently, though with the same stark terms:

> 'No trenches, nothing but holes . . . corpses as well which we'll need to bury . . . No barbed-wire, no entanglements, certainly no shelters . . . nothing . . . nothing! Gentlemen, don't ask for anything, I've nothing to give you. You'll have your rifles to defend yourselves, your bayonets to stop the enemy, and your hearts to hold on under fire . . . You'll have to submit to assaults, you will stand your ground. I wanted the 151st to hold the most dangerous corner of the sector. It will hold it. It will be the regiment's honour . . .'[11]

While he was speaking, his voice cracked several times, becoming hoarser as he finished. A bone-chilling dread sank into the silent and captive audience as the general ended with 'Good luck, gentlemen!' Deville quickly shook hands with Moisson and the two shared in an intense glance, an unspoken understanding. The general then abruptly departed, leaving his audience in a stunned silence.

First Rotation at Verdun (10–29 March)

Early in the morning of 10 March, an alert went out to the 151 to be ready to move out, giving the men only a couple hours of sleep following their gruelling march. As the men begin to assemble, some lucky ones enjoyed a bit of old vintage wine poured into their cups by the few local townspeople remaining. Others stumbled upon a sack of tobacco and crammed a handful into their pockets. To ensure the men were stocked up for their rotation to the front lines, both of their 2-litre canteens were filled with *pinard* (the rough red wine the troops were issued) and additional ammo was handed out, bringing each man's total to 160 cartridges. Forming up in front of Hôtel de Ville in the rue Saint-Sauveur, Lieutenant Cavallier brought his 6 Company to attention and cried out: '"The Boches have sworn to take Verdun. We swear that they will not take it." – "We swear it," came the reply from 170 chests.'

Yet it seems this was a classic case of 'hurry up and wait', as the regiment would spend the afternoon in town waiting for cover of darkness before proceeding up to the front. The units of the 42 ID would be relieving the severely battered 39 DI in the Bois d'Haudraumont, with the 151 replacing the 160 IR. They would be marching in with a strength of 67 officers and just over 2,800 men. As night fell, the regiment departed Verdun with nothing but the flames of the burning buildings to light the way, each company being provided with its own guide. Forming into short columns by platoon with intervals of 100m between each, they departed the town. The ranks were silent, no one spoke. Raymond Jubert, brevetted to second lieutenant upon his return to the 151, captured the eerie scene:

> We've crossed over the Meuse – broad, noisy, sinister-looking – its shifting, bloody mirror flowing past the last blazing fires. The ranks are silent. We seemed to be like ghosts, and perhaps tomorrow we will be. This procession of shadows leaving the ruins of the ghost town, this silent army of specters marching toward the guns, had an almost Dantesque grandeur to it.[12]

The regiment initially followed the course of the Meuse on the right bank until it reached Belleville, where they were greeted by the first German high-explosive shells. It was snowing heavily on and off as the regiment then turned right and marched towards Fort Belleville. Once reaching the fort, it took a left turn and headed northeast towards Fort Froide-Terre, about 2km distant. Campana noted:

> We marched across open ground that was covered with snow. It took six long hours. Our route was strewn with craters and all sorts of obstacles, and the ground beaten by the uninterrupted fire of the enemy artillery. The region was very hilly. We went down one hill only to immediately begin climbing another, and many men fell on the slippery ground. Yet the moon, full and yellow, shown in the clear sky . . . [I]n front of us . . . Bras, Samogneux, Vacherauville and Louvemont burned. In the distance you could make out the Meuse, which spread out in long bloody stretches. The snow reflected the light, intensifying it and we could see the heights and ravines that we still had to cross.[13]

The moon and the fires illuminated the ground with a pink incandescence. The temperature started to drop. At the battered Froide-Terre, the companies halted for a quarter of an hour before starting the final leg of the relief march. The 3 Battalion was held here in reserve and took up positions in the woods on Côte de Froide-Terre, close beside the fort itself. The 1 and 2 Battalions continued their march up the line, moving forward now with greater speed across the slippery snow. After some distance the legendary Fort Douaumont (now in German hands) hove into view on their right some 2km away atop its prominent height. It was around here that the men entered the first communication trench, or what passed for one in the chaos and devastation that prevailed here. In reality, the *boyau* was little more than a shallow ditch. Campana viewed the desolation around him:

> At times we passed the bodies of dead horses – from which emitted a horrible smell of putrefaction – shapeless debris, the remains of wagons

and caissons. From time to time, we passed numerous resupply parties as well as stretcher-bearers bringing back to the ambulances the dead and wounded. For in front, behind, to the right and the left, the shells fell, unnerving us with their quick detonation and blinding light. Soon we clearly perceived the sound of gunfire. Bullets began to whistle by and flares shot across the sky like meteors.

We stopped along the edge of a woods to catch our breath . . . A poison gas shell had burst near us. We felt as though onions had been rubbed in our eyes and tears began streaming down our cheeks. We retake our march forward: 'This is the last ravine,' my guide tells me, 'it's called the Death Ravine!'

The Death Ravine! An evil, dismal name but very apt! There, the grim reaper had made an ample harvest. Covered over with a blanket of white, hundreds of dead bodies were rotting on the ground. Slowly, softly, noiselessly, the snow was covering them over with its shroud. There, lying in their wool greatcoats, were the zouaves and Moroccans who'd held back the enemy and replaced the nonexistent ramparts with the impassable barricade of their valiant chests.[14]

An order was passed down from mouth to mouth: 'We've arrived! Silence! Pass it along!' Even with guides to lead the way, it took hours for all the companies to be placed in their designated positions. The relief was only completed in the early morning hours of 11 March. The 1 and 2 Battalions had taken up front-line positions about halfway up the southern slopes of the Bois d'Haudraumont (above the Bras–Douaumont road in the Goulette Ravine) in a general east–west line. The 2 Battalion went in on the right with three companies on the first line (5th, 7th, 8th) just in front of the lip that dropped 15m straight down into Haudraumont Quarries and the fourth company (6th) in support 100m back. Here the ground was open with the edge of the woods some 50m away. On the left was 1 Battalion in the same array (1st, 2nd, 4th in line, 3rd in support). On this part of the front the line ran into the woods. The machine-gun companies were in immediate support of the 1 and 2 Battalions, with additional guns positioned part way up Côte 295, behind and above the right flank of 2 Battalion. The 3 Battalion was kept in reserve 2km to the south, immediately to the southeast of Froide-Terre on the reverse slope. In liaison to the left of the 151 was the 162 IR, while to the right was the 150 IR (which would be relieved the next day by 94 IR). The Territorial Engineers Company 6/3 was also in the sector to provide entrenchment and construction support.

As the men took stock of their situation, the shock must have been profound. As Deville had warned, there were no trenches to speak of, only pathetic scrapes in the ground, knee-deep fighting holes linked together with a shallow trough. There was nothing between them and the German army, whose first line was very close, no more than 50m away. There were no wire entanglements out in front of them, no defensive accessory of any sort. They would soon discover that their first-line position was exposed to enemy fire from above as well as by enfilade from both flanks. And all around them lay the decaying bodies of French dead killed in the previous days' fighting and emitting their putrid stench. Yet, as luck would have it for the immediate present, the German advance had temporarily stalled out here just a few days before the 151's arrival and the enemy's artillery had yet to fully target the location of the fallback positions that now constituted the French first line. While merciless bombardments would soon eviscerate all of nature from the heights north of Verdun, at this stage of the battle the sheltered southern slopes of the Bois d'Haudraumont still remained largely populated with saplings and undergrowth.

Of course, trees and vegetation presented no real cover from German shells and bullets. The sector was effectively defenceless. In this light, the recent weeks spent constructing barbed wire entanglements in the reserve lines of Champagne now paid off. The 151 must continue the work on their pathetic entrenchments and turn the sector into a defensible fighting position capable of withstanding the next blow from the enemy. Despite the biting cold, gnawing hunger, and physical exhaustion, there could be no question of rest. Immediately the men set to work, furiously picking and shovelling away with their small entrenchment tools at hard ground before daylight would make such activity impossible. Their job was to deepen the trenches, and dig *boyaux* and advanced listening posts.

The orders for Campana's company were to throw up some lines of barbed wire between them and the enemy. Spools of wire were quickly brought forward and immediately the wire parties set to work. Campana would lead a guard detail with four others to provide security for the workers. Moving slowly from tree to tree through the undergrowth, the innumerable branches, felled logs, and dense foliage presented a barrier of snares and obstacles. After placing the men of the security detachment along a perimeter, Campana took cover behind a shrub and the vigil began. Only a short amount of time passed before he saw a dark mass move close by. Thinking it was one of his men, Campana, hands in his pockets, advanced towards the man and asked who it was. Immediately a gunshot rang out and a bullet zipped past – it was a German patroller! Campana instinctively reached for his revolver as the German quickly dashed back towards his lines. It was only then that Campana realized the fatal error he had committed – he had neglected to load his revolver! Right away a fusillade erupted from the German side. Forgetting that their comrades were out working between the lines, those in the French first line carelessly returned fire. A deafening inferno of gunfire erupted in the woods, as bullets smashed into tree trunks and snapped off branches overhead, causing a perfect rain of splintered wood and sticks. The wiring party managed to get back to their line and then gradually the firing wound down. Orders were reiterated to maintain the strictest vigilance. Those not sent back to work or put on watch soon wrapped themselves up in their blankets and tried to get some much-needed sleep, still wearing their equipment and with their loaded rifles resting beside them.

A grey dawn with low clouds and a heavy fog slowly materialized like a phantom and shrouded the land. The snow had ceased to fall but a light layer of white rested on the blankets of the slumbering men, lending them an eerie resemblance to the frozen corpses in the ravine below. As the morning light continued to spread its wan light, the fog dissipated and a new danger presented itself. On the right of their first-line positions, a German machine gun opened up, sweeping the top of the shallow ditch acting as their trench by enfilade. The slightest movement immediately called down a hail of bullets, angrily ripping up the earth around them. The lesson was simple: keep down and keep still. So the men hunkered down as best they could. Only darkness would bring respite, allowing freedom of movement and the resumption of the entrenching work. The regiment's position was certainly a precarious one. When Jubert's company moved up to the first line in a few days' time, he immediately recognized that the ground given to them to hold was *un mal coin* – 'a bad spot'. That was putting it mildly. The entrenchments were dug hastily, in spite of all tactical thought, on the exposed side of a hill that was open to enfilading fire from above. It was also isolated from the rest of surrounding trench system by 150m of open ground. During the day, no liaison was possible, while at night it was difficult at best. All of it screamed of desperation, of holding on by a thread.

Although it was not apparent at the time, in a way the regiment's arrival in the Haudraumont sector in the first week of March was fortuitous. At this early stage in the battle, the German army's effort had shifted to the left bank of the Meuse, with what could be considered by Verdun standards to be a lull in the fighting on the right bank. Aside from some occasional shelling and machine-gun strafing by both sides, the first line would remain relatively calm, a condition largely made possible by the spotty intelligence on the German artillery's part. At the same time, German commanders did appreciate the nearness of the French lines to their own. For the time being, they would focus their artillery on the more visible French supporting lines on the far side of the ravine and further back. From the first day the 151 had arrived, German 105s and 150s rained down on the Côte de Froide-Terre, snapping the large beech trees and smaller saplings, which came crashing down with loud cracks.

The companies of 3 Battalion, holding the reserve positions, were right in the middle of it. Jubert's simple shelter consisted of a roof of branches with a few shovelfuls of earth thrown on top and a tent canvas for a door. Jubert was getting some desperately needed sleep when he was rudely woken up by a salvo of 150s landing only 15m away. Instinctively relying on his keen sense of danger honed during the fighting in the Argonne, Jubert quickly perceived that the German artillery was firing in salvoes of six and were methodically progressing up the hill. His was the sixth and final position that would be targeted. Jubert started a count in his head to keep track of the salvoes. As he began emerging from his shelter, he once again heard the approaching shells. One . . . two . . . three . . . four . . . five . . . But this time he didn't have time to count the sixth salvo.

> A more deafening explosion, a more violent shock, then the sound of a hailstorm on my roof. An acrid smoke filled my eyes and nose. Suffocating, but conscious of keeping my wits in the midst of the disaster, I restrain myself from going into a coughing fit. In the agonizing silence that followed, the sounds of groaning rose up.
>
> Crawling forward, I put my head outside of my shelter, the opening of which was at the moment obstructed. Night had completely fallen. Before my eyes a smoking hole opened, out of which rose the voice of death. 'We have to clear that away quickly!' I yelled out into the night. 'Who is that there? Go look for picks.' The shadow didn't move. I shake him.
>
> 'Don't hurt me, don't hurt me.
>
> 'Why are you yelling? Go look for picks.
>
> 'I can only see flames in my eyes.
>
> 'Were you down in there?
>
> 'Yes, at the entrance.
>
> 'And who's with you?
>
> 'The adjutant was at the bottom with the Sergeant van Walleghem. Daniault and Arquillière were eating their soup. The shell entered from behind. It burst in the middle.
>
> 'Are you wounded?
>
> 'I don't know.'
>
> An hour passes as the shells continue to fall. We've cleared away the earth and pulled out the bloodied Daniault and Arquillière. Their limbs broken, groaning softly in a sad voice, they leave their flesh behind on the ground, the confinement stifling their cries of pain. Then with more trouble, at the bottom of their tomb we find Van Walleghem and Folliart, flattened and convulsed, their contorted hands thrown back behind them. On their swollen faces there is frozen the two-fold expression of terror and death. 'They could see it coming,' someone says. For the past several days, they'd been fearful and full of bitterness.[15]

While 3 Battalion positions at Froide-Terre were subjected to shelling, this remained relatively measured for the time being. The same could not be said of the neighbouring sectors. To the 151's right and left, the German bombardments were much more intense and the heights of the Meuse were transformed into erupting volcanoes. At night the effect was impressive, as Jubert wrote:

> For 3 kilometers all around, a distinct zone was created, where flares, spotlights, cannon flashes, and the flickering flames of fires, put on their display in the distant setting of a glowing fog. 'The Vestibule of Hell,' declares [Second Lieutentant] de la Ferrière. And it truly was that, a luminosity from beyond, a work of Dante, a fantastic vision on a field of death.[16]

Throughout their second night in the front lines, the men of 1 and 2 Battalions laboured away on their positions and threw up additional wire to their front. Anything that can be used to shore up the entrenchments was used: sandbags, scraps of wood and timber, ammunition crates. Progress could only be made slowly in the half-frozen ground. A cover trench was also begun just behind the first line to provide some improved means of defence. Work continued until dawn broke and then the men must once again take to the earth. In the surrounding sectors, violent bombardments fill the air with an incessant tearing, crashing, and thundering. To the right, Fort Douaumont appeared only as cloud of black smoke from an unending deluge of the heaviest calibre shells. At nightfall, orders came down to the companies to carry out reconnaissance patrols to better ascertain the enemy's positions. Henri Laporte was one of those who ventured out into the narrow no man's land in Bois d'Haudraumont.

> At 2:00 am, I left with two comrades on a reconnaissance patrol in front of our lines in order to learn the approximate position of the German advanced posts. We crawled along carefully in the greatest silence. The ground was frozen and made moving about very difficult. We skirted around a partially destroyed wire entanglement, then stopped to listen in the cover of a small fold of ground. The thousand noises of the forest, especially at night, prevented us from hearing very well. After waiting a little while, we set back off.
>
> About ten minutes had elapsed when two or three shadows emerged from the ground a dozen metres in front of us. They were definitely Germans coming out of a look-out post. Or were they in fact about to carry out their own patrol? We clasped tighter onto the stocks of our guns, remaining absolutely still, ready for anything. After a moment, the shadows seemed to evaporate. Without a doubt they were look-outs coming from one of the advanced posts we had set out to locate. We

remained long enough to be able to mentally mark the location of the emplacement.

We were just preparing to turn back when the barely perceptible sound of weapons clinking reached our ears. Indeed, one of the occupants of the German post was crawling off toward his lines, located a few metres behind. We saw him get up and jump into a hole (their trench without a doubt). Right away, we made out an upheaval of earth. Now we knew where the German first line was in front of us. To mark the position, we lay out two branches in a cross on the edge of the fold of ground with the greatest possible care. After we were certain that our landmark was visible, without losing any time we made an about-face and continued back toward our trenches flat on our stomachs. All went well. Our comrades, who were watching for our return, were happy to receive us safe and sound.

I immediately recounted my mission. From our trenches, we could see very clearly our two branches: the moon illuminated the ground like it was daytime. We were lucky that the sky was obscured by clouds during our reconnaissance.[17]

The excitement of Laporte's derring-do was balanced out by a small but painful tragedy. A section of the trench that was protecting Campana's company desperately needed to be shored up before it collapsed, and Campana called for a volunteer to leave the shelter in broad daylight to cut down several saplings to use for the purpose. Stepping forward to volunteer for the dangerous job was the suicidal soldier who'd confided in Campana about his unfaithful wife and departed child. Though moved by the gesture, he also knew the soldier's ulterior motive, and he reluctantly accepted the offer. In a moment, the star-crossed man leapt out of trench and began furiously hacking away at a nearby tree with a hatchet. After a few minutes the first sapling was down. He was proceeding on to the next, when suddenly he let out a cry. Stumbling a few steps back, he threw out his arms and then collapsed in a heap. Ignoring the danger, Campana sprung out of the trench with one of his corporals and dragged the wounded man back into the cover of the trench.

He had been shot in the face. After blasting apart his nose, the bullet had drilled through his right cheek and lodged into his shoulder, creating a gruesome flesh wound. Campana was convinced it was an exploding bullet, though more than likely he was simply seeing up close the damage that a standard Mauser round could inflict on the human body.

The blood gushed out in bursts; an artery must've been cut. All the efforts of the stretcher-bearers to stop the haemorrhaging were in vain . . . His face grew pale, his purple eyelids began to close, his discoloured lips trembled, his nose pinched up. His entire face showed that death had cast its hideous veil over him. He opened his eyes revealing dilated pupils:

'Lieutenant . . . there . . . in my jacket there . . . to the right . . . wallet . . . photo . . . my little girl.' I handed him what he asked, the portrait of his young daughter. He gave a passionate kiss to the face of the child.

'Give my money . . . comrades . . . *pinard* . . . Ah! My little girl . . . little girl . . . I'm coming to you . . . your mama, no . . . go away . . . your mama, your cruel mama, yes, crue– . . .' He suddenly threw back his head, he shook in a long shudder, and then it was over. [He] had ended his Calvary. In his clenched hand we left the photo of his departed child who he'd now gone to join. His body, wrapped in a tent-canvas, was put down in a ditch dug behind the trench, at the foot of a briar.[18]

Given the trajectory of the so-called 'exploding' bullet that had killed the man, Campana surmised that the German sniper who'd shot him must have been perched high up in a tree. To poilus, it was another example of German conniving and duplicity, further proof that the enemy fought dirty. They were more beasts than men. How else to explain the rape and killing of civilians, the wanton destruction of sacked villages, the aerial bombings of cities and hospitals behind the lines, the releasing of toxic gases, the exploding of underground mines, and now the use of exploding bullets. The list of German atrocities both real and perceived continued to grow.

A murderous rage had been ignited in their hearts and revenge was now on their minds. The only appropriate response was to retaliate against this heinous act. That night, having stuffed their pockets with grenades and taking only their bayonets with them, Campana led a small party of men out towards the German lines. Carefully crawling along the ground, the raiding party got to within 12m of the German trench, up until they heard the sound of picking and shovelling. Campana gave a signal and the men hurled a volley of grenades at the German line. Immediately they dashed back, not waiting for the grenades to explode. The bullets began to fly even before they reached their own lines, cracking and zipping by, tossing up the earth around their feet. One of the men had an even narrower escape when his helmet was struck by a round. Soon they arrived back at their trench, jumping in just as the shooting escalated into an all-out fusillade. Eventually the shooting died down, the occasional flare being sent up from the anxious German line. There were of course dozens of little dramas like this unfolding along the regiment's front. Though the *JMO* fails to record much of this low-level activity, incidents involving sniper fire, patrols, and bombing parties were taking place up and down the French and German first lines, and in the thin ribbon of no man's land separating them. For most of those occupying the tenuous positions in Bois d'Haudraumont, a pattern began to set it: the days were spent sheltering from German rifle and machine-gun fire, while the nights were spent deepening and strengthening the line. The first line continued to escape the wrath of the enemy's artillery. The same was not true for 3 Battalion in the reserve lines. Jubert bemoaned the sensation of feeling like helpless prey to the enemy gunners, who used their air power for eyes:

> These daily bombardments served as a lesson. We were under the eyes of the airplanes. The hawk, after spotting us, throws down a thunderbolt. We learned to hide ourselves out of view . . . security became the law of the land. The blood of the victims, which continued to spread itself further each day, wrote this lesson out on the soil. Lively now! Carelessness and laziness had taken the form of suffering and death all too frequently . . .[19]

The days on the Côte de Froide-Terre were difficult. During the daylight hours, as up in the first line, the men were forced to keep out of sight for their own safety. They passed the time toiling away at their meagre holes scraped into the trench walls, which were under the threat of collapsing from the enemy's shells. There wasn't much else to take comfort in. Only the occasional spectacle distracted them from the constant presence of death. Jubert witnessed several of these episodes. Some were almost comically absurd. From his position on Côte de Froide-Terre he could see the entire Fort Douaumont sector and to his right, the line of crests from Fort Souville to the village of Fleury. All of this remained under intense bombardment by German and French artillery. The heaviest calibre shells (French 380s and 420s) were slamming down onto Fort Douaumont in salvoes of ten and twelve at a time.

> In the middle of these bombardments, I repeatedly fixed my eyes on a cow which, to me, disturbed the scene. It came back each day and peacefully grazed in the middle of all these shells. The closest sound would momentarily draw the attention of its inexpressive eyes. But then with its slow powerful neck, it soon turned its head back and resumed munching the grass.
>
> I was not alone in witnessing this. One day, one of my men had a craving for milk and ran out through the bombardment to reach the cow. It was Maronne, now dead but still the most celebrated stretcher-bearer in the regiment. At the billets, he was a drunkard and a thief, insufferable to NCOs. But in the face of danger on the battlefield, he was the saviour of the wounded. Later in the evening, he chatted with his comrades about it, while I, hidden in the darkness, listened in:

'The cow, she didn't have any more milk. Not for lack of trying though, I tried milking her teats. So, I pushed ahead to Fleury, where there had to be some cellars. I see a farm. The door's closed. I throw my shoulder into it, then go down into the cellar. I light a match, it goes out, but I had felt a keg. I put my hand down on the ground, it's wet. Is it wine? It tasted funny to me. I light a second match. There were two corpses there and I saw my hand was covered in blood.

'And the keg?

'Just my luck, it was empty.'[20]

On another day, a thrilling scene unfolded in the skies above the 151's sector, something which both Campana and Jubert were witness to. Above the town of Bras, a French 'sausage' (as the French called observation balloons) snapped its tether and drifted helplessly towards the German lines. Two German fighter planes soon appeared on an intercept course, and then two French ones heading out to engage them. Staring up from their trenches, the men watched breathlessly as the balloon pilot – appearing only as a tiny black dot – leapt from the pilot box and plummeted to earth. A few moments later, a parachute blossomed and the balloonist slowly began to descend through a hail of German bullets. Adroitly, the balloonist dispersed his papers into the air and tossed away his camera. As he did so, the wind shifted directions and the lucky man drifted back towards French lines. Upon seeing this happy turn of events, Jubert and his men erupted into applause, congratulating the balloonist on seemingly beating ill-fate. Listening to the jesting of some of his men at the expense of the balloonist in his moment of peril, Jubert observed: 'The soldier is without pity. Himself a victim of misfortune, he laughs at the misfortune of others, which distracts him momentarily from his own.'[21]

And for his men, their misfortunes would return during the night, as Jubert's company was tasked with bringing up munitions and supplies to and from the first line. The fatigue parties travelled along supply routes that were known to the Germans and as result, were frequently the target of their artillery. In the confusing darkness and broken terrain, it was not uncommon for parties to become lost or to overshoot the French lines entirely. Jubert led several of these gruelling fatigues between the first and reserve lines. At one particular spot, an Austrian 88mm gun fired at regular intervals – three shells in three minutes – so the space needed to be crossed in a single rush. This was no easy task: '[You must] descend down 300 metres of a hillside with a steep grade, striding over the thousand obstacles made by a destroyed forest at night, including a multitude of branches, with a heavy, awkward load on your back, the restricted legs exposed to who knows what, and threatened by death that operated like clockwork.'[22]

From Côte de Froide-Terre, the fatigue parties typically passed through the Goulette Ravine and followed the Bras–Douaumont road. Alternately, the route involved following the Couleuvre Ravine (rechristened by the men as the 'Colonel's Ravine'). A brook ran along the bottom of the ravine, which was filled with the bloated carcasses of dead horses. Passing through this blighted land of smashed carriages and wrecked trucks, they reached the Bras–Douaumont road, in front 1 and 2 Battalions were in-line. On one occasion, the itinerary took Jubert's resupply party along this same route, past La Folie and the bombarded village of Bras. The village cemetery had been destroyed by shelling. The graves had been blasted open and the old human remains inside exposed. Passing Côte du Poivre on their left, they followed the progress of the German bombardment on the hill above. Suddenly, they came upon a group of bodies and one of the men shouted out: '"Boches!" There they are, a dozen lined up by our feet, motionless, stiffened eternally into the position of attention. I have to work hard to keep my men from snatching off buttons. "We'd like to make you a nice ring out of them, lieutenant."'[23]

By this time, Jubert and his men had been spotted and German shrapnel shells began to burst above them, obliging the group to hurry along to get out of view. Continuing along the road, they start to make out a group of dark forms ahead of them. As they approached, a sad scene presented itself:

> On the road, two vehicles with their slaughtered horses. Surrounding them, with ration sacks lying beside them, eight bodies: the men on a resupply chore from a different company struck down in the course of their mission. Among those inert masses, only two things move. One of the party is crawling off the road toward the ditch, crying. It's a wounded man with his legs broken, the only one of the group spared from death. And in the other direction, a small keg of wine rolls slowly down the road, coming to rest against a body.[24]

As noted, German artillery actively shelled known supply routes, which made the replenishing of provisions to the first line very difficult. The situation in the first lines was becoming more desperate, as Laporte reported:

> For two days, we have not received any rations resupply. The fatigue parties can't make it through the German barrages, which are unleashed ceaselessly behind our lines. Their plan was easy to see. They intended to isolate each sector and to puncture holes on each side, through the Ravin de Bras and our own position. Our meals consisted of only our reserve rations, which little by little got smaller. Already our provisions of wine and water were exhausted.[25]

On 18 March, it was Jubert's company's turn to rotate up to the front line. They were to replace the left-most company of the 94 IR, thereby maintaining the liaison between the 151 (8 Company) on the left and the 94 IR on the right. The rest of 3 Battalion would relieve a battalion of the 162 IR, which had been in the second-line positions on the southern side of the Goulette Ravine. The 3 Battalion had already been suffering casualties in reserve from the shelling, as the reserve positions had already become a target for the enemy artillery, and the men of 11 Company were eager to head up to the first line, which had managed to escape the heavier shelling. The situation had only marginally improved from the time when the unit they were relieving had first arrived. As the company moves up into its new position on the slope of Bois d'Haudraumont, Jubert was immediately struck by how exposed and isolated they would be.

> A man's well-being was no longer a question of shells. It depended on his vigilance: a little in his heart and a lot in his eyes . . . Here, no one passes during the day; death stops all movement. At night, it strikes at whim, any time it wishes. The slightest snapping of a twig under our feet freezes us for a long, agonizing moment. A flare in the sky! The entire length of this serpent of men freezes motionless.[26]

Jubert could see that the trenches had been dug haphazardly in great haste, with little thought given to the actual terrain or tactical situation. The trenches themselves remained dangerously shallow, no more than a metre in depth. To pass through safely, the men were obliged to bend over, while in certain sections, the only way to pass was crawling on all fours. The only shelters that existed were small niches scraped into the walls of the trench, which conversely served to undermine the walls and make them more prone to collapse under a shell blast. During the day, the men kept themselves hidden to avoid drawing enemy fire. As before, all work and movement had to be done at night. The officers of the 11 Company reminded their men of the tough lessons they had already learned at Froide-Terre: 'Only work will save you from death.' Desperately the men went about deepening and strengthening their deplorable positions as best they could. Meanwhile, the company officers had to make do with the only command post in the area, one woefully inadequate for the purpose:

> I lift up the four joined tent-canvases that hide the light inside from enemy view. A warm odour, a yellow light, dust-filled air . . . I get a glimpse of bare, stiffened, strained necks, torsos, ankles and thighs. Raised toward me as though in the grips of an agonizing hatred, blanched faces with bloody bandages, with mouths twisted and convulsed in a monochord moan . . .

> Everything is run out of here. The communication post, the officers' quarters, the troops' quarters for this platoon, the liaison's shelter, the telephone post, the material depot, the supplies room, the munitions shelter . . . and besides that it's also the morgue and the first-aid post, since we can only carry out the wounded at night.[27]

Jubert listened to the shells passing overhead, screaming and roaring without interruption. Most seemed to land on neighbouring positions. Nevertheless, casualties were suffered in the 151's ranks. Just as Jubert's men had begun toiling away on the shallow trench, a shell landed right on the parapet, exploding and injuring several men. This evening, just as they'd seen each of the previous evenings since they arrived, the procession of bloody faces slowly passed by on their way back to the rear. Ironically, it wasn't as much the barrages of shells that inflicted the most damage. Rather, it was the lone shell striking unexpectedly at night when the men were active, often catching an exposed resupply party as it was coming and going between the lines. As a commander, the burden of responsibility for his men weighed heavily on Jubert.

> Every evening, while assigning work to our men, we were filled with a sense of foreboding and we had to keep our voices from trembling. We managed to convince ourselves that we had chosen the first ones randomly, the preliminary drawing for this death lottery. It can't take an hour passing on your watch to count out the victims. A certain number of losses would then follow as determined by fate, and were added to those already suffered at Froide-Terre. It gave the company a tragic reputation in the regiment . . .
>
> We truly were those condemned to death. No one wants to hang around us for fear of being caught in the trap. The resupply men who come in the night care less about our needs than for their own safety. Even the verification of their job seemed unnecessary to them. They run off as quickly as they can. Anxious for our departure, only Captain Tison (commander of 2 MG Co.) is adamant about visiting this corner each night, at which time we report to him our losses . . .
>
> Nowhere else had I felt such a sense of isolation and stupefaction as I did at Haudraumont. Reduced to just [Lieutenant] Ganot and me, comradery no longer sufficed. At first we made small talk with each other. [But] the monotony of the days, even the permanence of danger, had brought an end to this. We remained quiet. We had lost our light-heartedness. Our faces were grave and tense. We had lost our appetite. The only way to relieve the boredom is to go to sleep.[28]

Raymond Jubert, *c*. December 1914. His insignia indicates this photograph was taken when he was still a private in the 91 IR prior to his transfer to the 151 IR. Source: L'illustration – Tableau d'Honneur.

Roger Campana, standing in the first-line trench at Bois d'Haudraumont, March 1916.

André L'Huillier, 1919. Source: 1KT 48 – Fonds L'Huillier, Service historique de la Défense de L'Armée de Terre.

Charles Auguste Bordinat, with his wife, Eugénie, and daughter, Solange, 1919. Source: Joël and Sylvie Le Roy.

Henri Laporte, *c.* 1915.

Second Lieutenant Roger Basteau, standing second from right. Also present, left to right: Second Lieutenant Lamothe de Mondion (KIA 10 September 1917), Second Lieutenant Le Gallo (KIA 20 May 1916), and Doctor Michaulet. Source: Pierre Jego.

Junior officers of the 151 IR. From left to right: Second lieutenants Camusat de Riancey (KIA 9 April 1916), Mesté, Noël, Richard (KIA 30 June 1915), and Captain Tison (KIA 25 September 1916). Source: L'Illustration – Tableau d'Honneur.

Second Lieutenant Arthaud de la Ferrière (KIA 9 June 1918).

Lieutenant Colonel Edouard 'Papa Victory' Moisson, commander of the 151 IR, photographed by L'Huillier, *c*. June 1917. Source: 1KT 48 – Fonds L'Huillier, Service historique de la Défense de l'Armée de Terre.

The 151 IR barracks, 'Miribel', in Verdun (Faubourg–Pavé), before the war. Source: author's collection.

The 9th Company of the 151 IR on manoeuvres before the war, c. 1913. Many of these young men would be dead by the end of 1914. Source: Florent Renaudin.

New recruits of the class of 1916 at the 151 IR regimental annex depot in Quimper, c. spring 1915. Source: author's collection.

Private Henri Joseph de Rivière (second from left) with his 37mm gun crew, *c*. 1917. De Rivière received his first wound after being shot in the arm in the Argonne Forest in 1915. During fighting at Saconin in July 1918, he was struck in the face by a shell fragment that inflicted a disfiguring facial wound. Source: Frederic Rivière.

The 151 IR delegate party for the Bastille Day ceremonies in Paris, 14 July 1917. Standing on the far left, left to right: Aspirant L'Huillier, Captain Adjudant Major Bourgoin, and Second Lieutenant Baillat. Standing directly behind the regimental colours is the stretcher bearer Private Henon (KIA 21 July 1918) and to his right, Lieutenant Coureaux (KIA 10 June 1918). Source: Bibliothèque Nationale de France.

The Haudraumont sector (Verdun) under bombardment, where the 151 fought in March 1916. At least fourteen separate shells can be seen exploding in this photograph, which was taken by a French aviator on 22 May 1916. The French first-line trenches are in the left background, the Carrières d'Haudraumont are at the centre, the Bois Nawé is in the left foreground, and the Ravin de la Mort is in the right foreground. Source: Bibliothèque Nationale de France.

Le Ravin de la Mort ('Death Ravine'), Verdun, part of the 151 IR's sector in March 1916. Source: *Le Miroir*, 10 December 1916, No. 159.

Summit of Le Mort Homme (Côte 295) on 22 August 1917 after being retaken by French forces. Source: Fonds des Albums Valois, Bibliothèque de Documentation Internationale Contemporaine (BDIC).

The village of Chattancourt, 16 June 1916. This perspective is looking northwest with the southern slopes of Mort Homme looming in the background. Source: Fonds des Albums Valois, Bibliothèque de Documentation Internationale Contemporaine (BDIC).

Monument to the 40 ID on the summit of Le Mort Homme (Côte 295), c. 1920s. This perspective is looking northwest towards the former German lines. It was over these slopes that German assault waves were mowed down by 1 Battalion on 9 April 1916. Source: author's collection.

Monument to the 69 ID on the summit of Le Mort Homme (Côte 295.4), 1920s. The figure of death stands cloaked in a French flag with the inscription '*Ils n'ont pas*' ('They Did Not Pass') inscribed on the base. Source: author's collection.

Three men in L'Huillier's platoon wearing M2 model gas masks at Verdun, August 1917. Photograph taken by L'Huillier. Source: 1KT 48 – Fonds L'Huillier, Service historique de la Défense de l'Armée de Terre.

Le Ravin du Helly (Verdun), where the 151 IR fought in 1917, photographed by L'Huillier on 20 August 1917. Source: 1KT 48 – Fonds L'Huillier, Service historique de la Défense de l'Armée de Terre.

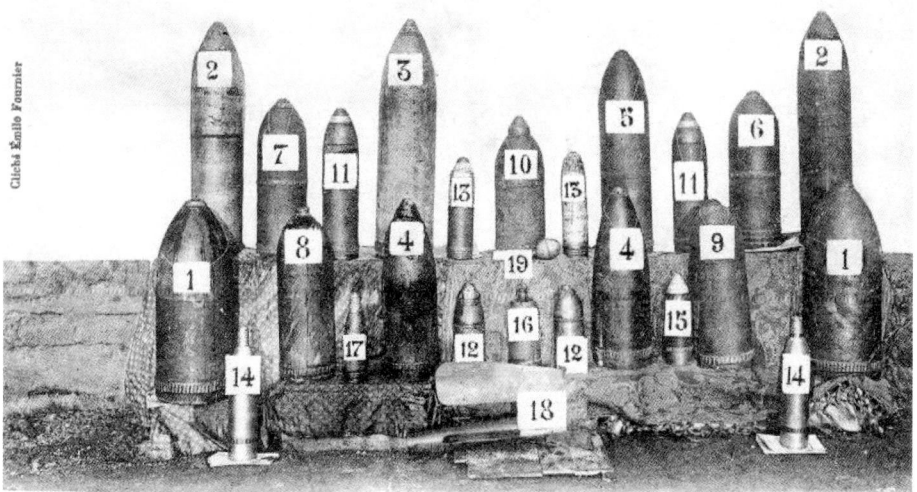

War-time postcard showing various calibres of artillery shells, from the French 75mm and German 77m up to the German 210mm. The men of the 151 were subjected to all of these projectiles. Source: author's collection.

The regiment receiving its Croix de Guerre fourragère from General Fayolle (far left) at Camp Mailly in Ramerupt, 28 June 1917. Lieutenant Donsimoni holds the regimental colours as Colonel Moisson, to his right, looks on.

Now in the first line, it was Jubert's turn to go out on night patrol. On one such evening, he ventured out with three men to ascertain what types of artillery pieces were left abandoned between the lines. Passing beyond the French advanced posts, they occasionally encountered gunshots as they skirted along near the top of the hill. He and his party came very close to German lines, and could soon hear the sound of enemy troops all around them. They are soon spotted and come under small arms fire and before long a battery of 88s also opens up. As they attempted to crawl away, the dark figure of a German sentinel suddenly materialized less than 2m away. They instantly froze. Yet the German, seated with his rifle in his hands, inexplicably remained motionless. As they cautiously approached, the reason became clear. The man was dead and upon being struck he'd tumbled forward into this odd position still clutching his rifle. Seated at his post overlooking the corpse-strewn valley, he now fulfilled the role of sentinel of the dead.

The 151 had been under fire for a week. Losses for the first seven days in the fighting line appear to have been light by Verdun standards. The regimental *JMO* recorded 34 killed and 100 wounded to date, though the divisional records put the losses closer to 170 (an average of 25 casualties a day). As usual, not included in the *JMO* were those evacuated for sickness, disease, or shell-shock. For example, there were recorded in the *JMO* of the 42nd Divisional Stretcher-Bearers Group 190 cases of men evacuated for illness between 13 and 24 March, an average of 15 a day. This number only rose for the final five days that the division would remain at the front. Based on combined casualty figures, it can be estimated that the total number of troops evacuated for illness from the units of the division was over 350.

Up to this time, German artillery had only occasionally bombarded the regiment's first line, and though the support line had been a more frequent target, this had been carried out without great intensity. Now, however, the enemy had good understanding of the new French front-line positions. Consequently, a continuous bombardment was unleashed using all calibres of shells. The first line mainly came under fire from 77s and 105s, while the second line was bombarded with heavy calibre shells. The bombardment of the entire sector steadily increased in intensity over the next few days. Losses continued to mount, including those in the sister units of the 151. On 20 March, the three companies of 3 Battalion still in reserve were rotated up to the second line to relieve a battalion of 162 IR. These positions were located behind (south of) the 1 Battalion, halfway up the slope on the opposite side of the ravine. Beyond the actual number of those killed and physically wounded, though, there must have been an immense psychological strain to account for as well. On top of the immediate physical threats from shells and bullets, there were the daily hardships wearing down the spirits of the men.

By now, the men had been under fire in the most difficult of positions for a week and a half. But time held little meaning for those burrowed into their dark holes, where the absence of latrines and the presence of danger often meant relieving themselves where they stood and tossing out the waste close by. Here, something as benign as answering the call of nature could mean death or disfigurement. Days and nights seemed to blend together. Resupplying those at the front still proved a difficult feat. Laporte lamented that over the last ten days his company had only received the most meagre of provisions on two occasions. Water was scarce, as was *pinard*, and food was low.[29] Sleep came solely in short periods, constantly disrupted by shelling, work assignments, and the myriad banal disturbances of living in holes in the ground with hundreds of others. Meanwhile, the German bombardment only continued to grow in strength, with the second-line trench occupied by the companies of 3 Battalion particularly targeted. Added to this was the rising threat presented by German snipers who had taken to climbing up into the trees still standing close to the French lines so they could fire down on the vulnerable French troops below. The poilus took to calling them 'parrots' and the number of victims shot down because of their temerity steadily stacked up. It was one of these parrots that had killed the suicidal cuckold when Campana's company had first arrived. A few days after his death, the regimental chaplain was likewise shot in the face by a sniper. The problem was exacerbated by the visibility of their helmets, which had a gloss to them that reflected the light and made for a conspicuous target. Indeed, while the 151 was in the front lines, the companies would receive a distribution of dark blue neck-covers (formerly intended for use with their kepis) to convert into helmet covers.

Campana would see another victim struck down on 21 March and this time it hit Campana hard. The victim was a young soldier who had always proven himself to be dependable in the past. Yet the man had received a terrible fright only a few days before when he was struck in the head by grenade thrown by a German raider. The grenade had failed to detonate and the only physical harm caused was a large bruise on the soldier's head. Nonetheless, he had clearly been rattled and since then had been acting rather skittish. After refusing to go out with a wiring party and then threatening the sergeant who'd ordered him to go out, Campana had to take action. As punishment, he ordered the bewildered soldier to stand watch in a listening post for twelve consecutive hours (normally the watches were done in two-hour shifts). Only a short increment of time had passed when Campana received word that he'd been shot in the head and was dying. Campana rushed to the scene. Lying stretched out on the ground, stretcher-bearers had already opened his blood-stained greatcoat. But there was little they could do: the bullet had passed through his throat and severed the jugular. When Campana arrived, the dying man looked up at him.

> Oh, the look [he gave me], I will never forget it. A look that revealed plainly at once gentleness, pain, and regret. A feeble smile weakly spread

across his terrified face. He held out his hand to me: 'L'tenant, you'll write to my mother?'

'Yes, dear boy.'

'You won't say anything . . . you won't speak of my mistake?'

'No, I will say you were wounded bravely.'

'Mortally wounded . . . I couldn't for a long time . . . Ahh!'

'But if, if you can get treated in time, you'll get better.'

'No . . . I can't . . . I can't breathe . . .' He coughed up a dark spurt of blood. 'L'tenant . . . L'tenant, don't be angry with me if I've done something bad. You'll say to my pen pal girl that I loved her very much . . . That she'll remember me . . .'

'Yes, dear boy, I promise, I give you my word . . . Your pen pal won't forget you, she'll never forget you. As for your mother, I'll take care of her. I'll fill her in on everything.'

'Thank you . . . Ahh, I can't breathe . . . I can't breathe . . .'

He coughed up two mouthfuls of blood, then a calm seemed to come over his poor face. He looked at us for a few moments, smiled again, closed his eyes, and then in the hands of the old stretcher-bearer, whose face was streaked with tears, his head gently eased down. I knelt down beside him and kissed his sweaty forehead, which death had already made cold. Then, so that my men couldn't see, I hid away in my shelter and let the tears I'd held back flow freely.[30]

Guilt bore into Campana like the bullet that had killed the young soldier. It was he who had ordered the man to listening post, his punishment which caused the man's death. Yet this was simply not the time to reflect on his decisions. As he struggled to compose himself, the sadness and guilt quickly burned away as a deep rage boiled up inside him. Vengeance, vengeance is what was needed now. Campana would punish those truly responsible and he swiftly resolved to take out the German sniper whatever the cost. All morning and all afternoon, he carefully surveilled all the ground in front of his section's front, scanning all the shrubs and tree tops he could see. He began to lose hope of ever finding the sniper when suddenly a bullet smacked into the parapet a few inches away from him, quickly followed by a second close enough to project pebbles into his face. Dropping down, Campana chose the more prudent option of continuing the search using a periscope, focusing on the area he believed the shots had come from. He soon spotted a suspicious-looking shrub. It appeared as though the branches had been spread out horizontally, with the openings then filled with artificial branches. At the base, there appeared to be some sort of object placed behind it on the ground.

Campana would use a simple yet effective ruse to take out what he suspected was the sniper. Taking up a rifle, Campana instructed one of his men to place a helmet on the end of a bayonet and, on his signal, to slowly raise the helmet over the parapet. Campana watched through his periscope as the man complied and raised the helmet. He perceived a dark mass shift slightly behind the bush. Flinging down the periscope, he fired off two shots from the rifle. Campana saw something dark spread out at the base of the shrub and remain still. The ruse was repeated an hour later but the dark mass did not budge. At night, he ventured out with two other men to confirm if he had in fact scored a hit. Circling around to approach the shrub from behind, the group got as close as they could, then made a dash and jumped onto the body. It was indeed a German sniper he had shot. Campana's aim was true: the bullet had entered the left eye and exited through the bottom of the skull, piercing the helmet close to the steel reinforcement plate. They decided to take the body with them back to the French lines. Campana also made sure to take the sniper's personal papers and send them to Lieutenant Colonel Moisson for intelligence purposes. The German turned out to be a 22-year-old corporal in the 117 IR, Hessian Guards. He took great satisfaction in knowing he had killed the man responsible for taking out three of his own. As war trophies, the vengeful Corsican kept some of the dead man's papers, along with his helmet, gas mask, and knife.

Meanwhile, German shelling of the support lines continued uninterrupted and conditions further deteriorated. Reprovisioning of food, water, munitions, and supplies could only be carried out very irregularly due to the incessant barrages on the ridge behind their positions. On some days, the increasingly diversified German artillery fire made resupply altogether impossible. To illustrate, on 20 March, Campana sent out a party of eight men; when they came back the next morning there were only five and they had no rations as the supply vehicles had been destroyed by shells. The next night another eight men were sent out and this time none returned. Their shredded bodies were found near la Folie Farm among the debris of their inverted bread wagons. The sensation of being isolated and abandoned only deepened.

For his part, Laporte had been transferred to 1 MG Company (1 Battalion) to serve as the *caporal-fourrier* ('quarter-master corporal'), as well as a liaison agent, a job he admitted was dangerous but full of excitement. On 22 March, with hunger gnawing at their empty stomachs and thirst clawing at their parched throats, Laporte volunteered to lead one of the hazardous resupply chores himself.

> For 48 hours, we've had nothing to eat. I asked the captain to allow me to go [on a resupply fatigue] in the evening. I gathered up six volunteers, a very small batch owing to the losses we suffered from the bombardments

every day and night, but still sufficient. Around midnight, we set off walking with each man carrying in addition to stew-pots anywhere from ten to eighteen 1 and 2-litre canteens on his back. At the time of departure, except for some bursting shells here and there, the sector was calm up to the moment when we arrived at the bottom of the [Haudraumont] ravine. There was a hundred metres of exposed ground to cross. This distance had to be covered at a quick pace, one man at a time, in order to avoid being spotted by the German observers at Douaumont. The moon was out, lighting everything up like it was daylight. A rain of shells, big and small, came down with an incredible racket in the ravine. We lay down and waited for the hurricane to pass.

After about a quarter hour, the bombardment stopped. Shells continued to fall but with less intensity. I started off again in the lead, crossed the zone safely and waited for my comrades. One poilu passed through, then two, then three, then four. We waited almost five minutes for the fifth. He finally arrived, collapsing next to us, very pale. His comrade had his head crushed by a shell fragment, killing him instantly. My first resupply fatigue had started off badly. Our fifth comrade got back on his feet but was badly shaken, still shocked from the sight of his unfortunate companion.

We waited a moment and then started off again and reached the crest an hour later without another incident. We then descended the slope of Bras Ravine [likely either the T-shaped Wood Ravine or the Three-Corner Wood Ravine]. We walked another hour across the shell-holed ground. We couldn't get very far along the route in an hour. We made out a gathering of people behind a fold of ground: it was the field kitchens. I gave the head-count of my company to the resupply chief and the distribution commenced right away. Some comrades from other companies had already gone back. Our canteens and stew-pots (beef and beans, very appetizing) now filled, we rested for another ten minutes, since it wasn't a good idea for all of us to depart at the same time on such a clear night. German shells are falling continuously in the plain.

After having drained a cup of hot coffee, we left again for the trenches, one behind the other. The explosions had gradually come closer as we approached the last ridge to cross over before getting to the Douaumont Ravine [the Death Ravine]. We paused several minutes on this crest, for keep in mind that the hike through the mud, shell-holes and explosions, with the weight of the canteens on the back and two stew-pots in each hand, meant it wasn't exactly a walk in the park. Taking cover beside tree trunks, we rested for a moment before setting off again towards the ravine.

The barrage fire was less violent than during our departure. A good thing too, for on the return trip it wasn't possible to run with our loads.

The ravine was crossed without hindrance and we arrived back in the trenches at 3.00 am. All our comrades welcomed us with joy. The coffee, still warm, felt good in all their poor stomachs to those subjected to such tough ordeals. The rations distributed to everyone, I went back to my shelter and, without eating any of my own portion, broken by fatigue, I rolled myself up in my blanket and fell asleep. Shell blasts both near and far didn't disturb me then.[31]

Laporte would only get a few hours of sleep after his exhausting trip when suddenly all Hell broke loose.

Around 6.00 am, I was awoken from my sleep by an intense fusillade. Our machine guns were in action. I ran with my captain and three liaison agents to our trenches on the top of the hill, about 50 metres away. The Germans were making a sortie. I made sure my revolver was ready to fire (my rifle had been replaced by this weapon because of my functions) and picked up a rifle which I loaded immediately. The first grenades were already exploding not far from us. Our own artillery opened up with an intense fire on the enemy trenches and our machine guns fired continuously.

The Germans didn't make it closer than 20 metres from our lines and all those who left their trench never made it back. Their attack had failed. They had suffered heavy losses; the number of bodies that could be seen, piled up in front of our lines, testified to this. All day long, their shells fell on our positions. We only took very light losses on our side and we were able to carry out an ammo resupply for our guns without incident.[32]

Under the uninterrupted bombardment, under attack from enemy sorties, deprived of both food and water for days, and with little rest, the situation for the regiment was starting to become critical. In desperation on the evening of 24 March, a hundred men pulled from all the companies were sent out to find food and *pinard* but were all massacred by concentrated gunfire. Because of this disaster, the men in the first-line would go another three days without any food or drink. Like shipwrecked survivors, they were now reduced to scavenging whatever scraps they could find off the bodies of the dead Germans in no man's land. The biscuits, sausages, and butter they found had been on the rotting bodies for a month and were permeated with the smell of rotting flesh. But hunger proved more powerful than their disgust and the men devoured the spoiled morsels all the same. By 24 March, the Furnace had been stoked to full blast as the shelling reached a point of 'extreme intensity', as the regimental

JMO notes, with Moisson's CP now specifically being targeted. Only the protection afforded by the industry of the men's labours kept the losses from being worse. To make matters worse, the weather turned foul and added to the general misery on the ground. Writing from his wet hole in the ground, Campana described the scene:

> It's raining. The water streams through the *boyau*, accumulates in long yellow puddles or passes across the roof of my shelter, falls with a dull and monotonous sound in the dented mess-kit, which is slowly filling up. The cannonade rages away. On the slopes of Douaumont, the smoke curls of the 210s are silhouetted against the backdrop of the pale grey of the sky. In the trench, the misery works away at my men. They remained squatting down on the fire-steps, wrapped up in their tent-canvas, silent, immobile, like statues. Where do their thoughts go, these poor tired minds, where do their minds travel off to? Oh, far from here certainly, to a cozy home, to a dear family, to the little kids whom they may never see again. So, I go and hand out a little booze, cigarettes, tobacco, some words of comfort, and in doing so, fight against the ravages of a formidable enemy: *la cafard* ['the blues'] . . .
>
> Certainly we've had to endure terrible suffering: the shells, the bullets, and sickness even, have decimated us. The 3rd Battalion is reduced to an effective of a single company, my platoon consists only of one sergeant, one corporal, and 19 men. When we arrived in the sector, the Boches had come to a halt 50 metres from us but couldn't advance further. Each time they tried to make a go at it, we nailed them back down into their holes . . .
>
> The 'parrots' and patrollers from the first days had now disappeared. The nights were calmer. They no longer came up to our lines; we went to theirs. But their artillery hammered us without cease. On the slopes of Douaumont, the earth seemed at times to boil and the village slowly changed form. Today it is only a mass of white stones, where it loomed like a ravaged church clock tower.
>
> All day we listened to 77s, 105s, 210s, 380s, even 420s passing over our heads, and the fire doesn't slacken at night. Sometimes the sky glowed red and for a little while, it looked like it was raining blood. It was the Boches firing off Bengal lights to mask the flashes made by their big guns. Their purple light coloured the sky. It seemed to us that our artillery remained powerless, there was only the continual angry barking of the 75s.[33]

Days and nights passed as the storm of shells raining down in the sector continued uninterrupted. It was proof enough to most of the experienced hands that the Germans were planning to mount a large assault on their positions. The slopes of

Douaumont were being plowed up over and over again. On Côte de Froide-Terre, the forest in front of them was disintegrating before their eyes under an avalanche of 150s. To the right, the village of Bras was completely obscured by the smoke of the fires burning there. At the foot of Côte du Poivre (to the 151's left front), the noxious gas dispersed by 105s spread out into large yellow and green blankets. French positions on the left bank were also suffering under a deluge of artillery fire. To the bewildered poilus, it was like being in the centre of a tempest. The ground quaked beneath their feet and the very air trembled with the reverberations of so many cannon discharges and shell blasts. It had now become a continual rolling of explosions. Campana and his platoon sat in awe of the sheer force of energy unleashed by man, while in the skies above another drama was unfolding.

> In the soft blue sky big white clouds still drift by and under them, within them, planes wage a pitiless combat. Three of our unfortunate Caudrons, were shot down by the Boches. The fight lasted no more than 5 minutes. When the first was attacked, it sought shelter in an enormous cumulus cloud but as soon as it did, one of the [German] Taubes pursued it into the cloud while the other waited at the opposite end of it. Soon the Caudron came out of the white vapours, its silhouette cleanly defined against the backdrop of the sky. The German planes swooped down on him with machine guns cracking away.
>
> Large red flames suddenly shot out from under its wings and an enormous black cloud of smoke enveloped it. As a wing snapped near the centre, the biplane went down in a death spiral. Soon two little dark spots separated off from the plane and tumbled into space. It's the observer and the pilot who, caught between two horrible fates, chose the least painful: to escape the agonizing biting of the flames, they had thrown themselves out into the void. Some moments later, they smashed onto the ground close beside the burning Caudron. In short order, two more French places were shot down by the Boches on the Côte du Poivre in the same manner. Sad day for our aviation.[34]

Losses on the ground continued to mount. Campana's platoon had gone in with forty-five troops. After seventeen days at the front, only twelve remained. As he had testified, the rest had been lost to bullets, shells, and illness. Casualties in 3 Battalion (which had been subjected to heavier shelling in the second lines) were particularly high, so much so that it was the first unit of the regiment to be sent off the line. It was relieved by a battalion of the 162 IR on 27 March. After slogging their way back down to the city of Verdun, the survivors boarded trucks at Baleycourt and were transported to Autrécourt, 25km southwest of Verdun. The 1 and 2 Battalions had another two days to suffer through. Finally on the night of 29 March, after three weeks under fire, the 1 and 2 Battalions were told they were being relieved by the 116 IR. (Moisson, along with the battalion and company commanders, remained behind for another day to brief the officers of the 116 IR and provide a tour of the sector.)

Being relieved didn't mean the punchdrunk, gutted survivors were out of the ringer just yet. They first had to make it back to the rear. Weak from lack of food and water, exhausted from the physical and emotional strain, the men had to contend with crossing the difficult terrain of shells holes and shattered trees, all the while under fire from the German artillery still pounding the support areas. Inevitably, as they struggled to escape the clutches of the battle, casualties were suffered and a handful more were hit by shell fragments. The itinerary of the relief march led from the *boyaux* at Bois d'Haudraumont, across the Death Ravine. From there they had to cross over the open country to the west of Boyau Remy, through Bois de Nawé and Bois des Trois Cornes, to Fort Froide-Terre, and then Fort Saint-Michel. Their end destination was the Verdun aviation camp and the town military hospital, where the battalions would spend the night. Through the mud, fire, and steel, progress could only be made slowly. The same was true for the companies of the 116 IR coming up to relieve them. In the case of 2 Company and one of 7 Company's platoons (de Riancey's), the relieving troops arrived so late that it left these units without the sufficient time to make it back to the rear before daylight returned, stopping all movement. To the dismay of the men, they were forced to take rest for the day in the 4 Chimneys shelters (beside Fort Froide-Terre). When it was time for his company to leave at nightfall on 29 March, Campana was charged with leading the company to the rear. It was a prospect he did not relish:

> Marching under bombardment was dangerous enough, but to lead the entire company across an area beaten by artillery of all calibres, from 77s to 420s, through a dark night with guides who suddenly confess they don't know where they are, that's a terrible thing. At 9.30 pm we received orders to be ready to leave. I told my men to put on their equipment and backpacks . . . At midnight, no one had shown up yet. At 3.00 am, a liaison agent comes up and lets me know that the 116 IR will be arriving imminently. As it was impossible to pass through the communication trenches, I made my men pass on top of the parados so that the 116 IR could replace us in the trench.[35]

At the moment that Campana's company was set to leave, salvoes of 77s rained down in the bottom of the Goulette Ravine, which they would have to cross. After waiting several minutes, Campana gave the signal and moved his men out. The hike down the slope of Bois d'Haudraumont was painfully slow. The thick wall of darkness was punctuated only briefly by the quick, blinding flashes of shell bursts. Passing through the bottom of the ravine, they began ascending the slopes of Bois de Nawé on the opposite side. As they did, the German artillery barrage doubled in intensity. Three 77s landed close to the column and one of Campana's men was struck by shrapnel in the leg. After quickly bandaging the wound, Campana ordered a stretcher-bearer and a corporal to remain with the injured man and bring him to the first-aid post. He then set off back with the company.

After passing over the first ridge and descending down the reverse slope, Campana halted the company to reform it. When he saw the stretcher-bearer and corporal who he'd just ordered to stay with the wounded man, his blood began to boil.

> 'What have you done with the wounded man?'
> 'We couldn't find him.'
> 'What! Do you have no shame!? To have abandoned in the woods one of your who needs urgent care! You'll go back immediately. I forbid you from presenting yourselves to me again without a pass from the Doctor-Major of the 116 IR attesting that you've brought the wounded man to his first-aid post. Come back tomorrow, or the day after tomorrow for all I give a damn, but I want you to find this man again.'[36]

The chastened men complied, retracing their steps back up the slope as Campana got the company moving again. As they arrived at the edge of Fort Froide-Terre, a volley of 77s welcomed them, knocking Campana to the ground and spreading panic in two of his platoons. Believing that their commander had been killed, the men quickly scattered and sprinted past his prone body.

> 'Where are you going?' Campana shouted. 'Let the 77s come down. You're not going to save yourselves by marching like a flock of sheep. Come on, rejoin your platoon.'
> Order was reestablished after a short time and we started back off again. After several minutes, night began to gradually fade. First we began to make out objects around us: splintered tree trunks, shell-holes filled with water, the carcasses of dead horses. Then the sky turned grey. To the East, the horizon silhouetted Douaumont on top of a milky band. A pale purplish light soon bathed the entire company in its light. Thin clouds stretched out in long bloody trails. And then the immense plain presented itself to us, pale, monotone, desolate, blotted here and there by the black smoke of the shell bursts. We would now be spotted by the Boches: the situation was becoming critical.[37]

Suddenly from behind them, a violent storm erupted: it was the start of a massive preparatory bombardment on the entire sector of Haudraumont, the Death Ravine, and Bois de Nawé. The hearts of the men of the 151 went out to their poor comrades in the 116 IR, who were now taking the full force of the blow that nearly landed on them. Though they were probably too ashamed to admit it, secretly in their hearts they must have been happy it wasn't them up there taking a shellacking. The only concern now was to get away, to escape, as fast as one could. With little time to waste, Campana formed the company into a column of twos and set them off at the quick march in the direction of Verdun. After a quarter of an hour at this pace, they reached the cover of a wood and filed down into the Tranchée d'un Decauville. There, covered with sweat, Campana halted them for five minutes to allow them to catch their breath. From there, they skirted around Fort Saint-Michel (where French heavy artillery was firing away) and shortly after, the town of Verdun could at last be seen. Cast in the pink light of the dawn, its disfigured buildings still proved a welcome sight to Campana and his men. Jubert's company had two days previously completed the same trek, making it to the outskirts of Verdun as day broke. In the morning light, Jubert was struck by the great change in appearance of his men after three weeks in the front lines.

> We've left our muddy shelters. We've spent twenty-two days in the mud, without any washing station other than the shell holes where the rainwater gathered. In this mud, we've run, we've jumped, we've slipped, fallen, been knocked over, sunk down, crawled along under gunfire, carried out work in all manner of positions. The mud clung to us, penetrated our clothing, each day more subtly, more masterly. It coated itself over the layer on our bodies formed the day before. Stiff, pasted onto our numbed skin, our clothes were nothing but a solid block of clay, which blended with our faces and hands that had taken on the same colour. Moreover, on the faces of those who normally went clean shaven, in the chaos of the environment a beard had grown out, the dense hair standing out from the clay layered on their faces.
>
> Under the ochre light and mournful yellow of the trenches, we blended right in. We had adapted. But in this different light, our appearance had changed. [Now we were] sharply contoured yellow masses, our picturesque silhouettes standing out starkly against the blue sky. Returned to normal life, with natural colours, we looked like actors who, with their play now over, still wore their costumes out on the street.[38]

With the exception of de Riancey's section stuck at the 4 Chimneys shelters most of the regiment had arrived in the suburbs of Verdun by the morning of 30 March.

The majority of the companies assembled at the aviation park, though some took shelter in an abandoned convent in town. After a couple hours of rest, the regiment marched out of Verdun and proceeded to the outskirts of Baleycourt. In the late afternoon, the men boarded trucks and after a long ride, were dropped off at the neighbouring villages of Autrécourt and Fleury-sur-Aire close to midnight. Once there, distributions of fresh straw were given out and the units assigned to either barns or tents erected on the hills overlooking the village. The officers by and large took up lodgings in the villagers' homes, including the local priest's house. After a frugal meal and a distribution of liquor, the men bedded down for the night.

The 151 IR had served an absolutely gruelling twenty days under constant enemy fire. They arrived in a sector where there was virtually no defensive cover or protection, tenuously hanging onto an exposed and isolated position. Conditions had been horrible and only continued to deteriorate as the seemingly endless days and nights dragged on, merging into one long agony. Both in terms of its duration and intensity, the regiment had never endured such a trial before. If it had anything to be grateful for, it was simply to have dodged the proverbial bullet of a large-scale assault launched by German forces soon after they had been relieved.

The number of casualties recorded in the regimental *JMO* put the unit's losses at an unconvincing 55 killed and 231 wounded. The divisional records indicate that the regiment was less 385 men compared with when they went up to the line, yet the accuracy of either of these numbers cannot be taken at face value. One glaring aberration in the *JMO* is the absence of men categorized as 'missing' despite both Campana and Jubert's frequent mentions of supply parties failing to report back or disappearing entirely. Added to the pathetically low number of effectives of the companies and platoons cited by the officers, there is also a report in the regimental records stating the regiment's total number of effectives on 26 March: 34 officers and 1,515 men. This would mean there were 1,300 fewer men present for duty. The discrepancy might lie with a high (yet unknown) number of evacuees who had fallen ill with bronchitis, strep throat, influenza, pneumonia, typhoid, frostbite, or shell-shock. The real number of casualties may never be known. In the days immediately following the regiment's escape, Lieutenant Colonel Moisson would award a number of individuals the Croix de Guerre. One of those who would eventually receive honorable mentions was Second Lieutenant Jubert, who would be cited in the Orders of the 42nd Division (dated 5 April 1916), for which he would win his first Croix de Guerre. The citation read:

> Volunteer for the duration of the war despite being exempted from military service. Has shown the greatest qualities of courage, energy and sang-froid. On 11 March 1916, thanks to his sang-froid, oversaw the quick removal of the bodies of the dead and wounded in the sap next to

his. On the night of 22 March 1916, lead a patrol under the difficult and dangerous conditions, providing valuable intelligence on the enemy.
–Signed: DEVILLE[39]

General Deville also came to pay the regiment a visit to personally congratulate the troops under his command. But his thanks came with a grave warning of things to come.

> From a non-existent sector, you made a sector of resistance . . . You were under the threat of a blow from an attack that your successors had to endure, but which they were able to hold back thanks to your earthworks. Thus, your efforts have aided France.
> Now, you must prepare yourselves mentally for the eventuality of a more serious battle . . . You're going to find yourselves in circumstances where, as never before, you'll have to rely on yourselves . . . Farewell, gentlemen, and good luck.[40]

At Autrécourt and Fleury-sur-Aire it seems a number of recuperated sick cases and lightly wounded returned to the ranks. These helped to replenish the depleted ranks, bringing the regiment's strength up to 2,416 men and a full complement of officers. But this did nothing to reassure the poilus. Having escaped the maelstrom with their lives, the arrival of reinforcements augured an ill omen, for it could only mean one thing. Four days. Four days of rest is all the men were given before being tossed back into the Furnace. For those who'd already received their initiation on the heights of the Meuse, General Deville's comments must have now hung over them like a funeral pall. Present among the new arrivals were the first contingents of the class of 1916. In a few days' time, these 19 and 20-year-olds would prove their mettle in one of the most pivotal moments of the entire Battle of Verdun. This time *le Quinze-Un* was being sent to the left bank of the Meuse to fight in one of the most infamous sectors of the war: Mort Homme.

Chapter 7

Shellography

What the 151 would face at Mort Homme was unlike anything the men had quite experienced before. It was not just the number of guns and shells they hurled but the sheer size of them. In the Great War, artillery was king and its mantra simple as it was brutal: to devastate, so that the infantry could infiltrate. It then perhaps goes without saying that the lethality of combat in this conflict stemmed in large part from the dominance of this weapon, which accounted for two-thirds of wounds inflicted. By 1914, artillery had reached its pinnacle and the principles of artillery fire applied even today are largely derived from those developed in the Great War. Since the early nineeenth century, artillery had become ten times more lethal in its explosive power. Even by the time of the American Civil War, the arc of technological advancement was measured. The M1857 'Napoleon', one of the deadliest cannon of that conflict, could throw a 12lb projectile 1,500m at the rate of 3–4 rounds per minute. Four decades later, the French M1897 75mm cannon, which constituted the bulk of the French army's field artillery pieces, could fire a 12-16lb shell 8,500m at a rate of fire of 15 to as many as 30 rounds per minute (with a well-trained crew).[1] By 1916, both the French and the Germans widely employed 120mm, 155mm, 210mm, 280mm, 305mm, 380mm, even super heavy 420mm guns (the shells of which were the height of a man and weighed over a ton).[2] The crudeness of the metallurgy in these shells though resulted in them shattering into fewer but larger, jagged and non-uniform pieces. While the smaller fragments were no bigger than a pen cap or wine cork, the larger ones were the size of hubcaps or wine bottles and weighed 5, 10, 20lb and more.[3]

The two types of shells in greatest use were shrapnel and high explosive (HE), although incendiary, smoke, and eventually chemical (tear and poison gas) were also employed. The shrapnel shell was composed of a hollow iron casing packed with small metal balls and explosive, and was intended to burst in the air showering its projectiles down onto the target. The effect of a 75mm shrapnel shell was exceedingly deadly to troops out in the open. In a single minute, a 4-gun battery firing shrapnel could deliver 17,000 balls over an area 100m wide by 400m long.[4] High-explosive shells were the projectile of choice against entrenchments, however. These shells were filled with powerful explosives that were meant to destroy a target through the force of its blast and, secondarily, by the fragments it projected. As is implied, more than just the size and weight of these fragments was the sheer kinetic energy of the shell.

> The shell expresses one idea – energy. The cylinder of iron, piercing the air at a terrific speed, sings a song of swift, appalling energy, of which the final explosion is the only fitting culmination. One gets too an idea of an unbending volition in the thing. After a certain time at the front the ear learns to distinguish the sound of a big shell from a small shell, and to know roughly whether or not one is in the danger zone. It was a grim jest with us that it took ten days to qualify as a shell expert, and at the end of two weeks all those who qualified attended the funeral of those who had failed.[5]

The German Skoda 305mm shell (which the 151 would be subjected to at Verdun) fired a delayed action fuse weighing 850lb capable of creating a crater more than 8m wide and 8m deep.[6] The fragments it threw up on exploding could kill a man up to 400m away. Even the less monstrous shells were extremely powerful. The 210mm howitzer was one of the workhorses of the German heavy artillery at Verdun. Its 8in diameter shell was 36in long and weighed 260lb. A direct hit by one of its shells on a trench could obliterate an entire platoon. An American volunteer serving in the Red Cross described the first time he heard a heavy calibre shell.

> There was a sound like the roar of an express train, coming nearer at tremendous speed with a loud singing, wailing noise. It kept coming and coming and I wondered when it would ever burst. Then when it seemed right on top of us, it did, with a shattering crash that made the earth tremble. It was terrible. The concussion felt like a blow in the face, the stomach and all over; it was like being struck unexpectedly by a huge wave in the ocean. It exploded about two hundred yards from where we were standing, tearing a hole in the ground as big as a small room.[7]

The experience of being under artillery fire, particularly the type of shelling so common in the Great War, is something which most will never have to undergo. The scale, intensity, and duration of the bombardments in this conflict were unprecedented and rarely achieved the same level again even in the Second War. The feeling of mortal terror and the violence of the shock forms a unique sensation that many soldiers of the period struggled to put into words. The previously cited Paul Dubrulle likened it to being overcome by extreme seasickness:

> When one heard the whistle in the distance, one's whole body contracted to resist the too-powerful vibrations of the explosion, and at each

repetition it was a new assault, a new fatigue, a new suffering. Under this regime, the most solid nerves cannot resist for long; the moment arrives where the blood rises to the head; where fever burns the body and where the nerves, exhausted, become incapable of reacting. Perhaps the best comparison is that of seasickness, but an 'aggressive' seasickness, caused by the unceasing attack of breakers sweeping over shipwrecked men on their raft. It's then that one gives up, that one can't even summon the strength to cover oneself with his pack for protection against shell fragments, that one can hardly manage to commend oneself to God.[8]

The worst bombardments could go on for hours or even days without interruption. Under such conditions, even if they were sheltered in underground dugouts, men could be driven mad.

There's no doubt about it, this is a bombardment, a real one, one of those artillery preparations which precedes an attack, when the ground to be taken must be completely churned up, where nothing can remain alive in the flattened trenches . . . Soon the noise becomes hellish . . . Impossible to make out anything. Shells fall without interruption. His head feels like it will burst, that his sanity is wavering. The agony is interminable. He calculates, seeking the least unfavourable place, cowers down, puts his head near the opening of his dugout so he can breathe more easily in case of a partial collapse . . . His ear notes each shot. He guesses the shell's trajectory, knows approximately where it will burst . . . If he realizes that the shell will fall near him, he closes his eyes, makes himself as small as possible, instinctively puts his arm over his head for protection . . . Flame burns his eyelids, bitter fumes suffocate him . . . it's over for this time, he is not wounded.

Suddenly, he is afraid of being buried alive. He sees himself, back broken, suffocating, digging at the earth with clenched hands. He imagines the excruciating agony, wishes with all his strength that the shelling would end, that the attack would begin, that he could choose where to wait for the enemy. But what has happened to his friends? Are they gone? Are they dead? Is he the only one left alive in his hole? Then there is the sudden vision of his loved ones: his wife, his mother, his child . . . Without knowing why he sees again some minor detail at home . . . He wants his final thoughts to be of those he loves . . . He will say their names out loud, quietly, piously . . . Then he is in revolt, with a mad impulse to leap up. It's too stupid to stay here, waiting for death! Anything is better than that! Oh, to look danger in the face! To fight back!!! To do something!!! The deluge continues. A blind force is unleashed. And the man remains in his hole, powerless, waiting, hoping for a miracle.[9]

As noted above, front-line soldiers who were fortunate to survive their first encounters became adept at discerning these threats. An experienced man could quickly identify the shell's trajectory, whether it was incoming or outgoing, its calibre, and probable point of impact, affording them enough time to take what cover they could. Those who'd experienced heavy shelling would attest that one *feels* the sound more than one actually hears it. The disturbances as the air was rent apart and the resulting shockwave caused by the explosion, passed *through* the body. So a bombardment wasn't something you just listened to, it was something you experienced in a physical way. The sound produced by the shell depended largely on one's position in relation to the shell's trajectory. The primary factor was whether the shell was an *arrivé* or *départ* – that is, 'incoming' when it was enemy's artillery or 'outgoing' when it was one's own artillery. Typically, though sadly not always, it was the former that represented the real threat. While an incoming shell could make a good deal of noise, that made by outgoing shells was often perceivable louder and longer if the listener was stationed behind its flight path, with the pitch gradually lowering as it flew away. Whereas the pitch of an incoming shell generally rose as it approached, though again, this depended on the location of the gun that fired it in relation to the listener.[10] The second factor that determined the sound of the shell was its calibre. The American writer and naturalist, Henry Beston, who volunteered as an ambulance driver for the French army, provided a description of the sound of a heavy calibre in a general way:

> Suddenly [the silence] was broken by a swift, complete sound, a heavy boom-roar, and on the heels of this noise came a throbbing, whistling sigh that, at first faint as the sound of ocean on distant beach, increased with incredible speed to a whistling swish, ending in a HISH of tremendous volume and a roaring, grinding burst. The sound of a big shell is never a pure bang; one hears, rather, the end of the arriving HISH, the explosion, and the tearing disintegration of the thick wall of iron in one grinding hammer-blow of terrific violence.[11]

Henri Laporte thought the sound of a salvo of outgoing heavy shells was like 'hearing right beside you a dozen heavy freight trains barrelling along with unbridled speed . . .'. The sound of 150s passing by sounded to Gabriel Chevallier like 'Rrran, rrran, rrran, vraoof, vraoof, vraoof-vraoof . . .', while the noise produced by 105 shrapnel shells was more of a dulcet tone that he expressed as a 'Vouuouou . . . Vrrroom . . . Vrrroom-vrrroom . . .'. Maurice Genevoix articulated the passing of 120s 'as a light rustling, a rapid rushing . . . growing more and more distant until it terminates finally in the explosion'. One man claimed he could tell if a shell was heading directly for him by the hissing sound it made. Gas shells on the other hand were distinguished by the whine they made that was followed by a dull crump, owing to the smaller amount of explosive contained in the shell. Some of the most dangerous shells, though, were the light calibre shells like the 75mm, 77mm, and 90mm, which travelled with a flat trajectory at tremendous speed, giving the soldier precious little time to take cover. British troops gave these the iconic nickname 'whizz-bangs' for the quick sound they made before bursting. The French equivalent was *zim-boum*, though more commonly the poilus called them *miaules/miaulants* ('meowers') for the cat-like undertone the metal casings had upon bursting. Of course, in a heavy bombardment where all types and calibres of shells were being fired, the projectiles often rose into a cacophony of sound. One French officer wrote: 'Thousands of projectiles are flying in all directions, some whistling, others howling, others moaning low, and all uniting in one infernal roar. From time to time an aerial torpedo passes, making a noise like a gigantic motor car.'[12]

As these terms indicate, front-line soldiers chose descriptive monikers for the types of shells they encountered. Indeed, an extensive lexicon of slang terms was invented by the troops to classify them. A generic label applied to all shells but particularly the heavy calibre ones was *marmite* ('stew-pot'), in reference to the large pieces of shell fragments produced after the shell exploded, which resemble those of a cast-iron cooking pot. By extension, shelling was frequently referred to as literally *marmitage* ('stew-potting'). More simply they were called *les gros* ('big ones'). Generally, shrapnel shells were simply called *fusées* ('timers') as they were equipped with time-delayed detonators, or simply 'shrapnels'. Aside from these generic labels, a virtual taxonomy was developed by the poilus, being derived from the physical qualities of the shell or the sound it produced either in flight or upon detonation.

The prolific light-calibre shells enjoyed a number of monikers. The notorious French 75mm shells – characterized by their quick high-pitched scream – were usually just referred to as the *soixante-quinze* but also went by *distributions* ('deliveries'). The German equivalent, the 77mm, typically went by the aforementioned 'zim-boom' or 'meower'. Another popular name for them was 'monkey cans', in reference to the epithet given to the French canned meat ration. The Austrian 88mm was referred to simply as the 'Austrian', while the 120mm was called the *pétard* ('fire-cracker') or the 'pipe'. Regarding the heavier calibre shells, the 150mm was called *gros noir* ('big black') in reference to the dark cloud of smoke produced from its explosion. Similarly, there was also a 'big green'. Starting around 1916 both sides' artillery relied heavily on the 210mm shell and this fearsome shell was called the 'metro', as it sounded most like a subway train rushing down a track. But it also went by the *intendance* ('quarter-master'), the *ravitaillement* ('supplies'), or the 'coal box'. The heaviest shells also got their nicknames, like the 280mm which was known as the 'Charles Humbert', a famous politician and newspaper proprietor who made speeches criticizing the inadequacy of French munitions before the war. The 305, 380, and 420 were invariably called the *train de permissionaire* ('furlough train') or the 'metro' again. Mortar shells were called *crapouillot/crapouillaux* ('toady'/'toadies'), in reference to their squat, toad-like form. The Germans called their mortars *minenwerfers* ('mine-throwers'), which the poilus quickly adopted (or shortened to *minens*). They also called them *saucisses* ('sausages') and *tuyaux* ('stove pipes') owing to their shape. The heavier calibres included the 170mm and 250mm, firing shells that weighed between 110 and over 200lb each. Poison gas shells were called perhaps a little too benignly *puants* ('smellies'). Finally, there were the shell fragments projectiles burst into. These went by as many names as there were types of shells, such as bonbons, pralines, prunes, or honeybees, just to name a few. All of these colourful terms worked as a system of classification, a lexicon, to help the combatants learn, share, and cope with the threats faced. But it should not be forgotten that they also helped to defuse the true nature of what were lethal projectiles capable of inflicting appalling injuries and death. Meowers could literally tear a man into pieces, toadies could pulverize him into the dirt like paste, while metros could vaporize bodies or bury them under tons of earth. It was these same projectiles that would be unleashed upon the 151 when ordered to hold their positions at Verdun.

Chapter 8

A Life of Battle

Second Rotation at Verdun (5–13 April)

When, on 6 March, the German VI and X Reserve Corps commenced their assault on the left bank, it was not conceived of as a long-running operation. Given the large gains the Germans had achieved in the first week of February, Falkenhayn had no reason to doubt that the hills that provided observatories and shelter for the French artillery could be taken similarly in a week. The ground in question was held by two French divisions (26 and 72 IDs) of the VII Army Corps. Once again, the attack was preceded by a powerful bombardment that destroyed much of the French positions. On the foggy morning of 6 March, elements of German 22nd Reserve Division stormed out of their positions above the Forges stream, crossing the stream using gangplanks, and advanced through snow flurries towards the lightly manned line of French outposts. At the same time, units of the 12th Reserve Division crossed the Meuse from the right bank on pontoons and gangplanks. Using an armoured train to punch through a massive belt of wire entanglements that had been erected across the railway line, the attack units rapidly skirted along the river bank. They certainly had numerical superiority, as entire German divisions assaulted regiments and battalions. The first objectives, the villages of Forges on the left and Regnéville on the right, were soon in German hands and the advance continued towards Côte de l'Oie. French rifle and machine-gun fire together with counter-barrages by the artillery slowed them down in the afternoon. But by the evening, the eastern half of Côte de l'Oie and Côte 265 were taken. The next morning, the Germans attacked the fortified village of Cumières but were stopped by a desperate defence of the troops garrisoned there. They now turned their attention to the Bois des Corbeaux and the smaller Bois de Cumières, which dominated the approach to the highest of the observatories on the left bank, Mort Homme. Repeated attacks and counter-attacks stormed back and forth around and through the woods over the course of 8–9 March. In the densely packed forests, the fighting at times was hand to hand. Yet by 10 March both woods were solidly in German hands. Assaults were also made against the strongly fortified villages of Avocourt and Béthincourt, as well as an initial foray on Côte 304, but all with little gain. Impatient to get results, a direct assault on Mort Homme was scheduled for 14 March.[1]

The origin of the name Le Mort Homme ('the Dead Man') has now been lost to time. Local lore had the name originating from a time centuries before when some forlorn traveller had become lost in a snowstorm and froze to death on the hill alone in the cold. In trying to understand its role in the battle, a good deal of confusion arises from the fact that Mort Homme is not a single summit. Rather, it comprises twin summits designated as Côte 286.4 and Côte 285.9 (their height in metres above sea level). These were separated from each other along a northeast–southwest axis by 500m. These summits were referred to collectively as Côte 295. Any literal reference to height of the summits would ultimately soon become irrelevant. The shelling unleashed on the heights was so extreme that it is claimed 10m of topsoil was blasted off the surface. Even at the time of the battle this became a source of confusion. On the maps used by German commanders, the words 'Toter Mann' (Mort Homme) were printed across the entire promontory. On other maps, and perhaps as a consequence, Côte 265 is included as part of Mort Homme, when in fact it is the westernmost point on the long ridge of the Côte de l'Oie situated about a kilometre from 295. Even before the battle, the hill was largely devoid of trees. By April, there would not be a single blade of grass or foliage to be found. Nothing but the unending undulations of a vast, static sea of muddy shell holes.

Beginning in the morning of 14 March, German artillery pounded the French front-line positions (now held by the 25 ID) on the northern forward slopes. The shelling lasted all day before the infantry attacked in the late afternoon. Losses were appalling on both sides, numbering in the thousands. The Germans had managed to get a foothold by taking the defences atop Côte 286.4 and repelling French counter-attacks, and senior commanders prematurely announced that Mort Homme had been taken. They were to be bitterly disappointed as news from the front reported that another summit (285.9) lay beyond them. After the 14 March attack, a stalemate had once again set in at Mort Homme, one marked by frequent shelling by both sides. Reinforcements were pushed up to relieve the depleted units, many having suffered 50 per cent casualties. From a distance, Mort Homme and the other heights of the left bank looked for all the world like a gigantic forest fire, smoking and bursting under the perpetual thundering of the cannonades and bombardments. Clouds of smoke and dust rising nearly a kilometer into the air obscured the sun and turned the light filtering through it into an ashen grey. The vision was even more impressive at night, when the horizon glowed for miles around like an infernal Aurora Borealis. For the rest of March, fighting raged back and forth through Bois d'Avocourt and Bois de Malancourt, and the fortified villages of Malancourt, Haucourt, and Béthincourt. By the end of March, the Germans had lost nearly 82,000 men in their attacks and the French 89,000 in holding them back.[2] Needless to say, General Deville's warning of a life of battle to come would seem prophetic.

The mood in the ranks of the 151 must have been dour, as men grappled with the gravity of their situation. They had been explicitly told to expect a pitched battle, and this held a special kind of terror in the minds of most. The symbol that historians Leonard Smith and Stéphane Audoin-Rouzeau so fittingly adopted to describe this terror is that of a scaffold. In a literal sense, the troops were often supplied with ladders to help them climb out of the trenches and go into the attack to enter upon the plane where death awaited them. But on a deeper level, the term implies the allegorical fear of the condemned who climbed the scaffold for their own execution. To prepare themselves for this trial, rituals were performed not unfamiliar to soldiers throughout the centuries. They wrote final letters to their families. Friends exchanged promises to retrieve each other's bodies if one were killed out in no man's land. Some arranged an unofficial will, decreeing who in the squad or company should receive what meagre possessions they had in their pockets or haversacks. The more religious prayed fervently. Many had developed a ritual routine repeated on the eve of entering battle. It might be quietly humming a certain ditty or reciting over and over a given verse. For some, it was arranging their kit in just such a way, checking and rechecking that their equipment straps were secure, or fastidiously performing weapon checks. Of course, chainsmoking and the liberal consumption of alcohol helped to alleviate the consuming fear as well. On the morning of 5 April, the regiment was alerted to prepare for its departure. It would be relieving the 150 IR (40 ID), which had just spent three weeks at Mort Homme in heavy combat. As usual, Lieutenant Colonel Moisson with his senior officers and machine-gun company commanders left in the morning to carry out a reconnaissance of the regiment's new sector.

In the wake of the German gains of 14 March, what had been a support-line trench (running along a southwest–northeast axis bisecting 285.9 and 286.4) had become the new French first line. This had been doubled by a covering line dug on the reverse slope immediately below the summit of 285.9. Beginning about 400m behind this was a series of intermediary support trenches – *Ligne 1 bis* (or, 'Line 1A') and the *Place d'Armes* – which extended along the western side of the Mort Homme's southern face. A final reserve line was situated a full kilometre from the summit of Mort Homme. This was referred to as the 'Second Position', though in actuality it was more of a third-line entrenchment composed of a series of interconnected strongpoints, or *ouvrages*, extending from the Hayette Ravine to Chattancourt. From east to west these were: Mollandin, Laborderie, Macker, and Gers.

The morning of 5 April dragged by as the men waited anxiously for their departure to the front. Around noon the transport convoy arrived and troops crammed themselves along with their haversacks and canteens into the back of the trucks as best they could. Travelling a short way along the narrow roads connecting Autrécourt and Fleury-sur-Aire, they soon turned onto *la Voie Sacrée*. Jubert reflected on the dualistic motion on the road:

> Everyday for two months there were two kinds of processions that passed each other continuously. In convoys by the hundreds, there were the endless lines of heavy motor trucks veiled in long green tarps. The convoys looked alike, but they are not the same. They follow each other like night follows day, like death follows life; those coming from Verdun and those going up to it.³

The convoy continued its slow, lurching drive along the critical artery until it reached Baleycourt, where the men were told to get out. The trucks could go no further without the risk of coming under artillery fire, so the rest of the journey was done on foot. From Baleycourt the regiment had to backtrack a short distance to Blercourt. Mobile kitchens were already waiting for the men there, though it seems only some companies were able to enjoy a final hot meal before heading up to the front lines. The 1 Company set off immediately without receiving any food. The 11 Company, on the other hand, fared better. They wouldn't depart Blercourt until later that night. The men quietly ate their soup in the darkness and then took advantage of the delay to get a little sleep in the damp grass and the icy wind. The relief march that took place on the night of 5–6 April was a long and difficult one. As always, the men had to carry their normal full marching kit with them to the front. Before setting off, a supplemental distribution of ammo had also been done – 200 cartridges per man, weiging close to 18lb. With 120 rounds in the cartridge pouches, the extra packages had to be placed in the pockets of their greatcoats which now weighed down like coats of chainmail on their shoulders. The first stage of the relief march was over the muddy roads that traversed up and down the rolling ridges. From Blercourt the regiment passed through Jouy-en-Argonne before proceeding onto Sivry-la-Perche. Massive German 380mm shells passed overhead with a tremendous rumble, causing the very air to tremble in their wake. A little further on columns reached the ridges overlooking Germonville, where the French heavy artillery ceaselessly thundered away, the muzzle blasts lighting up the column in a fevered flickering as it trudged silently by. Jubert recalled:

> The march lasts all through the night, slow and trying, toward the luminous zone that envelops the battle. Now and then, a hellish noise shatters one's hearing as big calibre cannons spit out a heavy shell. The flame erupts not 10 metres away from us with an earsplitting blast, and for a minute afterward we are completely deafened. The young new recruits were grave and silent. Even before encountering the enemy, the first

encounter with the brutality of death's workings makes an impression on them . . .

A shell bursts 10 metres away from my company causing disorder in the ranks. In the darkness, there was shouting and running, and we had to reorder the files and the ranks. But the ineffectiveness of the projectile had already reassured them. The new recruits retake their place without too much trembling. They've had their first lesson in the dangers.[4]

Upon entering Germonville the regiment had already travelled 13km, but the journey would only get more difficult from here. From the village the column left the road and took to the open country, skirting the western edge of Bois Bourrus before crossing over the plain that led towards Chattancourt and Mort Homme beyond. Laporte noted:

After having skirted along the edge of a large woods [Bois Bourrus] and by a few villages in ruins, we pass through the area of what had been Chattencourt [sic], this village being the closest to the front. The shells here fell without stop and numerous gaps were torn in our ranks before reaching our trenches.[5]

By the time Campana's company passed Bois Bourrus it was midnight, with the most difficult part of the trek still to come. The leather straps of their packs bore down on their shoulders and amplified the biting pain from their canteens, haversacks, ammunition pouches and rifles. Campana recounted the experience:

Our torture commenced. The waterlogged ground was strewn with telephone wires, barbed-wire, and especially shell-holes. The night was so dark you couldn't see a metre in front of yourself. The men, in single-file, held onto the bayonet scabbard of the man in front. We advanced blindly groping our way forward to the far off front lines. We were led by a guide who, fortunately for us, knew the terrain. At 2 am we rested for a few minutes. On the horizon, flickering pale-coloured lights appeared and then disappeared. A low roar reached our ears as we approached the battlefield.[6]

The regiment entered the first *boyau* while they were still several kilometres from the front lines. Running along a north–south axis, Avenue No. 3 would become the central artery for the 151 in its passage to and from the summit of Mort Homme. The winding, seemingly interminable communication trench became shallower as it entered the real danger zone, where it was gradually and continually levelled by shelling. Already death-dealing songbirds could be heard singing overhead and smacking into the earth around them – stray bullets fired from the German lines up on the summit.

> Kilometres followed kilometres. The darkness became less thick as the dawn light began to bathe us, the sky taking on an ashy gray, then violet to pale green, and finally a bluish hue. The morning clouds were burned away by the first rays of the sun.
>
> It was now 4.30 am. We had been marching since 9.00 pm the previous evening and we still hadn't arrived at our position. We passed over several defensive lines of entrenchments, followed a line of batteries, passed the brigade CP, and at last arrived at the trenches we were to occupy on the top of Mort Homme at 6.00 am.[7]

The 1 and 2 Battalions had been assigned to the front-line trenches on Côte 295, with the former along the western summit and slope and the latter on the right along the eastern summit. The companies of 2 Battalion were arrayed with (from left to right) 5, 6, and 8 Companies in the first line (Tranchée Perrenet, Garçon, and Zouaves). The 7 Company was in support in the cover trenches (Boyau des Zouaves and Chattancourt) together with the guns of 2 MG Company. On 2 Battalion's front, the opposing lines were in close proximity to each other, varying between 50 and 100m distance. The German first line was located on the north counter-slope of the hill, though the two sides' advanced listening posts were separated by merely 10 to 20m. His second line traversed Côte 265. On 1 Battalion's front, where the French line angled down the northwest slope, the German first line was further off, about 200m. The companies were similarly arrayed with (from left to right) 4, 3, and 1 Companies in the first line (Tranchée Guilbert and Perrenet) and 2 Company and 1 MG Company in the cover trenches (Tranchée Gilbert and Molina). Detached from the rest of 1 Company in a portion of the cover trench Molina, just below the summit of Côte 285.9, was Campana's platoon. The remainder of 1 Company was in front of them, which provided relative security and afforded Campana's men the luxury of a little rest: 'They didn't even have the strength to find shelters. They laid down randomly, wherever they could – on the fire-steps, in the *boyaux*, in the mud – and immediately fell asleep, wiped out by the dreadful march. I followed their example, stretched out on the ground and passed out.'[8]

Interspersed among the rifle companies in the adjoining cover trenches was Laporte and the guns of 1 MG Company. As they had experienced during their first rotation on Côte de Froide-Terre and the Death Ravine, the situation here was in fact worse than being in the very first-line trench closest to the enemy: 'We took up our positions around 5.00 am . . . in the middle of a violent bombardment. Wracked night and day by the bursting of shells of all calibres, only the remnant of trenches now remained. In reality, we were connected simply by a line of holes (or more accurately, excavations). Only a few shelters still remained."⁹

Because of the inevitable slow progress and endless delays faced by 3 Battalion in its approach to the front, it was unable to reach its assigned reserve positions before daylight arrived, forcing it to halt its movement until darkness returned the next evening. In order to avoid the risk of being spotted by enemy aircraft and artillery spotters, it would spend the day at Germonville. Up on Mort Homme, Campana had managed to get a few hours of sleep before waking up on the morning of 6 April and setting off to conduct a quick inspection of the lines. This done, he went to find one of the few remaining shelters and was pleasantly surprised with its soundness – it was halfway interred in the ground with railway ties as a roof, which were in turn covered with a layer of stones and earth. He noted:

> It was an old artillery command post very solid and comfortable, even luxurious I must say. It contained two suspended frame beds made with wire mesh, a table, two stools, and a stove with a stove pipe, all of which had surely been taken from Chattencourt [sic] by a poilu who was fond of the material comforts. Since I've been at war, it's the first time that I was the temporary proprietor of such an agreeable abode.¹⁰

As the morning fog dissipated, Campana discovered he had a commanding view of the surrounding landscape from his position. Far away on the horizon he could make out the towers of Montfaucon church, the Crown Prince's Observatory, atop on its dominating height. In the shell-ploughed plains below him he could make out the Forge spring winding its way through the devastated countryside. To his right was Chattancourt, partially obscured by the yellow smoke of 105 shrapnel shells bursting over it. On his left was Esne, or rather the ruins of it, which were bathed in the soft light of the morning sun. And rising high above this village was Côte 304, where large plumes of dark smoke created by the impact of German 210s and 305s could be seen spurting up on its slopes.

Several hundred metres off to Campana's right was Sergeant L'Huillier. After establishing liaisons to his right and left, and setting a plan of fire, L'Huillier went to reconnoitre his new sector. He found two listening posts to his front, one of which was at the end of a trench extending into no man's land and protected with an overhead screen of chicken-wire to prevent enemy grenades from being tossed into it. Reporting to Captain Le Boulanger at the 2 Battalion command post (at the entrance of Boyau de Chattancourt in the Chattancourt Ravine), L'Huillier was told he would reprise his role as battalion's primary observer. Posted in the shelter of 5 Company's stretcher-bearers between the first and cover line, in the ominously named Boyau de la Mort (likely the upper portion of Boyau de Chattancourt), his job was to ensure that the liaison was maintained between the companies in line and battalion command. Since the telephone lines were constantly being cut by the the shelling, he was provided with runners to assist him, which he placed at intervals of 200m. In case of attack, L'Huillier was charged with centralizing the orders and reports, and ensuring they made it to the appropriate destinations. While the first-line positions were largely spared the heavier shelling, the same could not be said about the 151's covering positions. Laporte was with 1 MG Company in their assigned support position and complained:

> Our first day at Mort Homme was bad. The German artillery along with the French artillery gave us no respite. At nightfall, the bombardment lightened a bit . . . But the artillery duel continued to rage away over by [Esnes]. Our first-line trenches were very well situated and didn't suffer as much as the second-line, which was a hundred metres away from it.[11]

L'Huillier noticed the same and that the German heavy artillery fired on the supporting line every five minutes. Their fire appeared to be well adjusted by observation balloons floating high above the German rear lines. Regardless of the fire, the rest of the day was spent with the units settling in and organizing their new positions. As dusk arrived and darkness again obscured the land, the 3 Battalion resumed its final approach march and went into reserve along the southern slopes of Mort Homme. The 12 Company took up position in the *Place d'Armes* traversing Côte 259 some 300m behind Line 1A. The rest of 3 Battalion's companies posted in the 'Second Position', the final line of strongpoints at the base of the hill, about a kilometre from the summit. Jubert and his 11 Company was posted on the left end of this line in the Ouvrage Laborderie.

> The earthworks of the Second Position were dug below [Mort Homme], separated from the mother-summit by a set of twin, angular ravines. A company occupied this position, together with machine guns. On its wings it was joined to a line of trenches heading off to the east toward Chattancourt, and to the west across the Hayette Ravine. Dominated from afar by Montfaucon Heights (thereby threating our lines), to the west by Côte 304, and to the northwest by the top of Mort Homme, referred to as 295 . . .
>
> Under the view of these two hills, each offering mutual protection for the other, the Second Position wasn't really all that dangerous a place. The shells fell around it. Though there were no shelters to protect us from the rain, the majority of men rested in the *boyaux* under their tent-canvases, despite the daily bombardment that enveloped us with smoke.[12]

By the evening of 6 April, the disposition of the regiment was as follows: on the left, 1 Battalion with three companies in the first line; on the right, 2 Battalion with three companies in the first line; 3 Battalion in the support and reserve positions. The 162 IR was in liaison to the left of 1 Battalion and the 8 LIB in liaison to the right of 2 Battalion. For the next several nights, the companies would be put to work reorganizing and improving their positions. As soon as it was dark enough, the men set about deepening the trenches or digging new connecting ones, fortifying the Second Position into a line of strongpoints, erecting barbed wire entanglements, strengthening dugouts and munition shelters, installing machine-gun platforms, building traverses in the *boyaux*, and throwing up sandbag barricades in those leading to listening posts. Going into their second night, Laporte again volunteered to lead a ration resupply party despite the danger presented by incoming artillery fire. His harrowing tale is recounted here in full:

> Not a metre of ground escaped the shelling and it was a miracle that any human being could survive under this deluge of hell-fire. Everything was flashes, detonations, smoke. That evening around midnight, I took advantage of a light lull in the firing and went out on a rations resupply, accompanied by eight poilus, all volunteers. The 'promenade' was certainly hazardous. We were just leaving our positions when a rain of shrapnel pelted us. One of the poilus in our party was thrown to the ground, killed instantly by a shrapnel ball that struck him right in his forehead. We stopped for a moment and after relieving our poor comrade of his load of canteens, we set back off on our route right through the bursting shells.
>
> Countless times we had to throw ourselves down to the ground to avoid the huge fragments whistling their death cry as they plummeted down in all directions! After much excitement, we finally reached the small village of Chattencourt [*sic*], which we passed through without incident. A small village! In reality, imagine piles of bricks and scorched beams with streets made of water-filled shell-holes. It was no easy task to walk through on this black night, amidst all this chaos.
>
> About 2 kilometres past the entrance to the village we found the mobile field kitchens. And how happy our cooking comrades were to see us: 'So, up there? How's it going?' etc. Our provisioning complete, we rested a moment before heading back fully loaded, bodies draped with canteens and stew-pots. While moving back through the village, we pass other fatigue parties. We weren't entirely alone out here and this route was the most practicable. After each spectacular chute of mud [tossed up by bursting shells] rained back down, the curses of the men always

ended in laughter. The most important thing was to not lose the slightest portion of the precious rations.

We left Chattencourt in the direction of Mort Homme around 2.00 am [on 6 April]. The bombardment was going stronger than ever, gradually increasing in intensity as we advanced. Once again we re-entered Hell. We walked in a zigzag in order to avoid (so we believed) the fire of the German batteries, which sometimes continued firing on the same point. We trudged on like this for more than an hour when all of a sudden, believing to be in our trenches, we heard shouting in a voice we knew all too well: we were at the edge of a German trench. In the pitch-black night, we had lost our way. Needless to say (with no weapons and only the precious rations in hand), we quickly all huddled up in an enormous shell hole. After we could no longer hear anything suspicious, we turned back in the direction from which we came with the greatest speed despite our load.

I've never been able to explain how, but an hour later we arrived back safe and sound in our own trenches this time (if we hadn't had the death of a comrade to mourn, we would've had a good laugh). It was around 5.00 am. We were given a good welcome. Our comrades were afraid that we had all been laid low in this fire-filled wasteland. A chore duty of this type made it back one time out of two. That's why we had to call on volunteers. Anyways, we hadn't been knocked around all that bad this time. I recounted our story to the captain [Captain Antoine], who couldn't help from laughing despite the circumstances. We have to keep our spirits up after all, don't we?

The rations distributed, the men of the fatigue went back to their places in their platoons. Separated from us by about 100 metres was a platoon that only had an effective of fifteen men at this time. Our comrade who had been killed during the course of the fatigue was from this platoon and as the resupply volunteers from the other platoons were going back to their emplacements, I took the stew-pots and canteens myself to hand out the rations for this neighbouring platoon. The 100 metres that separated me from them wasn't easy ground. It was a true obstacle course: nothing but shell-holes. Fortunately, the bombardment had calmed down some. I had hardly gone 20 metres when I fell flat on my chest. I had collided with a big poilu, who I had also knocked off his feet. He let out a curse which brought me back to my senses!

With my helmet in my hand, and before he had the time to get back on his feet, I landed a strong blow on his head (his helmet, by good fortune, had rolled off onto the ground). It was in fact a German who, without being fazed by the blow he had received, lifted his hands into the air and stammered out: '*Kamerad Français.*' The only weapon I had on me was my revolver, but it had been covered over by the canteens when I took my tumble. Worse still, I had let half the stew-pots, which held meat and vegetables, tip over. I first made sure that he didn't have any weapons – he was a young German of 18 or 19 years who was leaving his lines to surrender. I made him get in front of me and brought him to the captain. He wasn't the first one who had come over to our lines during the course of the last two days . . .

[Returning later] the interrogation of the prisoner was still going on. The 'Fritz' seemed at ease. He confessed that they had suffered enormous losses. They'd been sent up as reinforcements, being previously on the Russian border, and were told that they were being sent to take Paris. For them, Verdun was Paris! . . . And the only thing they'd taken up till now were unending shells of every calibre. The interrogation over, the prisoner was lead to the rear, accompanied by a liaison agent.[13]

This wasn't the first deserter that made a desperate escape to the French line. It was a harbinger for things to come, and in the days that followed more would flee to try to cheat death. The next day (7 April), the men were put to work organizing the sector, with the regiment on high alert in expectation of a big enemy attack. As if to confirm these suspicions, German spotter planes circled over Mort Homme, hawks looking for their prey. In the Second Position, work on the strongpoints was handed off from the engineers (who had originally constructed it) to the companies of 3 Battalion. Each night, a platoon would be tasked with carrying on the work all night. The nights were brisk and those off-shift slept huddled up with a comrade, sharing blankets to keep warm. Otherwise, Jubert's men had little to concern themselves in their sheltered position. As a distraction from reading letters and books, they could watch the spectacle of destruction unfolding on Côte 304 and Mort Homme, both of which seemed to be erupting like volcanoes under the storm of German shells. This curtain of iron and fire continued to increase in intensity, a box barrage saturating the first and second lines as well as all the ground that lay in between. Laporte was up in the first-line cover trench under the avalanche of steel and remarked: 'I have never witnessed such a deluge of fire. It was so bad that that those who still remained standing were losing their hearing.' All types and calibres of shells rained down by the hundreds – high explosive, time-fuse shrapnel, poison gas – 77s, 105s, 120s, 150s, 205s, and 210s. Most seemed to be fired from the Bois de Forges to the northeast.

The fire would slacken somewhat in afternoon of 8 April, with the lull lasting into the night. Campana was sheltering in his dugout when a liaison agent arrived inquiring whether he had a candle he could lend to Lieutenant Olivier, another platoon officer in 1 Company. The 27-year-old Marcel Olivier from La Réole (Gironde) had been a student in the sciences at the École Normale Supérieure before the war. Yet even at the front, in his moments of downtime, the former student enjoyed solving maths problems from an arithmetic book he kept with him.

> It would be charming if he wasn't constantly exposing himself out in the moonlight in order to complete a new theorem. Science was his passion. When he was searching for a solution, the shells could fall but he didn't hear them. He didn't think about war, or the privations, or the possibility of death. He only saw his numbers, his equations, his logarithms. At Haudraumont, in the light of a beautiful morning, he could think of nothing better than to lay out in the sun on the parapet, pencil in one hand and notebook in the other, tirelessly scribbling away in the pages. He should have been killed twenty times over . . . but he didn't catch a single bullet, and it took an order from the captain to get him down. He was reckless.[14]

Now, upon returning from a nighttime patrol, Olivier hoped to get back to his love. All through the night, Olivier huddled in his tiny shelter, working away on his formulas by the flickering light of Campana's candle. But the calm was deceptive. Around 7.00 pm, a German soldier was spotted coming over to the 2 Battalion's first-line trench with his arms raised in the air and was allowed into the lines. Jumping down into 8 Company's listening post, the prisoner was subsequently escorted by Lieutenant Couplet to Captain Le Boulanger's battalion command post. There, it was revealed that German was in fact of Polish origin (Poland at the time was annexed to Prussia) of the 6 Reserve Jäger Battalion. He declared that he'd deserted his post after learning that his regiment would be attacking the next day. He also said that another comrade had planned on surrendering that night as well. Though it is stated in the *JMO* that the deserter did not know the time of the attack, Campana and L'Huillier both claimed the man professed that zero-hour for the preparatory bombardment was set for 8.00 am, with the infantry scheduled to attack at noon. Artillery of all calibres, heavy *minenwerfers*, and flamethrowers were to be unleashed on the French positions. In the event that the infantry attack failed, the bombardment was to continue unabated until the evening. After initial questioning, the prisoner was taken back for further interrogation to regimental and brigade command posts. L'Huillier personally escorted the prisoner down through the Boyau de Chattancourt, now almost completely levelled by the heavy shelling. After dodging several salvoes of 210 shells, he and his terrified prisoner eventually made it to Chattancourt where the brigade command post was situated.

From there, the telephone lines came alive as the invaluable intelligence quickly shot out across the French lines of communication.[15]

L'Huillier reported back to Moisson at his command post in the *Place d'Armes* trench before heading back up to the front line. No sooner had he arrived than he was told that, sure enough, a second Polish deserter had come over to the regiment's line and corroborated the statement of the first. The French wasted no time. Extra stores of ammunition and grenades were rushed up to the units in line and placed in easily accessible spots. As a precaution against poison gas, bundles of straw were brought forward (which, when soaked with water and held over the mouth and nose, could act as a makeshift filter). Laporte reported that in his section of the line, machine guns had been placed every 10m with all fields of fire pre-sighted. The anticipation among the men was palpable – they were spoiling for a fight. In the previous month, they had suffered a relentless beating without being able to strike back.

This degrading experience of utter powerlessness went even further back though. Campana was one of a small portion of *anciens* remaining in the ranks who'd witnessed the massacre of the regiment on the plains of Champagne. Campana himself had arrived after the bloody opening day assault on 25 September 1915, when whole companies were cut to pieces in the impenetrable barrier of barbed wire. But he did go over the top on 6 October in a similarly senseless bloodbath. Though there were many new replacement troops with him, Campana had passionately recounted to them the events of that dark day, when the Germans had mowed down entire lines of their men, and then went on to pitilessly rake with their machine guns the dead and the wounded lying helplessly on the ground. Those who tried to crawl away, including the badly injured, were coldly picked off by enemy marksmen throughout the long day. The searing memory of those events inspired a deep and abiding lust for revenge, one that he passed on to his platoon. The thought that they would at last have the upper hand and be on the giving end of a brutal blow was deeply satisfying. Not everyone was as eager as Campana, though, to engage with the enemy. When Jubert was told to be ready to move his men forward the next day for a possible counter-attack, he quipped to a fellow officer: 'This will be good for us. We were starting to get out of the habit of dying.'

Attack of 9 April

The German operation scheduled for 9 April would be the largest assault at Verdun since the opening day of the offensive on 21 February. This was to be a general assault against both the left and right banks simultaneously, something which General von Falkenhayn had failed to commit to before. The mission to take Mort Homme was given to the German XXII Reserve Corps. Throughout the night of 8–9 April, on the German side things remained eerily quiet; it was the calm before the storm. The same was not so in the French lines, where thorough preparations were actively carried out. Trenches were deepened, parapets strengthened, and *boyaux* intended only for circulation were changed into fighting trenches. Campana's platoon had been placed on the south side of Côte 295 in a cover trench just below the summit. While it was sheltered from direct frontal fire, the position was open to enfilade fire from the German guns from the far off Côte de Talou on the right bank. Moreover, German aircraft had already surveilled and photographed their trench, all but guaranteeing they would make an easy target for the German artillery. To make matters worse, Campana had no view of Lieutenant Olivier's position in the first-line trench that traversed the ravine on the western face of 295. Nor could he see the enemy's trenches, save the profile of his second lines on Côte 265. Not all was lost though. Campana could see an advanced post 30m from his own trench that was situated on the summit of the hill and enjoyed a commanding view of the surrounding area. Seizing the initiative, he shifted his men to the post and resolved to have it enlarged during the night. Having distributed picks and shovels, Campana explained the purpose of their work, the importance of which was lost on no one: they were literally digging for their lives. All through the night and into the early morning hours of 9 April, the men dug energetically without a break. And when daylight finally came, the advantage of the new position was obvious. The post overlooked the ravine between Mort Homme and Côte 265 to the northwest, affording unobstructed views of Lieutenant Olivier's positions immediately in front, the entire German defensive system, and the positions of 7, 8, and 9 Companies to the east. To the west Campana could see Côte 304 and off to the north Montfaucon, where the German Crown Prince would observe the battle.

The early morning of 9 April remained calm. As he awoke, Jubert gazed upon his slumbering men: 'They were sleeping, with no suspicion that death hovered over them. Like condemned men, they would be awoken only so that they could die.' Up on the crest above him, L'Huillier was making his rounds, accompanied by an artillery spotter from the 61 FAR. Not as single gunshot or artillery shell could be heard. As he passed through 6 Company's line, a soldier quipped in a northern accent, 'They've stuffed our heads again. The Poles have pulled our leg!' L'Huillier quickly retorted, 'It's the calm before the storm. Wait until 8 o'clock and quickly get down into your saps once the bombardment starts, leave a few lookouts in place.' All the units were ready and now waited for the hammer to drop. The 1 Battalion was in place on the western summit and forward slope with (from left to right) 4, 3, and 1 Companies in the first line of Tranchée Guilbert and Perrenet. The 2 Company was in support in Tranchée Gilbert and Molina, along with the 1 MG Company and Campana's platoon from 1 Company. In liaison to their left was the 162 IR, holding the first-line trenches that extended down the northwestern slopes of

Mort Homme and into the Ravin de la Hayette. On the regiment's right was 2 Battalion holding the summit of 295 in a similar array, with (left to right) 5, 6, and 8 Companies in the first lines in Tranchée Perrenet and Garçon. The 7 Company was in support in the Boyau des Zouaves and Chattancourt along with the guns of 2 MG Company, which were interspersed between the first and support trenches. They were in liaison to the right with the 8 LIB holding the trenches stretching northeast to the Bois des Corbeaux. The companies of 3 Battalion remained in reserve. The 12 Company was furthest forward, holding the *Place d'Armes*, while the rest of the battalion was back in the Second Position: 11 Company in Ouvrage Laborderie, 9 Company in Ouvrage Mollandin, 10 Company on the far right beside Chattancourt, and the guns of 3 MG Company interspersed throughout.

Finally, the fateful hour arrived. The intelligence gleaned from the Polish deserters had the start of the operation at 8.00 am. All units in the 42 ID were on high alert and the troops all at their combat posts, nervous but ready. Campana was sitting in his newly enlarged advanced post with his section. He had already ensured his men had their rifles ready and placed stockpiles of grenades within arm's reach. Now they waited.

> As the sun rose, the day revealed itself to be clear and the sky free of clouds. Suddenly, at 8.00 am as anticipated, a single 105 shrapnel shell burst in the air, producing a yellowish-green cloud of smoke and breaking the serene calm. It was the signal for the attack. Three more shells burst, one after the other, while on Côte 304 huge plumes of smoke burst out of the ground. Innumerable shells now roared overhead. At Chattancourt, a veritable storm of 150s plummeted down. Then from all around, columns of smoke – black, grey, white, and yellow – shot up from the earth as the general bombardment of the entire sector began. The ground under our feet shook as hundreds of shells detonated around us.[16]

Along a front 6km in width and more than 2km in depth – from Côte 304 to Mort Homme to Cumières – the world erupted into smoke and flame and steel. It was unprecedented in its severity. Indeed, it was the strongest bombardment since the initial one on the first day of the battle but confined to a smaller space. So as to feign ignorance of the impending assault, the French artillery, contrary to the normal practice, fired only a few numbers of shells and these were aimed at targets far away from the interior of the German lines. On Mort Homme there were two distinct zones of fire: one pounded the trenches along the line of Côte 304 to Côte 295. The other blocked the Chattancourt Ravine below 295, where the enemy judged the reserves had been built up. From his sheltered position of the second line, Jubert watched the spectacle unfold.

> I have rarely seen such a sight. It was massive in scale and had a life of its own. It spread out like a game of death in the serenity of the morning... Brushstroke was being added to brushstroke in quick succession, dozens at a time. So heavy it felt as though it could suffocate you. From a distance they looked fresh, even harmonious to the eye. Thunderclouds floated across the sky, touched with the colour of the morning. The sun has this virtue: beneath its rays, death takes on pure beauty.[17]

The men of the 151 had suffered under bombardment on many occasions, including during their twenty-day stay on the right bank just a few weeks before. But they had experienced nothing like this. After action reports speak of the bombardment as being of hereto 'unknown intensity'. Eyewitnesses described uninterrupted curtains of flame and smoke. Raining down from the sky were 77s, 105s, 120s, 130s, 150s, 205s, and 210s. The conflagration continued unabated for hours and then somehow increased in intensity at 11.00 am, the final hour before the German infantry was to attack. In the trenches only a small number of lookouts were posted, the rest of the men were sheltering in their cramped shelters. None of these could hold up to a direct hit by a heavy shell and many were crushed in just such a fashion. On the 1 Battalion front, the first-line trench was largely spared from the heaviest shelling owing to its proximity to the German lines. The fire was worse on the covering trenches and 1 Battalion command post. The real beating came on the regiment's right, where 2 Battalion held the line. L'Huillier fell back on a term so frequently used when speaking about the shelling at Verdun ... the scene was 'Dantesque'.

> We thought the German artillerists were literally hand-dropping the shells down on our positions. The ground is thoroughly saturated down to an area of 20 m^2 by 20 m^2. I see arms and legs flying through the air. The wounded can't find the way to the first-aid post ... In a few hours, it's a lunar landscape where only enormous, smoking holes can be seen ...[18]

The 8 Company, on the right flank of the battalion where the opposing lines were closest, was particularly targeted by heavy calibre *minenwerfers* – 170s and 250s. With a deep, dull thud, the cylindrical bombs shot up into the air, before hurtling back down and exploding with devastating violence. But orders had been issued and no ground could be given. It was imperative that the line be held. And so the poor souls of 8 Company would have to suffer their fate, remaining in their position as one murderous projectile after another came crashing down on top of them. Here, the definition of courage and sacrifice was simply to stay put, to not run away, even in the face of an inevitable brutal death. All movement to and from the front lines was made suicidal by the intensity of the fire. Yet, orders had to be sent out and received, and L'Huillier watched in awe as his dedicated runners dashed off to deliver them. Losses in 5 and 6 Companies were already mounting, as the trenches were pounded into nothing more than shallow ditches affording little to no cover. Men were slashed, gouged and smashed by shell fragments and, unable to be evacuated, were struck and wounded again or killed outright. Many suffered for hours with shredded flesh or splintered bones, lying in puddles of their own blood and urine. Fathers, sons, brothers, husbands, boyfriends, burning with fever, wracked with headaches, tortured with thirst, suffering, dying.

As Campana watched the brutal pounding of 2 Battalion unfold, eight shells suddenly exploded simultaneously behind him in the trench he'd abandoned the night before. A close escape indeed! Meanwhile, in the skies above, German aircraft were highly active, reporting back to their artillery the effects of their fire. One of these was shot down by a French Nieuport and crashed down in the French lines, the pilot burnt to a crisp. Around 11.30 am, French artillery commenced a counter-fire on the German departure positions. To the cacophonous din of passing German shells and explosions was added the unmistakable high-pitched scream of French 75s, along with the howls, whistles, and moans of medium and heavy calibre shells all raining down on the masses of packed men in the opposing lines. At noon, the German heavy artillery lengthened its fire to hammer the support areas and the bombardment achieved its maximum ferocity. The sound of the explosions now seemed to change into a demented confusion of noise. This stepped up barrage would only last about a quarter of an hour. It proved to be the final preparatory fire from the German side. To those on the ground those fifteen minutes must have seemed an eternity. Then, at 12.15 pm, the fire died off as suddenly as it had descended. In that moment, a flare shot up from the German lines. It could mean only one thing: it was the signal for the start of enemy infantry assault. From his advanced post atop 295, a dazed Campana, having survived the onslaught, quickly jumped up and looked down the forward slope:

> Suddenly, waves of German infantry now jumped out of their trenches. A company of German infantry with bayonets fixed now charged against our line. It pressed on a few metres, then under the tac-tac of our machine guns, it collapsed. Some men having escaped our volley of bullets fled back in disorder towards their jumping off positions. None made it back. Our merciless fire stopped them in their tracks and the survivors threw themselves to the ground.[19]

Working in support of 1 Battalion, Laporte witnessed the same scene as his company's machine guns burst into action and turned the slopes of Mort Homme into a killing field:

> They [the Germans] were all superb, strapping fellows. When this mass of men in tightly packed ranks had gone a dozen metres, the cross fire of our machine guns literally mowed down the first ranks. The second wave then took its turn and immediately suffered the same fate as the first. Those Germans, and there weren't many, who managed to pass through this storm of metal were taken down by rifles or grenades.[20]

Further east on the regiment's right (2 Battalion), L'Huillier looked on from his observatory just behind the first line as the enemy assault waves raced up the slopes towards their lines.

> In tightly packed ranks, elbow to elbow, I see German companies advancing. Our poilus come up out of their saps. The machine guns crackle away and at less than 100 metres, mow down masses of Germans who fall upon each other in heaps. To my left, they are stopped by a section of barbed-wire entanglements that (unbelievably) remain intact. They're the perfect target for our machine-gunners. What a massacre![21]

Yet with its trenches completely flattened by well-sighted heavy artillery fire, the situation for 2 Battalion was rapidly deteriorating. Despite suffering heavy losses, wave after wave of German assault troops broke against the dazed survivors of 5, 6, and 8 Companies, and enemy troops began to infiltrate the first-line trench. To 2 Battalion's right, heavy plumes of evil looking black smoke billowed up into the dusty air – the Germans were using flamethrowers against the 8 LIB. Refusing to flee their trenches, the chasseurs were transformed into living torches, their uniforms, hair and flesh were set aflame. Some burned alive in the shallow remains of their trenches, writhing in agony like embers in a fire-pit. Others ran about wildly, flopping to the ground and squirming like fish out of water, until the flames sucked the air out of their lungs.

Just as it seemed to Campana that the enemy assault troops were about to break through the 2 Battalion's lines, a machine-gun crew of 1 MG Company shifted its aim to the 2 Battalion's front and let loose with a withering enfilade fire.

> Gunner-Sergeant Dufour pointed his weapon on the teeming horde: the Hotchkiss spat out 300 bullets a minute. Under the rain of steel, the Boches tumbled down like toy soldiers and in a few seconds, many green-grey clad bodies lay scattered on the ground. Seized with panic, the survivors scattered in all directions. So each of my men chose his victim and did his best to knock off another pretty target. Not a single German made it back to his trench. In front of us, a calm settled in, but

to the right and left waves of enemy advanced toward our positions and on the side of the 8 Light Infantry, the hideous black smoke continued to rise up.²²

The world seemed to be ripping itself assunder as thousands of rifles and machine guns continually crackled like endless bolts of lightning, creating an auditorium of ear-splitting noise. Men shouted, swore, cursed, laughed. Shells continuously whistled and roared overhead. Laporte was awestruck by the sheer fury of the fighting.

> What an inferno of fire! What an infernal noise! The unending German waves were all composed of tightly packed ranks, which gradually grew larger. Heaps of bodies were already laid out in front of us. The muzzles of the machine guns turned red. We fired without stop. For their part, our 75 canons created enormous devastation in the German trenches just behind the assault waves, while our heavy artillery rained down on the German reserves without stop. The Germans continued to fall in front of our lines. It was a total slaughter . . .²³

Savouring the carnage unfolding before his eyes, Campana's thoughts raced back to the visions of butchery he'd seen the 151 subjected to in Champagne the previous autumn. 'Remember the 6th of October!' he cried to his men.

> Angrily, hatefully, but with calm, they chose their prey. Rifle placed in the crook of the elbow, attentive, they scan the slopes covered in dead bodies. Under our violent bursts of gunfire, many Germans were pinned to the ground, hoping to escape the massacre by playing dead. But sometimes, either taken by a sudden panic or profiting from a moment of calm, they leapt up and ran back towards their trenches. Amused by this new type of hunt, my men take careful aim and shoot them down like rabbits.
>
> I had taken the rifle of my orderly and spotted a big German hurtling down Côte 265. I fired in repetition. On the third shot, he threw up his arms and collapsed with his body stretched out. I continued to empty my magazine on him. Out of the six rounds that still remained, four hit his body, the other two throwing up little clouds of dust behind him. I was certain that he was truly dead.²⁴

German planes now hove into view in the smokey air and took account of the regiment's positions. One came down in flames having been struck by a 75 mm anti-aircraft gun. But most remained airborne, providing accurate reporting back to their batteries for fire adjustment. And soon after appearing, a volley of 105s and 210s began to slam down around the 1 Battalion positions. Campana's men jumped down from the fire-steps to shelter in the bottom of the trench. To boost their confidence, Campana remained standing where he was and, taking out his camera, began to photograph the shell bursts. As a 210 struck down in front of him, he quickly snapped a picture of the explosion just as a fragment from the shell struck him in the chest. Fortunately for Campana, the careless act didn't result in serious injury as the flying piece of metal lacked the force to penetrate his skin. Shortly after this lucky escape, the company commander, Captain Carrère, arrived, tranquilly smoking his pipe.

> 'How's it going in front of you?
> 'Not bad. See for yourself.
> 'Oh, hey, that's nice work. I'm coming from the 3rd Platoon. They already have three killed.
> 'For the moment I don't have any killed or wounded.
> 'Gontran has had his second machine gun buried by a 150.
> 'He's doing marvellously. Look at this whole line of Boches, it took less than two minutes to mow them down.' The Captain advanced toward Sergeant Dufour to congratulate him:
> 'It's a pleasure to see you haven't wasted any time!
> 'The pleasure is all mine, sir. It's wonderful stopping these bastards right in their tracks and to see them come tumbling down like wood chips. There was an officer leading them, making big gestures with his arms to give his men nerve. I shot him down with my musket. He must be over there, in the group of dead. I'm going to try to find him with my binoculars . . . I see him, hold on, sir, would you like . . .'[25]

Just as Dufour was uttering these words a dry crack rang out and the gunner collapsed into Campana's arms, his skull blasted open. A bullet had struck him square in the forehead, cracking his head apart and splattering Campana's greatcoat and those around him with bits of brain. Recovering from the shock, Campana could see the German communication trenches that led back to the enemy's support line teeming with little green men, like branches of a tree: it was Prussian chasseurs. They were over 1,000m away (on 265) and either presumed they could not be seen by the French or were simply obeying orders to march across open ground in order to move up quicker. The Prussians advanced carrying their rifles in one hand, their bayonets glittering as they reflected the sunlight. Campana ran over to the corporal-gunner manning the nearby Hotchkiss to ensure that he'd spotted this superb target. Right away the gun began angrily spitting out bullets by the hundreds and a great agitation could be seen among the enemy columns. The German chasseurs quickly jumped down into their communication trenches but the storm of bullets continued to rain down mercilessly on the tightly packed enemy troops, cutting them down like fish in a barrel. Suddenly there is a loud explosion on Campana's right and a corporal comes running up to him.

> 'Mon lieutenant, the 210 fell close to us, the machine gun is in pieces, the aimer and the loader have been killed. I'm done for too.
> 'Are you wounded?
> 'I am in the chest, I'm screwed.'[26]

After calling over a stretcher-bearer to take care of the wounded corporal, Campana tells his men to fire as if they were at the shooting range, with calm and taking care not to waste ammunition. They had already gone through an entire sack of cartridges and their muzzles were burning hot. Yet with their machine gun out of service, the thirty to forty bullets that the rifles could fire a minute weren't enough to stop the rapidly advancing German troops. The swarms of enemy troops moved both across open ground and up through the *boyaux* and into the the front-line trench before throwing themselves forward.

> My men fired without stop and each time they knocked off a Boche, they laughed like big kids . . . I carried out target practice for more than a quarter hour, while my orderly reprovisioned his comrades with ammunition. I'd hoped that our artillery fire would open up on them soon, but their fire appeared to be concentrated to the right where the Prussian chasseurs had taken the first-line and were moving on to the second.
> In front of us the Boches came on but en masse this time. In a few minutes the slopes of Côte 265 were covered in enemy rushing toward us. This time, we only had our rifles to stop them, and that was not sufficient. At our feet, in Lieutenant Olivier's trench, the fighting was already hand-to-hand. On the off chance, I sent up a red flare to request artillery fire. The situation had become critical. The green horde had already overwhelmed our first-line and was advancing toward us . . . Suddenly a terrifying barrage was unleashed on the German waves: 75s and 155s rained down as thick as hail on the hundreds of men packed elbow to elbow. My soldiers screamed in joy while this fire continued.
> 'Bravo! Bravo!
> 'Go on then! Bing! Bing and bing! Oh, *mon lieutenant*, take a look at this omelet!'

> The bodies were piling up. Whole lines of Boche were dropping like wheat before the scythe. Others under the explosions of our shells were thrown several metres up into the air, mixing with clouds of earth and stones before crashing back down. German grenadiers, with greatcoats rolled around them in bandolier fashion, advanced toward us. Barely thirty metres separated us from them.
> 'Fix bayonets! Get the grenades ready!'
> The fire of our 75s doubled in intensity. Fortunately one gun fired too short and several shells fell on the enemy grenadiers. Seized by panic, the survivors tried to about-face but in the violence of the bombardment, they ran around as though completely lost. So they made the 'Kamerad!' [to surrender] and headed toward us. There still were about forty of them but we were too over-excited to have pity on them.
> 'No prisoners, boys! Shoot all these vermin!'
> Caught between our rifle fire and our bursting shells, they ran panic-stricken to the right and left. My men cold-bloodedly shot them down. Soon . . . the last grenadier collapsed. For the second time the enemy fell back in disorder. Heaps of corpses lay on the slopes of Côte 265. It looked like a field recently harvested where bales of hay wait to be collected.[27]

They were euphoric. There was no better feeling than at last giving better than they'd received. There was a new lull in this part of the regiment's line. For his part, Laporte watched the progressive destruction of his regiment and the bravery displayed by so many.

> One of our platoons had lost all of its men except for one, Faglain, who was able to save his machine gun and continued to fire into the enemy waves. We suffered some losses, but nothing compared to the bloodshed across from us. Thousands of their men were stacked up one on top of the other in front of our lines. Further back the bodies were countless and way off in the distance, the Meuse carried along streams of bodies. Those of us who had survived looked like filthy chimney sweeps after this terrible massacre.[28]

In contrast, on the right the situation had become critical as 2 Battalion literally disintegrated. The 5 and 6 Companies had been conducting a desperate fight to hold on to their front-line trenches. With most of the regiment's machine guns out of action, a dwindling number of crazed, hopeless riflemen fired away into the swarms of German attack troops. They could see the writing on the wall. Trying to reach his own 6 Company in the first line to determine where the enemy was, L'Huillier suddenly heard German voices not 20m away.

Real fast, I instruct Corporal Gabert and five of his men – Guillois, Grenet, Martin, Petot and Doucet – to make a sandbag barricade. Their platoon leader was missing. Gabert fires his automatic-rifle admirably and stops a German assault less than 50 metres from us. I fire, the Boches fall. I try to understand the situation as I return to my post. Through the binoculars it seems like I see Fritz practically everywhere, mixed together with the debris of my battalion's units.[29]

More and more enemy troops pressed down upon them and overwhelmed the first line. The handfuls of men that constituted the remains of 5, 6, and 8 Companies had to give ground, the survivors escaping back through the crumbled remains of Boyau de Chattancourt or scrambling down over the cratered slopes. The battle had devolved into small isolated groups of soldiers, their commanders either dead or cut off from them, fighting and dying to the last man. In the raining confusion and chaos, L'Huillier sent off his last runner to report on the dire situation to battalion command. An hour passed as he waited anxiously for the runner's return – nothing. With all his couriers killed, wounded, or missing, L'Huillier decided he must leave his post and attempt to reach his battalion commander no matter what the cost. Physically and emotionally exhausted, he failed in his first two endeavours when he spotted and engaged groups of Germans occupying nearby shell holes.

Yet, somehow L'Huillier managed to run, dive, and crawl his way back down into the Chattancourt Ravine to the battalion CP. There, Captain Le Boulanger was astonished to see him, especially in light of the intercepted German radio messages announcing that Mort Homme had been taken. Lieutenant Colonel Moisson had even passed the news on to the division. L'Huillier emphatically set the record straight, telling his commander that elements of the 151 were still clinging onto Côte 285.9. Moreover, the enemy had not managed to take the regiment's covering line nor his own observation post. The situation could still be corrected! Le Boulanger immediately telephoned Moisson and urgently requested that reinforcements be sent up to plug the gap and stabilize the situation. At this point, 5 Company, with all of its officers (including its commander Lieutenant Liethou) now killed or missing, had been reduced to a fraction of men. The 6 Company, with its commander Lieutenant Guilbaud killed, had disappeared completely. Under the weight of the German infantry attack, the remnants of 7 Company were no longer able to hold onto the recaptured trenches and fell back. The 2 Battalion was gone and the liaison between it and 1 Battalion was consequently broken. Meanwhile, to the 151's right, the 8 LIB had been forced to abandon its first line too, leaving a large gap between the two units.

The situation was dire in the extreme and could spell disaster for the French line as a whole if exploited by the enemy. In desperation, Moisson now committed his final reserves. The companies of 3 Battalion had remained in the Second Position at the southern base of Mort Homme. Now, around 1.00 pm, orders went out to 12 Company that it was to counter-attack to retake the lost positions of 2 Battalion and seal the gap in the line. Many of the troops in this company had only just arrived at the front two weeks before. Now these new recruits of the class of 1916, 19 and 20 years of age, were about to face a severe baptism of fire. Assisting 12 Company in its counter-attack was a mishmash of elements patched together from the remains of several companies. The largest contingent was from 7 Company, which until now had remained in its support position just below the summit, sheltering from the avalanche of shells as best they could. A brave handful of survivors from 5 Company that could be gathered joined them. For 7 Company, two platoons would advance on the left while the other two would attack to the right to plug the gap left by the withdrawal of the shattered 8 LIB from its first line. In order to not delay the advance, orders specified that the units were to advance across open country. This was near suicidal, as the counter-attack force would surely be spotted by German observation balloons as soon as it left its positions. But the situation was critical.

From his post, Campana could see the units deploying into the attack. Taking out his binoculars he recognized one of the officers of 7 Company to be his fellow Saint-Cyr cadet friend Second Lieutenant Pierre Camusat de Riancey. Suddenly Campana was struck by a small detail. He could hardly believe his eyes when he realized that his classmate was wearing his white dress gloves! Saint-Cyr cadets swore an oath in 1914 to wear white gloves into their first battle. But this was not the young officer's first time under fire. He had already seen plenty of action the previous year in the Argonne, where he was wounded – struck by two bullets – while leading his platoon in a bayonet attack. His bravery had already earned him two citations and the Croix de Guerre with two stars. French 75s screamed down on the lost first lines for several minutes to soften the enemy's defence before lengthening its fire. As they did, the men of 12 Company, bayonets fixed, climbed out of the *Place d'Armes* and bounded forward in two waves. Observing from his position, Campana watched his Saint-Cyr comrade climb out of the trench only to immediately collapse on the parapet, already struck by a bullet. Taking a moment to recover, he got back up on his feet and ran another dozen metres before being struck a second time and falling down again.

For Campana, the image of seeing his friend spread out motionless on the ground with his white-gloved hands resting crisply on his Horizon Blue greatcoat seared itself into his mind. He would learn later that evening that his young friend had not been killed outright. Thrown to the ground by a bullet that had torn open his side, he had the strength to get back up again and continue to lead his men. But he was struck by three more bullets in the belly and collapsed a final time. A gut shot is always agonizing and promises a slow death. De Riancey was evacuated by stretcher-bearers to a first-aid post, and then transported back to an ambulance at Jouy-en-Argonne. There he suffered in great pain throughout the night, finally dying the next morning. For his action, de Riancey would be promoted to the Chevalier de la Légion d'honneur posthumously.

On the east side of Chattancourt Ravine, the platoons of 7 Company had quickly exited Tranchée de Foix, formed into short columns and rushed up the slopes. Upon reaching the summit, they pressed on, eventually abandoning the open ground and dropping down into the shallow *boyaux*, where they encountered the German defenders. The fighting was hard and costly. Leading his section forward, Second Lieutenant Mattei is shot in the forehead and falls dead. Second Lieutenant Basteau and his section managed to take back a portion of the trench lost by 6 Company but casualties were high and only continued to climb as the men fended off multiple enemy counter-attacks. Meanwhile, 12 Company led by Lieutenant Le Gallo had deployed into a double line of skirmishers and advanced across open country in a northeastern direction, obliquing across Chattancourt Ravine and back up the eastern slope of Mort Homme. Multiple eyewitness accounts stated that the 12th moved in perfect order. Immediately, German observation balloons spotted the formation and soon shells begin to fall all around the company. Yet, the men advanced and managed miraculously to arrive at the 2 Battalion command post without suffering any casualties. Lieutenant Le Gallo found Captain Le Boulanger to receive his orders: "'Follow L'Huillier, he knows the sector and the situation better than anyone. He'll lead you. Relieve 5th Company. The mission: hold the position no matter the cost. I'm waiting for the 11th Company which will counter-attack on your right . . .'"[30]

Deploying back into its skirmish line, 12 Company advanced as if on manoeuvres. They had only gone a short distance up on the crest when bullets began to whistle and crack around them by the hundreds. Taken by an enfilading fire on their left, the men took cover and then continued the advance, rushing forward in small groups from shell hole to shell hole. Men were struck and cried out before collapsing to the ground. The 12 Company suffered heavy casualties but nonetheless managed to retake 5 Company's abandoned line, or rather the series of holes that constituted it. Those who managed to make it to the objective now jumped down into what remained of the trench to engage the enemy up close. For several minutes, a short but brutal hand-to-hand fight ensued. Soon the remaining Germans fled the trench, pursued close behind by the French attackers and their now bloodied bayonets. Few in number, the survivors of 12 Company consolidated on the retaken line. However, despite their valiant efforts, 12 Company had been unable to reestablish contact with the 8 LIB on the right. As the German assault troops consolidated their gains along the summit of Mort Homme, they signalled back to their artillery to cease firing on the hill to avoid striking their own men, and a relative lull in the storm settled in. From Ouvrage Laborderie, Jubert with his 11 Company remained largely out of touch with the events going on above them. They took the slackening of the enemy artillery fire to mean that the German attack had been thwarted. Believing they had been spared, the men vented themselves in hysterical relief. They had escaped the noose! Soup was served to the men who feasted voraciously. As the smoke filling the air started to dissipate, the rays of the spring sun managed to break through the pall. Jubert stretched out with his comrades to play some cards as they awaited further orders.

The time was now around 2.30 pm and Jubert was doing quite well for himself having a lucky run when a message arrived from the 3rd Battalion commander, Commandant Coltat. Lieutenant Ganot, in command of the company, opened the note, read it slowly, and then handed it to Jubert without saying a word. The news blew away the illusion of comfort like the sudden arrival of a 77 shell. The top of Mort Homme had been overrun; they were to retake it immediately. Their prospects seemed dire indeed. The 11 Company – reduced to 100 effectives, most of whom were raw recruits – would be moving uphill against an enemy that was quickly entrenching in the newly conquered positions. Like their comrades in 12 Company before them, they were told to not take the *boyaux* but to advance nearly a kilometre out in the open. 'Rarely have I seen less hesitation, more calm as in this moment. The adjudant gave the orders, the men assembled without a word spoken. Leaving the packs behind, we loaded ourselves up with plenty of ammunition, and took an extra day's rations.'[31]

The 11 Company's instructions were to counter-attack to the right of 12 Company's advance in order to retake 8 Company's positions and reestablish contact with the 8 LIB. Climbing out of the trenches, the company formed up into line by platoons in single rank and began advancing towards the zone of death marked by bursting smoke and flame. The faces of the men were grave. A few managed a thin, taut smile when Jubert caught their eye. Their approach march took them in a northeasterly direction towards the eastern crest of Mort Homme. As they continued forward, fear scraped away inside the men. What else could one do but act brave, to put up a front that they would not be cowed by their fear, to be indignant to death. Spontaneous shouts of encouragement were exchanged:

'We'll show them what the boys from the North are made of, sir!
  'And those from the Ardennes too!
  'And the kids from Paris!'[32]

It may well have been pure bravado but it helped steel this small line of humanity that steadily advanced in well-dressed lines into the maw of battle. Passing over the top of Côte 259 the company descended into Chattancourt Ravine.

> [It was like] the bottom of a furnace, explosions and smoke converge in hellish roar that deals out death. We go another hundred paces. Now we're in the real danger zone. The shells fall all around us. The men were silent. With grave faces, they advance in the prescribed order and pace. When we get to the Colonel's CP, where salvoes of shells were concentrated, a wall of fire and steel stood before us.[33]

As Jubert turned around to check that he was being followed, a shell exploded on the ground, the force of the blast hurling one of his men several metres into the air like a rag doll. As the limp body plummeted down, it was immediately caught by the fresh blast of a second shell and jerked back up into the air. With the arrival of this second shell, one of his half-platoons dived to the ground. Jubert could see their faces were palsied with fear. Yet, as soon as the danger had passed, they rose back up one by one and resumed their place in the line. Incredibly, the skirmish line had made it through the wall of shell-fire still intact and had arrived at a point just below the top of the hill. As they did, Jubert spotted an officer gesturing to them. It was Second Lieutenant Mollet, who'd been posted by 2nd Battalion Leader, Commandant Le Boulanger, to give last-minute directions.

> 'The Boches are up at the top or just behind it. One section will progress with grenades through the Boyau des Zouaves, the rest of the company will take the crest obliquing to the right.
> 'Where's the enemy?
> 'You tell us!'
> We platoon leaders are at our posts several paces to the front. I look upon an admirable line to my right, Noël, Dubot, Buisson. 'We're going to give them a thrashing!' a man shouts, laughing as he does. 'The bastards won't get past us.'
> More voices join in, boosting their confidence. Letting out a laugh, I appease and then calm them down with a gesture. 'We'll sing when we get up there! Forward, boys!'
> Making an assault like this gives a real sense of satisfaction. We're moving forward, Noël, Dubot, Buisson, and me. We maintain good order. It feels good to face death this way.[34]

The men followed behind them, many with smiles on their lips and laughing. The shelling had been bad but they had made it through and now they were going to take back their regiment's positions. Carrying their rifles in one hand down by their side, they had still not encountered any enemy troops. In the smoke and devastation, they'd been unable to spot any indications of a trench line. Jubert and the other platoon leaders reminded their men to maintain their pace and order for the final push, which they did, just as they had in training, as they continued towards the eastern crest. They had another 100m to go as their eyes continually scanned the ground for enemy troops.

Suddenly, on their left flank, a machine gun opened up on them from about 500m away. The German assault troops had set it up near the lost command post of 8 Company. It was at this moment that one of the men in 11 Company struck up a popular cafe concert song in an attempt to bolster his courage. His neighbours joined in and soon the entire line of men had picked up the tune in a stirring display of élan. The singing was indeed corroborated by multiple sources at the time. Yet, here is one of those great incidents of war that has become ensnared in murky myth. From his post atop 295, between the brief moments of silence punctuated by explosions, Campana said he could hear the singing of 11 Company as it reached the summit. However, Campana believed the song was 'La Marseillaise'. A number of official accounts produced after the attack reported the same. The French *Etat-Major* and the French press seized on these reports, trumpeting them as displays of the patriotism and zeal of French troops. The reality, as clarified by the officer leading the attack, was something different yet no less compelling and inspirational. The poilus of 11 Company, many of whom were just receiving their baptism of fire, had joined together in a song of life to help steady themselves under the hail of steel. But the enemy's machine gun sputtered its own mechanical song of death and its notes quickly began to cut the men down. Jubert could hear the cries of his fellow officers – Noël, Dudot, and Buisson – as each were struck and fell. But he continued to press on all the same.

> 'Watch your alignment!' I yell.
> 'Forward!' someone is repeating behind me. 'We've got them!'
> My men follow my command. Bullets patter down by the hundreds, burrowing 20 cm into the earth and causing puffs of smoke to rise around me. That's from the rounds striking the ground, kicking up a cloud of dust. They brush past my feet and graze past the others around me as I dodge about.[35]

In a matter of seconds scores of men had been mowed down, just as the Germans had been a short while before. The momentum of the charge had hurtled the survivors of 11 Company to top of the hill. But the singing had died out as men were cut down, the melody replaced by the discordant cries of the wounded. Those remaining fixed their eyes on the final objective. The rain of bullets continued to whistle by. They were almost there, only a little bit further to go. Thirty paces left, then fifteen, then five. Jubert turned around and asked himself where his company had gone. Finally, he reached the trench and jumped down into it and then braced himself to be set on by the enemy. But the trench was deserted, the German troops holding it had fled. Where had they gone, Jubert's men asked. Jubert quickly took count of his men. There were a handful of his old soldiers and a few new recruits from the class of 1916 (he'd still not learned their names). In all there remained only ten – ten out of the hundred or so who had started off. Looking back over the ground behind him, he could see only the dead and wounded, the latter of whom were trying to drag themselves up to the trench while enemy machine guns continued to target them.

In the momentary lull and relative safety of the trench, one of Jubert's men named Vandervoode offered him some fancy tobacco he took into combat as a tradition. Jubert shared it with the survivors around him. But in the uneasy calm, a sense of dread now began to seep in, as the cries of the wounded and their calls for help reached their ears. To help boost morale, Jubert seized an envelope lying on the ground beside a dead German and ceremoniously recorded the names of the ten survivors, declaring that they would be awarded the Croix de Guerre for their good conduct. Only after the battle would Jubert, reflecting on the bravery of his men, come to a searing revelation: 'In the middle of combat, one is little more than a wave in a sea . . . a stroke of the brush lost in the painting . . . Courage, in our days, is a currency that is not depreciated, but tarnished by usage'.[36]

A quick exploration was made of the position and they realized that they were occupying an undefended trench system, entirely empty except for the dead. Everywhere there lay the mangled remains of French zouaves and chasseurs mixed together with the bloodied bodies of German assaulting troops. Adjudant Dudot, crawling up to him with a bloody chest and holding out a broken hand, asked Jubert where they were. Jubert replied that he had no idea but believed they were entirely cut off from the regiment and could be scooped up by an enemy force at any moment. Yet, he immediately recognized the importance of the position. Quickly he jotted down a brief note to Moisson: 'I don't know where I am, but the position is of the first importance, and I have only ten men to hold it. I request that two companies be sent up immediately.'[37] Jubert handed it to one of his men who set off back down the hill with instructions to deliver the note to the commander. Jubert then carried out a short reconnaissance with the injured Dudot and one other man. Proceeding 200m down the remains of a communication trench that seemed to have been literally turned upside down by the gunfire, they strained to make out any human sounds among the bullets and shells striking down around them. Suddenly they came upon an entire platoon of heavily armed German grenadiers not 20m away and heading up another trench perpendicular to their own. They held their breath, Dudot with his broken hand and Jubert with an empty revolver. Luckily, the enemy's attention was fixed straight ahead and the tiny party of Frenchmen went unseen. After allowing the enemy platoon to pass on, they beat a quick retreat back to the centre of the position. Once back, Jubert was informed that the runner he had sent out was wounded shortly after departing and had returned unable to deliver the message. So Dudot volunteered to go to deliver the message himself. When Jubert protested, the man insisted he be the one to go since he was effectively out of the fight. The two shook hands and Dudot departed. As Jubert watched him scale the parapet and head down into the ravine, he couldn't help but say aloud to himself, 'There goes another dead man.'

The small band of survivors of 11 Company had advanced over a kilometre and had effectively taken back about 600m of ground. As Jubert's impromptu roll call had confirmed, of the 100 men who had begun the counter-attack only 10 were left. Most had been cut down by enemy machine-gun fire in the final moments of their advance. The rest of the afternoon Jubert continued his reconnaissance of the maze of trenches, sometimes discovering only empty trenches, other times coming upon enemy troops at places where they least expected. All the while, a deadly game of hide-and-seek played out as Jubert and his men dodged the shells that continued to plummet down around them.

Following 11 Company's counter-attack, 10 Company was sent in its turn into the counter-attack, moving up to the left of 11 Company. The 10th deployed into the skirmish line and advanced in the same perfect order as the 11th had. And just as before, it too came under the fire of the same hostile machine gun placed in the old CP of 8 Company, forcing it to halt its advance to the left rear of the 11th. Once night fell, 10 Company would make a final attempt to advance but would be unable to progress further and retired back to the line it had reached along the route of Esne–Cumières road. As the sun set, the German bombardment diminished in intensity. A few final salvoes fell on Chattancourt, one last salvo of shrapnel shells, and then an impressive silence settled over the land. The last rays cast a pale-yellow light on the heaps of mangled corpses that now covered the slopes of Mort Homme. The sky gradually transformed into a bluish-green, then pale green, before fading to violet. Soon there appeared in the sky the moon cast in a fitting blood red. As it continued its ascension, the light changed to yellow and at last to white, as though it had been cleansed of the blood soaking the earth it had risen from. The landscape was illuminated thereafter in a blue ethereal light.

Isolated pockets of poilus held the line, including Jubert's small clutch of survivors. His request for reinforcements had seemingly gone unanswered. Taking advantage of the darkness, he decided he would try to reach the regimental CP himself, struggling down the ravaged, shell-hole strewn landscape, scrambling up and down endless craters. In one large crater, he encountered a group of wounded, among whom was Second Lieutenant Noël. His leg broken, he'd been lying there abandoned since noon. Noël begged Jubert to take him with him. It wrenched his heart to leave his friend but his first duty was to get to the colonel. Jubert pressed on and encountering a group of stretcher-bearers, and directed them to the group of wounded he'd just left behind. When he finally arrived at the colonel's CP, Jubert was greeted like a man returning from the grave and showered with congratulations. Second Lieutenant Courreaux informed him that both General Deville and Lieutenant Colonel Moission had observed his company's counter-attack and were brought to tears by the moving spectacle.

Yet, to Jubert's call for reinforcements, there were none to give. After some further discussion, eventually Jubert was promised that a company would be sent up as soon as one was available. Dejected, Jubert headed back up the hill and on the way passed the stretcher-bearers carrying Second Lieutenant Noël, who'd grown very pale. Without exchanging a word, the two embraced each other. In the heartbreaking silence, his friend's fate was all too obvious. Jubert also recognized Second Lieutenant Mesté, who appeared to be completely dazed and for good reason. Struck in the arm by a shell fragment, he had refused to give up command of his machine-gun platoon. While maintaining his platoon's machine guns in the face of direct enemy contact, he had been projected into the air by a shell blast and thrown violently to the ground. The shell had landed so close by that he'd lost most of his hearing. But this was no time to ponder their losses. Jubert pressed on to the summit where he found his men still nervously holding on to their position, munching on their reserve rations of bread and tinned meat.

The fighting was over on the regiment's front for the time being. Thousands of German dead lay scattered over the slopes, on their parapets, in their trenches, in the shell holes. Campana counted just the number of dead in front of the immediate span of his platoon's front to a depth of 200m and reckoned there to be over 180. On the left, the 1 Battalion had been strongly pressed but still managed to hold the line. At the end of the day, all companies remained in their original positions. From left to right then were 4, 3, and 1 Companies, all holding the first line (Tranchée Guilbert and Perrenet) and the covering trenches. Additionally, two platoons of 2 Company had moved up as reinforcements to the left of 1 Company. The situation on the right was far more serious, where the companies of 2 Battalion had been pounded into dust. The 6 and 8 Companies had been annhiliated. On the left of the line, the remains of 5 and 7 Companies were back in their former position (Tranchée Perrenet), or rather the series of holes that constituted the trench now. The shredded 12 Company held the top of the Boyau de Chattancourt, while on their right the few handfuls of men that made up 10 Company occupied a line of shell holes along summit. A dangerous 150m gap then existed between 10 Company and the remains of 11 Company (now with only eight men left).

Aside from the gap between 10 and 11 Companies, regimental commanders were also keenly aware that a gap of unknown length existed between the right of the 151 and the 8 LIB. Moisson sent one of his staff lieutenants up to investigate and report back what he found. In the meantime, up on the hill Jubert was taking matters into his own hands. Bringing one of his men with him, he summoned the energy and courage to conduct a reconnaissance to his right. As he moved across the shattered terrain, undulating up and down through the endless shell holes, they encountered not a living soul. There were only the bodies of the dead and dying, which he stumbled over continually, his boots kicking into chests, the hobnails treading on legs, arms, and faces. Disembodied moans, cries, and sobs rose up from all around and seemed to merge into one discordant hymn. But pressing on Jubert at last managed to make contact with the battered remains of the 8 LIB. Jubert's reconnaissance presented a frightening revelation: there existed a 600m gap between the 151's right flank and the 8 LIB's left. The situation wasn't much better on the 151's front either. There were gaps between 7 and 10 Companies and between 10 and 11 Companies.

As he learned more about the situation, Moisson immediately ordered 9 Company (the only element of the regiment still held in reserve) to the left of the 11th to help plug the gap. Meanwhile, during the night the first elements of 83 Brigade began to arrive as desperately needed reinforcements. A company of the 94 IR was sent up as reinforcement to the left of the 8 LIB to help close that hole. Later that night, a company of the 162 IR would be rushed up the hill to join the company from the 94th and thus form a modest patchwork defence. Even with the meagre reinforcements, there still remained 150m of ground with no significant force to guard it. The distance was only covered by a scattered line of men placed in shell holes. Measures were also taken to improve the defensive works. It fell to the Territorial Engineers Company 6/3 to complete an important itinerary of work on Mort Homme. The engineers worked hard throughout the night in digging a trench to connect the positions of 7 and 10 Companies and a second one a remarkable 150m in length to reconnect those of the 10 and 11 Companies.

As would be expected, casualty reports were sketchy at best. As the situation stabilized somewhat in the evening, those in charge of the companies and platoons began jotting down their figures. Total casualties as compiled in regimental reports and the *JMO* differ. One report had the losses tentatively at 29 killed, 158 wounded, and 316 missing. The *JMO* recorded 51 killed, 149 wounded, and 229 missing. The divisional record has the total number closer to 500, and when compared to regimental rolls, this number would seem closer to the mark, though still dubiously low given what is known of the losses suffered at company level. The 2 Battalion was practically wiped out. The 3 Battalion had also suffered heavy casualties, especially among 11 and 12 Companies, which had each been reduced to just a squad. Only 1 Battalion was still intact. As is the custom when considering the losses of missing in Great War combat, it can be assumed with a degree of certainty that most of these were in fact dead. There are few reports of

French prisoners being taken and given the nature of the combat at Mort Homme, that is not surprising. The fate of most of the missing was likely that of a horrific demise – blown to atoms or pulverized by the shells, or buried underneath the geysers of earth thrown up by them, or simply struck down and unaccounted for in one of the thousands of craters that punctuated the landscape. Losses among the officer cadre were severe, especially the lieutenants and second lieutenants acting as company and platoon leaders. Second Lieutenants Mattei along with Guilbaud and Maurel were confirmed as killed in action. Among the wounded were Poussière, Depoilly, Bertrand, Langlois d'Estaintot, Noël, Erkens, and Camusat de Riancey, the last mortally. Meanwhile, Cavallier, Chazot, Couplet, Blondet, and Loubere were all missing and presumed dead. Again, this official tally was tentative. Added to the butcher's bill were Buisson and Mesté, who Jubert attested as being wounded. With so many officers incapacitated, this left sergeants and corporals in command of the companies and platoons.

The rest of the night of 9–10 April passed without further infantry attacks and only intermittent shelling. From the enemy's side, a regular display of illumination flares was sent up and shot across the sky in their long parabolic arc. From the French, reconnaissance patrols set off to retrieve any significant documents from the German dead. All along the line, the exhausted battle-worn men of the 151, their ears still ringing from the din of the day, waited vigilantly through the night fully expecting another German attack, but it did not come. Though there were occasional firefights that erupted sporadically here and there along the line, these amounted to nothing significant and quickly died out. In the face of the onslaught, the 151 along with the other units of the 42 ID had managed to hold back the mighty German assault. Their stand inspired General Pétain's Order of the Day:

> April 9th is a glorious day for our arms. The furious assaults of the Crown Prince's soldiers were broken everywhere. Infantrymen, gunners, sappers, aviators of the Second Army competed for heroism. Honor to all! The Germans will likely attack again. Let each man work and watch to achieve the same success as yesterday. Courage, we will have them (*on les aura*)!
> –Signed: PETAIN.

In fact, General Nivelle commanding Second Army would explicitly cite the 11th Company of the 151 IR in the Orders of the Army:

> The 9 April 1916, ascended into the assault in admirable order, the men laughing and singing. Thusly it crossed under an intense fire of machine guns and heavy calibre shells the four hundred metres separating the

departure trench and the trench to be conquered. It was successful in spite of its losses, and remained in-place for thirty-six hours under a furious bombardment.

–Signed: NIVELLE

As day broke over Mort Homme on 10 April, the German artillery again came to life and focused its fire on the unbroken positions of 1 Battalion. The same was true along the old 2 Battalion front, where the shelling and gunfire continued until the evening. Enemy machine guns kept up a harassing enfilade fire over much of the ground on this part of the front as well. Evidence of the continued intensity of activity can be seen in the regiment's consumption rate of munitions, with a report recording nearly 5,000 rounds of ammunition and 1,000 grenades being expended throughout the day. Despite the pounding that the regiment and the other units of the division had taken, adequate reinforcements were lacking and the defenders would have to hold on for several more days before their relief would come. And that meant that more blood would be shed. In the next three days, the regimental *JMO* would record another sixteen dead and forty-two wounded. As the sun went down on 10 April, several forays were made by bands of German grenadiers against 10 Company's position. These were met with a lively fusillade by the vigilant riflemen posted in their shell holes and quickly repulsed. The sector remained fairly calm for the rest of the evening until midnight when the German bombardment started back up more violently than before. In Laporte's mind, the shelling this time was one of 'unequal strength'.

> We were forced to make the most of the smallest shelter or fold of ground in order to stay alive, all the while holding the ground with which we had been entrusted. Not an inch of ground escaped the explosions. And this time we had considerable losses. It seemed the Germans wanted us to pay for their failure and this was their revenge. At 5.00 am, the bombardment was still just as intense. One heavy calibre shell, then two, then three, then by the hundreds. The 1st Platoon placed beside us, with thirty-five men, was completely crushed. I was sheltered with my captain and several poilus in a dugout constructed of interlaced logs and rails, which up till then had held up against the shots, despite some material giving way.
>
> We stood guard in turns behind a small mound of earth to watch the front lines. Around 10.00 am [11 April], it became impossible to remain in this position. We were forced to stay at the entrance of the dugout. How had it resisted so long under a deluge of fire so formidable? Heavy shells exploded right on our shelter, shaking it more and more with each new detonation.

As I said, the ceiling of our shelter was composed of railroad irons (at least five or six layers thick) interlaced with wood beams as big as tree trunks. It was an ex-German command post. The entrance of the shelter began caving in more and more. We continually had to scoop out the earth to keep from being buried alive! And I must admit that as time wore on, we started losing faith and were close to giving up on this convict labour altogether. Our strength left us. We were left completely dazed by this bombardment, which continued with the greatest intensity on both sides. The Hell of gunfire, explosions. The air that we breathed was simply smoke impregnated with the smell of gunpowder, which made us sick and we suffered from violent headaches.

What's more, there was an uninterrupted rumbling above us. Imagine hearing right beside you a dozen heavy freight trains barrelling along with unbridled speed: this was the passing of French heavy shells on their way to reap death across from us. Around noon, still in the middle of the bombardment, a poilu from a regiment on our left in liaison with us [likely the 162 IR] fell in front of our shelter entrance, stricken by an awful wound in the back. The poor man howled in pain, called out for help, but it was impossible for us to give him the least bit of assistance owing to the violence of the explosions. Alas, his suffering was prolonged ... His dulled eyes reflected the approach of death. In the few words that he still muttered, which alternated with vomitings of blood, he called out for his mama. Though accustomed to seeing similar terrible fates, it was heart breaking to watch. None of us could speak ...

We were still excavating and tossing out earth over our unfortunate comrade sprawled out, lifeless, close by. Right at this moment, a heavy calibre shell exploded almost on the entrance of the shelter and we were buried inside. Our comrades at the bottom of the shelter were already yelling at us to search for air. Those of us who were at the entrance, now feeling the approach of death, felt our strength suddenly increase ten fold.

Scraping at the earth with our fingernails, we soon were able to create a hole for air, which allowed us to breathe again, albeit that the air was foul. It was a gas shell that had exploded. Working in shifts, we had to enlarge the hole and excavate the shelter entrance. The survival instinct had won through! Sometime in the evening, the bombardment became less violent and with nightfall, we could finally leave our hole, which had nearly served as our tomb.[38]

When the Laporte's 1 MG Company was finally relieved two days later, Laporte recorded that there were only six men remaining. The fragments of companies from

2 and 3 Battalions (together with the reinforcement elements of the 162 and 94 IRs) were relieved by a battalion of 254 IR (69 ID) during the night of 10–11 April. For the time being, the 2 and 3 MG Companies that accompanied them would have to remain in place as the machine-gun companies of the 254th had still not arrived. Heavy rains had arrived, lashing down in the darkness and quickly turning Mort Homme into a quagmire of thick mud and water filled shell holes. It would not stop raining for another twelve days. The conditions only slowed the movement of the relieving battalion from the 254th. Up on the summit, the men grew more and more anxious as time wore on without their relief showing up. As the hours dragged on, one can only imagine their frustration as they sat shivering in their flooded mud holes, cursing the tardy unit and their rotten luck in low voices. It wasn't until 3.00 am that the relief would get underway. Fearing they would be unable to reach the rear before daylight returned to stop all movement, the exhausted, mud-covered men struggled back down the hill as quickly as they could. As luck would have it, a heavy fog settled in, obscuring their movement and allowing them to at least make it off the summit. But they would be unable to reach their objective of Fort Bois Bourrus and would instead have to spend the day at the Netter shelters to wait for nightfall. Perhaps it was for the best, for one report put it that these poor souls 'were utterly incapable of expending any further effort'. That same night, the remaining elements of 3 Battalion would go into reserve behind 1 Battalion. Less fortunate was Jubert who would have to stay behind for a while longer.

> I was wrapped in my blankets in a deep sleep when there was a hubbub of voices around me, which didn't fully wake me until it was nearly over. I opened my eyes and cleared my head. Deffer was in front of me, fully equipped with helmet on and ready to go. Behind him, the liaison men had their packs on their shoulders.
> 'Is there an alert?' I said.
> 'No, it's the relief.
> 'And no one woke me up!'
> 'You have to stay here, sir, to pass on the orders.'
> 'Just my luck!' I cried. I folded my blanket down over my face but couldn't sleep. To pass the time, I counted the minutes, the seconds, impatiently waiting till six o'clock when the Germans would begin their bombardment.
> We had suffered under it all day the day before, protected by good luck rather than by our shelter, for death slammed down a hundred metres in front and a hundred metres behind the line we were occupying. Following the road to Chattancourt, it had enveloped the Colonel's Ravine [Chattancourt Ravine] with a veil of smoke all day long. But this

time, as soon as the first shell arrived, we realized that the bombardment was moving. The masses of copper and steel were set against us and burst in our midst. The corrugated iron which vibrated above our heads announced at every moment the smack of shrapnel.

I felt more alone than ever. In this place of Hell, far from all human life, the thought came to me that I'd be hit and be left left until death came to take me . . . the misery that took hold of me was unbearable.[39]

In the afternoon Jubert finally departed the first line and made his way back to the Second Position hoping to find his commanders. For some time, he wandered along through deserted trenches, poking his head into the dark shelters that he encountered in his search to find a familiar face. But each time he only found troops belonging to other units. At last, he spotted a man at the entrance of a sap bearing the '151' insignia on his lapels. As he neared, a horrifying sight presented itself: the man was seated at the entrance with his shoulders resting against the dirt, his skull blown apart and his brains tossed beside him. He was still going through his final death spasms, indicating that he'd only just been struck. Jubert took his wrist and felt that the pulse was very weak. Jubert's only comfort was in knowing that he was at least on the right track to finding his unit. A little further on he came upon a bunker in which several officers from the regiment's 2 MG Company were taking shelter. Surprised to see Jubert, they offered him a cup of hot coffee. To pass the time as the shells continued to fall outside, one officer invited him to play draughts. As they did, they traded the little happenings and stories of the day, one of which they took to calling 'Tison's Surprise'. Captain Tison was the commander of 2 Machine-Gun Company. The day before, Tison was standing in his little shelter when he felt something suddenly strike down behind him. Turning around he saw a terrified look on the faces of his men. Lodged in a hole was a 150mm shell, still hot and glowing, that had miraculously failed to detonate. In the roof was a clean hole where the shell had punched through. On the night of 13 April, the remaining units of the 151 were relieved of their positions by two battalions of the 150 IR and were at last free to make their escape from Mort Homme. The going would not be easy.

We left Mort Homme at night but the sky opened up on us . . . Lashed and soaked by rain, for a long while it was slow going across slippery ground and through liquid sticky mud in which we sunk up to our ankles.

It seemed as though, jealous of leaving us alive and not wishing for us to hope we'd escape the ever-expanding mass grave, Mort Homme made one last effort to keep us from getting away. After a ten hour march first through the nocturnal torpor of night, then in a foggy pale morning, and finally under a light rain in the azure blue afternoon

... we had arrived at the place [Blercourt] where we had to board trucks.⁴⁰

On 14 April the men of the 151 were again crammed into trucks at Blercourt and transported to Saudrupt (10km south of Bar-le-Duc), the neighbouring hamlet to Brillon-en-Barrois where 2 Battalion was billeted. During its second rotation, the 151 had lost perhaps around 700 killed or wounded; the real number is likely never to be known. The badly worn regiment would be given five days of rest to recuperate. Campana remarked about this period:

> We were in great need [of it] for the 2nd and 3rd Battalions are entirely decimated. In fact, all the regiments of the division had submitted heavy losses, but we could take pride in the having held our ground entrusted to us, having carried out our duty to the utmost.
> ...
> We're now billeted in a wonderful village to the southwest of Bar-le-Duc. It is nestled in an island of greenery, a clear stream as our bath, wooded undulations encircling it with a curtain of foliage. All exercises have been temporarily suspended in order to give the men time to recover from the difficult endeavours that they had endured. It's a splendid peace, and in the freshness of shaded forests, daydreaming as I lay on beds of moss and turf, I forget the hellish days that I've lived through.⁴¹

The restorative powers of nature on the poilus, most of whom maintained a strong connection to the land, could not be underestimated. The first days were spent cleaning off the layers of mud plastered to their skin, uniforms, equipment, and weapons. But Campana feared the effect that consecutive days of idleness off-duty would have on his men. At first there was only a numb shock, a stupor that had flooded over their minds. But soon after a debilitating depression had overcome many. Some spent all day getting drunk at the wine shops in the village, while others took advantage of nearby train stations to go AWOL for several days. One of those was a 20-year-old soldier in Campana's company who had left his billets without permission when they arrived in Brillon and had gone missing for four days. On the fourth day, the young man returned accompanied by his mother, who attempted to explain to Campana the reason for her son's apparent desertion. The mother explained that their home town was located in a region that had been invaded by the Germans in August 1914 and occupied ever since. Her son had fled to his aunt's house in Rodez, where he waited for his class to be called up. He had dutifully reported and served for twelve months, but during all of that time, he had not seen nor heard from his family. He was completely cut off from those he loved. After the brutal trials endured at Verdun, with the regiment's arrival at Brillon, the soldier took a train from Bar-le-Duc all the way south to Rodez to go see his mother. But once he confessed to her that he had not received permission to go, she insisted they return together to beg pardon. Normally desertion from the army automatically meant facing a war council. Yet, Campana was sympathetic to the young man's story and assured them both he would argue in favour of leniency.

Beginning on 21 April, the regiment resumed a regimen of physical exercises and instruction in the latest combined arms fire and movement tactics, including specialist training in the use of hand and rifle grenades, the automatic rifle, 37mm cannon, trench mortars, and signalling. In part for his exemplary conduct leading his platoon at Mort Homme, Campana would be given the post of battalion grenadier officer. In this role, he would have under his command 4 sergeants, 16 corporals and 128 men. While these days and evenings were employed in rigorous training, replacements for the losses suffered at Verdun began arriving to the regiment, including several hundred new recruits of the class of 1916.

With so many gaps in the officer cadre, a number of promotions were made among the lieutenants and second lieutenants. Campana, who'd previously been brevetted to the position on Christmas Day 1915, was definitively promoted to second lieutenant along with over a dozen of his compatriots. Several more were promoted to captain, while a half dozen others were transferred into the 151 from other regiments. This included two new battalion leaders as well – Commandant Simon Chamousset (transferred from the 16 IR) who took command of 2 Battalion and Commandant Malochet (transferred from the 15 IR) who took command of 3 Battalion. Accompanying the arrival of new junior officers were successive detachments of reinforcements to fill the ravaged ranks of the enlisted men. Over a 10-day period, 6 adjudants, 35 sergeants, 58 corporals, and over 830 privates flocked in. Out of these replacements, only 250 had originated from the regions where the regiment traditionally drew recruits, subsequently passing through the 151 relocated depot at Quimper. The rest came from a multitude of regiments and by extension a multitude of regions, from Brittany in the northwest to Tours and the Central Loire Valley, to Montpellier and Alpes-Maritimes in the southwest. After the murderous fighting in the Argonne in the summer of 1915, the 151 saw its first significant influx of replacements from areas outside of the peace-time recruiting grounds. Now another levee of troops arrived to fill the empty ranks of the regiment. Campana spoke about this period of rebuilding:

> There weren't many of my old poilus from October [1915] left. Sickness and bullets had taken almost all of them. We've received new reinforcements recruited from all the depots of the army . . . and my platoon is entirely reformed. I see only new faces around me, many are

the new young recruits of the Class of '16 along with some recuperated wounded . . .[42]

Though the original local identities embodied in the 151 were increasingly replaced with those of other localities, it was concurrently becoming more reflective of France as a whole. And together with the survivors of Flanders, the Argonne, Champagne, and Verdun, the history and fighting traditions of the regiment were kept alive. Indeed, for its heroic actions on 9 April, the 151 had rightfully earned its second battle honour of the war, giving it the privilege of inscribing 'Verdun' on its regimental colours. For Citation in the Orders of the Army, the 11 Company was awarded the Croix de Guerre and its company fanion decorated with the fourragère, the traditional braided cord attached to the staff. There were also a number of individuals who received citations for their conduct in the fighting at Mort Homme. The commander of 2 Battalion, Captain Le Boulanger, was awarded one of the highest honours in being promoted to the Chevalier de Légion d'honneur. Joining his commander in distinction was Sergeant L'Huillier, whose tireless efforts in reporting to Le Boulanger won him the Médaille Militaire. Another reward awaited L'Huillier as well. For the first time since the start of hostilities, regimental commanders were invited to appoint two soldiers (privates, corporals, or sergeants) who were decorated and possessed honourable qualities to be sent to complete the Saint-Cyr *elèves-aspirants* ('officer-candidates') training course. The course would be held at the military academy outside of Versailles from May to September 1916. To his great surprise, L'Huillier was one of the two Lieutenant Colonel Moisson had recommended. He would join the promotion class of Verdun, returning to the regiment as an aspirant.

For his resourcefulness and temerity on 295, Second Lieutenant Campana was awarded the Croix de Guerre. On the sunny morning of 2 May, the regiment held a *prise d'armes* attended by General Deville himself. Formed in a large square in a vast huge meadow, the blue of the men's greatcoats seemed to match the bright blue expanse of the sky. Like amputated limbs, two dreadful gaps were left in 2 Battalion's line to mark the places of the annihilated 7 and 8 Companies. Galloping at the head of his staff, Deville passed before the arrayed troops and headed to the centre of the square, where those who were to be decorated were standing at attention. Bringing his sword up before his face in salute, he briskly dismounted and approached the recipients. Campana could barely contain his emotion as general pinned the Croix de Guerre to his chest and shook his hand. It would remain for him as the most beautiful day of his life. When the ceremony concluded, his eyes fell irresistibly down to the red and green ribbon suspended from his chest.

The decoration symbolized more than the young lieutenant's personal bravery. The Croix de Guerre also came to affirm Campana's zealous conviction in the war and the ruthlessness with which he prosecuted it. Evidence of this was reflected in a conversation Campana held with a long dark-bearded corporal who'd arrived with one of the newest batch of replacements. The man, with the appropriate surname of Dubondieu, had been a missionary in the Congo before the war and, upon arrival with the 151, was put in command charge of the 1 Company stretcher-bearers. Learning of what had transpired at Mort Homme, the holy man related to Campana his experiences of living in a part of the world where cannibalism and the slaughter of prisoners taken from other tribes was common. Anger, vengeance, and lack of faith had led to horrible acts, Dubondieu recounted to Campana:

> 'And so I'm told that on April 9th, on Mort Homme, a certain lieutenant I know gave the order to take no prisoners, even though about forty German soldiers were ready to surrender.
>
> 'Thanks for casting stones, but on October 6th [1915] the enemy acted even worse and I swore to avenge the victims of their barbarism. For a Corsican, such an oath of vendetta is a sacred thing.
>
> 'But these men you killed, or had killed, had nothing to do with those from October 6th.
>
> 'They wore the same uniform, they share the same blood, consequently they were responsible for the crimes committed by their comrades, and under the same circumstances they would have surely acted in the same way. And even if I had ordered my men not to shoot, they would've been too overexcited to obey me.
>
> 'I would have obeyed you, out of pity's sake.
>
> 'In combat you don't think about pity, only about how to do right by the country. That alone counts and takes all other consideration. And to your criticisms, I'll respond simply with these three words: That is war. And we must win and win at any price! . . . We can't understand each other on these grounds, for you are a machine of prayer and I am a machine of killing . . .'[43]

Verdun was changing the men of the 151. For his actions at Mort Homme, Second Lieutenant Jubert would receive his second citation, this time in the Orders of the XXXII Army Corps (dated 19 May 1916), which read in part:

> On 9 April 1916, went into the counter-attack against trenches taken by the enemy with leadership and an absolute disregard of danger. The only officer left in his company, taking command and holding his position for thirty-six hours.
> –Signed: BERTHELOT

Jubert would continue to distinguish himself in battle, receiving further citations and medals for his conduct under fire. But something had clearly begun to change inside the sensitive young man. A sort of moral torpor had seeped into his warrior's heart. In part, he captured this internal shift in an ironic catechism he put down in his memoirs:

> 'What sublime feeling took hold of you as you went into the attack?
> –'I was thinking only of pulling my feet out of the mud they were stuck in.
> 'What heroic cry did you utter when you had recaptured the crest?
> –'I echoed the words of Cambronne.
> 'What feeling of power did you have when you had defeated the enemy?
> –'I grumbled because the soup wouldn't get to us and I'd spend several more days without any *pinard*.
> 'Was your first act to give thanks to God?
> –'No, I went off alone and relieved myself.'[44]

The statement is even more striking in its obvious cynicism towards his previous notions of honour, duty, even righteousness, all of which were defining motivations for Jubert before the war. Jubert had discovered that the war could also possess a sort of banality to its horror. In a tragic accident that occurred on 3 May, Commandant Simon Joseph Chamousset was killed in a live grenade training exercise along with several other soldiers. Though Chamousset had only just arrived to two weeks before, he had quickly made a great impression on those who met him. Campana spoke of the highly decorated commander, who would receive full military honours when buried, with great esteem. So too did Jubert, who witnessed the bloody aftermath first-hand: 'I went to the firing range where Commandant [Chamousset] was lying dead, his mouth agape, eyes rolled back, guts ripped out . . . I felt then how death is cruel in its games. It would seem more humane if it only killed in combat. This man, with his numerous past glories and magnificent past achievements, fell victim of a blunder.'[45]

Two weeks had passed at Saudrupt and Brillon when dispiriting rumours quickly spread that they would be returning to the front soon. The rumours proved all too true when on 4 May the regiment was put on alert – it was being sent back into the Furnace the next day, back to Mort Homme.

Chapter 9

The Infernal Machine

Third Rotation at Verdun (5–24 May)

The 151 IR had been severely tested during their nine days on Mort Homme in April. Up until then, it was the most extreme fire the regiment had endured after nearly two years of war. Indeed, this sector had cemented its reputation as being one of the most violent sectors of the war. Those who had managed to escape with their lives the first time had no illusions of the life that awaited them at Mort Homme. What deep sense of dread those two words must have conjured in the hearts of those men who, having somehow survived the hellish hill once, were told that they must return to it. Even among the many new arrivals who had yet to experience the fighting at Verdun, the infamous hill had earned a reputation. Some 930 replacement troops had come into the ranks since mid-April (bringing the total number of effectives to 57 officers and 2,793 men).

One of those going up to the front for the first time was Private Charles 'Auguste' Bordinat, class of 1904. Bordinat was fortunate to have been spared from the trenches until now, having passed the first two years of the war mainly in the territorials, assisting farmers with their farming and harvesting near Bar-le-Duc and then being detailed to work at a mill in Dijon. In the back of his mind, perhaps he continued to hold on to the dangerous hope that he would make it back to his wife safe and sound. But in March 1916 he received his inoculations for typhoid in preparation of being sent up to the front line. Weeks passed while he awaited his sentencing. Finally, on 5 May, he was assigned to the 151 as a replacement together with fifteen others from the depot. He took a train to Bar-le-Duc, where he arrived before dawn on 8 May. Bordinat had two brothers currently stationed in Bar. His oldest brother, Paulin, was at the airfield at Behonne just outside of town. But Albert was at Exelmans Barracks (the garrison of the 94 and 294 IRs), not far from the train station. Taking advantage of the stopover, he ran over to Exelmans to see Albert.

> I surprised my brother around 5.00 am and got a little food. He waited till the last minute to leave and again I took the Meusien [small gauge railroad] I knew so well in the direction of Verdun. Alas, it was with a heavy heart that I listened to sound of the terrible cannonade off in the distance. In a few hours, it would be my turn to face them.[1]

Disembarking at the terminus of the Meusien at Lemmes – to go any further put one in range of German long-range artillery fire – Bordinat and his companions were told to proceed on foot to Jouy-en-Argonne. There he would be assigned to 6 Company now commanded by the mathematician-officer, the recently promoted Captain Olivier. 'All the same, I don't lose heart, since fate will decide, as it does for all those who have not yet done service in the field. To listen to my comrades, I wonder by what miracle one can come back alive. But there was nothing to be done for it, I'd have the time to judge for myself.'[2]

On the same morning that Bordinat had received his assignment to the 151, the regiment was making its way back to Mort Homme to relieve units of the sorely tested 40 ID. At Brillon, the 1 and 2 Battalions were loaded onto trucks and driven back up to Blercourt. From there they proceeded to the Bois des Clairs Chênes (northwest of Blercourt) and waited for darkness to make the final approach march. The 3 Battalion (together with the HQ Company Territorial Engineers Co. 6/3) boarded a troop train at Baudouviliers in the afternoon. Disembarking at Baleycourt, they then marched to the Bois des Clairs Chênes and rejoined the rest of the regiment. After the evening soup, 1 and 2 Battalions resumed their march. As they entered the battle zone, it seemed as though a curtain had risen to reveal a scene which had not ceased unfolding ever since the 151 had gotten its short reprieve. Persistent French counter-attacks following the 151's relief had retaken the entire summit of 295 by 14 April, reversing all enemy gains from the 9 April attack. For the next twelve days, it rained without let up and with the battlefield turned into an almost impassable swamp, operations on the hill were temporarily suspended. A new attempt by the Germans to take Côte 304 was slated for the beginning of May, to be preceded by a barrage similar to the one on 9 April. This time, however, the fire would be more concentrated over a smaller portion of ground. On 3 May, the bombardment by over 500 heavy calibre German cannon opened up along a 1,500m front – one gun for every 3m of ground. For two days and a night, the shelling continued uninterrupted. French pilots flying over the battlefield reported columns of smoke rising to an altitude of 760m (2,500ft).[3]

The infantry assault was sent forward on 5 May, just as the 151 was marching back up to the neighbouring Mort Homme. On the heights beyond, it looked as though the earth was being ripped apart and the fires of hell erupting to the surface. The French first lines on 304 had already been flattened and overrun with German forces now pushing down the southern slopes as a mismash force of French reinforcements were rushing up to meet them and plug the gaps in the line. At the same time on Mort Homme, a murderous see-saw fight over the ground between Côtes 265 and 295 was taking place, leaving hundreds of dead in its wake. The first German effort on 30 April to recapture the summit of 286.4 that had been lost two weeks before was unsuccessful. Over the next several days, the French counter-attacked repeatedly, most recently on 3 May when units of the 69 ID attacked with their own flamethrower units in the lead this time. The French assault waves rapidly swept over the western slopes of Mort Homme, reclaiming most of their former positions. A German counter-attack the next day was thrown back with heavy losses, but the firing had not ceased since. As the 1 and 2 Battalions got within a few kilometres of the devastated slopes of Mort Homme, the roar of rifle and machine-gun fire could be heard – like water passing over a giant falls – under the oppressive thundering of the cannonade and bombardment. Not to be outdone by the storm unleashed by man, Mother Nature let loose a gale with gusting winds and a battering rain that made the night darker still.

Since the 151 had last occupied Mort Homme, the trench networks had morphed and expanded on both sides of the line. French forces had recaptured their old first line, including portions of the Trapèze, the Guitoune, Tranchée Lassalle, and Tranchée Garçon. In places the lines were less than 50m apart or even nearer still. The trenches themselves had multiplied, with new lines being dug and existing lines extended so that the positions were more interconnected. The reserve line known as the Second Position had especially been strengthened and was now a formidable position all of its own. These enhancements would prove critical in the days ahead. But all of these positions were constantly under fire and degraded. The best trenches were less than 6ft in depth. Most were shallower still, only 4½ to 5½ft deep. In such conditions, the 2 Battalion relieved elements of the 150 IR and again took up the eastern side of Côte 295, on the same ground where so many had met their end in April. Three companies (from left to right: 5, 7, and 8) took up the first line and covering trenches.[4] The 6 Company was in support in Tranchée de Foix. The 1 Battalion went into reserve with two companies occupying the *Place d'Armes* and the other two in the Ouvrages Laborderie and Mollandin in the Second Position. For the time being, the 3 Battalion, regimental staff, and HQ Company remained bivouacked just outside of Jouy-en-Argonne (10km to the southwest).

Campana had not been back on Mort Homme long when he was struck by a grenade fragment in the chest, a clear indication of how close the opposing lines were to each other. Though it appeared not to have penetrated his clothing, the iron shard caused significant bruising, and made breathing difficult. As was his habit, Campana refused to be evacuated, failing to appreciate the severity of his injury. In actuality, a small piece of metal had lodged itself into the top of his lung. But there was no rest for the weary. After an exhausting relief march, his platoon was detailed to transport supplies from the depots to the front lines. Throughout the long night, they carried ungainly logs, ponderous spools of barbed wire, hazardous crates of grenades, and swollen sacks of ammunition. Twice Campana nearly passed out from the excruciating pain in his chest, which was only exacerbated by his habitual stomach pains. But he pushed himself hard and saw the job done before allowing himself to crash in his shelter. Despite his fatigue and the overwhelming need for sleep, he was kept awake by the torturous pain in his belly. Soon, he began coughing up blood. Yet again, the stubborn Campana refused to abandon his post, instead sending one of his men to request a vial of opium from the doctor to relieve his discomfort.

The next day the companies of the 1 and 2 Battalions worked hard to deepen the existing trenches and *boyaux*. In concise terms, the *JMO* simply notes that the German artillery remained highly active. But what does this brief note truly signify? Campana helps provide a window. At noon on 6 May he could see that the bombardment was intensifying in volume and accuracy, with shells not only falling around his trench but actually in it. Weakened from his injury and unable to stand on his own, he was obliged to lean on one of his men to exit his shelter. Just as he did, a 210 shell landed in the neighbouring *boyau*. The force of the blast collapsed the parapets, propelled skywards whole cubic metres of earth into a geyser of dirt and rocks, shattered rifles and equipment, and killed or wounded a dozen men. One of the victims was standing close to Campana when he was hit by a shell fragment as big as a bottle. Crumpling to the ground with a soul-tearing wail, the victim's belly had been torn open by the large hunk of metal. Rushing up, Campana could see that his abdomen had been split open from navel to pelvis while his intestines lay strewn upon the ground about him.

> 'Oh, lieutenant, don't let me suffer like this, it's unbearable! Put a bullet from your revolver in my head. I can't stand it any longer. You know I'm screwed, why let me suffer for no reason . . . Or if you're afraid to, give me your weapon and I'll do it myself!'
>
> I looked at his gasping body and gory entrails and saw it was all torn to shreds. He had no hope of recovering.
>
> 'Well what are you waiting for . . . my friends you're as scared as the lieutenant to kill me off. Take pity on me . . . kill me with a rifle shot damn it . . . Why don't you do something? Bunch of cows . . . bastards . . . you're as much as a bastard as the officer!'
>
> I exchange a look with my men. They were quiet, but I saw in their eyes that they understood what I was thinking and agreed with me. With a heavy heart, I drew my revolver:
>
> 'Finally,' the wounded man groaned, then closed his eyes. I placed the revolver against his ear . . . Suddenly a hand grabbed my wrist, pushing the weapon away and causing it to drop, as a low voice murmured in my ear:
>
> 'Lieutenant, you don't have the right to play God.' I turned and recognized the missionary.

'I don't have the right to let this soldier suffer needlessly.' . . . The wounded man opened his eyes again:

'What are you going on about, you dirty crow!

'Try to put his innards back in his body and bring a stretcher,' I tell Corporal Dubondieu. 'Then bring him back with one of your men to the first-aid post. Try to avoid as much as possible jolting him and then come back quickly since I think I'll need you again before too long. At least I have morphine on me!'

'You'll kill us all,' [cried the man] 'goddamned lieutenant . . . goddamned priest . . .'[5]

Incredibly, the soldier would remain alive for at least a few days more, thus sparing Campana from the guilt of having to kill one of his own men. But the effect was devastating on the morale and Campana's moral turmoil smouldered in his heart. There was little time to contemplate his actions. The air was literally filled with flying cleavers of steel and iron. Another 210 slammed down, shaking the ground and killing a corporal standing beside him. Moments later, a 105 hit close by and glancing over, Campana could see his orderly hurriedly digging away some earth, ignoring the blood streaming down his own face. The shell had caused the parapet to collapse on top of someone. No sooner had they cleared the earth away from the unconscious victim than another shell fell on a small shelter where two others were taking refuge from the storm. One escaped with only a few scratches but the second had both his legs broken. Right after this, another shell fragment buzzed in and tore the arm off a stretcher-bearer. This is what is meant when the *JMO* states 'German artillery remains highly active.'

There was nothing for the men to do but hold on once more, to retreat inside themselves, to endure. And to dig, to dig because their lives depended on it. The shelling went on unabated in an unbroken line stretching 6km, from Côte 304 to Mort Homme to Cumières. By the morning of 7 May, another eight men in Campana's platoon had been killed or wounded. A fusillade of small arms fire crackled above the fracas, while to his right he could see thick, ominous black smoke slowly rising up from the French positions, indicating that the Germans were hitting them with flamethrowers again. Captain Carrère instructed the men to be ready to counter-attack to assist 2 Company if the need arose. Just then, two men, Corporal Ducoeurjolly and Private Verluys, ran up in an absolute panic, saying that another shell had landed squarely in the trench a short distance away. They knew they would be next, that they were done for. He did his best to calm the men down, telling them they could stay by his side if it made them feel more at ease. The fusillade in the ravine to his right erupted again as German troops, having taken a portion of the French first line, now moved towards the second line. Campana set off down the trench to find his liaison agent when suddenly – obliteration! There was a brief sensation as though his head and body had physically exploded, then everything went dark. As he regained consciousness, he opened his eyes to see his men surrounding him. His eyelids felt heavy as he gradually regained his bearings and observed that his greatcoat had been unbuttoned and was saturated with a dark slurry of blood-soaked dirt.

> 'Am I wounded,' I asked weakly.
> 'I don't think so, lieutenant,' my orderly said to me. 'After we unburied you, we looked you over and couldn't find any wound. It must be their blood . . .'
> I turned and made out a ghastly sight. At my feet lay two bodies viciously mutilated. One was missing the head, with the backbone and shoulder blade projecting out of the bloody flesh. The other was split open from shoulders to hips like quartered meat at the butcher's stall. The skull was split apart and the right eye torn out, and from the gaping eye socket, a thin trickle of dark blood flowed.[6]

The victims were Corporal Ducoeurjolly and Private Corluys, who had fled to their lieutenant's side for protection seconds before. In that moment, Campana took out his vest-pocket camera and macabrely photographed the mangled bodies as a record of his close call with death. It could just as easily have been his body broken and torn lying in the bottom of the trench. It was certainly a morbid impulse, though he wasn't alone in feeling compelled to capture such a grisly memento mori. On the fateful day of 9 April, Lieutenant Boissin in command of 2 Company photographed the body of one of his men who'd been cut in half by a large shell fragment. He later wrote on the verso: 'Souvenir of 9 April 1916 – Mort Homme / Killed during the counter-attack by a heavy shell: Darras – Cyclist, Lebarqy, Troushill, Delattre / To the Memory of my brave liaison agents.'

In the end, Campana concluded it had been a 210 shell that had exploded behind him, with the blast and avalanche of falling debris burying him and badly contusing his body. Only later would he be told that the pressure from the crushing earth burst his thorax muscles and caused a tear in the linea alba. In the evening fever and nausea overtook him and the pain from his combined injuries became unbearable. In the early morning hours of 8 May, Captain Carrère ordered Campana to report to the first-aid post on the outskirts of Chattancourt. So began Campana's personal Stations of the Cross. The 1½km journey back down the *boyaux* to the first-aid post was excruciating. Once he eventually arrived and was examined, he was told his injuries required an immediate evacuation to Jouy-en-Argonne. However, because of the overwhelming numbers of wounded, there weren't enough vehicles to transport all the injured there. And so he would have to walk the 3km to the ambulance at Marre, along with any others who could manage to walk. Along the shell-pocked road, he passed scenes of destruction – trucks wrecked and tossed over by shell-fire, and the bloated carcasses of horses, the putrefying bodies of which filled the air with an overwhelming stench. Late in the afternoon, Campana finally reached the ambulance – a large open room, poorly lit and covered in filth. The place was packed with about fifty seriously wounded men, all of them hurriedly bandaged and now waiting impatiently for their turn to be evacuated. A chorus of cries of pain and wails of agony filled the space. And just as soon as one body was removed, another injured victim would be immediately brought in to fill the spot. Sleepless, hungry, dehydrated, wracked with pain, Campana believed he had been dropped into a pit of hell.

Hours passed in this tiny world of suffering, madness, and death. When at last a doctor had a chance to inspect Campana, he was told that the ambulance trucks would not go past Fromeréville and that he would have to cover the last 6km to Jouy on foot. In the early morning hours of 9 May, Campana was loaded into the back of a truck and transported to Fromeréville, where he then began a seemingly endless journey to Jouy. With each step he took it felt as though his chest was collapsing in on itself, as a sharp cutting pain produced a sensation like his intestines were being ripped apart inside of him. From time to time, his thoughts turned to a dark place. Maybe he should just kill himself and finally end this unbearable martyrdom. But ultimately he knew this would be a cowardly act, so he kept on pushing himself. Every step taken was a small battle of its own, a fight as hard as any he had made on the battlefield. Campana's luck improved when a passing artillery battery let him ride atop one of the caissons for the rest of the way to Jouy. While being treated at the ambulance, Lieutenant Colonel Moisson came to see him. Kneeling by his side, Papa Victory tried to offer some comforting words, informing him that he would be evacuated to the interior. The news crushed Campana with the force of a 210 shell. Despite all of the trials and tribulations endured, he didn't wish to be sent away from the front, away from his men. Moisson reassured him that there was still plenty of fighting to do, in which Campana would play a part once he'd fully recovered. But this was not to be. After six months of convalescing in a hospital at Lyon, he was sent to the depot at Quimper and underwent physical inspection. His injuries had left him unfit for active service. Campana's war was over.

While Campana was busy in his struggle to reach the various medical posts, the bombardment on Mort Homme had continued unabated. The men were put to work improving their positions, mainly deepening trenches and, at night, setting up barbed wire entanglements across the regiment's front. A thin trickle of replacements would arrive from various depots, a meagre 135 who were sorely needed. By 10 May, German artillery began stepping up its fire, first in precision and then in intensity. Disturbingly accurate heavy calibre shells landed on the regiment's positions, reminiscent of the fire on 9 April, which completely flattened portions of the first and second-line trenches and rendering them practically untenable. Two days later the bombardment doubled in intensity, obliterating whole stretches of trench. French artillery responded in kind with 155mm howitzers, 270s, 280s, and 58mm trench mortars firing their large winged bombs down onto the German first lines. On the night of 12 May, 3 Battalion (which had been in reserve at Jouy-en-Argonne) relieved 2 Battalion in the first line, with 9, 11, and 12 Companies in line and 10 Company in support. The 2 MG Company remained behind in the first line as 2 Battalion rotated back to the supporting trench lines and the Second Position to relieve 1 Battalion, the latter marching back to Jouy-en-Argonne in ready reserve. Joining 2 Battalion was Territorial Engineers Company 6/3, which took up the trenches between Ouvrages Laborderie and Mollandin. With 3 Battalion's return to the trenches, Jubert was now back on Mort Homme to the east of Côte 295.

> Are beetles fond of corpses? In the first lines at Mort Homme, after the relief march I spent all night surrounded by their constant buzzing and whirling. We took up the trenches at midnight in an inky black night that seemed to swallow up the relief. Where were we? I couldn't say. The night kept us from investigating further. Even the flares only let out a weak sort of light, a pale halo drowned out in the distance. We only had our groping hands to fill us in on what we could not see and were unaware of.
>
> In his haste, my predecessor could only bother himself with a single terse word to indicate where the enemy was: 'There!' I tried questioning him in vain. I'd hardly thrown out my first question when he'd already made off into the night. He was gone, leaving me to my own devices to figure things out.
>
> With my men in place at randomly chosen spots, passwords exchanged, and recommendations made, I was left alone, separated from the last elements of my platoon by a traverse. No niche to shelter in, no firing-step to sit on, tired of war, and with a nervous mind from being in an unknown sector. I remained awake, standing up with my back resting against the parapet, blanket tied about my knees, feet sunken into the mud of Mort Homme.
>
> Men called out to me as they passed. They themselves were lost and only got annoyed with me when I couldn't give them directions. Others in groups, brushed up against me or outright crashed into me. They were carrying heavy loads, which swept past my face. The suffocating smell emitted as they passed by and which will impregnate my clothes for eight days, reveals they're carrying corpses.[7]

As the sky lightened the next morning, Jubert was able to gain a better understanding of their new sub-sector. The rest of 11 Company had taken up the line closest to the enemy (Tranchée Garçon) several dozen metres to his front. His own platoon had been assigned to the covering trench (Tranchée des Zouaves), which was at the top of the reverse slope and thus seemingly out of the line of direct fire. This false sense of security led Jubert to make a careless mistake that nearly cost him his life.

> At dawn, I stick my head above the parapet. Appearing in the sad grey of the morning and now from a new perspective is the vast battlefield that I've come to know well. We are twenty metres below the main summit of Mort Homme. To the east of here, roughly two kilometres away, I could make out German positions, which lead to the Bois des Corbeaux. On our side, and facing them up to the Bois des Caurettes, are our gains from 9 April.
>
> . . .
>
> What an appearance this battlefield has! For two months it had not stopped. Is the trench we're in not one of the most disputed? Ten times, perhaps twenty times, it had changed hands. And across this vast field of death gouged full of craters like a lunar landscape, everywhere you look, bodies of the enemy dead stick out of the ground.
>
> A helmet glinted thirty paces away from me, one belonging to an officer I surmised. I jumped up to go retrieve it. Just at that moment, a machine gun opened up. By the dozens, the bullets smacked down around me with the crack of a whip. I threw myself down, right on top of a corpse. I rested against it at the bottom of a crater, a singular neighbour under hovering death. An elastic-like chest stuck out of the ground, which my stretched out hand pressed upon. The jet-black mass let off a vile stench and I was overcome with utter disgust.
>
> The obscene ugliness of it all was revolting. There's no stronger human feeling than that of disgust. Helmet under my arm, I lept up and making my way from mud hole to mud hole, gradually building up my speed. I bent down under the bullets with uncertain footing, stumbling over the corpses. I could see the trench – two more paces – then I'm safe.[8]

Jubert and his comrades were all in agreement: it was another *mal coin*. Their position had changed hands more times than could be counted, occasionally in savage hand-to-hand combat where men slayed each other with bayonets, knives, shovels, fists, and feet. Machine-gun fire and heavy shelling was a constant threat. Mort Homme had become one huge charnel house, an open mass grave. Scattered about and jutting out of the earth all around were arms, legs, feet, hands, heads, limbless torsos, entrails, brains, and bile. Bodies that had been buried were disinterred by shells, then reburied by others, halved, and then quartered. The trenches were in constant need of repair from this shelling but as the men set about digging, they often found their positions to be made up more of flesh and bone than earth and stone. The dead had been embedded into the entrenchments and as they worked, a shovel or pick buried into the ground would often strike human decay in various states of rot. The prevailing sensation was that they weren't shovelling soil as much as they were meat. But the need to dig only grew by the day with the increase in artillery fire. Beginning on 14 May the bombardment increased in scale across all of Mort Homme and the neighbouring heights. Jubert and his comrades amused themselves by lighting matches and watching the flames be extinguished with regularity each time a large calibre shell detonated nearby with an ear-shattering thunderclap and reverberating shockwave. In their first day back in line, Jubert's company already had fourteen men killed or wounded. But with the opposing first-line trenches so near to each other, it was once again the second-line trenches that were targeted by the largest shells. And it was there that the losses had been the heaviest. By 15 May, after ten days of being on the line, the 151 had lost 70 killed and 140 more wounded – an average of over 20 a day. By 18 May the total number of casualties had climbed to over 270. A perceivable change in enemy activity now began to be observed.

> Since the first evening we'd arrived, we'd carried out reconnaissance missions every night. We crossed over the summit and got into an abandoned trench that was completely filled with dead bodies. Returning two days later, Vandevoorde made out a living form five paces away. He hesitated for a moment just as a gunshot rang out right in front of him. [Second Lieutenant] Erkens went over next and saw that the enemy had cleared away the bodies. Lanckmans and I decided to try to take a look. No sooner had our silhouettes been cast against the sky as we crested the summit than two machine guns opened up a crossfire on us. We took cover in a crater until dawn and spotted a working party. In Erkens' opinion it was apparent that the enemy had cleared out the old positions in preparation of making it into a departure trench.
>
> . . .
>
> Our advanced posts and trenches were too close to the enemy. A shell lands twenty metres behind our lines and green flares by the dozens shoot up immediately from the enemy's, requesting the range be lengthened. This added to our conviction that the enemy was getting ready to make a push. Barricade us in before an attack on our front. They had sealed the approach routes with a curtain of steel. We were in the mousetrap. They felt so masterly that they'd neglected to strike us. They'd broken the branch to pick the fruit. We would be in their hands whenever they wished to come over.[9]

For the first two weeks on the line, the shelling had not yet achieved the cataclysmic fire seen on the 9 April. Until now it had come in storms, flaring up for hours and then abating into periods of light shelling, like the action of a battering ram, slamming hard and then easing back before the next blow. Still, it required being constantly on alert, bringing about a continual nervous strain. This began to change on 18 May as the shelling became continuous both day and night. It was a bad sign.

> We secured our interior lines by doubling the watch. Our reconnaissance only served to prove to us that we still had a day or two of respite. Our artillery now hit the works that constituted a threat. We felt the blow coming when our relief was announced. It was 18 May. This was the last time I would see several of my friends. We'd shook hands . . . I left with heavy heart. The danger held two-thirds of the regiment in a circle of steel. Closing in on them, it would be in less than two days' time that my friends would be crushed.[10]

On the night of 18–19 May, the 151 conducted another internal relief. The 1 Battalion, which had been rotated down to Jouy-en-Argonne, made the climb back up to Mort Homme to relieve 3 Battalion in the first line, the latter going back to support in the *Place d'Armes* and the Second Position. When the relief was complete, the 1 Battalion was arrayed from left to right with 4, 3, 2, and 1 Companies on line along with the 1 MG Company.[11] Two platoons of 10 Company moved back to Tranchée de Foix. The other two platoons of 10 Company were placed in reserve of a battalion of the 162 IR occupying the Netter shelters on the western end of Line 1A. The 11 and 12 Companies were occupying the *Place d'Armes* for the time being, while 9 Company was in the Second Position holding Ouvrage Laborderie, in liaison with the Territorial Engineers Company 6/3. The 1 MG Company in the first line was supplemented by a platoon of 2 MG Company. The remainder of this company was holding the Second Position, where the 2 Battalion had just been relieved.

While Private Bordinat had arrived at Jouy-en-Argonne on 8 May, his assigned company (6th) had been up on the line with the rest of 2 Battalion until now being rotated back to Jouy, accompanied by the 3 MG Company. He would now have some time to get to know his new comrades, or so he thought. For events were rapidly unfolding at Mort Homme that would forever shape Bordinat's life and those of thousands of others. The 151's relief had only just been completed around 4.00 am when the German artillery commenced a new harassing fire on the regiment's positions. There was a marked change in the nature of the bombardment now. The shelling, regulated by a number of German observation aircraft, seemed to be both highly responsive and deliberate, moving progressively from target to target. It was a methodical destruction fire, a tactic typically employed before an infantry attack.

Beginning around noon and lasting into the evening, the bombardment steadily increased in intensity, with the enemy fire consisting exclusively of heavy calibre shells that struck with remarkable precision. What's more, the French first line, until now largely spared, was targeted by showers of rifle grenades joined by devastating heavy *minens*. In his new shelter in the *Place d'Armes*, Jubert had just managed to get a few hours of sleep. When he awoke in the morning of 19 May, it was to the sensation of the ground trembling beneath him. He looked upon his sleeping comrades and was struck by how tranquil they appeared, their exhaustion allowing them to go undisturbed by the detonations. At first he thought that perhaps he himself was still asleep and was caught in a dream. The sudden bursting of a salvo of shells close by yanked him back to harsh reality. Word came that three of his men had already been killed. New detonations shook the ground, followed now and then by a shower of earth. Suddenly there was a commotion in the trench and a surge of panicked men pushing and shoving their way into the entrance of Jubert's shelter. Shoving them back out into the trench, he ordered them to return to their positions. As soon as he cleared his entrance and emerged into the trench, Jubert saw the cause of the panic.

> Coming from the enemy lines in an unbroken chain were a number of Taubes [German airplanes] hovering overhead and strafing us with machine guns. They were transmitting by prearranged signals step-by-step instructions in order to correct the fire of their heavy calibre batteries. Arriving four at time, the shells completely flatten our line of shelters. At this moment they were localizing their fire to the southern end where my platoon is located.[12]

Before this looming danger the men of 11 Company – their faces stricken in terror, with wide eyes and open mouths – reflexively ebbed back to the centre of the position, like prey trying to escape a predator. There was no stopping the flow of the crowd and Jubert reflected on what real purpose it would serve to hold on to these 40m of ground in the face of such destruction. Slipping back into his shelter, he couldn't help but smile with self-pity as he mused that 8in of earth piled on top of a thin piece of corrugated steel was all that protected him from certain death. The situation continued to worsen, as news arrived that both of his sergeants were missing. There was nothing for it, other than to wait in his trembling shelter for the imminent enemy attack. When there was a brief lull in the shelling, Jubert ran out with several of his men to check on the dead and wounded.

> First there were the survivors, lying flat at the bottom of the trench with rounded backs and their faces buried in the earth. Then there were the wounded, their heads and hands covered in blood, eyes wide with terror, forgetting even to cry out, waiting for the reprieve that would allow them to suffer. Here, a collapse of earth with a blanched face protruding out of it, the face tossed back with eyes closed and mouth open to the sky. At the same level were two pale hands jutting out of the earth, outstretched and rigid with open palms. The first dead man I come across.
>
> We find others now lying in groups in the churned up and collapsed trenches. The position my two platoons were occupying had been erased. I couldn't see any blood, and all of the dead were at least partially buried. There was now only enormous masses of loose soil in pyramid-shaped holes, out from which stuck bare arms, faces, and hands – all white like bleached marble.[13]

Grabbing some tools, Jubert and his men did the best they could to disinter those buried who were still alive. For some, help came too late. Unable to move, they'd suffocated under the crushing darkness of the piled soil. The respite in the shell-fire was short-lived. A voice groaned, 'They're coming back', and once again the chain of Taubes hovered into view. Right away, heavy calibre shells began slamming down four at a time, sending shockwaves reverberating through the air and ground alike. This time the fire had shifted to the northern end of 11 Company's positions, onto the line of shelters missed in the earlier barrage. The German aviators had reported this intelligence back to their artillery. Now, along with the localized zone fire, an advancing progressive fire began as well, which seemed to sweep back and forth over the same battered stretch of ground like a garden hose. New batteries positioned both to the left and right joined in this time. The resulting enfilade fire sent shells crisscrossing behind the 11 Company's line, right where the flock of panicked men had retreated to earlier.

> Fifteen paces away, without any other protection above them except for a piece of corrugated steel thrown across the top of the trench, twelve or fifteen men are huddled together. They stood beside each other – arms wrapped around their torsos, their backs exposed – in one solid block against the danger. Men belonging to the company, liaison agents of the colonel [Marathel of the 162nd] commanding the sector, and those from three different regiments temporarily under his orders.
>
> A shell bursts right in the middle of them. There is a powerful explosion, which for a second obscures the view. In a single blow, without there being a single shout, all of this living flesh is turned into a mass of death.[14]

As the earth tossed up by the explosion rains back down to earth, someone began shouting to get Jubert's attention. One of the Taubes had been shot down by a French fighter and was now crashing to the ground. It provided the briefest of distractions as up and down the line men who had been rendered mute by an oppressive sense of terror now vented in hysterical relief. 'Bravo, aces! Bravo!' they shouted and applauded. 'Lucky pilots!' Jubert quipped. Whether victorious or beaten, he mused, either outcome won the applause of the poor poilu stuck in their holes and dying like the cannon fodder they'd become. The downed Taube was simply a small emotional victory but it did nothing to stop the shells from falling. At any rate, Jubert wasn't given the time to reflect further. Jubert was ordered to report to Lieutenant Colonel Marathel's command post. To reach it, he would have to pass through the very spot where the shell had just turned the pitiful group of cowering men into a gory pile of flesh and bone.

> I had to climb over the recent victims, still pouring out blood and going through their last spasms. Two bodies had been quartered, with all their entrails torn out. Then a huge round pile of earth, with a pyramid-shaped hole gouged out all around. Sticking forty centimetres out of it and in a symmetrical fashion were legs, arms, hands, and heads, like the bloody cogs of some monstrous capstan.[15]

Once at the command post, both officers acknowledge that 11 Company had suffered too many casualties to be able to carry out a counter-attack if it was needed. In Jubert's platoon, there were only eight men remaining from the original forty or fifty. Marathel instructed that the company was to be relieved that night, when it would be sent back a short way to the Second Position. Returning to his platoon, Jubert gave them the good news but was shocked by the utter indifference expressed by his men.

> 'What's the use of moving, sir?' someone says. 'Here or someplace else, we're all cursed.' All day these words followed me, tormented and agitated me. I hid it from my comrades. It's already enough that I should be so self-obsessed with it. At night through the mist, I lead my men out, the head of a procession of shadows, while off in the distance quick bursts of flame shot up one after another. They were docile and mute, with empty eyes and spellbound stares, their heads lowered, like people who'd not fulfilled their destiny. Like a sheepherder of ghosts wandering through the night of ages, the blind guide of fate, leading the silent flock of victims to their new stage of death.[16]

By day's end on 19 May, the 151's positions were in a deplorable state. The trenches were mostly filled in and the *boyaux* no longer existed. Repairing either of them was made nearly impossible because of the shell-fire. Telephone communications were also down, the wires being shredded in numerous places. Every day since their arrival, men in the 151 were being killed and injured in unspeakable ways. Most were struck by shell fragments. The smaller pieces lacerated flesh, punctured organs, and shattered bones. The larger ones did far worse, tearing bodies apart, severing men in half widthwise or lengthwise, or flattening them into pancakes or pulverising them into pulp. Many others were buried alive by tons of falling earth or tossed up by the force of exploding shells, or within collapsed trenches and shelters. These sorry souls had their bones and organs crushed or just as horribly suffocated slowly in a dark prison of earth over minutes or hours. Just 14 days into its second tour at Mort Homme, the 151 had already lost almost 300 men. That was the cost of simply holding the line in the Furnace of Verdun. Yet things were about to get far worse.

Attack of 20 May

The shelling continued unabated through the night. Salvoes of 77 poison gas shells (diphosgene known as 'Green Cross') only served to make the environment that much more hellish. An internal rotation among the regiment's machine-gun companies – during which 1 MG Company was to relieve 2 MG Company in the first line – could only be partially completed. The shelling had been so violent that the very landscape had changed and liaison agents no longer recognized the way and became lost. One liaison agent who had taken care to erect place markers using stakes topped with empty ration cans found that every one of these had been swept away by the storm. As dawn broke on the morning of 20 May, Jubert and his friend Erkens stood beside each other in Ouvrage Laborderie a kilometre from Côte 295. With heads above the parapet and elbows resting on the firing ledge, they gazed up at the sky with sunken eyes watching the stars gradually extinguish themselves in the slowly brightening sky. The purple light of the early morning cast its fairy-like hue over Mort Homme, which loomed above them like a gigantic emerald. Both men were restless and despite their fatigue were unable to sleep. Jubert confided to Erkens: 'All of my men who've died crowd my thoughts. I've never felt more haunted by ghosts.' It struck Jubert in that moment that he was standing in the same position from where he had lead his company in the 9 April counter-attack. In fact, in his after-action reports for 20 May, Jubert would mistakenly write 20 April on several occasions – a testament to the depressing similarity of the events at Mort Homme.

As the light of early morning spread, the mighty beast of battle roared back to life. The bombardment quickly picked up in tempo. High in the air 105mm shrapnel shells burst with their clouds of ochre as all calibres of high explosives crashed to the ground, spewing up heavy chutes of white, grey, and black. Gradually the smoke from the explosions thickened, forming a cloud that spread over the hill and rolled down into the ravines. By noon, the bombardment erupted with even greater force and expanded to encompass all of Mort Homme and surrounding areas. The men of the 151 had been under fire many times before, even at Mort Homme, but nothing like this. Never had such a powerful concentration of fire been witnessed. The German artillery was using almost primarily heavy calibre shells – 170mm and 250mm *minens*, together with 105s, 150s, 210s, even behemouth 305s. In the first line, 77s and large numbers of rifle grenades (nicknamed 'Rat Tails') were thrown into the mix. Further back, gas shells saturated the Second Position, causing a large number of men to become overcome with its hellacious effects. For those underneath it, their state of passivity coupled with the sense of complete powerlessness was a devastating force of its own. The blind, mechanical, industrialized killing engendered a profound feeling of ignominy and worthlessness. Gabriel Chevallier perfectly captured this in his mostly auto-biographical work *Fear*:

> The artillery thunders, obliterates, disembowels, terrifies. Everything is roaring, flashing, shuddering. The sky has disappeared. We are in the middle of a monstrous maelstrom, pieces of sky come crashing down and cover us with rubble, comets collide and crumble, sparking like a short circuit. We are caught in the end of a world. The earth is a burning building and all the exits have been bricked up. We are going to roast in this inferno . . .
>
> Bodies whimper, dribble, soil themselves in shame. Thought prostrates itself, begs the cruel powers, the demonic forces. Tormented minds throb weakly. We are worms, writhing to escape the spade. This is the consummation of ignominy. There is no disgrace we will not accept. To be a man is the depth of horror. Just let me get away. Let me live in shame and infamy, but let me get away . . . Am I still me? Is this piece of jelly, this stagnant human puddle, really me? Am I alive?[17]

The sound and fury of it was stupefying. It had become a single demented cacophony of roaring, hissing, howling, whistling, wailing, booming, rattling, cracking, and tearing. The very air and ground trembled spasmodically from the percussive blasts. What was left of the first and second-line trenches was now completely obliterated and the number of dead and wounded soared. The survivors now occupied a line consisting of nothing more than amorphous holes. Rifles and machine guns became buried under the avalanches of falling earth or otherwise rendered inoperable. With the telephone lines shredded and runners dropping like flies, communication between the front lines and regimental and divisional commands was poor to nonexistent. All signs indicated that an infantry attack was nigh and orders were passed down to the junior officers and NCOs to be ready to repel the assault as soon as the enemy's artillery lengthened its fire. Jubert was approached by a liaison officer from the 267 IR (69 ID) who provided intelligence pointing to a possible enemy attack from the north–northwest via Hayette Ravine, which would advance up the western slopes of Mort Homme. He immediately set off to inform his battalion commander, Commandant Malochet, who confirmed the intelligence. Malochet ordered the 9 and 12 Companies to advance across open country in front of their current positions up to the regimental command post of the 162 IR in the *Place d'Armes*. There they were to deploy to the west and form a defensive line in front of the Second Position.

The 11 Company was to remain with Malochet to defend Ouvrage Laborderie and its right wing, together with the pioneer company and two machine-gun groups from 2 MG Company. With his platoon reduced to less than a squad, Jubert and his men were detached from the rest of 11 Company to help ensure the defence of the left wing of Laborderie. Small pockets of men to hold back hordes of attackers. All along the line, machine guns were set up in position and the ammo crates opened beside them to allow for continuous resupply. The men stood with their rifles loaded and ready, heads above the parapets and nerves on edge as they awaited the coming assault. At 1.30 pm, 9 Company began its movement by platoons. One of them, despite already having lost its commander (Second Lieutenant Bouchard having been mortally wounded) sent patrols up to the top of the 285.9 to watch for the enemy's approach. At 2.00 pm, the German artillery lengthened its fire, signal flares shot up from the enemy first line and thousands of German infantry (composed of the 203rd IR on the left and the 204th IR on the right) supported by flamethrower units leapt out of their departure trenches and rushed up the smoking slopes of Mort Homme. Few accounts remain of the attack from the perspective of those in the first line; so few survived to tell the tale. Only fragments remained. It was reported that the bombardment had knocked out a number of the regiment's machine guns. Even those that remained operational had to be dug out from the earth they had been buried under and quickly cleaned.

As waves of German assault troops surged forward, the remaining gunners from 1st Platoon of 2 MG Company frantically fired and refed their guns, pouring fire into the rushing enemy troops at point-blank range. In minutes, they had burned through 2,100 rounds, until one by one all the crews and their guns were taken out. Most of 1 MG Company and its weapons had been destroyed even before the German infantry attacked. Only one gun remained, operated by the gunner Private Albert Faglain who was posted in the covering line, at the intersection of Boyau de Chattancourt and Tranchée Couplet (named after the deceased lieutenant of the 151). Faglain was a decorated hero from the fighting in the Argonne who again proved himself at Haudraumont in March and Mort Homme in April. With the rest of his crew killed, Faglain now operated his weapon alone, continuing to fire on the enemy even as they overtook the first line and closed to within 40m of his position. After expending all 1,200 rounds at his disposal, the gunner displaced, carrying his 50lb Hotchkiss back down Boyau de Chattancourt while stepping over the countless bodies of dead and wounded from 1 Battalion that filled the bottom of the trench. Arriving in Tranchée de Foix, Faglain set the gun up on the parapet and after procuring more ammunition, resumed firing on the attacking troops on the summit above. His actions drew down a hail of gunfire upon him, until at last the gunner was himself struck and collapsed dead on his gun.[18]

Despite suffering heavy losses, German troops managed to gain footholds on the regiment's right front relying once again on flamethrowers. Shooting liquid flame into Tranchée Garçon, the men in 1 and 2 Companies were ignited into human torches, shrieking and howling as they died in unspeakable agony. This was followed by a rain of hand grenades wiping out any last resistance. Worse still, to the regiment's left the enemy had broken through the 162 IR's first line, thus threatening the 151's flank and the rear. From afar, Jubert and his comrades watched as the lines in front of them were overwhelmed, their comrades blazing away with every rifle and machine gun that could be brought to bear. German troops were shot down by the hundreds, yet additional waves continued to follow behind and bore down on the jumbled French line. Dozens of hand grenades were lobbed back and forth between attacker and defender. It was now 3.30 pm as two company size German elements arriving from the northwest appeared on the peak of 285.9. Cresting the hill, they rushed down the southern slopes of 285.9, heading towards Chattancourt Ravine. Right in the path of their advance was Commandant Oblet, 1 Battalion commander, who still held his command post behind Tranchée de Foix. His guard consisted of only a few liaison agents and two machine-gunners, who were now working feverishly to set up the one remaining machine gun. Gathering a handful of able-bodied men he could find close to the post, Oblet had 4 riflemen and 1 working machine gun to hold back some 300 Germans.

From his position in Ouvrage Laborderie, Jubert could clearly see this body of advancing troops and quickly directed fire onto it. A withering crossfire and a storm of 75mm shells pummeled the attackers.

> The enemy line wavers, disperses and breaks. They try to advance again, this time in singles, progressing from shell-hole to shell-hole. But our rifle fire blazes away, the machine guns adding their voices to the din. The gun barrels get hot in our hands. We get all worked up. In this moment, we

are masters of death. The enemy stops, recoils, then hunkers down. Our gunfire roots them out and they withdraw now behind the summit. Still, I can't help but admire them in the minutes that follow when, under our unrelenting fire, I see some of them go out to retrieve their wounded.[19]

The sense of mastery was short-lived, however. Soon two Taubes appeared overhead once more in what was now taken as a certain harbinger of death. The planes shot down signal flares right over Jubert's position, marking it for the German artillery. Shortly thereafter, a furious storm of shells descended on Ouvrage Laborderie. In degrees Jubert's trench was blasted open, then flattened and mutated by an unending cascade of explosions. Despite all of this, the survivors stuck to their loopholes, maintaining their fire on the enemy up above them. The gunners of 2 MG Company – with three guns already knocked out of action – set their remaining three up on the parapet, knowingly exposing themselves to enemy fire. Unsettling news arrived that the Germans had progressed through the Ravin de la Hayette and taken Ouvrage Gers to their left. Their own position was in danger of being encircled by the enemy. The only recourse was to counter-attack and retake Ouvrage Gers. But with so few effectives remaining, Jubert went in search of reinforcements to accompany him and his handful of men.

Orders were sent at the same time to 9 Company in front of the *Place d'Armes* to front to the southwest and advance towards Gers. But just as it began its movement, it was taken by artillery fire and machine guns placed on 285.9 and quickly decimated. Having lost both its commanders, the survivors fell back to Line 1A, which 12 Company was occupying. Those still left uninjured in 12 Company were fighting for their lives, as Lieutenant Le Gallo directed the fire of his men on the German attackers to their front and flank. Soon after, Le Gallo was himself shot in the head and collapsed dead. Everything descended into noise and chaos. The fear increased ever more that the Germans were about to encircle the French line on Mort Homme. Rushing along in search of any able-bodied troops he could muster, Jubert found only the dead. They lay everywhere, some piled in groups others lying alone. One machine-gun crew lay dead around their destroyed gun, their bodies seeming to form the shape of the cross. At last he comes across something living. It was his friend, Erkens, who informed him that the 332 IR from the neighbouring 69th Division had already retaken Gers. Jubert breathed a sigh of relief.[20]

The check at Gers was the last significant development of the day. As daylight faded, the German attack on Mort Homme came to a halt. Darkness allowed for reconnaissance patrols to venture out and ascertain the enemy's positions. These confirmed what was already all too obvious, that the French had at last lost the summit. German troops were occupying all of Côte 295 (including 285.9) and they were in firm control of the western slopes as well. Though they'd been forced to withdraw from the southwestern base of of the hill, they maintained the gains they'd made through the Ravin de la Hayette and now threatened the Second Position. On the eastern side of the hill, they had advanced to a point overlooking the Ravin de Chattancourt and set up positions in shell holes south of Tranchée Couplet. Meanwhile, 200m below them, the tattered remains of 1 Battalion – now reduced to a platoon-size band about fifty strong – were rallied by Commandant Oblet. A ragtag defence made up of sixteen men from 10 Company was organized by Second Lieutenant de la Ferrière in Tranchée de Foix.[21] Any movement was made impossible by enemy machine-gun fire that enfiladed the entire Ravin de Chattancourt. The survivors were completely isolated. All of Oblet's liaison agents were gone and any runners he sent out to gather intelligence were killed by the shell-fire. Requests for counter-battery fire went unanswered. Liaison with any units in the first line was also impossible. The only thing they could do was to defensively organize the positions that were still in friendly hands. At night, they would be reinforced by an understrength company of the 94 IR, but even with this supplement no advance could be made in the face of enemy machine-gun fire coming from above.

The 94th was just one of many French units that had been hurried up to the front as the mighty onslaught slammed against the French positions. Over the course of the day and into the night, reinforcements were thrown piecemeal and headlong into the fight in a desperate attempt to help bolster the crumbling line. Elements comprising eight different formations (287th, 306th, 332nd, 151st, 251st, 254th, and 94th Regiments, and the 16th LIB) from three different divisions (40th, 42nd, and 69th) formed a patchwork line of defence at Mort Homme. The units themselves were all jumbled together, the troops sharing what meagre protection they could find in the same ditches and craters that had once been trenches. And like marooned sailors from a shipwreck, here and there along the line, isolated from their units and each other, handfuls of men still clung to small churned up portions of ground they'd been ordered to defend. Tiny islands of resistance, surrounded on all sides by enemy troops. Under cover of darkness, some tried to make their way back to friendly lines, as was the case with a clutch of soldiers from 1 Battalion who'd constituted the last defenders of Tranchée Couplet.

Casualty reports for the 151 on 20 May were understandably sketchy. Initial figures in the 151 *JMO* put the total losses at 48 killed, 169 wounded, and 462 missing. However, the more accurate figures are likely those recorded in the divisional records. These had the total loss for the regiment at 1,060, including 50 killed, 231 wounded, and 762 missing. Some of these last were taken prisoner. But as was too often the case, the vast majority of those unaccounted for were likely dead. Among the officer cadre, three officers were confirmed killed and six wounded, with another eight missing and presumed dead.[22] It is worth remembering that these losses were limited only to the two battalions of the regiment that were currently on the line – 1 and 3 Battalions – and were thus felt more severely. The 1 Battalion had been truly decimated, with little more than two dozen survivors. From the battered ditch that was his trench, Commandant Oblet sent a report to Lieutenant Colonel Moisson earlier in the day in which he wrote: 'Of my battalion there remains only a few scattered elements. It sacrificed itself in defending it's position. All have done their duty. I have no more than 41 riflemen with me. They lay where they fell: dead, wounded, or missing. This time is very painful for us all, the tears flowing with each passing moment.'

The trial was not yet over. The debris of 1 Battalion would have to hold on for another two nights and two days. All through the long night of 20–1 May, the bombardment continued with the same intensity. The darkness was punctuated by quick stabs of light from bursting shells, which then alternated with long moments where green and red flares cast their eerie light to complete the apocalyptic vision of a blasted landscape of smoke and fire and death. Strewn across the slopes in long lines or in heaps, piled on top of each other in the trenches, and scattered singly in the shell holes, were thousands of French and German dead. Thousands more wounded men were intermixed with them, bloodied and broken and alone. In their pain and isolation, their thoughts fled to memories of home, to their mothers and fathers who could not help them, to their wives and children or sweethearts who could not comfort them. Maybe they tried to envision the warmth of the sun on their face, or the feeling of soft green grass under their feet; the refreshing coolness as they dipped a hand into a local stream or the peaceful idleness of lying under the shade of a tree. Too many would never again get to enjoy these simple pleasures.

When the Germans attacked on 20 May, 2 Battalion was still at rest at Jouy-en-Argonne after returning from two weeks at Mort Homme on 19 May.[23] Now on the morning of the 21st, it was called up as reinforcement and ordered to report to Fromeréville. It would be relieving the beleaguered 3 Battalion in the supporting lines that now constituted the French front line. Even with the small supplement of replacement troops it had received in Jouy, 2 Battalion counted a diminished 625 troops. In the ranks of 6 Company was Private Bordinat, who would finally receive his baptism of fire and be forever marked by it. Under a broiling noon sun, he now started the long hazardous journey up to the line.[24] To avoid observation from enemy aircraft, the battalion moved under cover of a tree line as far as possible. Despite being a good 8km from the front line (as the crow flies), it wasn't long before the column entered the rear zones targeted by intermittent German long-range guns. To minimize the potential destruction from the shells on their ranks, the companies deployed into single-file columns. Even still there were a few hit by shell fragments. In command of a platoon in 6 Company with Bordinat, Second Lieutenant Basteau was struck by a small one in the left hand. At the time, it didn't look bad so he carried on. In a few days' time this would change. Arriving at Fromeréville in the early evening and already drained from the march, 2 Battalion made a brief halt to eat one last meal and to wait for darkness before making the final 10km approach march to the line. They were also urged to top off their canteens with water for a final time, as they were warned they'd find none at the front. As day faded to dusk, a light mist spread over the land like a thin funeral shroud. At 9.00 pm, 2 Battalion resumed its march and soon began passing batteries of heavy artillery firing away without stop. Long red flames shot out of the gun muzzles like dragon tongues, shaking the ground with each blast. All around, arrayed across the fields and hidden in the wooded ravines, the big guns flashed and thundered away. Bordinat was awestruck. 'The further we go along, the more frequent the noises became and you couldn't help being shook by the repeated yet unpredictable discharges around us. These guns that delivered death from afar with every passing second. We took it all in humble silence.'[25]

The 2 Battalion had already been marching for hours. Around 10.00 pm, the column made another brief halt. Under their heavy loads, the men were already exhausted and they had not yet reached the line. Taking advantage of the short break, Bordinat joined his comrades in quickly dropping on the ground to get a fraction of rest.

> And God, what silence! No one talks, no one complains. What's running through their minds? Who can say? Probably many things. I (as a novice) nervously watch the flares shooting up from the lines. The entire sky is lit up. All of these things are new to me. It reminds me of the 14th of July festivities out in the country. At this moment, one of our dirigibles, having likely assisted with directing our bombardment is returning from a trip over the enemy lines.
>
> What a sight! Everywhere, in the air, on the ground, in the distance, there is only fire. And to our left, the flames in a neighbouring area help to illuminate these sad plains. What a pitiful sight![26]

Heavy shells fell around the battalion as they descended into the interminably long *boyau*, Avenue No. 3. Within the claustrophobia of the winding communication trench, Bordinat struggled to make sense of all the sights, sounds, and smells assaulting him from all sides. The one imperative he'd been made keenly aware of was that they must arrive before daylight or else risk being spotted by the enemy. And even in the relative protection of the *boyau*, men were still struck by shell fragments, sowing more chaos in the narrow confines of the trench. The pace was quickened as the danger increased.

> Moving in single-file at the double, from time-to-time we call back to each other to make sure the man behind is still there, though the man ahead doesn't bother to wait for the response to check. For there are already many men who've been killed or wounded. There's no time to stop and care, we don't want to lose the rest of the column. The scene becomes more and more terrifying. Many don't even reach our destination and besides, the boyau was already filled with bodies who'd been dead for some time now. We keep moving up. We stumble and fall over the dead again and again, and again and again we pick ourselves back up.
>
> Despite our physical fatigue, our nerves alone carry us forward like the spirit of the poor, beyond feeling the weight of our heavy packs. Despite our concerns otherwise, at the briefest stop we take a swig of water from our canteens, which are already nearly empty. And now we smell a pungent, nauseating, overpowering stench [of death].[27]

As Bordinat and the men of 2 Battalion were moving up the line, Jubert, tasked with ensuring the liaison between units, had spent a miserable night waiting and waiting for the relief to arrive. As low clouds rolled in over the land, the night sky took on an eerie aspect, illuminated in yellow by scores of red and green flares shooting up from the front lines all along the horizon. To bolster his eight-man platoon, a miniscule reinforcement of eight young recruits from the class of 1916 had been thrown up into the line and told to report to him. At last, a company from the 332 IR arrived to relieve them. Jubert was getting his men ready to move out when a shell came crashing down close by, throwing Jubert and three others to the ground. One being killed outright, another was gushing blood from his buttocks and ran off screaming into the night. After recovering from the shock, Jubert quickly organized the survivors and started leading them back to the rear. These men were no longer from the world of the living. Jubert saw in them all a zombie-like stupefied look. They were incapable of speaking, half-mad, completely detached from the events going on around them.

> We collide and bump into men from other relieving units that line the trenches for more than a kilometre, stepping over hundreds of corpses as we go. It's a trial of slaughter. Yesterday my platoon had been targeted to the full extent. What does this new ordeal really matter to me though? All it is is horror piled on top of horror.
>
> 'Oh if you saw the *Place d'Armes*, lieutenant! The 2nd Battalion found its grave there.
>
> 'Any news of the business from yesterday?

'The 1st Battalion is gone. We only know that Commandant Oblet hasn't been captured by the Germans, but anyone sent out to look for him ran into the enemy.

'No survivors?

'A few loners, their minds so gone they can no longer speak. Captain Ritter, wounded, missing. Captain Boissin, Lieutenants Castet-Baron and Jubien are missing; Captain Detrais was crushed. But I'll stop there, lieutenant. Have your men eaten their tins of reserve food? There won't be any resupply tonight.'[28]

Minutes turn to hours, as Jubert waits for his relief to arrive, eventually falling asleep alongside his men.

When I wake back up, the dawn light is spreading. 'How about the relief?'

'We're still waiting, lieutenant.'

'Get on your feet quick! Ask around. Go to the commandant's command post, to the lieutenant's shelter. Maybe they've forgotten us?'

'There's no one here anymore,' the man says upon returning. 'I went into the commandant's CP and an officer from another regiment threw me out. I asked this lieutenant where the 151st was, he told me: "Over there, on the ground". I lit my lamp and saw a heap of men. I thought they were asleep, so I shook several of them. Nothing doing, they were all dead.'

'Clearly we've been left behind,' I pronounced. 'Assemble the platoon.'

My men formed up, I point out that it's dawn:

'In half an hour, the bombardment [will resume again]. It's a waste of time to go through the obstructed trenches. We'd wouldn't make it far before we're pounded. So, a bit of courage; jump up on the parapet. The bullets won't hit us but in a little while, the shells surely will.'

Through the shell-holes, running, stumbling, tumbling into craters, we cross the vast plain. A machine gun spots us but doesn't deem us to be a good target. Only a few bullets whistle past us. That came as a happy surprise to us all, so we're happy fellows. Even six kilometres away from Mort Homme, reliefs are not made until night. Crowded by ghosts, it seemed that the field of the dead would only let shadows escape by accident.[29]

They were racing against time, racing against the light that would betray them. After covering a few hundred metres of ground, Jubert granted the escapees some rest in a little wood sheltered behind a ridge. As they caught their breath, they took a quick headcount: there were only nine present. Of the eight new recruits who'd just arrived the day before, only two had made it out.

> During the pause, I thought about this miserable war that kills at random, both while danger is at its highest as well as when it has subsided. And now I have in my head a picture from the day before: at the entrance to my shelter lying face-down in his own blood is this kid. His face is pale, his eyes clear, his lips let out a little pink drop. I lift him up. I hug him in order to put him on his back. On his collar is the number of our regiment. 'One of my reinforcements,' I thought. Death is blind! He barely came into the service. How many kids of his same age have died like this with no glory, taken by surprise on their first day, without enthusiasm in their hearts. Back at the depot in the rear, they'd waited stifling tears of anger, impatient to not yet be under fire at the front. They gave their lives, and no one knew their name. Their mothers will weep for them, but their commander will have only the memory of a corpse he'd kicked with his foot one evening during an assault . . . I thought of my brother, [Maurice].

The official butcher's bill for 11 Company as a whole was frightful. Having gone in 117-strong, it had been reduced to just 40 men.[30] After finally making it back to Jouy-en-Argonne, Jubert was informed of the deaths of several more officers he had shaken hands with only a few days before. His response: 'War's a sad thing. Give me some *pinard*.' His men followed his lead and guzzled down the wine. With so many gone, there was plenty to go around. It was the last blessing of the dead – their rations were shared out among the living. As the battered companies of 3 Battalion had been struggling back to the rear, those of 2 Battalion were going through the endless delays, difficulties, and dangers of a relief as they struggled to take their turn in the meat grinder of Mort Homme. It was dawn on 22 May as the companies occupied the Netter shelters, sections of Line 1A still in French hands, the *Place d'Armes* and the tenuous positions in the Chattancourt Ravine. As Jubert was gathering his men to make their pre-dawn dash to safety, Bordinat and 6 Company was at last reaching the Second Position. There they found a motely crowd of men from three different units – fractions of the 3 Battalion of the 151 IR, together with elements of the 332 and 251 IR.[31] But this was not their assigned position, so 6 Company had to force its way through the forlorn flotsam. Their eyes were hollow, betraying the unspeakable scenes of terror they had witnessed. From their mouths arose again and agin the same two beseeching questions: 'Are you our relief?' – 'Do you have any water?' – 'Are you our relief?' – 'Do you have any water?' Bordinat and his comrades were keenly aware that they would need to conserve every drop they had. It was a matter of their own survival now. So they lied, responding that they had none and with sharp pangs of guilt, pressed onwards up the hill.

Troops from the 162, 94, 251, 287, and 332 IRs were scattered all over, the men crammed together into trenches now reduced to incongruous lines of shallow ditches and deep holes. Packed in elbow to elbow, stretcher-bearers and liaison agents had to physically climb over the men to pass. The air itself was almost unbreathable, filled with clouds of dust and smoke, reeking of death, explosives, and gas. Frequent explosions sent showers of earth and broken stones raining down like hail, which bounced off helmets with a sharp rap. As the sun rose, the day grew hot. Bordinat and his friends had already drunk all the water in their canteens and it was only their first day on the line. To help relieve their parched lips, a small bottle of mint liqueur was passed around. By the end of the day this too was gone. Left to their own devices, the only recourse was to wait for nightfall in the hope that a search could then be made for water. The German bombardment once again doubled in intensity (concentrating principally on the *Place d'Armes* and the Second Position) and reached – as noted in the 332 *JMO* – 'proportions heretofore unknown'. Bordinat was stunned:

> It is a deafening din of wailing. In this dry air, smoke mixed with dust to form a dark cloud that choked us and left a bitter taste that made us thirsty. But there was nothing to drink. If only we still had water! And this feeling got increasingly worse.
>
> By noon, we are totally wiped out by the heat of the sun and the smell of rotting corpses around us. But what can be done? The suffering doubles the feeling of thirst. What terrible malady. What we wouldn't give for a little water.[32]

Another in 6 Company undergoing the same hell alongside Bordinat was the telephonist and radio telegrapher Private Pierre Rouquet. In an interview many years after the war, Rouquet (aged 19 at the time) recounted the horrendous conditions on Mort Homme.

> You couldn't describe the deluge of fire that swept down on us. Every second, I was conscious of the danger of being killed. I was lucky to make it through those first fifteen days. But I ended up stupefied. I felt as though my brain was jumping around in my skull because of the guns. I was completely dazed by the severity of the noise. At the end of fifteen days we came back down, seven to eight kilometers from the front to [Jouy-en-Argonne]. And that we thought was the end of our spell at Verdun as far as we were concerned. We had one quiet night's sleep, just one, that's all, then the next day the battalion that had relieved us was

wiped out. They had lost as many killed as were taken prisoner. There were five or six left out of a whole battalion. No more.

We were sent up again in all haste to face another bombardment, one worse than ever before. 210mm shells were come coming over four at a time and we were getting buried with every volley. Men were being completely entombed. Others came to dig them out. This lasted all day during the preparations for a German attack. My moment came on the stroke of 7 o'clock. It was my turn to be buried, and you must understand that I suffered greatly because I was unable to move. I could do absolutely nothing. I remember saying to myself, 'Well, that's it at last!' and I lost consciousness. I was dead ... And then I was being disinterred with picks and shovels and they pulled me out. [I was] totally exhausted. My captain [Captain Olivier] said, 'Lie down over there.' Later he sent me to a first-aid post two kilometres back.

Night fell and I could see the red flashes of shells passing in front of me. At the first-aid post there was a major engaged in looking after a German whose leg had been badly smashed. The major put a dressing on him, and the German begged him, 'Finish me off!' The major told me, 'I don't have the time to see to you. Go over there.' I went over to where he pointed. I hadn't been there five minutes when a shell landed on the major and the German. That's destiny. You're marked by fate. After that we were sent down to the field kitchens. I was evacuated. I gather I stayed four days in a corner, exhausted, in total shock.[33]

The 2 Battalion's job was to simply stand its ground and block any further enemy advances. Yet as German troops occupied Côte 285.9 and 300m of ground along Line 1A immediately below the height, a gap was created between the right subsector and the Netter shelters. In order to close this gap, the 7 Company of the 151 together with mixed elements of the 287, 306, and 332 IRs were ordered to attack from the west, south and east respectively, and thereby encircle the German forces on 285.9. For its part, the 7 Company managed to take 100m of trenches between Line 1A and the Boyau de Chattancourt, setting itself up in the latter. In addition to reestablishing the liaison with the 332 IR, their advance allowed machine guns to be set up and, subsequently, to engage enemy troops in the area. These would inflict serious losses on the enemy and effectively shut down all enemy movement in the Chattancourt Ravine. On the left, the attacking companies of the 332 IR were able to make some progress but were ultimately unable to link up with the 287 IR. At various points, sandbag barricades were erected in the trenches and were all that separated friend from foe. Throughout the day and night, local attacks erupted sporadically on the summit. Small groups pushing forward only for the gain of small patches of churned up, seemingly inconsequential ground.

The hours dragged by as day faded into night. It wasn't until the early morning hours of 23 May that the bombardment slackened somewhat and allowed several of Bordinat's comrades (who were familiar with the ground from their last rotation) to venture out to try to find water. Bordinat handed them his canteen and hoped luck was on their side as he watched them set off down the slope. His friends would never be seen again. Meanwhile, the shelling went on and on, a relentless pounding, hammering, gouging, convulsing. Tranchée de Foix and Boyau de Chattancourt – where a number of men were sheltering – were singled out and caused scores of casualties. At one moment, eleven heavy calibre shells were observed landing in a space of a hundred metres almost simultaneously. As night slowly turned back to day, a pale grey light filtered weakly through the smoke and dust that enveloped the ridge. The temperature began to climb again. Life was reduced to dry mouths, parched throats, fever, heat, dust, explosions, smoke, fire, blood.

> The infernal machine continues. We're being observed by enemy planes which direct the fire of the guns. Now the shells get closer to our trench; big 210s. One of my comrades tells me we've been spotted. He's right. It's total destruction, total carnage. Many are swallowed up, pulverized, decapitated. Our trench is half filled in. Those who aren't wounded, like me, remain impassive, stoic, waiting for our own deaths. We endure the terrible shock of the explosions, often only a metre or two from us. One shell lands no more than a meter and a half from me and my fighting buddy, Boisson, but miraculously does not explode. Nonetheless, the force of it still causes our trench to cave in.
>
> By now all the survivors are more or less exposed without any cover. Finally the enemy calls off its big guns at 8.00 am. Only 77s continue to burst, but this is a mere play thing to us now and we pay them no mind. Tools, shovels and picks are brought to us. Where did they come from? We have no idea. We scoop away this disastrous mess to try to dig out, if possible, those comrades who've been buried alive. But that accursed thirst that brought so much suffering has still not left us.[34]

Desperate to relieve their nagging thirst, Bordinat and a young soldier from the class of 1916 decide something must be done. Collecting the abandoned canteens that lie scattered about, they set off at a run across the desolate plain. The empty canteens bounced around their torsos as they rushed to cover the 1,500m of ground from their position to Chattancourt. Though it was forbidden to pass out in the open, the *boyaux* had been so levelled that sticking to them was a moot point. Bullets whistled past, indicating that the enemy on the high ground above had spotted them. A mad lust for water drove them forward despite the prospect of death, made all the more real by the countless bodies of French and German dead they must jump over in the course of their race. Eventually Bordinat and his young companion come across others who'd likewise gone in search of water and knew where to find it. Following these guides, they are led to a small muddy brook running through Chattancourt. Crawling up and dropping on their stomachs, they guzzled down the dirty water in large gulps, unphased by the muddy flavour. After quenching themselves, they filled up the mess of canteens strapped around them and headed back up to their positions. Once back, they were welcomed like heroes. But the relief would be short-lived, for soon salvoes of 210 shells begin thundering back down.

> The awful business starts up again. The living burial continues. Armed with shovels and picks again, those still standing set back to the task of saving the victims who may still be alive by clearing away the earth and stones. At last we manage to pull out a few survivors, the others having been asphyxiated after ten minutes under the earth. In turn, the captain's command post is caved in with his entourage – the lieutenants and a few men – all slowly suffocating in their airless hole. We go to work digging them out and after a little while we can hear cries and groans, which gives us a little more hope. Eventually, we get them out. The captain and lieutenants are unharmed but our commander tells us to keep digging as several others are still further down. We keep on picking for a little while longer but our strength leaves us and we're simply unable to continue. We're all so exhausted and have to give up. Of the twenty of us still alive, not a single one is capable of exerting any more energy. What can be done? And so, despite our best efforts, the bodies of our buried comrades remain under the soil of this cursed ridge.
>
> The same infernal bombardment goes on. You could say it was like a tremendous reaper sweeping back and forth from right to left and razing everything. We are totally demoralized, unable to budge. This rolling thunder completely stupefies us. Eventually we are lulled to sleep by the noise, until the moment that an explosion goes off very close by and wakes us back up from our reverie.
>
> For a moment, the jolt pulls you out of your stupor, gives you a shudder, and then five minutes later you doze right back off. How long these frightful days were, waiting for death while uncontrollably nodding off. And when sleep abandoned us, this damned thirst gnawed at us and had to be equally endured. We could eat but no one wanted

to put anything in their dry throats, burned by the alcohol that we had previously drank. And the stench of the dead we couldn't get out of our noses. These proved to be the real enemy. It wasn't the Boche. On the contrary, how happy we would be if only we could see this detested race of people coming at us on days like this.

...

Those still clinging on in the trenches are silent. Their minds think of everything and nothing. They had been transformed into living statues, their skin taking on a yellow waxy look. The trenches are reduced to nothing more than shallow ditches. With no other form of protection, some men pathetically shelter under their packs to protect against the razor sharp chunks of steel that slice through the air. The constant landslides and showers of earth caused everything to be buried: equipment, rifles, men. Occasionally stretcher-bearers carry away a sad wreck of a human being, filthy, crumpled, and bleeding. And despite the unfortunate fate of the injured man, those who remain cast an envious eye to those who've seemingly escaped the furnace.[35]

To those like Bordinat, this was as near to the end of the world as one could get. One of those who could count himself more fortunate among the injured was Second Lieutenant Basteau. The small shell fragment that had struck Basteau's left hand on the approach march to Mort Homme several days before had now become inflamed and dangerously infected. On the evening of the 23rd, he set off with a group of wounded to the regimental first-aid post. But on the way back, a heavy shell came crashing down close by. 'I find myself half-buried, mouth full of earth, my right ear bleeding. I'm deaf, or at least believe I am. No one else from my group remains. I pull myself together and head off alone in the night. The shells continue to fall. Many times I have to fall flat on my chest.'[36]

Arriving at the first-aid post, he first sees the bodies of those who'd expired piled up on top of each other at the entrance, while inside it's crammed with wounded moaning and writhing in pain. Beleaguered doctors moved automatically among the injured, quickly dressing their wounds and giving them a tetanus shot before moving onto the next. After his turn, Basteau was sent on his way to the divisional first-aid post for further examination and eventual evacuation. Luck or fate was on his side. Basteau had escaped the Furnace. Back at Mort Homme, the firestorm continued unabated, mercilessly smashing, crushing, churning, destroying. Suddenly, at 7.00 pm the shelling rapidly subsided and for a few moments, a deafening silence fell over the smoking churned up land.[37] Bordinat sat there in stunned disbelief.

'Get up!' our captain shouted. 'Fix bayonets. Everybody get up on the parapets, the Boches are coming!' The sharp cry reverberated in this moment of calm and had the effect on us like a spring. Rifle in hand, all ready and loaded, with a bound we climb up and wonder where all these human wrecks around us have emerged from. No matter, everyone is determined to make the enemy pay dearly for these nameless sufferings we've had to endure since our arrival.

Red flares go up all along our line. It's to signal our 75mm guns, which now come alive and in their turn, play the tune the Boches know well. And this change in noise, mixed with the crackling of our remaining machine guns, moves us. We let loose with shouts of 'bravo' after our long period of silence. The enemy wave is decimated, doubtless leaving behind only desolation and the dead. I wonder when it will be our turn.

The thunder was in full swing. Arms and legs were flying through the air and in five minutes, everything is swept away. Five or six make it to us, unarmed, running with their arms up in the air crying out '*Kamerades, kamerades*'. Each of them was wounded one way or another, and just like us, were pale and looked exhausted.[38]

A strong German infantry attack had been mounted on the French line between Avenue No. 3 and Boyau Bourré. On the right, the dense enemy formation that rushed down the southern slope appeared to be almost a 1,000 strong. It had been quickly mowed down by the combined rifle and machine-gun fire of elements of the 332 IR. On the left, another battalion-sized enemy force had attacked with flamethrowers. After initially pushing back the French defenders, an immediate counter-attack was carried out by 7 Company and the Germans repulsed. The remaining elements were cut down by French machine-gun fire just as the other group had been. Yet the sense of satisfaction Bordinat and his comrades felt of having been able finally to act, to do something, was immediately wiped away. As they dropped back down into their holes, the German artillery opened back up to exact revenge. The maddening thirst returned once more. The same brief burst of enthusiasm was quickly extinguished by the malaise and dispiritedness which crept back into their hearts. The only saving grace came with the news that 2 Battalion would be relieved that night by elements of the 150 IR. An end was at last in sight. They just had to hang on a little while longer.

The torturous hours dragged on. By midnight, 2 Battalion's relief had still not arrived and the men wondered anxiously if they were still coming. Finally, around 2.00 am, poilus from the 150th silently filed into their position. Conscious of the terrible condition of their men and the difficult relief ahead, the officers simply told them to make their own way back as best they could to the Bois Bourrus where they would reassemble. Huddling together in small groups, the survivors – the living dead – lurched and stumbled down the churned up wasteland, winding around double and triple shell holes, tripping and trampling over the hundreds of bodies, parts of bodies, and pieces of flesh and human innards, making for the rear before daylight arrived. The occasional arrival of salvoes of German shells obliged them to throw themselves flat on the ground until the storm of shell fragments and shower of earth and stones passed. And with considerable effort, they would quietly pick themselves back up and continue the slow trudge away from the death zone. Bordinat reached the Bois Bourrus at dawn (24 May), surprised he was somehow still managing to stand upright. Reassembling with the rest of the company, they plodded forward in short jerky steps, zigzagging as if intoxicated, eventually slogging the 10km to the Bois des Clairs Chênes south of Jouy, where the 1 and 3 Battalions had been bivouacked. There, 2 Battalion dragged themselves up into the back of the trucks that would take them to Brillon-en-Barrois for rest and reorganization. What was left of the 1 and 3 Battalions boarded a train at the Baleycourt station, where they were taken overnight to Robert-Espagne. From there, they marched to their billets at Saudrupt, a neighbouring village of Brillon.

The 151 had gone up to Mort Homme on 5 May with 2,850 officers and men. They came back down with 1,517. During its third rotation at Verdun then, the 151 had suffered over 1,300 casualties, half its total strength. The other units of the 42nd and 69th Divisions suffered similar losses.[39] Most were lost on that single dark day of 20 May. Though the French had lost the summit of Mort Homme, the sacrifice of the 151 helped to limit the German advance that day. Jubert later clarified: 'War today is an effort in time, not an effort in space. It is less a matter of gaining ground than of simply holding one's ground.' In this regard, the 151 had done its duty admirably. And though it would not be codified until 23 June in General Nivelle's Order of the Day, the iconic phrase '*Ils ne passeront pas!*' ('They Shall Not Pass!') was already in use by the men of the 151.

The May rotation would be the last it would undergo during the Battle of Verdun proper. For now, the 151 would be given a period of rest before once more reorganizing, rebuilding, and retraining. After a brief time in a peaceful area of the Vosges far from the front lines, the regiment would be sent to a quiet sector in Lorraine where it would spend the entire summer of 1916. When they arrived in the Embermenil sub-sector, those in the unit they relieved asked where the rest of the 151's men were, the response was at once tragic and terrifying: '"Go to Verdun," we responded. There you can find them sleeping forever.'[40]

Chapter 10

Closing Operations at Verdun (May–December 1916)

The units of the 40th, 42nd, and 69th Divisions had held back the enemy assault by the skin of their teeth. Yet, there could be no denying the German successes. By 24 May they were in firm control of the summits of Mort Homme and Côte 304, together with the village of Cumières. Just how many men were sleeping forever at Verdun, to echo Bordinat, will never be precisely known. By the end of the month of May, French losses totalled 185,000 and those for the Germans close to the same mark.[1] By the late spring, Verdun had morphed into a shapeless battle that seemed beyond the control of those senior commanders who had ordered it. The violence inflicted on the land beggars description. The earth had been turned into a lunar landscape of double and triple shell holes, the land devoid of all vegetation. The forests had largely disappeared, the trees systematically blasted into a sparse collection of jagged toothpicks. Whole towns had been wiped off the map, many never to be rebuilt again (though this didn't stop them from being fought over as critical objectives). To help bolster their forces, a number of German divisions had been transferred from the Eastern Front during the month of April. Through April and May, intense combat had been unfolded on the right bank of the Meuse as well. With preparations for the Somme offensive well underway, pressure was exerted on both sides to quickly achieve a conclusive resolution to the fighting at Verdun. At the same time, and for the same reason, fewer resources (mainly shells and men) were provided to accomplish this. As a consequence, the scope of the fighting was scaled down and the objectives to be attained more limited.

German attacks in April around the village of Vaux, the Bois de la Caillette, and Côte du Poivre had led to progressive but costly gains. On the French side, Pétain's efforts to spare his troops from excessive losses by remaining on the defensive had not been viewed favourably by Joffre. Having saved the army at its most critical time, Pétain was removed from direct command over the Verdun operations vis-à-vis a promotion to command Army Group Centre on 1 May. His replacement was the more aggressively minded General Robert Nivelle, who wasted no time in ordering a counter-attack to retake Fort Douaumont. For the job, he tasked General Charles Mangin, commander of the 5 ID, a tough-minded fighter in his own right. Originally, Mangin had envisioned a large attack by multiple divisions across a 3km-wide attack front. Yet to preserve the troops for the Somme, Mangin was given only one division for the attack and one to use as a reserve to be used on a front just over 1,000m in width. The assault was preceded by a five-day artillery barrage that inflicted a great deal of damage on the fort and neighbouring entrenchments. The infantry attack was launched on 22 May and though the assaulting French forces suffered high casualties, by nightfall half of the superstructure had been retaken. The next day a German counter-attack forced them to back off. The attack had been a bloody failure with 5,600 of the 12,000-strong attack force becoming casualties.[2]

Meanwhile, with the summits Mort Homme and Côte 304 being captured, the Germans shifted their attention back to the right bank, launching repeated attacks to expand on their earlier gains around Fort Douaumont. By the 3 June, to the west of Douaumont they had taken the Côte du Poivre, the Carrières d'Haudraumont (where the 151 sheltered its units in March), along with the Ravin de la Mort and de la Couleuvre. South of Douaumont they'd reached the northern edge of Ferme and Ouvrage de Thiaumont, while to the east they took the Ravin de la Caillette and de la Fausse-Côte. With the capture of the village of Vaux, the Germans commenced the assault on the fort. After driving back the French defenders around the outside of Fort Vaux, they forced their way in through the coffers of the counter-escarpe using grenades, smoke, and flamethrowers. A savage combat erupted through the underground corridors and galleries. For days the fight went on from barricade to barricade with grenades, smoke, flamethrowers, poison gas, and point-blank rifle and machine-gun fire. The situation for the walled-in defenders became desperate when they ran out of water. At last on 7 June, Commander Raynal surrendered the fort, the Germans paying the defenders full military honours for their heroic struggle.

With the fall of Fort Vaux and the capture of Thiaumont, the situation for the French was getting critical. With reserves being withheld for the coming effort on the Somme, the same divisions were being sent back to Verdun and for longer periods. The heat and dust made the lack of water and the resulting thirst and dehydration even more unbearable, as clouds of enormous black flies engulfed the battlefield and feasted on the dead. Around this time, Lieutenant Henri Desagneaux was with his unit occupying a line not far from Ouvrage de Thiaumont. He had hunkered down with his company in the shell holes that constituted his position, feverish, dehydrated, and having gone days without sleep due to the tremendous shelling.

> Impossible to eat, our nerves can't stand it. If we have a call of nature to satisfy, we have to do it in a tin or on a shovel and throw it over the top of the shell hole. It's like this every day . . . We don't know where to put ourselves, we are powerless. Isolated from everything with no means of communication. There's blood everywhere; the wounded have sought

refuge with us, thinking that we could help them; the blood flows, the heat is atrocious, the corpses stink, the flies buzz – it's enough to drive one mad. Two men of the 24th Company commit suicide.[3]

Morale was running low and for the first time in the war acts of indiscipline and outright disobedience began to manifest themselves. In certain units already sent up to slaughter, singly and in small groups men refused to go back to Verdun. In most cases, the insubordinate soldiers were sent before courts martial but typically received light sentences from sympathetic officers. After the fall of Fort Vaux in June, the sector to the right of Ouvrage de Thiaumont was targeted for attack. Following days of being subjected to heavy shelling and equally heavy losses, German infantry moved in. When it did, practically an entire battalion of the 291 IR surrendered together after its commander was killed. In liaison with this unit was the 347 IR, which had suffered under the same terrific fire. Even when it had been reduced to 6 officers and 350 men, the 347 put up a fight when the enemy attacked. When one of its companies (with only thirty-five survivors) began to be encircled, the commander Second Lieutenant Herduin ordered a tactical withdrawal. But when his movement was seen by others, other elements of the 347 broke off too and for a period of time, a dangerous gap had been opened in the French line. News of the incident quickly made it up the chain, and in light of Nivelle's orders to hold positions no matter the cost, Herduin and a fellow officer were ordered to be summarily shot for cowardice. The execution was agonizingly carried out by their own men. Shortly thereafter both the 291 and the 347 IRs were disbanded and the men transferred to other units.[4]

On 22 June, after firing over 100,000 'Green Cross' poison gas shells, Fort Froid-Terre was captured and the villages of Fleury and Chapelle Sainte-Fine overrun. With the German line now on the boundary of Fort Souville, they were now within 5km of the Verdun citadel. Yet, at this critical juncture, French units were thrown into the counter-attack and pushed the line back from Chapelle Sainte-Fine, marking the furthest point reached by German forces in the Verdun offensive. On 24 June, the Allied preliminary bombardment on the Somme commenced – it would last for seven days and nights uninterrupted before the British and French infantry attack set off on 1 July. As German units were now siphoned off to meet the threat to the north, Nivelle ordered repeated counter-attacks along the right bank. The village of Fleury, long since erased from the face of the earth, changed hands sixteen times between 23 June and 17 August.

On 11 July, the Germans mounted what would be their final attack at Verdun with the intention of finally taking Fort Souville. If they succeeded, they would have control of the last set of heights overlooking the city of Verdun. Over the course of two days, French defenders held them back, with thousands mowed down by French machine-gun fire for no gain. By now, the French had lost 275,000 men at Verdun. A lull set in for several weeks but by August both sides were back at it again, with a series of attacks and counter-attacks around Fort Souville and Fleury heights. While the fighting would go on, it was clear that the offensive had failed in its objective, stated or otherwise, of capturing Verdun with respectively lower casualties than the French were to suffer. On 29 August, Falkenhayn was replaced by Chief of the General Staff Paul von Hindenburg and First Quartermaster-General Erich Ludendorff. With the Germans thrown back on a defensive stance both on the Somme and at Verdun, Nivelle again wasted no time in countering the enemy's advances over the previous six months. Planning began in September for a strong counter-attack the next month in an effort to recapture Forts Douaumont and Vaux. The attack involved a four-day preliminary barrage using some of the most powerful guns in France's arsenal, coupled with a 'rolling barrage' on the actual day of the assault, scheduled for 24 October. With the rolling barrage (known also as the creeping barrage), the infantry would advance behind and in close proximity to a barrier of shells according to a precisely coordinated timetable. In the case of the 24 October attack, the infantry would advance 50m behind a barrage of field artillery progressing at a rate of 50m every two minutes, beyond which a heavy artillery barrage progressed in 500–1,000m lifts, as the field artillery barrage approached to within 150m, forcing enemy infantry to remain sheltered.[5] On the morning of 24 October, three divisions went over the top and by the end of the day, Fort Douaumont had been retaken along with thousands of German prisoners. Following the fort's recapture, the French advanced 3km, retaking Côte du Poivre, the Carrières d'Haudraumont, Thiaumont, Douaumont village, and Bois de la Caillette. After days of pounding by the heaviest French guns, the Germans abandoned Fort Vaux, which was subsequently back in French hands by 2 November.

The final French offensive at Verdun (in 1916) was slated to begin on 5 December over a 10km front on the right bank with the goal of retaking the entire former French second line lost on 24 February. The preparatory bombardment began on 29 November but bad weather and poor visibility delayed the *jour-J*. The Germans, now aware of the plans, launched a preemptive attack of their own on 6 December, which resulted in the total capture of Côte 304. With the return of good weather on 9 December, the preparatory barrage recommenced. Over the course of 6 days, 827 guns fired over a million shells, with the shelling being directed by spotter planes. The infantry attacked on 15 December behind a double rolling barrage of shrapnel and HE shells. Despite the deplorable weather, the French reached their objectives at Vacherauville, Côte du Poivre, and Louvemont. The fighting went on for another three days but at the end, the French had advanced 2½km, recapturing all of Bois d'Haudraumont, Ferme des Chambrettes, Bois des Carrières, the Bois d'Hardaumont, and the defensive works in front of Bezonvaux. Having rectified the front lines close to where they had been in the first days of the enemy assault, the Battle of Verdun drew to a close

The human cost was catastrophic. The precise number of fallen will likely never be known. Commonly accepted casualty figures today put the total at roughly 709,000, of whom about 305,000 were killed. The French lost around 379,000, with 162,000 dead.[6] Other estimates put the numbers higher still, with as many as 800,000 killed and wounded. This number represents more than three times the number of combat deaths than the United States lost during the entire war.[7] These figures it should be noted only apply to the cost of the fighting in 1916. The armies had clashed over this same ground in 1914. Moreover, to speak of the Battle of Verdun ending on 18 December 1916 is to draw an arbitrary line. Though Forts Vaux and Douaumont had been captured in November and the old second line in December, it wasn't until the fall of 1917 that something close to the original battle lines was achieved. Even then, the Germans weren't pushed back fully to their 1915 starting positions until November 1918. The real number of those killed and wounded on the heights of the Meuse may well be nearer to 1 million.

Chapter 11

From the Somme to the Armistice: 1916–18

Battle of the Somme (September–November 1916)

Verdun had been the worst ordeal the regiment had yet undergone in the war. It would become the bar against which all other battles were measured and few surpassed. Those who'd fought there might liken future combat experiences to it, where for a few minutes or a few hours, such and such had achieved something comparable to Verdun. And the 151 certainly had plenty more fighting to do, for the war was far from over. The French had contained the German army at Verdun. In the summer of 1916, they turned the tables on the enemy. The 1 July 1916 marked the start of the massive offensive of the Battle of the Somme. Primarily thought of as a British battle, the French would take up a large portion of the offensive front and ultimately contribute fifty-seven divisions to the effort. In the 5 months of fighting, the French army lost 209,000 men, half of whom were killed. This compared with 420,000 British and between 450,000 to 500,000 German casualties. While the French lost fewer men at the Somme than Verdun, these losses were suffered over a much shorter period of time (five months versus ten). Thus, French soldiers fell at a quicker rate in the 'Meat Grinder' on the Somme, as their army was on the attack. The heaviest casualties were suffered in September, when the French lost an average of 19,000 killed or wounded a week.

At the end of September the 151 was sent to fight in the Battle of the Somme, after receiving four months' reprieve in a quiet sector of Lorraine.[1] On 20 September the regiment – still depleted from its days at Verdun and having only 2,070 men in the ranks – sloshed its way up to its front-line positions under a torrential downpour. The trenches had already turned into a quagmire of stagnant liquid mud knee-deep in many places, while the shell holes had been transformed into lakes. Taking up positions opposite the village of Rancourt, the 151 would lead the attack for the 42 ID. Its objective was to take the fortified village and a series of adjacent enemy trenches. This time it would be the Germans on the receiving end of the sledgehammer and in the days leading up to the attack, the French bombardment had achieved in Henri Laporte's mind something like the level of intensity equalling that of Verdun. The attack was scheduled for 25 September – the first anniversary of the 151's disastrous assault in Champagne in 1915. A year later, the extent of the logistical preparations, advances in weaponry and communications, and sophistication in training and tactics all pointed to a great probability of success. Aircraft, artillery spotters, and infantry would work in coordination with each other. On the day of the attack, Laporte watched as the German first-line trench 100m away appeared to be literally blown into the air.

> A quick command is passed down: 'Fix Bayonets!' We're going to attack. The rain has stopped. The sun, as if to mark the occasion, suddenly appears. In the tumult of explosions, a bugle sounds the charge. We all leap out of our trenches to rush forward. Our machine guns follow, carried in the arms of the men. It's a marvellous sight to behold: all the way to Mont Saint-Quentin, as far as the eye could see, an entire line of poilus running across the sea of water and dodging around shell-holes with the sunlight glinting off their bayonets.[2]

It was the complete inverse of the regiment's experience at Mort Homme. Lieutenant E.R. Bourgoin in command of 10 Company was in the first wave of the attack now surging across the flooded no man's land:

> For the first time we left the trenches following a rolling artillery barrage, and in less than eleven minutes we had taken Rancourt. The defenders, literally exhausted and stupefied by our preparatory artillery fire, looked like ghosts who had neither the time nor the energy to fight.
>
> After starting off with the first-line lead by Second Lieutenant de la Ferrière, I turned back to see if our two platoons of the second wave had set off well. With utter stupefaction I saw the artillerists in shirt-sleeves coming up behind us with their horses at the gallop, unlimber their guns, set up in battery, and begin firing! What great temerity they showed in order to send their shells far enough ahead to cut off the approach route of the German reinforcements! . . . The advance is made in perfect order with no stopping.[3]

Losses were relatively light as the regiment continued on to take its second and then third objectives. The crews of German 77mm batteries desperately tried to limber up and escape to the rear as waves of French soldiers bore down on top of them, but before they could they were caught by French 75s and quickly cut down. Hundreds of German prisoners came flocking up to the men of the 151, hands held high up in the air, and were herded to the rear. The men immediately set themselves up in the newly conquered positions, constructing fire parapets and machine-gun positions. As the men went about their work, Laporte observed a grim episode unfold in the old no man's land behind him.

The German batteries far away from our new lines, bombarded our rear with heavy calibre shells in order to block our reserves moving up. But it was the uninterrupted column of German prisoners who took all the fire intended for our troops. The day following this attack, piles of German corpses by the hundreds littered the resupply route, three-quarters of which lay in the water-filled shell holes and would never be buried.[4]

Rancourt and the surrounding environs had been taken by the 151 with a comparatively small number of casualties, some 500. Among this number were two distinguished officers. Lieutenant Bourgoin had received his fourth wound of the war when he was struck in the jaw by a small shell fragment that broke several of his teeth. Bourgoin would recover and return yet again to the unit in November, when he would take command of 10 Company. The second was the mathematician-officer, Captain Olivier, commanding 6 Company. Seriously wounded in the attack, he was transported back to a field hospital. Two days of suffering passed as his body struggled for life. It was a battle he would not win. The young student whose passion for arithmetic drove him to work through algorithms by the light of the moon, oblivious to the dangers, died of his wounds on 27 September — he was 27 years old. His actions together with the hundreds of others dead and wounded had contributed to the 151's achievements that day. The regiment had advanced over a kilometre, seizing multiple lines of enemy trenches and taking hundreds of prisoners in the process. For its accomplishments, the 151 was given the unofficial moniker of the 'Rancourt Regiment' and received its first Citation in the Orders of the Army as a unit in the 42 ID, which read:

> Elite division which has played the most glorious part in all the most important operations of this campaign – the Marne, the Yser, the Argonne, Champagne, Verdun – under the energetic direction of General Deville, demonstrated once again in September 1916 its offensive spirit and brilliant manoeuvring abilities on the Somme, taking strongly organized and bitterly defended positions. The 8th, 16th LIB, the 94th, 151st and 162nd IR have acquired new titles of glory.[5]

Through its actions, the unit had earned its third battle honour of the war and the right to add 'La Somme' to it's regimental colours. The assault would continue the next day on the trenches north of Rancourt and against the Bois Saint-Pierre-Vaast to the northeast. Though the 151 was able to take a foothold in the woods, with the neighbouring regiments unable to make headway in the face of heavy fire and serious losses, the 151 was forced to halt its advance. The delay was a harbinger, for it followed the pattern of combat on the Somme (and indeed the

Western Front at large). After an initial gain was made and lines of trenches taken, the attackers faced ever more lines of trenches to the rear and the enemy's resistance grew stronger. The battle would then devolve into a slow, grinding slugfest, where eventually casualties among the attackers became exponential and no further progress could be made. This was the case for the 151 and other units of the 42 ID. For another two days, the attacks on Bois Saint-Pierre-Vaast continued, with gains measured in tens of metres costing hundreds of lives. As was so often the case, provisions like food and water did not reach the front lines. Even though the rain was pouring down, the familiar torture of thirst returned. Eventually the scourge of dehydration became too much to stand and in desperation men drank from filthy water collecting in the shell holes. Bordinat and his friends drank from a scum-covered pond, adding in a few drops of mint liqueur to help mask the nasty flavour. The troops were told to start digging in where they'd been stopped.

> The holding of a conquered position is always just as murderous if not more so than the attack. The enemy now having recovered and seeing our defensive works, was avenging his setback by furiously shelling us. We took shelter as best we could in our hastily dug trenches and constantly struggled to improve them as best as possible.[6]

While hunkering down in his trench, Auguste Bordinat was half-buried by an earth collapse caused by a shell that killed or wounded eight of his friends. Although freed, he had suffered internal injuries and was vomiting blood. When he eventually chose to head back to the first-aid post, he led a blinded adjudant back with him.

> To recount the way I took would be impossible. Leading my unfortunate comrade by the hand, he begs me to move along as quickly as possible, moaning from his horrible wound, insulting me when I had to wait after the nearby explosion of shell, telling me that I must have lost my way, that I was going to get him killed, and that the journey was never-ending.[7]

They crossed over what seemed an endless passage of ravaged ground ceaselessly beaten by gunfire and asked the shortest way from the rare person they encountered, who were always seemingly in pain and in a hurry, and who responded evasively: 'You're headed the right way, keep going,' or more often, 'I have no idea, *débrouillez-vous* [keep trudging on]!' At last, Bordinat arrived at the first-aid post, where he delivered his charge into the hands of the doctor. The adjudant gave him a strong embrace, thanked him, and wished Bordinat all the best of luck. At the first-aid post, Bordinat was inspected but the doctor had no way of treating him, so he was sent back to his company. Once back, he quietly settled in as best he could, taking strange comfort in the fact that at least there was the filthy slime water from the pond to drink – at the first-aid post there was absolutely nothing.

When the 151's relief started on the night of 28 September, its effectives had already been reduced to around 1,050 troops. The regiment was given two weeks of rest and received a boost of replacements. L'Huillier (now an aspirant serving under Second Lieutenant Basteau in 6 Company) noted of these new arrivals:

> Our battalion is topped off with reinforcements coming from the Divisional Depot. In our company, we received those who'd been shirkers since 1914 in the depots of different regions and even factory workers who'd been sent to the front for disciplinary reasons. We must not only teach them how to be soldiers but also instill our wonderful esprit de corps![8]

New recruits from the class of 1917 would soon follow. With these men incorporated into the ranks, the unit was sent back up to the front on the night of 17 October to occupy the trenches skirting the western and southwestern border of Bois de Saint-Pierre-Vaast. The hope of a breakthrough now suffered the same fate as many of the wounded and drowned in the mud. The mission was simply to hold the line against enemy bombardment and counter-attacks. By then, the weather had made a distinct change for the worse. Gone for good was the hot sunny weather experienced on those fateful first days when they'd launched their heady attack. The rainy autumn season had set in, as the clay earth turned into an ocean of liquid mud.

> [The trenches] have transformed into rivers, the slippery soil of the Somme no longer able to absorb the water. The duckboards [the 162nd] have put down serve absolutely no purpose. Many poilus cut off the bottoms of their greatcoats at knee height. They sink in the yellowish water as they move about. My poilus are burrowed into shelters that are about to collapse. The tent-canvases can no longer protect us against such a deluge of water.[9]

For twenty-one days, the men lived in the filthy slurry, which in many places was waist deep, under a never-ending rain. The trenches were completely inundated and the walls of the trenches collapsed in small mudslides. Much of the time was spent bailing out water and trying to fix the cave-ins in what must have seemed like a Sisyphean task, as maddening as it was dispiriting. In addition to rain and deep liquid mud, the position was poorly placed, with the enemy line hidden just inside the wood line at a slight elevation. German mortars and artillery remained active and the mud often made it difficult for the men to get out of harm's way. In the 151's support lines, an uninterrupted barrage of tear and poison gases was fired.

In October, the 151 would have to carry out several piecemeal attacks by battalion or company against enemy positions. Though these large raids were well planned and prepared – led by automatic riflemen and hand and rifle grenadiers, with the support of flamethrower units and 37mm gun crews – they still only succeeded in capturing small portions of the enemy trenches and at significant cost. The Germans in turn counter-attacked with similar results. Laporte was present for one of these attacks.

> We were on high-alert. The guns were pre-sighted on each of the combat sectors. Suddenly the [German 77mm] cannons stopped, replaced by bursts of machine-gun fire. Immediately, flamethrower units jumped up. The Germans were leaving their trenches to come and roast us like rabbits. Despite some losses already suffered on our side, our response was furious.
>
> Flares sent up from our lines – signalling the 75s to lay down a barrage fire – had only just gone up when the rapid and heavy fire of our machine guns stopped the Germans cold just as they were arriving at our trenches. [The flamethrowers exploded] and we watched the Germans burn with their death machines strapped to their backs. Those passing through the barrage who'd managed to escape were shot down before reaching us. A second German assault wave suffered the same fate.[10]

The dangerous and deplorable conditions at the front made carrying out even routine chores the most difficult and dangerous of endeavours. Bordinat had to go on these resupply parties where:

> At every moment, we plunged into the water-filled shell holes and were unable to climb out on our own without assistance. Otherwise we would have drowned, as was the case for many.
>
> Often the supplies were lost in these holes. When we got back to our lines, we shared with our brothers what we managed to bring up (wine or bread) to keep from starving to death. Often I was forced to share a cup of wine and a small piece of mud-covered bread with four comrades as our meal for the day.[11]

Laporte had to suffer through these ordeals as well. One night late in October he was ordered to lead a resupply party to retrieve crates of machine-gun ammo. This meant struggling through oceans of water and mountains of mud, all while under fire from the enemy's shells, which threw up towering geysers of water as they burst in the swampy ground. Laporte's luck had at last run out. A shell screamed down and burst in the midst of the resupply party. Laporte was struck in the head by a shell fragment which ruptured his right eardrum. One of his comrades, his arm nearly cut off at the elbow, grabbed on to Laporte and both men fell into the muck of a water-filled shell hole, where they began to rapidly sink. The two would have drowned in the mire like so many others if not for their comrades coming to their rescue and dragging them out. Bleeding profusely from his ear, Laporte and his wounded comrade helped each other along as they made their way several hundred metres or more back to their lines. From there they were evacuated to the first-aid post where they were bandaged and received injections against infection. Outside the post the shelling remained intense, further exacerbating Laporte's wracking headaches. There was no question of being evacuated by stretcher in the trenches at this time, and they had to get to the ambulance at Le Forest farm before daylight. This meant covering the 2km on their own through the shell holes, in the rain and under fire. It was no easy task but once they'd arrived at Le Forest, Laporte and Karoff were loaded into a truck and driven to Amiens. The long ride over heavily potholed roads was filled with jarring jolts inflicting more pain on the injured evacuees inside. Arriving at Amiens, they were moved into the Hall of Justice, now converted into a temporary hospital. Even there Laporte was not out of danger. Soon after arriving, long-range German bombers flew overhead and dropped their payload on the hospital, killing and re-injuring a number of wounded. Laporte was quickly evacuated from Amiens and sent to Bordeaux, where he was operated on and a small shell fragment removed from the side of his head. Laporte's war had come to an end. He would serve out the rest of the conflict at the regimental depot in Quimper before being discharged at the beginning of 1919.

It was not long after Laporte was evacuated that L'Huillier was injured in turn. It marked his third wounding and evacuation. He received his injuries in yet another German attack. After enemy troops managed to infiltrate a part of 6 Company's trench, L'Huillier led his men on a push to kick them out. He dashed forward through the trench lobbing grenades into the attackers, who fled back rather than be killed or taken as prisoners. As he pursued them, a German grenade suddenly exploded near him, which sent fragments flying into his face, and left thumb and thigh. L'Huillier fell into a water-filled shell hole just as a German shell burst close by, partially burying him with wet earth. With machine-gun bullets whistling overhead, he was forced to remain where he was until nightfall, when his orderly came and pulled him out. When he made it back to the company command post, Basteau consoled him saying, 'My dear L'Huillier, you've been recommended for a citation in the Orders of the Division for your good conduct on the 25th of September. Get back soon.' He was evacuated to Rouen, where he had grenade fragments removed from his left thigh, above his sciatic nerve. While recovering he developed bronchitis, which put him out of action for even longer. L'Huillier managed to recover, returning to the 151 once more in late April 1917. Outside the moments of excitement and terror experienced by Laporte and L'Huillier, the real enemy was the rain and the mud. Many in the 151 were now approaching the limits of endurance. Bordinat lamented on the state of the men:

> The ranks were visibly diminished, half of us having frostbite [from having our feet submerged in] the water. Everyone was grumbling. We're told to stay put a few more days. Despite the goodwill of all, the situation is demoralizing. If the weather was nice we'd be bored but not a day went by without it raining. We are in a terrible state and covered with mud from head to toe. Our limbs are numb and we bemoan our fate.[12]

At last, after twenty-one days under fire and wallowing in the mud, the regiment was relieved on the night 5–6 November by elements of the 40 ID. During their two rotations in the autumn of 1916, the 151 had suffered 1,900 men and 26 officers killed and wounded in the mud of the Somme. Those who were left in the ranks as they pulled out of the line were in rough condition. 'Walking on our swollen feet is done with the greatest of difficulties . . . a few who had the misfortune to lose their shoes and, unable to recover them, are forced to go barefoot. It feels like you are walking on thorns or small sharp stones. Such terrible pain!'[13]

Nivelle Offensive and the Crisis of Morale (April and May 1917)

After leaving the Somme, nearly a thousand reinforcements coming from the depots of various other regiments would arrive to once again rebuild the 151 into proper fighting force. Organizationally a change was made on 5 December when the 151 and the 162 IR were broken off from the 42 ID, its original division since 1898. Both regiments were reassigned to the 69 ID, under the command of Colonel de Marathel, the former commander of the 162nd.[14] The division would then be sent up to a portion of the front north of Reims along the River Aisne, where the 151 was assigned to the Ferme de Choléra–Miette sector. A kilometre and a half to the southeast was Berry-au-Bac, while immediately to the west rose the Chemin-des-Dames plateau. Here the regiment was once again put to work improving the existing trench networks for reasons that would only become clear in the spring of 1917.

The winter of 1916–17 passed with the normal mundane and monotonous rotation to and from the trenches, as the regiment once again assumed the role of work battalions. But increasingly signs were pointing to retaking the offensive.

The build-up of the regiment's sector over a period of several months was taking place up and down the line along what would be the attack front of the French army. At the beginning of April the regiment underwent instruction and training for its role in the coming push. These incorporated the latest developments in fire and movement combat tactics. Lectures were also given demonstrating how the enemy was exhausted and tired of war, possessing worn-out equipment, and running low on food. The coming offensive, they were told, would bring about a decisive end to the war. And the men had reason to hope. Aside from all the reassurances from their commanders, reinforced by reports in the press, the materiel build-up around them was astounding. New roads were built and existing ones widened, railway lines were laid down to transport supplies and ammunition, and depots constructed to stockpile it all, including the millions of shells that were required. Gun emplacements were dug to receive the hundreds of cannon that would be used to destroy the enemy's strong defences and aviation parks for aircraft and observation balloons were created. Bordinat was greatly impressed by all the preparations, as well as the fighting spirit of the men, though they came at a price:

> Let us not forget that the preparation of an attack at this time was a monster of a job that took at least a few months. The enemy's aircraft provided intelligence on our sensitive points, slowing our progress at the price of immense sacrifices from our part, costing us as many losses as the attack. Having organized the terrain, after the advance is kicked off, so often one does not think on the immensity of this task fulfilled by those units involved and the suffering endured.
>
> On our side, our aviation, perfected and augmented, was beginning to make headway and stand up to that of the enemy, so superior to ours up until now. We hoped that it would prove itself in this coming great offensive. It was praised a bit too much by the people in the rear at that time. In the eyes of the infantrymen, airpower was regarded as a novelty weapon. They didn't trouble themselves in the least about its practicality. Nevertheless, some of these airmen, as they were called at that time, were bravely doing their duty, and seeing the great numbers of planes flying over our heads, we began to expect they would indeed provide both material [sic] and moral support in our difficult days to come, whereas we had so often been abandoned to a sad fate.
>
> ...
>
> I rarely saw afterwards the morale of all the men, though already tired of this futile struggle, elevated to this degree and with such faith in the final success that was within reach. We were practically singing as we waited for

the tremendous assault to come. It was with joyous hearts that we watched the endless arrival of cannons of all calibres day and night, whose crews boasted of their efficiency and likewise expecting success to be guaranteed. From our billets filled with the greenery of the spring of 1917, we were already making plans for the return to our families in the near future.[15]

In reality, the operation referred to alternately as the Second Battle of the Aisne, the Chemin-des-Dames Offensive and more commonly as the Nivelle Offensive after the general who envisioned it, was entirely compromised from the outset. To start, General Nivelle's original objective was rendered moot when the Germans withdrew the large salient they had held and moved back to a newly constructed series of lines known as the Hindenburg Line. The French would now be attacking one of the strongest fortified lines of the war. At the same time, French intelligence on the enemy's new positions was poor, with little detail about the organization of what they would be assaulting. Moreover, the attack objectives and general plans were known to the Germans well in advance. His plan involved replicating on a grand scale the same tactics he'd employed at Verdun successfully on a local scale, principally using the rolling barrage as a defensive shield to the infantry advancing behind it. The self-assured arrogance of the man responsible for the operation, General Nivelle, had led him to disclose his plans and preparations publicly, and these were well published in the press. Operational security was further undermined by the capture of detailed attack orders and maps. On top of everything, the weather was horrible as well, with heavy snows alternating with rain showers, causing the roads to turn into seas of mud and the trenches to flood with icy water. Much of this discouraging information was known to the French political leaders, who at this stage in the war were very conscious of squandering the lives of France's soldiers. As late as 2 and 6 April, with less than two weeks before *jour-J*, Minister of War Painlevé was scheduling meetings with Nivelle to postpone or cancel the offensive. In attendance was Premier Ribot, among other important political ministers, all concerned about reports coming from within Nivelle's subordinate generals that expressed concerns about the upcoming operation and a lack of confidence in success.[16]

The 151 would be in the first waves of the assault. Its mission was to take three successive lines of enemy trenches, following the course of the Miette, and then seize the Bois Claque-Dents to the west of Prouvais. It would be assisted in its mission by two groups of Schneider tanks (under Commander Bossut), sixteen in all. On the dark night of 15 April, the 151 moved up to their jumping-off positions. The weather was dreadful with an alternating wintry mix of snow and rain. After struggling all night over muddy roads heavily congested and under fire from enemy artillery, the battalions trudged into their flooded *parallels de départ* just before dawn. Despite all of the trials encountered, spirits remained high, the men being certain of the victory to come. At 6.00 am on 16 April the entire regiment bounded out of the trenches in a single mass and dashed towards the German lines.

At first the advance went well, with the German first line taken in five minutes. But as they moved on to the German second line, things begin to derail. The speed of the rolling barrage in front of them started off too slow and hindered what could have been a more rapid advance. They'd lost all element of surprise and this gave the enemy machine-gunners, well-concealed in the plain and in the Miette valley, ample time to prepare their fields of fire. Matters were made worse when German spotter planes observing the 151's movement began signalling back to artillery observers on Côte 78. Immediately an intense and well-regulated fire from German heavy artillery came down on the regiment's assault waves. Much to his dismay, the much-vaunted airpower the infantry had been promised seemed to Bordinat to be absent from the fight:

> We didn't see any of our planes at this early stage . . . The same was not true for the enemy who had already sent his aviation up over us, and was strafing us. His aviators had soon defeated our sad ineffective planes, which to us had earlier been so highly praised.
>
> . . .
>
> Now the enemy, alerted in all areas, was pouring fire into us. The bullets whistle past, while we come under machine-gun fire from the nasty little birds flying only a hundred metres above us. We take shots at them but with no effect other than to make us feel good. What comfort we would've had if we saw our planes chase away these damned dogs above our heads, but still nothing.[17]

As the crossfire from machine guns and artillery intensified, the 151's progress slowed to a crawl before being forced to halt entirely and the men ordered to start digging in place. To the experienced troops, it was an ill-omen. Frustrations rose as morale began to sink. After only a few hours, things were once again resembling all the other bloody and ultimately futile assaults they'd made in the past. Bordinat was now pinned down with the rest of 1 Battalion in the German second-line position, unable to advance in the face of the withering fire.

> We're wretched martyrs and once again we are left to fend for ourselves, suffering it all without recrimination . . . Paying a heavy price in sacrifices and through force of courage, advancing by leaps and bounds under fire and through poison gas, we arrived at the Boche [second position] called the Tranchée [du] Ruisseau at half-past eleven. Now our rolling barrage

is at least 3 kilometres ahead of us where, according to the calculations of the general-staffs, we were supposed to be at this point. Wonderful planning, I swear.[18]

Spirits momentarily lifted when, to much amazement, Bossut's tank groups appeared and slowly lurched their way towards the regiment's advance line. Their mission was to support the infantry attack by punching gaps in the German wire that lay between the second and third lines, and to provide direct fire support against enemy machine guns and points of resistance. Some had broken down before even getting beyond the German first line. As the Schneiders approached the German second line, they were spotted by enemy observation planes, who signalled their locations back to German artillery. Disaster ensued. An avalanche of shells slammed down around them, with shell fragments striking and igniting the exposed fuel compartments. One by one, the Schneiders were hit and quickly made into flaming death traps for the crews inside. Most crew members burned alive inside their tanks, including Commander Bossut himself. Some managed to climb out of the crew compartments, even while they're clothes, flesh, and hair were on fire, but soon collapsed only a short distance from their tanks. Bordinat and his comrades watched the horrific scene unfold before them, powerless to help. At the same time, they were awestruck by the bravery of the doomed tankers, particularly by the coolness displayed by those who salvaged the weaponry from the vehicles not set aflame all while under a terrific fire.

By then it was perfectly clear to the troops what the outcome would be. Experience taught them how small the window for capitalizing on their initial gains was and it had already closed before their eyes. Bordinat's earlier prognosis was sadly correct. The regiment was left to fend for itself for a week under furious bombardment, without proper supplies, clinging desperately to their dearly paid-for gains. Every day, dozens were cut down by shell-fire. Another deadly nuisance revealed itself as well, for though the initial advance had swept quickly over the enemy first line at Choléra, a number of enemy troops singly or in small groups had still not been cleared out from the network of underground tunnels. These stubborn defenders refused to surrender and kept up a harassing fire from behind, even as fire swept down from the front and flanks. Trench cleaners had to be sent back in, whose special mission was the no-mercy-shown nasty work of rooting out the last pockets of resistance. With grenades, pistols, and medieval-looking melee weapons, a brutal hand-to-hand struggle unfolded in the underground rooms and passages, until the remaining Germans were wiped out. Days passed as the men in the new first line hunkered down and tried their best just to hold on. The morale of the troops plummeted, with many falling back without orders to the shelter of the former German first lines at Choléra, where they marvelled at the subterranean village the

Germans had built, replete with electricity, electric pumps, and comfortable rooms with sleeping bunks – all unknown luxuries for the poilus. Meanwhile, each of the 3 battalions had less than 300 men reporting for duty. When they were finally relieved on 3 May, the discontent in the ranks was widespread and visibly perceptible, the men doing nothing to hide their feelings on their poor treatment.

Regimental losses are not precisely known. From 16 April to 2 May, the 151 suffered between 1,000 and 1,200 casualties, with 360 killed and over 500 wounded on just the opening day of the assault. By 22 April, regimental rolls reported the total number of effectives as 1,547 men and officers, less than half the amount it had gone in with. Among the losses were seventeen officers killed or wounded, including Second Lieutenant Jubert who had been shot in the left arm. For his bravery and leadership, his actions in the attack would earn him a Médaille Militaire. After two months of convalescence, Jubert would return once more to the regiment in June.[19] By Great War standards, the 151's attack had not been entirely unsuccessful. The regiment had succeeded in taking two lines of enemy positions encompassing more than 3km of ground and in doing so had captured a number of German cannon, mortars, machine guns, and hundreds of prisoners.[20] For its accomplishments on this day, the 151 would receive a Citation in the Orders of the Army, which read:

> Elite regiment which came to affirm once again its reputation during the course of recent fights. On 16 April 1917, under the orders of the brave and energetic Lieutenant Colonel Moisson, it composed itself in perfect order into the assault against the powerfully organized and fortified enemy trenches. Taking the first and second positions under machine-gun fire and heavy artillery barrages. Entirely breaking the enemy counter-attacks and holding on to the conquered ground under an extremely violent bombardment. Taking numerous prisoners, taking cannons and machine guns.[21]

The 151 had done well for itself in comparison with many other French units. Yet, below the surface, the picture was much bleaker. This attack had been billed as a war-ending breakthrough, with minimal losses and massive gains over a short period of time. Nivelle had promised an advance of 5 miles in the first day. Instead, many units were able to advance only 500m. The general had also promised to call off the attack after forty-eight hours if not immediately successful, and yet he plowed ahead for ten days as the offensive devolved into yet another grinding slugfest, where gains were measured in tens of metres and paid for in thousands of lives. On the first day alone, 40,000 French soldiers were killed or wounded. After 4 days the number stood at nearly 120,000, including 30,000 killed and 4,000 missing or captured. By 9 May, the butcher's bill had climbed to 187,000.[22] The French army had been pushed to its breaking point. As regiments that had already completed one rotation on the Chemin-des-Dames were ordered back to the line, at first groups and then entire units began categorically refusing to re-enter the trenches. Even before the mutinies of 1917, cracks had begun to show. Verdun had inflicted irreparable damage on the poilus' morale. Starting at the end of 1916 and continuing into April 1917, the rate of desertions gradually rose. As April turned to May and then June, the frequency and severity of mutinous acts increased. A private in the 36 IR succinctly sums up the serious concerns of the troops:[23]

> We refused to go up to the line on Tuesday night, we didn't want to march. You might almost say that we went on strike, and many other regiments have done the same thing. It'll be easier to explain when I come home on leave. They drive us like animals; they don't give us much to eat and they want us to get ourselves killed for nothing. If we'd gone into the attack, only half of us would have come out alive and we refused to go forward.[24]

There would be no gross displays of insubordination in the 151 during the height of the mutinies that affected the French army in April, May, and June. However, when the regiment was told it was being sent back to the fighting two weeks after its first rotation, the men did not hesitate in protesting and airing their grievances openly to their officers. They demanded rest, an end to useless assaults, better food and pay, improved living conditions when not in the trenches, and the resumption of regular furlough. Bordinat reported that in the 151 men were particularly irritated with troops serving in rear echelon services, whom they regarded as shirkers. They argued that these men should be dragged out of their comfy posts and sent to share the burden in the combat formations.

> It was not not uncommon to see people already wounded several times, be sent back to the 'field of honour' to get killed, while workers fresh and available, full of health and wanting of nothing (including arrogance), lived peaceful lives with nothing to do.
> And it was the same thing with the officers: the officer of the trenches was a zero compared to that of the rear. It was because of all these shameful injustices that the poilus sang of their mental and physical suffering in front of our very commanders, who tried not to encourage us, as was their duty not to. Nonetheless, the officers couldn't help but be all ears, constantly warning [their superiors] of the ever-increasing danger. I still remember some inflamed couplets of songs composed by people who had done a turn on the front in the years 1916–1917, as well

as some stanzas composed in the trenches during days of despair. [At the back of Bordinat's memoirs is a version of the infamous 'La Chanson de Craonne', which he called 'Les plateaux Lorette, Somme, Verdun']

. . .

I think that if you had asked for a vote for the continuation of the war from the combatants, there would have been a good chance of a 'no' vote at this time. Only one hope remained for us when we saw the official declaration of America's entry into the war. But how would these Americans arrive here, with submarines? After what was happening to England around this time, there's no way the American army could get a million men to our shores in a year. In short, we would have to overcome all these difficulties on our own.'[25]

The mutinies in the French army had shaken it to its core. As civilian factory workers went on strike in support of their fighting men, it became clear that drastic action needed to be taken, which addressed the grievances of the troops and avoided any draconian measures. To do otherwise would have likely backfired and resulted in a violent revolt. To their great surprise, many of their demands would be met, starting with a period of rest in May. Much of this was thanks to reforms introduced by General Pétain, Nivelle's replacement as Commander-in-Chief. Pétain sympathized with his soldiers' concerns. He also agreed that a change was needed in how the French were waging war if France wanted to keep its army from falling apart, let alone be victorious against Germany. Pétain immediately called an end to the attacks on the Chemin-des-Dames and reinstated regular leave. Directives were issued that focused on improving the quality of and access to food, increasing pay, improving rear area living conditions, and creating military canteens and rest stations. Gradually, the reforms rolled out by Pétain led to the poilus feeling that they were at last being treated with human decency and not simply as cannon fodder. Tactical changes were made as well. Temporarily abandoning any idea of a general offensive, the commander-in-chief instead adopted the concept of 'limited offensives', whereby limited objectives would be attained only after an intense, meticulously prepared opening bombardment using predominantly heavy calibre guns, working in coordination with aerial reconnaissance and observation.

The 151 began another long period of instruction at Camp Mailly to improve upon their previous combined arms and fire and movement training. There, the men honed their skills with automatic rifles, heavy machine guns, hand and rifle grenades, trench artillery, and signalling. They ran through numerous combat exercises in coordination with aircraft. Aside from this immediate goal, though, was the underlying objective of re-instilling an *esprit de corps*. On 26 June a large regimental party was held, the day beginning with a *prise d'armes* followed by Mass. The rest of the day was spent at rest in social gatherings, games and recreational distractions, capped off by a torch-light march at night. For its action in the Nivelle Offensive, the 151 had also earned its fourth battle honour to be inscribed on the flag: L'Aisne. And with it, the regiment was awarded the Croix de Guerre. As a unit distinction, this entitled all men serving in the regiment to wear the fourragère of the Croix de Guerre around their left shoulder. On 28 June 1917, with the regiment formed up on the Camp Mailly parade grounds, General Fayolle (in command of Army Group Centre) was joined by General Passaga (XXXII CA commander) and General Monroe (69 DI commander) in decorating the regimental colours with the fourragère of the Croix de Guerre. At the time, it was only the eleventh infantry unit to have received this distinction.[26] Fayolle would also decorate the fanion of the 3 Machine-Gun Company (commanded by Captain Gelly) for its citation in the Orders of the Army Corps for its conduct at Choléra, along with the fanion of the Jubert's 11 Company (commanded by Captain Wébanck) for its citations in the Orders of the Army and the Orders of the Army relating to its conduct at Mort Homme and Choléra, respectively. As the national holiday of 14 July approached, orders went out to regimental commanders instructing them to select a platoon-size group of men to act as a delegate party for the unit at that year's Bastille Day march in Paris. The recently promoted Captain Bourgoin, who'd recovered from the jaw injury he received at the Somme the previous autumn, was chosen to lead it, along with Lieutenant Baillat. L'Huillier had also been picked, as had the stretcher-bearer Henon. All agreed it was a thrilling event that made a powerful impression upon them, as they paraded down the Grands Boulevards of Paris in dense marching columns, cheered on by enthusiastic crowds of civilians throwing flowers. It was a welcome, rejuvenating distraction for the forty delegates given the honour of representing *le Quinze-Un*. For two days later they were back aboard a troop train being shuttled back to the front – back to the Furnace of Verdun.

Second Battle of Verdun (August and September 1917)

In what would be the first of Pétain's limited offensives following the rebuilding period after the turbulent spring and summer of 1917, the French army would be going back on the attack at Verdun. On the left bank of the Meuse, things had remained quiet for the first six months of 1917. But in June 1917, the Germans unleashed assaults on the southern slopes of Côte 304 and Mort Homme, as well an attack on the fortified towns of Avocourt and Cumières. These proved partially successful and the fighting continued into July. A back and forth of bloody attacks and counter-attacks ensued, lasting until the end of the month. This was the aim of the coming French offensive, to rectify the recent gains made by German forces, re-establishing a tactical advantage that, at the same time, would hold heavy symbolic value. A massive coordinated assault would be launched on both banks of the Meuse along a 25km front. For the execution of the operation, select formations were chosen which had already distinguished themselves in various sectors at Verdun: XIII, XV, XVI, and XXXII Army Corps. It would be the fourth rotation to Verdun for the 151.

On 16 July the regiment was transported to its home garrison, where it would spend the night in its old barracks, Miribel, the roof and walls now punctured and pocked by shell-fire. From there, it would take up positions on the right bank, in the Bois des Caurières – Ferme des Chambrettes sector (north of Fort Douaumont). The regiment completed its first two-week rotation digging trenches while under bombardment in what was largely an uneventful period, after which it returned to the outskirts of Verdun. But the rest was deceptive as the battalions were put to work transporting heavy loads of munitions and supplies to and from the Forts Souville and St Michel, a tedious 7km round trip. There were even a few days in between the work fatigues where the companies of 2 and 3 Battalions would take shelter in the famous Fort Douaumont. Despite it being under bombardment by the most massive shells, life was fairly comfortable in the protected subterranean galleries of the fort. The same could not be said for the coming and going in order to carry out the various assignments, during which time the men had to run through the devastating fire of 1-ton German shells while heavily burdened. In the end, they preferred to avoid the fort altogether. Just before being sent back out to the trenches, L'Huillier wrote out a short ode:

'To the One-Fifty-One – There's no need to worry.'
There are two ways to be, you're at the front or you're not. If you're not, there's no need to worry.
–If you're there, there are two alternatives: you're at rest or you're in the trenches. If you are at rest, there's no need to worry.
–If you're in the trenches, there are two alternatives: you're in reserve or you're in the first line. If you're in reserve, there's no need to worry.
–If you're in the first line, there are two alternatives: all hell's breaking loose or all hell's not breaking loose.
–If all hell's not breaking loose, there's no need to worry. If all hell's breaking loose, there are two alternatives: you're wounded or you're not.
–If you're not wounded there's no need to worry. If you are wounded, there are two alternatives: you're wounded gravely or you're not.
–If you're not wounded gravely, there's no need to worry. If you're wounded gravely, there are two alternatives: you survive or you don't survive.

-If you survive, there's no need to worry. If you don't survive and if you've heeded my advice, you'll never have made it anyways.[27]

On 18 August, the regiment was sent back up to the Ravin du Helly, where it would support an attack by its old division, the 42nd, on 20 August. The relief up to the line was very hard, made so by the incessant fire from German artillery firing HE, shrapnel, and copious mustard gas shells. The men had no other choice but to don their stifling gas masks, which made breathing a labour and seeing almost impossible. Groping their way up and down the heights in the darkness punctuated only by the briefest stabs of light from the bursting shells, they somehow managed to reach their starting positions. On 20 August, the units of the 42 ID attacked and reached their objectives quickly, almost immediately the German artillery unleashed a strong bombardment on the entire sector. This included a barrage of poison gas shells that proved particularly devastating to the 332nd. With one of its battalions practically wiped out by the gas, the 3 Battalion of the 151 was ordered to advance into the Bois des Caurières in support. For forty-eight hours, it was subjected to one the most powerful bombardments the men had ever experienced even by Verdun standards, with nothing but shell craters in which to shelter.

A small consolation for the veterans of the 151 came with the news that after two days of hard fighting, units of the XVI Army Corps had taken Côte 304, Cumières, and most significant of all, Mort Homme. While there was an obvious sense of satisfaction upon hearing the news, there was little time for celebrating.

> Out of 450 we had [in 3 Battalion] on the 20th, there were barely 250 of us left by the 26th on the morning of the attack. At times like this, each man looks within himself and after this cruel, deadly period out in the open, the morale of the men and even the officers right now is pretty poor and no one has much confidence in success. Our goal is to take the Tranchée du Chaume and the Ouvrage de Lama, which was a den of machine guns. Fortunately, provisions had arrived that night – that is to say wine, water and a strong ration of booze – which helped to raise morale of everyone that had only just been so low.[28]

On 26 August, 3 Battalion participated in a new attack in the Ravin l'Hermitage sector, led by the 42 ID against Tranchée du Chaume and Ouvrage de Lama. Though exhausted from the tremendous efforts already expended, the men threw themselves again into the attack with energy. The battalion quickly took all of its objectives and then fought off several Germans counter-attacks, suffering heavy losses during the course of the fighting. By the evening, as rain began to fall from the dark skies, 3 Battalion had been reduced to only 230 effectives.²⁹ Among the dead was Second Lieutenant Raymond Jubert. By then, Jubert was a Chevalier de la Légion d'honneur and the recipient of the Croix de Guerre with two palms and stars of bronze, silver, and gold for his multiple citations in the Orders of the Army, Army Corps, and Division. His promotion to the Legion of Honour in May 1917 read:

> Brilliant officer of high moral character, a true leader of men. Distinguished himself in the Argonne, at Verdun and on the Somme for his wonderful conduct under the fire. Twice cited in the orders [of the army]. On 16 April 1917, lead his platoon brilliantly into the assault. Wounded, he nonetheless continued to direct the advance and only let himself be evacuated after having received permission.
> –Signed: DEBENEY

More than just being an excellent officer, Jubert was a gifted writer who possessed a mastery of language, a calibrated internal sensitivity, and a genuine empathy towards his fellow human beings. Of the principal eyewitnesses in the 151, he was one of the few who provided a true glimpse into how the war affected his mind and soul. What he saw on the battlefields destroyed him spiritually long before the bullet that cut him down. While recuperating from the gunshot wound he'd received in the previous April, Jubert wrote:

> After twenty months of fighting, where twenty times I should have died, I have not seen war as I had imagined it. No, none of those grand, tragic tableaux with sweeping strokes and vivid colours, where death would come as a quick blow. Only these small painful scenes, in obscure corners of small compass, where one cannot possibly distinguish if the mud were flesh or the flesh were mud.³⁰

Now the 27- year-old Raymond Jubert lay dead in the mud on the devastated heights above Verdun. He left behind two grieving parents who now had to mourn the loss of both their sons. Added to their pain was that neither of their boys would receive a marked grave, or any real grave for that matter. With a serious lack of officers, L'Huillier was promoted from aspirant to second lieutenant and transferred to 10 Company to help fill the gaps in leadership roles. On and on the killing went. After two weeks of hardship and suffering, the regiment was given five days of rest off the line. There was just time enough to receive a small number of reinforcements before again being pushed back up to the front on the night of 6 September – their sixth and ultimately final rotation at Verdun. Orders came down: the 151 was going to assault the heights of the Bois des Fosses and Bois le Chaume. It must have truly seemed like there was no escape from the Furnace, no way out but death. Indeed, Bordinat attested that there were grumblings from many of the men, especially among those who'd just arrived as replacements. On the morning of 8 September, with a heavy fog mixing with a thick shroud of smoke from the barrage, the regiment attacked. Despite their fear, the men fell back on the training that had just been instilled in them in June.

> After a short and intense artillery preparation, at 7:30 am we attack. We cross the starting position without difficulties. We advance at the pace of 100 metres every three minutes (just like in our training at Camp Mailly!). Some haggard Boches come out of their shelters. My 1st and 2nd Squads had taken some losses: Corporal Thuret is killed as is Chapon. I'm at the head of 3rd Squad. Gahery and his crew inflict heavy losses with their automatic-rifles on some Boches who were attempting to counter-attack.[31]

L'Huillier's company commander, Second Lieutenant Basteau, seemed to be running low on luck. At the beginning of the attack, he lost one of his boots to the mud and had to improvise one out of a piece of canvas. Later, his helmet was knocked off after being struck by grenade thrown by a sergeant who was aiming for a group of Germans. Basteau continued the rest of the attack helmetless with only one shoe. Confusion was the order of the day owing to lack of visibility and chaotic nature of the terrain so devastated and churned up by the artillery. Some platoons went off course or got entirely turned around in the fog. At one point, Captain Bourgoin's platoon came under grenade attack at his command post by an aspirant from 3 Company. Fortunately, the misguided officer was using less powerful offensive grenades and no one was injured. Despite the poor conditions, in a short time, all the assigned objectives were taken, including the formidable Ouvrage de Lama and Tranchée de Mésopotamie. They had also taken over 460 haggard-looking prisoners whose pale, sunken faces resembled their own, though the Germans wore an obvious expression of relief as well for having escaped. The regiment would once again be cited in the Orders of the Army for its actions: '[The 151] Regiment composed itself very well under fire. Under the command of Colonel Perchenet has checked the enemy advance and has contributed through its obstinate resistance to the breaking of the Germans' efforts.'[32] Yet, despite the official unit citation, for those going through these nightmarish days, it must have all been so horrifyingly similar to every other attack. Moving up into the Ravin d'Hassoule with 1 Battalion the week before Captain Adjudant Major Bourgoin experienced scenes that were depressingly familiar to those who'd been at Mort Homme the year before.

Approached the north slope of [Fond] des Rousses, encountered a bombardment of an inconceivable intensity. My battalion felt like it was cut off from the other defence sectors. The telephone line was constantly being cut, the TPS [ground telegraphy] unusable, only one liaison agent with the artillery limited to signalling with flares and with the commander using light optics to Fort Douaumont. But smoke and fog often made these two means of communication insufficient. There were some carrier pigeons as well, but these were reserved for emergencies.

The bottom of the ravine was being ceaselessly churned up by shells. The bodies of French and German dead which had been buried were constantly disinterred. Our stretcher-bearers faced great risks to rebury them each night and with evacuations made so difficult, our wounded were also left. We'd been sent up into line for four days but were left for ten. And we had no trenches. The units occupy lines of shell-holes, all mixed up together. The central boyau in which we arrived is dug out each night, as every day it was levelled by the *minenwerfer* opposite us sending over bombs weighing 200 kilograms [440lb]. Despite our strength in artillery (six groups of 75mm comprising seventy-two cannons and two groups of 155mm, 1 battery of 220mm mortars, and one battery of 58mm mortars) the battalion still felt like it was insufficiently supported.[33]

Having once again run out of water and with no provisions making it up their positions, the men tried to collect rainwater using their tent canvases but the taste of it made it almost undrinkable. For another five days, the depleted battalions of the 151 grudgingly fought on, mostly out habit, trying unsuccessfully to take more ground while fighting off multiple enemy raids and counter-attacks.[34]

Unfortunately, 1 Battalion had neglected to search all the dugouts, the enemy being a master in this art. These were usually dug deep underground and were well equipped, sometimes sheltering whole companies. Believing that the enemy was completely driven out, they began to dig and to organize the trench, leaving their weapons in order to wield shovels and pickaxes instead. Suddenly they came under attack by the enemy seemingly emerging from everywhere, including from the rear.

Within the great struggle, there were innumerable acts of bravery displayed. There was Corporal Caillet (1 MG Company) who was encircled with a handful of his men by a dozen Germans who'd taken his machine gun. Caillet put up a fierce fight to get it back using grenades and his revolver, and even the legs of the gun's tripod after disengaging the gun barrel. He succeeded in getting the gun back, along with taking several enemy officers and men prisoner. For his actions he would be promoted to sergeant and to the Légion d'honneur, his medal being pinned by General Pétain personally. Aspirant Ponchon (10 Company) didn't realize he had advanced beyond the flattened German first line and pushed on ahead. Isolated from the rest of his unit, he was forced to shelter in a shell hole for the entire day under a terrific fire of enemy shells before eventually navigating back to friendly lines by compass. Later, when his unit's advance was checked by the fire of an enemy machine gun, he set off on his own and circled around the gun before closing in on it from the flank and capturing the gun crew and the captain commanding the unit.[35]

It was while leading his platoon through a *boyau* that L'Huillier was wounded yet again, his fourth time and and this time much more seriously. L'Huillier was fighting with his platoon, using grenades to wipe out enemy defenders, when he spotted a very young German in the *boyau*. At the same moment as L'Huillier pulled the pin on his grenade, the German boy threw his own. Calculating that it would fall to the left of the *boyau*, L'Huillier committed to throwing his own grenade. Just as he released it, the German grenade exploded on the edge of the trench close beside him. L'Huillier's entire left side was riddled with fragments, one of which broke his left arm. He'd received multiple wounds to the face, including a deep cut above his left eyebrow penetrating the sinus. His arm and leg were badly lacerated and his knee fractured. Bleeding profusely from his face and arm, he told his orderly to cut the leather lace from one of his leggings to use as a tourniquet for his left arm. The man then used L'Huillier's handkerchief to bandage his left eye, from which he could no longer see. It was impossible at that moment to be evacuated with the enemy all around. L'Huillier began issuing instructions to his men, telling them to block the *boyau* with anything they could find, and when Aspirant Ponchon arrived to take over command of the platoon, he provided him with counsel too. An attempt was made by several men to get L'Huillier out of there, but one of the men was quickly struck in the shoulder by a bullet. It was still too dangerous to attempt an evacuation, so he ordered them to leave him where he was. His wounds continued to haemorrhage profusely as he bled through three dressings. Feeling certain he wouldn't survive, he began praying as his thoughts drifted to his mother and sister. As night fell, L'Huillier was still counted among the living, and he was at last taken back on a stretcher to the regimental first-aid post, located beside Colonel Moisson's command post. Moisson came over to check on the wounded and seeing the badly mauled L'Huillier, did his best to comfort him:

> 'So my dear L'Huillier, another glorious wound?'
>
> I had enough energy to smile and reply, 'Alas, you won't see me again in the regiment. I've lost my left eye.'
>
> 'Good luck to you all,' the colonel responded.[36]

From there, L'Huillier was taken on a long and painful journey back to the divisional first-aid post at the Carrières d'Haudraumont, where the 151 had sheltered during its first tour the previous March. After his wounds were dressed (his eyesight returning to his left eye after the blood had been washed out), he was loaded into an American Red Cross truck and driven to a hospital in Verdun before being sent on to Château du Petit-Montheron. In a final turn of luck, L'Huillier happily discovered that he would be treated by one of his own cousins who happened to be the chief surgeon. L'Huillier would finish up the rest of the war in convalescence, gradually recovering from his wounds, which left him permanently scarred. For his actions, he would receive a Croix de Guerre with palm and a promotion to the Chevalier de la Légion d'honneur with citation that read:

> Young officer of courage, ardour and temerity. On 9 September 1917 at the Bois des Fosses, energetically maintained his platoon at its post by his good example despite a heavy artillery fire. Then led his platoon into the attack against a strongly held German trench, where he was seriously wounded. Has made a superb example of coolness, decisiveness, and bravery to all. Four times wounded and three times previously cited.
> –Signed: DEBENEY

According to the *JMO*, between 8 and 13 September the 151 had 71 confirmed killed, 393 wounded, and 162 missing. All in all, during its 3 rotations in July, August, and September totalling 35 days in the front lines, 1,065 had fallen on the ghastly heights above Verdun.

> We leave with what remains of our sad battalion, once again torn to pieces, giving a last farewell to the comrades who will lie forever in this place of suffering and desolation around Verdun, a true graveyard.[37]

Training Americans and the Return to the War of Movement – Battles of Compiègne, Soissons, and Lorraine

After the terrible days at Verdun, the 151 would be given several months reprieve off the line. The 151 was now counted among the elite units in the French army, reviewed by General Pétain, Marshal Joffre, and General John Pershing. Many of the veterans would be given a much-deserved furlough at this time. One of the lucky ones was Bordinat who was granted a week's leave at the start of October 1917. Returning home, his would apparently be an amorous time. For without wishing to delve into taudry speculation, nine months later he would receive the happy news of the birth of a baby girl, whom he would name Solange. In the same month, in recognition of their experience and conduct under fire, the 151 was chosen as an advising and instruction unit to newly arrived American troops. For the months of November and December 1917, the 151 would help to train the 104th US Infantry Regiment (26 ID, I Army Corps) and the 5th US Marines (4 IB, 2 ID) in the region south of Neufchâteau (Vosges). The instruction would cover the roles of the various specialists, mainly hand grenadiers, signallers, and pioneers, as well as training on the Hotchkiss machine gun, the Chauchat automatic rifle, and Viven-Bessières (VB) rifle grenade launcher. They would also run through combat exercises on the platoon and battalion levels, 'passage of lines', attack on an 'island of resistance', and relief rotations in a mock sector of entrenchments. The time spent with their American comrades and the hospitable townsfolk of the Vosges was a happy memory despite the freezing cold and heavy snow. The regiment would return to the trenches in January, taking up positions around Flirey, Limey, and Regnéville in the St Mihiel salient. It was a fairly quiet sector when they arrived with only occasional light skirmishes. With US forces taking up a portion of the front, American led raids picked up in frequency, along with constant harassing fire on the enemy, causing the sector to become 'hot'. The German form of retaliation for the American hostilities was typically to send over mustard gas shells to make things unpleasant for everyone.

As winter turned to spring, Germany prepared to mount its final win-or-die attempt to break the deadlock and knock the Allies out before the arrival of millions of American troops. What followed was the vision of a single man, General Erich Ludendorff. In what was called the Kaiserslacht (the 'Emperor's Battle'), and now known more commonly as the German Spring Offensive, the German army would let loose a series of successive punches falling along different portions of the front. Taken together it remains one of the largest battles of all time. The massive onslaught would be led by assault divisions formed from elite troops, who were highly motivated, provided with the best equipment and specially trained in infiltration tactics. On 21 March the first of the blows was unleashed with the commencement of Operation Michel, which targeted the British 3rd and 5th Armies. It began with the largest cannonade in human history – 10,000 artillery pieces firing 1.1 million shells (including copious amounts of poison gas) in what was a 5-hour 'hurricane bombardment'. This new technique was meant to stun the enemy so as to allow the assault troops to infiltrate and inundate the positions, while avoiding the self-made impediment of battering the ground so badly that the speed of the advance was hindered. Under the onslaught the line bent back as British forces fell into full retreat. The front line was practically broken and disaster seemed to be inevitable. Yet as German losses mounted exponentially and supply lines became over extended, the momentum slowed. The weight of British and French reinforcements rushed up to bolster the faltering line stopped further enemy advances and ultimately prevented a complete breakthrough. Undeterred, German commanders launched the other successive operations as planned: Georgette on 9 April, Blücher–Yorck on 27 May, and Gneisenau on 9 June. This last, also know as the Battle of the Matz, struck the French 3rd Army between Mont Didier and Noyon and would require intervention from the 69th Division among others. At this time, the 151 was already in a weakened state due to a strong epidemic of Spanish flu sweeping through the ranks. The coming battle would be the regiment's first under a new commander. Colonel Moisson had been promoted in May to take command of 39 ID, leaving the regiment he'd commanded for three brutal years. Lieutenant Colonel Perchenet was his replacement. On 8 June the 151 was transported by rail and then trucks to Compiègne, arriving at Gournay-sur-Aronde the next day. With the French line bending back on itself, the 151's mission was to stop the enemy advance no matter the cost. The units struggled at night in the middle of a tall corn field to make contact with their liaisons. The next day, after crossing the Compiègne–Ressons-sur-Matz road, they were met with a hail of machine-gun fire and then fleeing survivors from other units, who told them that the enemy had attacked en masse and, incredibly, without artillery preparation or support. The 151 soon runs into German formations south of Bois de Ressons and counter-attacks (supported by FT-17 Renault light tanks) against vastly superior numbers. Without artillery support of their own, the battle was purely an infantry on infantry fight.

> We shoot into this human wave without stop, which then hesitates in the face of our rifle and machine-gun fire crackling away from all sides. The Boches stop and we do the same. For two hours, there was only the whistling of bullets, no cannon shots at all, on either side. We don't see anything else, no planes nor cannons. Our ammunition runs out and we have to rummage for more from our comrades killed beside us. Our fire slows, as we now have to make each shot count.[38]

The companies hold their ground, advance, then retreat, in a seesaw type of fighting not seen since August 1914. After his company commander is shot in the wrist, Bordinat is sent back to inform the commander of 2 Battalion that the company would begin a withdrawal.

> I set off wearing my pack with my rifle on my shoulder, in the middle of a storm of bullets, running through the wheat and oats that are sprinkled with a fine rain and slowing my pace. Splash, splash, flac, flac I go in my clodhoppers. No bother. I cover the 1,500 metres in haste. On the way, I am taken to task by a machine gun, probably guessing at my plans. The bullets cut down the ears of corn around me and pierce my greatcoat.

> For a second, I hit the dirt, pretending to be hit. Rest a little bit, then I set off again . . . through the oats. I close my eyes and tell myself, whatever happens will happen. I run to the right without making use of cover. While going through a field of alfalfa, I find two beautiful quail eggs in a nest. In the turmoil, I pick them up and put them in my empty ammo pouch, for what purpose I couldn't say.[39]

Gradually the 151 had to give way and began to conduct a fighting withdrawal towards Ferme Portes, inflicting heavy casualties on the German infantry. Eventually the weight of German troops and the threat of being encircled forced the 151 back. Though the unit had conducted itself well and delayed the enemy's advance, the feeling in the ranks was that the Germans were close to a breakthrough. After falling back further the next day, the shattered remains of the regiment dug in on a ridge and awaited the enemy's continued assault.

> Suddenly, at around 4.30 pm, this large grey mass emerges onto the Gournay – Compiègne road. We stiffened up waiting to receive them, finger on the trigger, waiting for the signal to fire. Suddenly, an artillery barrage of all calibres is unleashed against them, while we open up on them with rifles and machine guns. In light of this good trick played by the artillerymen, we laugh and even dance about. Arms and legs fly through the air as the terrified Boches flee backward and try to pass through our barrage. Almost all are blown away by the savage barrage.

The 151's tenacious defence, together with the rest of the 69th Division, had limited the enemy's gains to around a kilometre. Its conduct had also earned the regiment its third citation in the Orders of the Army but at the cost of nearly 640 men and officers. Among the dead was Lieutenant Arthaud de la Ferrière, the last of thirteen original Saint-Cyriens who'd first joined the 151 with Campana in January 1915. He had fought alongside Laporte in Slaughter Wood on that terrible day of 30 June 1915, emptying his revolver at point-blank range as enemy footsoldiers overwhelmed the lines. When the 151 first arrived at Côte de Froide-Terre above Verdun in March 1916, he had stood beside Jubert and muttered in awe at the 'vestibule of Hell'. From Mort Homme to the Somme, Choléra, and Chambrettes, he had done his duty valiantly. As a wave of German infantry bore down on Lieutenant de la Ferrière's company posted on the Gournay–Ressons road, he had ordered his men to stand firm and cover the retreat of the 2 Battalion. The two sides collided and hand-to-hand fighting ensued. As a German officer rushed up a few feet away, De la Ferrière raised his revolver and pulled the trigger just as his opponent did the same. De la Ferrière was killed instantly. He was 22 years old.

With the German advance brought to a decisive halt, it was the Allies' turn to strike back. On 15 July, the 151 was sent to Compiègne and proceeded over the next several days eastward to make a push on Soissons, this time supported by tanks, armoured vehicles, heavy artillery, and planes. They'd received little in the way of reinforcements and with the units so depleted from combat losses, the 151 would primarily be used as a supporting unit and mopping up force working in coordination with American elements. With the exception of a powerful thunder and lightning storm on the evening of the 17th, the nights were clear and the days hot. The men ran out of water and with the swollen corpses of men and horses choking up the streams, there was little that could be done to replenish their canteens. To make matters worse, German artillery regularly sent over Phosegene and mustard gas shells. Over the course of days of hard fighting, the 151 retook the villages of Saconin-Breuil, Vauxbuin, and Villeneuve-Saint-Germain, and was now within striking distance of Soissons. A period of desperately needed rest and resupply was given. The hot humid days of July were accompanied by frequent rain showers, turning the ground into a muddy morass. By August, with the enemy firmly dug in on the north bank of the River Aisne, the 69th Division was ordered to take back the industrial outskirts of Soissons, which had been solidly in German hands since the start of the war. The 151 would take the lead of the division in what would be the first true urban combat experience for the regiment. In another first, the assault was to begin with an amphibious assault. The 151 was to cross the river, secure the bridgehead, and then push north on to the Crouy plateau. The operation would mark the last great pitched battle for the regiment in the war and was also perhaps the most remarkable.

While the 3 Battalion (detached to the 72 ID) had orders to take Vauxrot, 1 and 2 Battalions together with an accompaniment of engineers were to conduct the amphibious assault, crossing the River Aisne (some 50 to 60m wide) on rafts and then footbridges. Once across, the regiment would have to conduct a house-by-house and street-by-street fight that constituted some of the most intense urban combat of the war. At 7.00 am on 28 August, the engineers dashed down to the river embankment carrying the rafts in their hands. When these men were quickly cut down by machine-gun fire, volunteers from the 151 stepped forward to finish the job. Stripping off their coats, shirts, and any unnecessary equipment, the men dashed down to the river. Bullets ripped up the water all around them. Despite suffering many losses, volunteers managed to make it to the opposite bank and (presumably) establish lines across the river to allow for the troops to be ferried across by their comrades. Countless acts of bravery went unseen or unrecorded, though a few were captured. There was Corporal Mérel (1 MG Company) who, at great personal risk to himself, set up his machine gun on the river embankment in a dangerously exposed position so as to better direct fire against the enemy guns and to draw their fire away from his comrades crossing on the rafts. At the same time, Corporal Le Guével and Private Coppier of the 2 Company jumped on a boat to cross over the river, along with a third man who was soon wounded. Despite the shells striking down nearby and bullets zipping past, the two managed to make it to the other side and take cover in a shell hole. There, the two men fixed bayonets and made a dash on an enemy machine gun that had temporarily brought the regiment's movement to a halt. A few moments later, they emerged with the German gunners as their prisoners. Soon the entire 2 Company, followed by 1 Battalion, was across the river and fighting through the streets of Saint-Waast before pressing on to Saint-Médard.

The 2 Battalion fared less well in its crossing with only 5 Company managing to make it to the other side. The 3 Battalion was also facing difficulties, as it came under fire from numerous machine guns on Côte 129. It was only able to advance in small groups from street to street and building to building. The fighting would drag on for three more days. It was savage and close-quarter, raging through the streets and buildings, from room to room and cellar to cellar. Grudgingly and only after suffering and inflicting severe losses, the enemy began to lose its grip. The 1 Battalion took the ruins of the Vauxrot distillery while the 2 Battalion carried out a rough fight with grenades to take out multiple machine-gun nests. Eventually, the town of Crouy was conquered as well. On the evening of 31 August, other units of the 69 ID would take over the lead but only after the 151 had advanced over 3km, earning it yet another citation in the Orders of the Army:

> During the course of very tough, sustained fighting from 28–31 August 1918, under the command of Lieutenant Colonel Perchenet, [the 151 IR] had forded in quick action a river in the crossing of a town, despite the organized defence of the north bank and the presence of numerous machine-gun nests placed in the houses.
>
> Has conquered, foot-by-foot and house-by-house, the suburbs north of the town, capturing it through three days of bloody fighting, from the point of departure to the subsequent attacks and holding on to it despite five enemy counter-attacks.[40]

The Battle of Soissons was some of the most challenging combat in which the 151 had ever been engaged, and it chewed up another 890 poilus killed or wounded.[41] For its actions, the regiment had earned a fifth battle honour (Soissons) for its regimental colours. Mercifully, the 151's war would start winding down after this last operation. From the smoking ruins of Crouy, the 151 was sent in September to the north of Nancy, below Pont-à-Mousson and alongside the River Moselle. There it took up the Sainte Geneviève sector, relieving the 326 US IR, where despite its reduced effectives it had to hold an extended portion of line. Though the 151 had been sent to the sector for rest, its lines were subject to frequent heavy calibre artillery barrages often mixed with mustard gas shells. The endurance required to withstand such conditions after its severe trial at Soissons should not be overlooked. Things were also kept active through periodic raids. On 25 September – a date that had repeatedly seared itself in the collective consciousness of the unit – the 151's *groupe franc* joined together with those of 162 and 287 IR, engineers, a company of Senegalese and another of Americans from the 326 US IR to carry out a large raid against German positions.[42] In a demonstration of the advance in firepower now wielded on the small-unit level, they brought with them four 37mm guns, eight Stokes mortars, and ten machine guns. The raid was at first successful but the German response in artillery and infantry counter-attacks eventually obliged the raiders to fall back to friendly lines, though not after a rough hand-to-hand fight. Twenty-nine were missing and the 151's *groupe franc* commander taken prisoner after being dealt a rifle butt stroke to the head. On 13 October the 151 shifted south to the Bouxières-aux-Chênes sector on the left bank of the Seille. Over the next several weeks, numerous reconnaissance patrols and ambushes were carried out.

As the war entered its fifty-second month and peace negotiations between the major powers were unfolding, military commanders were still actively prosecuting a war against an enemy whose forces in the field were still very capable of fighting back. Chilling orders came down to the 151 stating that preparations were to be made for a new offensive through Lorraine in the direction of Bensdorf set to begin on 14 November. While the troops readied themselves for the coming battle, one they assumed would take the war into its fifth year, incredible rumours began to circulate that a formal ceasefire was to be called on 11 November. It was something that many would not, or could not, believe. The dark fatalism so deeply rooted in the hearts of many poilus made them unable to fathom that the war would ever stop. Some had resigned themselves to the fact that even if it did someday end, they would not be alive to see it.

All through the afternoon and evening of 10 November, the German forces on the opposite side of the Seille sent up an abundance of flares and signal rockets. The unit commanders of the 151 were convinced that the enemy was planning a retreat. To ascertain the German plans, Lieutenant Basteau (who'd been given command of 5 Company) was ordered to take his unit on night reconnaissance from their positions at Armaucourt and, crossing over the Seille, determine whether Manhoué was occupied by the enemy. If it was not, he must hold it with his company and await the advance of the rest of 2 Battalion the next morning. Unbeknownst to Basteau at the time was that he was leading the final operation of the war for the 151. Having brought along a specially trained sentry dog, Basteau deployed his platoons into the frigid night. Through a thick fog, he quietly pushed his patrol parties up to a belt of German wire. As they began clipping the wire, a flare immediately shot up from Manhoué, piercing the heavy fog below. Ahead of them a submachine gun let loose a burst of gunfire, the rounds passing high overhead. Waiting a few hours, they tried clipping the wire again to see if the enemy was still there and the answer came in a second burst of fire, with one of the bullets sadly killing the sentry dog. As dawn approached on 11 November, a liaison runner arrived and told Basteau the operation had been cancelled. An armistice had been signed. Basteau was skeptical of this news and he ensured his patrols took all the usual precautions as they crossed back over the river. There a mobile field kitchen served them hot coffee spiked with liquor before returning to Armaucourt. Once arrived, the news was confirmed – there was to be an immediate cessation of hostilities starting at 11.00 am. The men of the 151 now waited anxiously for the fateful hour to arrive. Finally, at eleven in the morning, on the eleventh day, of the eleventh month, the war ended. At the appointed hour, the regimental band struck up the 'Marseillaise' and then played the 'Marche Lorraine', while from every chest came the cry 'Vive la France!' That afternoon and throughout the night, all along the line impromptu firework displays lit up the sky from both the French and German sides, as the troops shot off stockpiles of signal rockets and flares.

For the next week, the 151 waited for its orders to cross the River Seille, which had marked the border between France and Germany since the end of the Franco-Prussian War almost fifty years before, when Germany had claimed the territories of Alsace and Lorraine as spoils of war. To pass the time, soldiers from both sides went 'grenade fishing' in the Seille, tossing the explosives in the water to stun fish to the surface. On 17 November, the 151 marched in column with the rest of the 69 ID to make its triumphal return to Lorraine, bayonets fixed, regimental colours unfurled, and the band at the front playing 'Sambre et Meuse'. They first passed through a desolate land of empty enemy entrenchments and abandoned cannon, the inhabitants long since forcibly removed by the Germans. As they marched further, they began encountering civilians. The first village they stopped in for the evening was Bacourt, where the townspeople came out into the street and embraced the men as they marched in. Many of them were weeping with joy at seeing the liberating French soldiers, and knelt down to thank God and their patron St Martin for having delivered them.

> We set out early the next morning for Faulquemont, which the Boches had rechristened Falkenberg. In all the little villages our music played, the inhabitants, after having decorated with garlands, and make-shift homemade flags, cried out 'Vive la France, vive les soldats!' In all these villages it was more or less the same touching welcomes.

> Thousands of Lorrainers sporting our Tricolor flag, hastened about to organize receptions for us both big and small. This went on for a week, as they organized balls, and played old Lorraine airs. Young and old alike, girls and women danced joyfully in the arms of the poilus who were overwhelmed on every side . . . Everywhere we went, there was feast after feast. In many houses the statue of Napoleon was set up in the windows.[43]

In the final weeks of November, the 151 passed through Faulquemont, Saint-Avold, and Freymingen, close to the original German border prior to the annexation of Alsace-Lorraine. At long last, on 1 December, the unit marched into Germany, crossing the River Saar at Völklingen with bugles sounding. The inhabitants closed their doors as the Frenchmen passed, and from there on, the reception grew understandably colder. After billeting at Puttlingen, the 151 marched on to Homburg and began its mission of occupation. Though no hostilities would manifest itself between the German civilians and their French occupiers, the poilus were made to feel unwelcome. On 21 January 1919, the regiment was given one final award when the fourragère for the Medaille Militaire was added to the regimental colours by General Fayolle at Deux-Ponts (Zweibrücken), Germany. The 151's mission as an occupational force would continue into 1919, with the 151 garrisoning in Kaiserslautern and Germersheim until the end of June, occasionally rotating back over the border into several picturesque Alsatian villages in the Vosges mountains.

Meanwhile, Bordinat probably summed up well what was on the minds of many in the ranks when he said his 'thoughts were far from this country, our only wish was to be forever rid of the nightmare that had weighed on us for so long'. His wish would be granted on 15 March 1919 when Bordinat was at last sent home to his wife and baby daughter after four-and-a-half years of being away at war.[44]

Conclusion

What Men Call Victory

The scale of loss for France was of a magnitude well beyond what the nation has ever experienced in its long history. Casualty totals vary. Of the 8.4 million men who had been mobilized between 1914 and 1918, 65 per cent had been killed or wounded. Over 1.4 million French soldiers had died, nearly 17 per cent of those who went off to war. Other historians put the number closer to 2 million, especially given that those who died of Spanish flu are not traditionally included in the accounting despite dying while in the service. The picture becomes worse when looking at the most exposed branch, the infantry, in which fully three-quarters of all French soldiers served. One in four poilus did not survive the war. For infantry officers, it was one in three. On average, 900 soldiers died every day from the start of the war to the finish. On top of the number of dead were over 4 million wounded cases, or 48 per cent of all the men mobilized. Of these, half were wounded twice; 100,000 were wounded three or more times.[1] One only needs to look to the officers of the 151 as an illustration – L'Huillier and Basteau were wounded four times, Campana three times, and Jubert twice before being killed. Among the injured were hundreds of thousands of amputees and tens of thousands bearing monstrous facial wounds. Not counted among the casualties were those injured psychologically. The term shell-shock was coined in the Great War and the conditions encountered on the battlefields of the Western Front produced thousands, perhaps tens of thousands, of cases of severe psychological disorders (PTSD in today's parlance).

The exact number of dead and injured in the Great War will likely never be known. The same must be said of the 151's losses, where the figures again vary from source to source. On 16 May 1919, Lieutenant Colonel Martin tallied the total casualties of the 151 IR at 108 officers and 3,917 men killed (a quarter of whom would were still reported as 'missing') and 165 officers and 6,807 men wounded. Using the average war-time number of effectives as a yardstick, the 11,000 total casualties meant that the regiment had a total casualty rate of nearly 400 per cent.[2] In an unofficial regimental history published in 1997, Jean Lieffroy arrives at a higher count. He put the total casualty figures at 300 officers and over 16,000 men, of whom more than 6,100 were dead. Verdun alone was the location of where many of them fell. Over the course of its 6 rotations totalling close to 85 days at Verdun in 1916 and 1917, the 151 lost 3,200 soldiers killed or wounded on the right and left banks of the Meuse. Though it cannot be known for certain, the last recorded death for the 151 was Private Paul Metge, who had just passed his 29th birthday a week before, but who would die of his wounds at the ambulance at Villers-Cotterêts (Aisne) on 11 October 1918.

Le Qunize-Un had fought in many battles and occupied a number of horrendous sectors between 1914 and 1918. Yet, Verdun was not just another big battle among many. Verdun was a complete war within the Great War, a symbolic struggle, an ordeal of body, mind, and soul. And with three-quarters of the army having rotated through this titanic crucible of humanity, it became something of a national experience. In that context, it was only fitting that the main artery into the battle was coined the Sacred Way, even as the battle was unfolding in the spring of 1916. The name stuck and still appears as such on maps today. Yet, at the heart of this tremendous conflagration between two industrialized societies is a much more intimate struggle, one that was ultimately fought by small groups of isolated men. As L'Huillier proclaimed afterwards, 'It is above all a battle of infantry. Dug in, under fire, asphyxiated . . . a battle of devoted anonymous men, the sacrificed who have no story . . .'. Combat at Verdun was primarily composed of hundreds of tiny Thermopylaes fought in rude ditches and amorphous shell holes.

Outside of the trauma inflicted by witnessing so many horrors there was added a feeling of utter insignificance and a deep sense of powerlessness. To them, war was composed of a series of humiliations, stemming from one's filthy appearance and lack of hygiene, lack of autonomy and recognition, and from deep feelings of terror and fear and solitude. It wasn't long after leaving Verdun that men realized it had changed them. But just as words failed to convey what Verdun was really like, its effect on the individual also proved elusive. Veterans of the battle understood a change had occurred but at the same time they were unable to articulate it adequately through words. Jubert first seemed to realize the change when he once again returned to civilization shortly after leaving Mort Homme in April.

> Gund and me were at Bar-le-Duc. After being in combat, we felt here how much we'd lost touch with the ordinary world. Things and beings took on an unfamiliar aspect that was new to our eyes. We were like Iroquois [Indian] savages. We passed by fancily dressed servicemen in amazement, those whose uniforms made them appear to our eyes as though they were out of a festival, and we were foreigners. Our faded greatcoats, our worn boots greased with polish, our pathetic appearance that we could see in the reflection of storefront windows made us even pity ourselves. In the glances from these distant and lordly men, the gap that separated us from them became apparent. In the heart of the soldier there is a spirit of humility that comes out of being in combat.[3]

What is evident is not just the gulf between poilu and civilian but between who Jubert himself had been before Verdun and who he had become afterwards. And rushing in to this fissure there was depression, apathy, and a vague sense of bitterness and anger. Much of this stemmed from a strong feeling of disillusion, between what Jubert had envisioned war to be and his role in it, and what the war and his place in it really was.

> [The war] disappointed me from the very first day. I imagined it differently, and as popular conception may still see it today, as the fanciful and naïve Epinal prints will doubtless try to re-depict for us later. I imagined the magnificent role of the infantryman, heroism in action every day, the bitter joy of combat, the dangers defied and overcome, the wondrous leading role of the man who exposes his chest to bullets, heroic charges, the bright uniforms colouring the field of death. And in this immense movement all lit by the bright of day, small scenes would unfold where the lives of men would be glorified and then brought to an end. In the evening, under the light of a rising moon, the pale faces of the thousands of dead would cover the ground. But my mind has now changed completely.[4]

On display is the disparity between what he'd imagined war would be and what the war really was, from the mundane dreariness to the extreme revulsion. Even in April, as he benefited from seeing Mort Homme under bombardment from afar, he still saw grand beauty in the scene, a cascade of brushstrokes lit up by the serene morning light. That was before he went up to the summit himself and there is no similar scene when he returns in May. By then, there were no 'grand, tragic tableaux . . . Only these small painful scenes, in obscure corners of small compass, where one cannot possibly distinguish if the mud were flesh or the flesh were mud.' Upon leaving Mort Homme for good at the end of May, Jubert had resigned himself to the dreary, disheartening reality of the war.

> The greatest sadness of this war is that it does not speak to the imagination. It does not inspire our hearts, it reduces us to trembling flesh. Honour, that haughty exaltation of self, and which imposed itself on others, does not enter into its frame. Honour is reduced today to simply doing one's duty. Yet it is not a far-reaching duty. Our role is small. It is a petty, regular, continuous effort, requiring humility. It demands of us only our mediocre virtues . . . War was once noble and wondrous. It engendered vanity. Our war engenders humility. Heroism isn't a virtue, it's patience . . . simply having endured.

> . . .
> The foot-soldier serves no other purpose than to get himself crushed. He dies without glory, without élan in his heart, at the bottom of hole, and far from any witness. If he goes into the assault, he serves no other role than to place the marker flag indicating the zone of superiority established by the artillery fire. All his glory is reduced to recognizing and affirming the merits of the gunners. He sheds his blood to honour a caste who, to him, has no skin in the game.[5]

To have endured was enough. To him the war was 'not an effort in space, but an effort in time. It is less a matter of gaining ground than of holding fast onto one's spot.' This concept was epitomized in a single word: *tenir* – to hold on. This is what was at the heart of the phrase *ils ne passeront pas* ('they shall not pass') and it soon became a catchphrase for the entire French war effort at Verdun. There was victory in holding on, in surviving, perhaps the only victory. It is notable that even as Jubert experienced the horror of Verdun and the resulting disillusion, there was still no doubt in his mind that Verdun *must* be held. It must be held because France must be preserved. In this way, the prosecution of the war was a necessary thing.

> Our mission was to get crushed. The divisions followed each other, holding back the steel of the enemy with the flesh of men. They had no other role than to every day raise in front of him a veritable wall of corpses. This was our fate for six months. The whole challenge of command was thus reduced simply to allotting just enough of an amount to the Minotaur, his meagre ration. History will later speak more about our role and the tragic grandeur of our sacrifice.
> . . .
> Above all is the will to be victorious. It was necessary that France on its own should affirm that it will not to be defeated. She pledged her word to this. For six months, before the eyes of the whole world, Verdun was what was at stake for French honour.[6]

Jubert projected a patriotic pacifism that at once celebrated both the nation and peace. And while he hated the war and longed for peace, this did not stop him from holding his trench on Mort Homme, fighting back, and even attacking the enemy. What comes through in many accounts of those who fought at Verdun is a certain grim pride. As horrible as the experience was, it was also a rite of passage, albeit one that so many initiates did not survive. Verdun carried with it the weight of a terrible prestige. It was an ordeal that had to be undergone, and to the initiated it was a mark of identity. This was not simply an internal status symbol. After the war, the French military even commissioned a special medal for all those who'd served in the sector in 1916 to recognize this distinction. And since a majority of French troops – and by extension a large portion of the French male population – who returned home after the war could state *J'ai fait Verdun* ('I did Verdun'), it was a bloody badge worn of honour that many could claim. Certainly Roger Campana was one who took particular pride in being able to say he was one of *Ceux de Verdun* ('Those of Verdun'). His love of his country was not shaken by his experiences in the war. To the contrary, as was evident following the massacre he'd witnessed in Champagne, Campana became a more zealous nationalist. 'I loved war before I knew what it was. Since coming to know it, I hate it. But my hatred comes from contempt for it and not from fear of it. By contrast, I love liberty more than life . . .' The fervent patriot completed his memoirs in May 1919 while back at Saint-Cyr, just outside of Versailles, where he followed the events of the treaty deliberations closely. For the second printing of his book in 1963, now with the bitter memory of a second world war, he wrote:

> Having won the war, in five weeks we managed to lose the peace by signing this famous treaty, which, thanks to the naive ideology of the American President Wilson and the francophobie of the English Prime Minister Lloyd George, planted all the seeds for a new world war in which so many of our people would fall.[7]

Campana would continue his career in the army after the war, where it is clear he derived his sense of purpose. Indeed, while he would marry the 26-year-old Marguerite Bailly in August 1918, he fathered no children. Instead, it was the boys serving under his command that he would help raise to manhood. He went on to serve as a captain under Commandant Charles de Gaulle in the 1/2 Alpine Light Infantry Brigade in occupied Germany in 1927 and again in Metz in 1939. Campana was not alone among his comrades of *le Quinze-Un* in remaining in the army after the war. L'Huillier ended the war as a recipient of twelve decorations, including a promotion to the Chevalier de la Légion d'honneur, a Médaille Militaire, and a Croix de Guerre with two palms and two silver stars. After recuperating from the wounds he received from an enemy grenade at Verdun, the young war hero was sent on a final mission on 30 November 1918. Not to Germany but to the United States on behalf of the French Republic in order to raise funds for the reconstruction efforts. Who better to chose as an advocate than a wounded veteran whose original hometown of Somme-Py was destroyed in the war. Upon his return to France in 1919, he was promoted to lieutenant. Between 1919 and 1940, L'Huillier would serve in a number of formations and in multiple capacities, including on the Austrian-Italian border occupation force, command staffs, as an English instructor, and as an instructor at combat infantry and tank schools. He would marry in 1927 and father two sons, Jacques and Guy. L'Huillier was promoted to captain in 1930, a rank he would hold when he was assigned in 1937 to the 2nd Bureau of the 3rd Army General Staff as a Special Services Commander.

In the long term, the legacy of Verdun continued to play out in French political and military circles throughout the 1920s and 1930s. To the French, the lesson learned from Verdun was a defensive one. As early as August 1916, the assessment of the French High Command stated: 'One fact dominates the six-month struggle between concrete and cannon; that is the force of resistance offered by a permanent fortification, even the least solid, to the enormous projectiles of modern warfare.'[8] The take-away was that forts played a large role in France walking away victorious. Pétain, who would be Inspector General of the Army in and Minister of War, was a strong proponent of defensive works and advocated a 'Wall of France' to be built to hold back her traditional enemy if they should ever consider or attempt another invasion in the future. This wall would consist of a continuous chain of retractable gun cupolas, like the kind that had proved nearly indestructible at Douaumont, connected by tunnels burrowed deep underground. Eventually Pétain's vision was supported by the Minister of War André Maginot, himself a veteran of Verdun who'd been seriously wounded there. Construction on what would be called the Maginot Line would last through the 1930s and be largely complete by 1939.

As war with Nazi Germany approached, France placed her hopes in the indomitable Wall of France. When this barrier failed to stop the German Blitzkrieg in May 1940, the citizens of France turned to the Saviour of Verdun and the man who'd brought the army back from the brink in 1917: Marshall Pétain. Pétain had once wrote of the French soldier of Verdun: 'The constant vision of death had penetrated him with a resignation that bordered on fatalism.' This same fatalism had crept into his heart as well and by 1940 it had soured into defeatism. Faced with the deepest of moral dilemmas, Pétain could not bring himself to lead the country into another Furnace that could easily result in the annihilation of France. Better to survive, to endure, even if that meant surrender. When the bombs began to fall on Metz, Campana and the French forces would beat a retreat. Campana would go on fighting to defend the country he loved, eventually rising to the rank of colonel. L'Huillier was still serving in his capacity of Special Services Commander in the 3rd Army General Staff when the war came. On 25 June 1940, he was taken prisoner with the rest of the general staff and imprisoned in a series of prisoner of war camps. He would be repatriated for health reasons in May 1941 and receive the rank of battalion leader a month later. In September 1942, he departed for Casablanca to command the instruction battalion of the 7th Moroccan Tirailleur Regiment and in January 1943, he took command of the 1st Battalion/7th Moroccan Tirailleurs on the Tunisian front, which was attached to the US Army's 1st Division. L'Huillier would end his military career in 1956 at the rank of colonel.

When France quickly collapsed in 1940, Campana pinned the reason for this on the moral lassitude of the nation. The roots of this moral torpor, though, lie in the lasting imprint of the previous war. The telephonist and radio telegrapher, Pierre Rouqet, who was with the 151 at Mort Homme in May, admitted in his radio interview long after the war: 'These were the most tragic moments of my life. They have marked me forever.' Marc Boasson echoed Rouquet in even starker terms when he wrote to his wife immediately after serving a tour at Verdun, 'I have changed terribly. I did not want to tell you anything of the horrible lassitude which the war has engendered in me, but you force me to it. I feel myself crushed . . . I am a flattened man.'[9] Many of those who'd survived the war did their best to move on from the emotional and spiritual trauma it had inflicted. Upon completing his memoirs in July 1919, Bordinat wrote that he was now 'forever rid of this nightmare'. To him and countless others, the war was like a bad dream that he needed to move on from. To cope with memories that were too painful to recall, Bordinat did his best to shut them out of his mind. After transferring his experiences into words on the pages of a book – a book that could be closed and shut away – he never spoke about the war again. Resuming his civilian life, he eventually purchased a *café-tabac* in the Marsauceux district of Mézières-en-Drouais and focused on the daily operations of running a business. One wonders how successful Bordinat was in forgetting the nightmare of Verdun given that he had recorded in his memoirs:

> Laid low by our thirst, we remained under this storm of steel and fire passing over our heads, on this blood-soaked ground. What horrible existence and horrendous sights we've seen. How do you ever get these terrible things out of your head? It wouldn't matter where we went, we could never forget the memories of this awful life that had been engraved in our minds.[10]

Bordinat certainly wasn't alone here. Before being killed near Mont Kemmel on 29 April 1918, Marc Boasson asked rhetorically 'What kind of nation will they make of us tomorrow, these exhausted creatures, emptied of blood, emptied of thought, crushed by superhuman fatigue?'[11] Echoing this sentiment, Jubert wrote before his death: 'They will not be able to make us do it again another day; that would be to misconstrue the price of our effort. They will have to resort to those who have not lived out these days . . .' Inherent in his message was a warning, that the lesson of what happened at Verdun should not be misconstrued to mean that the army of citizen soldiers would be willing to march back up another *la Voie*

Sacrée. The same ordeal must be avoided at all cost. After all, the poilus had fought the war with the express purpose of ending war, referring to it as *la der des der* ('the last of the last') – the war to end all wars, as it goes among anglophone audiences. This had to mean something. It was precisely for this reason that the sacrifices made in the Great War and at Verdun in particular could be justified.

The effects of the Great War on French society are immeasurable. Statistics dealing with material destruction, loss of life, and economic decline do not suffice to assess the moral and psychological impact of the war and the trauma inflicted on society. And while nations taken together can be highly resilient in the face of catastrophe, at the same time this resilience can end up concealing deeper injuries that have subtle but long-lasting ramifications. Nations that are victorious and overcome the catastrophe consider themselves stronger for it. The belief among the people that the storm had been weathered and that blue skies were ahead is assumed and becomes self-reinforcing. The preeminent American historian on French history, Gordon Wright, astutely pointed out: 'Such lesions are more likely to be concealed when a nation seems to triumph over disaster – when the long strain of war ends in what men call victory.'[12]

The psychological scars inflicted by the Great War on the nation of France and its citizens still manifest themselves in physical form on the landscape of France today. Vast swaths of French territory are legally off-limits to the public and farming due to the tens of thousands of human remains and unexploded explosive and chemical munitions lying on and under the soil. The French call it *la Zone Rouge* ('the Red Zone'), a blighted land originally covering more than 1,200km². Today the area ecompasses around 100km². Nowhere is this dead zone more encapsulated than at Verdun, where it is estimated that a quarter to a third of the 60 million shells fired at Verdun in 1916 alone failed to detonate. In the 1930s, when all other attempts at cultivation failed because the land was too poisoned to support agriculture, forests of pines were planted across the battlefield. The clearing work has been going on ever since the war ended. Each year, hundreds of thousands of tons of munitions are hauled out of the ground by brave and dedicated French bomb-disposal crews. As recently as 2012, two *démineurs* were killed attempting to remove a shell for disposal. The problems are not limited to unexploded munitions. Recently, hunting and the consumption of drinking water were once again forbidden across large portions of the Verdun battlefield because of the danger of consuming deadly toxins released by the weapons still lying in the earth. A century ago the weapons of man turned Verdun into a strip of murdered nature. Yet, this is not some long-forgotten past. The scars of the Great War remain there: the unending sea of shell holes, the cuts of trenches slashed into the soil, the crumbling concrete shelters and wrenched steel bars, the rusting equipment, and decaying yet lethal ordinance.

What happened on this battlefield can still be seen and felt. Nowhere perhaps is the explanation of what Verdun did to the hearts and minds of men better illustrated than in the encounters between the columns of reinforcements heading up to the front and the shattered remains of those they were relieving. As Ian Ousby reflected, 'Somewhere in the contrast between themselves and those they came to relieve lay the contrast between life before Verdun and life after Verdun.'[13] When the men who'd endured the ordeal professed that they'd been marked forever by the experience, there was something else that they were communicating as well. That even for those who'd survived, a part of them had never left Verdun. As Jules Romains understood from the men who'd been at Haudraumont, 'now something's been broken that can never be replaced'.

What happened on those barren heights of the Meuse above the ancient and grim city of Verdun? Journey there today on a pilgrimage, walk the dark woods that now shroud the lunar landscape, speak with the ghosts that hold the ground there still, and bear witness.

Appendix I

Orders of Battle

Order of Battle: 42nd Infantry Division
(January 1916)

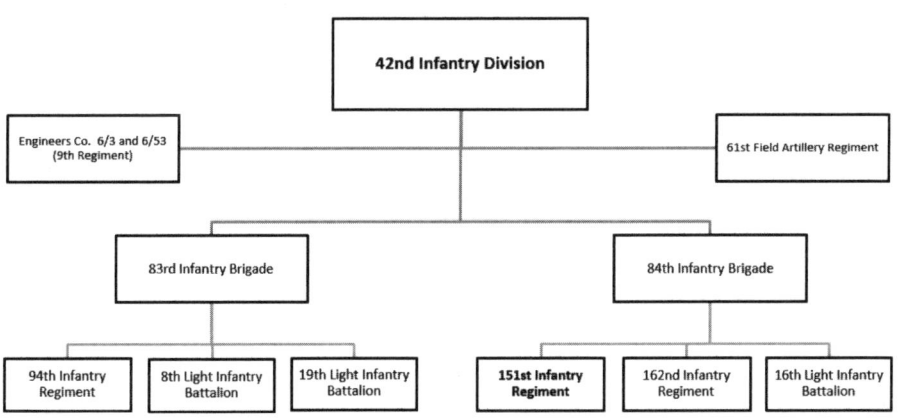

Order of Battle: 69th Infantry Division
(January 1917)

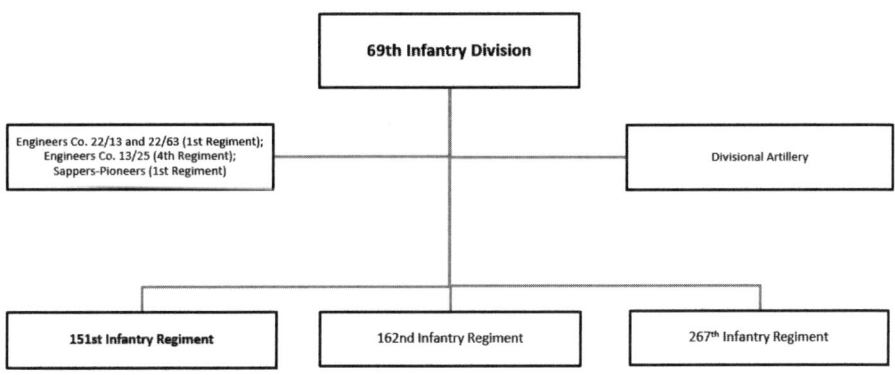

Appendix II

Organization of the 151st Infantry Regiment

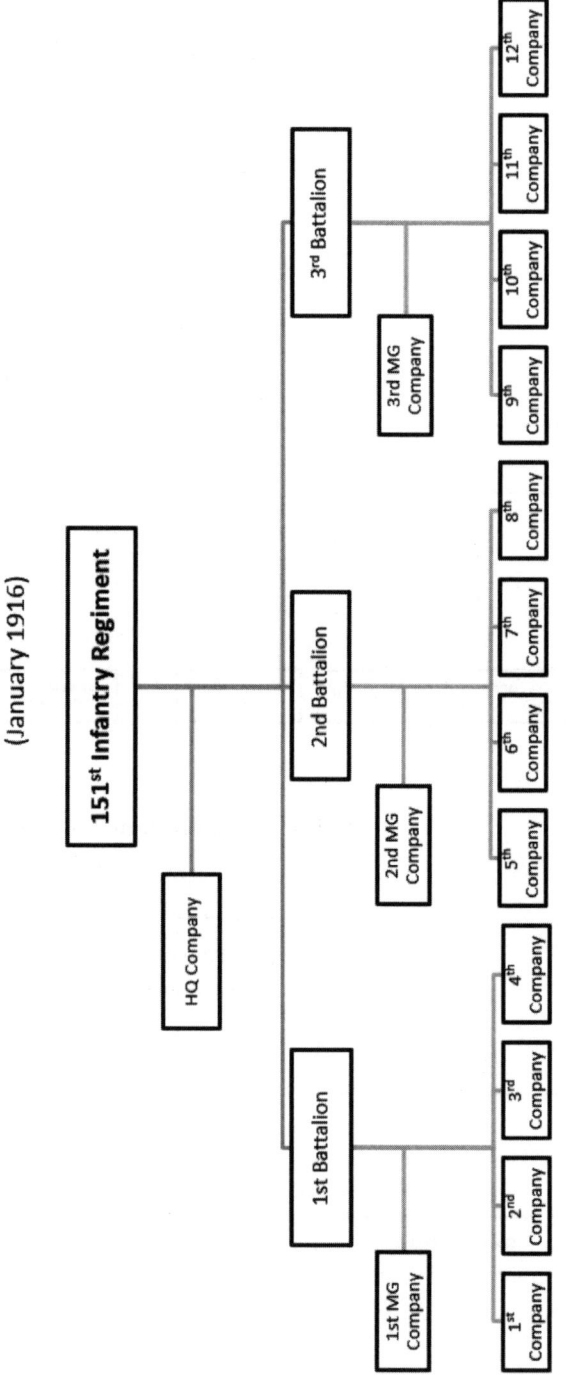

Notes

Preface

1. The 151 was one of two infantry regiments comprising the 84th Infantry Brigade, known as the Verdun Brigade. The other was the 162nd Infantry Regiment, also based in Verdun. The brigade also had a light infantry battalion attached to it, the *16e Battalion Chasseurs à Pied*, garrisoned at Labry. In 1914, the 84th Infantry Brigade was assigned to the 42nd Division, 3rd Army.

Introduction

1. This translation is the author's amalgamation of two versions of Deville's address, which were recorded by Raymond Jubert and Roger Basteau ex post facto, likely from memory. Overall the two accounts largely align with only slight differences in phrasing and details.
2. Raymond Jubert, *Verdun: mars–avril–mai 1916* (Payot: Paris, 1918), 84.
3. Joseph Auguste Constant Schmitt, *Historique du 151e régiment d'infanterie, rédigé en 1893: Complété jusqu'au 1er mars 1901* (1901). Each of the 173 active infantry regiments in existence in 1914 had a corresponding reserve regiment of two battalions, which took the number of their 'sister' active regiment addended by 200 (i.e., 201 to 373). The sister unit to the 151 was thus the 351st Reserve Infantry. Once a recruit's period of active service had ended, generally speaking the man served out the rest of his reserve service in the sister reserve regiment. At times of mobilization, the younger reservists were transferred to the active regiment to boost the effectives to a full complement. Beginning in 1915, the distinction between the active and reserve regiments was formally erased and the reserve regiment became entirely autonomous from its active sister.
4. Ian Ousby, *The Road to Verdun: World War I's Most Momentous Battle and the Folly of Nationalism* (New York: Anchor, 2003), 12.
5. H. Herwig, *The Marne, 1914: The Opening of World War I and the Battle that Changed the World* (New York: Random House, 2009), 157.
6. Paul Dubrulle, *Mon régiment dans la Fournaise de Verdun et dans la Bataille de la Somme, impressions de guerre d'un prêtre soldat* (Paris: Plon-Nourrit, 1917), 34.
7. Ousby, *Road to Verdun*, 13.
8. Jules Romains, *Men of Good Will: Verdun* (New York: Alfred A. Knopf, 1939), 431–2.

Chapter 1: To Arms

1. The French army's system of recruitment was based on regional conscription. Each regiment was assigned a home garrison and drew their men from the municipal districts in the vicinity of that garrison. This meant that, in general, recruits were assigned to a unit in the same region in which they lived and often to one based in or close to their home recruiting district. As much as possible, the men of each recruiting district were kept together and sent to the same army corps units. Though new recruits did not necessarily fulfill their active service with the unit closest to their homes, when transferred to the reserves, they were normally allotted to regiments as near to their homes as possible. The territorial army operated under the same basic principles as the reserve army, with an added focus on keeping men as near to their homes as possible. An exception to these rules came with what was designated as the Covering Corps. This was something like a ready reaction force constituted by supplementary battalions of regiments based in the army corps regions that faced the Belgium–German–Swiss border. The regiments in these regions were required to maintain a state of war readiness and consequently a higher number of men under arms in peace time than those of the 'interior' regions. As the less populated frontier regions could not supply enough men to fill the ranks of their corresponding unit, the shortfall was compensated by the allotment of additional recruits from more densely populated urban areas of France to the Corps de Couverture. In addition, a circle was drawn around each frontier garrison encompassing a certain number of rural districts. These districts had to then supply a portion of their reservists to the Corps de Couverture. British General Staff, *Handbook of the French Army, 1914 edn* (Nashville: Battery Press, 1995), 107, 120–1.
2. Ian Sumner, *French Poilu 1914–18* (London: Osprey Publishing, 2009), 10. In the winter of 1914–15 the *brassage* (or 'mixing') of recruits from the various regions of France began. No longer would men from the same subdivision region be sent to the same unit. Instead, they would be dispersed into units not solely dependent on their military region of origin but on wherever the manpower was most needed. The mixing was accelerated starting in the summer of 1915, when special unit depots and instruction battalions (and later, instruction centres) were formed and served to further shuffle around contingents coming from the regimental depots.
3. This information is based on the author's analysis of the population of *annotated* (emphasis added) death certificates found in the 'Mémoire des Hommes' online database, a site operated by the French Ministry of Defence. While this site contains digital scans of most (though not all) of the death certificates associated with French military war dead, an unknown number have not been digitally indexed to allow for filtered searching. As such, the analysis is based on a population of

3,324 records associated with soldiers killed while serving in the 151st Infantry Regiment between 1914 and 1918. Therefore, this does not reflect the total number of soldiers killed or, moreover, the total membership of the regiment. Nonetheless, the population serves as a good representation of the make-up of the regiment.
4. 'Every soldier a citizen, every citizen a soldier'.
5. More than half of the soldiers killed in action while serving in the 151 were between the ages of 20 and 25.
6. Jubert, *Verdun*, 225–6.
7. His brother, Maurice, was also eager to go to war. Even before the war he wanted nothing more than to kill a German up close. In August 1914, the 19-year-old was enrolled in the École Centrale des Arts et Manufactures but beat Raymond to the punch and volunteered for service that month. Administrative issues led to months of delays and Maurice was only at last incorporated into the 91st Infantry Regiment on 12 December. Maurice would be killed on 13 July 1915 not far from where Jubert received his first war wounds two weeks before.
8. The system of universal conscription had been in place in France since the time of the Revolution. The disastrous outcome of the Franco-Prussian of 1870 led to a complete overhaul of the army and its methods of recruitment. The fundamental organization of the French army under the Third Republic was shaped by the Law of 24 July 1873, which divided metropolitan France into self-subsistent army corps regions. In theory, Frenchmen (or naturalized Frenchmen) judged physically and mentally fit were required to serve in the military. Until 1905, not every man of the qualifying age was called up: selection was by ballot of those eligible to serve, and there were many exemptions. With the passage of the Two Years Law of 1905, nearly all exemptions were abolished with service being virtually obligatory. As the name implies, each man served two years' active duty, with his total obligation of twenty-five years, including service in the reserves and territorials (i.e., auxiliary forces). A man's obligation for military service universally began the year in which he turned 20, which was subsequently referred to as his 'recruitment class' and, by extension, his 'class year'. For example, a man born in 1895 belonged to the class of 1915. The mobilization date for each class of young men was 1 October but incorporation into the army actually took place the following year (when the recruit turned 21). The Three Years Law of 1913 effectively changed this so that recruits were incorporated into service in his actual class year at the age of 20, with the total requirement of active duty service increasing to three years. Philippe Boulanger, 'Espace Militaire, Recrutement et Commandement en France de 1873 à 1923' (Paris: ISC-École practique des Hautes études, 1998–2002).

9. Alfred Adrien Debon, *Faut-il transformer l'armee francaise? Etude sociale et militaire de la loi de deux ans et des troupes dites coloniales avec conclusions* (Paris: Henri Charles-Lavauzelle, 1911), 69. In addition to eliminating reduced service periods for students or diploma holders, the Three Year Law of 1913 mandated that those admitted to the special military schools after passing the competitive entrance exams were now obliged to serve a year in the ranks before definitively becoming graduates of Saint-Cyr or the École Polytechnique. After spending a year in a regiment learning practical skills and the life of the soldier (whom they would later command), the candidates entered the military school for two years as a student officer. Jean-Paul Bertaud and William Serman, *Nouvelle histoire militaire de la France, 1789–1919* (Lille: Fayard, 1998), 552. Source: British General Staff, *Handbook of the French Army*, 59–60.
10. Since 1829, every class (or promotion) of Saint-Cyr chooses a name for itself. This can be a nickname, the name of a famous battle, or the name of a famous soldier or general. All thirteen of the Bordeaux contingent that Campana was among belonged to the 1914 promotion class of *la Grande Revanche* in reference to the revenge they would get against Germany's invasion of France in 1870 and subsequent annexation of Alsace and Lorraine. Of the 797 cadets in this promotion class, only 344 would survive the war.
11. His sister, Marcelle, shared a similar sense of patriotism and duty and volunteered as a nurse in the Secours aux Blessés Militaires, the predecessor name to what would become the French Red Cross. Later, his mother and aunt would do likewise. The work of caring for the injured was no easy task, as Red Cross nurses assisted caring for men often hideously wounded and eased the pain of the dying. Unofficially, they also provided crucial emotional support to soldiers who were both homesick and traumatized.
12. L'Huillier's experiences during the war filled the pages of twelve notebooks, seven of which cover the period he was in the service. Stuffed inside the pages were postcards, letters from his commanders, and pressed flowers and clover he had picked (which still remain in the pages today). L'Huillier also took a number of photographs with his Kodak vest-pocket camera. He stored all of these souvenirs in a chocolate tin at his parents' house after the war. He never intended to do anything more with his diaries, which he considered to be too personal for publication. Yet, on the occasion of the 60th anniversary of the Battle of Verdun, L'Huillier had been invited with 300 veterans of Verdun to take part in ceremonies on 13 June 1976, which was attended by President Valery Giscard d'Estaing and the writer and veteran Maurice Genevoix, among other notable figures. President d'Estaing asked L'Huillier about the circumstances under which he had won his Légion d'honneur medal, to which he briefly recounted his small part in the fighting at Mort Homme. Upon the urging of President d'Estaing and Maurice Genevoix, L'Huillier transcribed his diaries two years later at the age of 82 despite suffering from semi-paralysis in his arms and legs.

Chapter 2: 1914: To the Hilt

1. Dubrulle, *Mon régiment dans la Fournaise*, 26.
2. Peter Young, 'Battle of the Frontiers: The Ardennes', in B. Pitt (ed.), *Purnell's history of the First World War, Volume I* (London: Purnell and Sons Ltd, 1969–70), 154–5.
3. Maurice Genevoix, *'Neath Verdun. August–October, 1914* (New York: Frederick A. Stoke Company, 2010), 47–9.
4. Maurice Genevoix, *Ceux de 14* (Paris: Flammarion, 1950), 34–5.
5. Over four months in 1914 alone, the French army executed at least 216 (summary executions on the spot being unknown) of their own men for charges of cowardice, abandoning post, and failing in one's duty. The charges were often dubious at best and certainly overly harsh given the reasons behind the alleged lapses and crimes. The number of those shot 'to make an example' was highest in the first two years of the war. Anthony Clayton, *Paths of Glory: The French Army 1914–18* (London: Cassel, 2007), 94.

Chapter 3: The 'D' System: French Trench Networks

1. Henri Desagneaux, *A French Soldier's War Diary, 1914–1918*, trans. Godfrey Adams (London: Pen & Sword, 2014), 18.
2. Roger Campana, *1914–1964: Treize de Saint-Cyr dans la Grande guerre de 1914–1918* (Paris: Debresse, 1964), 132–3.
3. Louis Barthas, *Poilu: The World War I Notebooks of Corporal Louis Barthas, Barrelmaker, 1914–1918*, trans. Edward M. Strauss (Yale: Yale University Press, 2014), 163.
4. François Déchelette, *L'Argot des Poilus: Dictionnaire humoristique et philologique* (Paris: Jouve et Cie, 1918), 206.
5. Gabriel Chevallier, *Fear*, trans. Malcolm Imrie (London: Serpent's Tail, 2011), 41.
6. Jacques Meyer, *Les soldats de la Grande Guerre* (Paris: Hachette Littératures, 1998), 66.

Chapter 4: 1915: The Killing Year

1. Roger Basteau, 'Carnet de route du lieutenant Roger Basteau du 151e RI (Jan. 1915–Nov. 1918)', 1KT 187 – Fonds Basteau, Service historique de la Défense de l'Armée de Terre, Vincennes, 1.
2. Campana, *Treize de Saint-Cyr*, 78.
3. *Ibid.*, 79.
4. *Ibid.*, 82.
5. *Ibid.*, 85–6.
6. In the face of unsustainable losses, the theoretical total number of effectives of an infantry unit began to change, first perceptually and then formally. By September 1915, the 42 ID records started referring to a total complement for an infantry regiment with

3 battalions as consisting of 75 officers and 2,793 men, and a HQ company and battalion staffs of 257. It is worth noting here, on 21 February 1915, a machine-gun company was constituted in adherence to the orders of general commanding the Groupe des Armées d l'Est (conforming to order no. 9267 of 30 January 1915), two platoons of St Etiennes and two others with the new Hotchkiss model. This was then augmented to two MG companies in the summer and finally to three by the start of 1916. In addition, at the start of 1915, a few dozen men were transferred out of their companies to form a brigade-level machine-gun company. In the case of the 151, a machine-gun company of 146 men was also provided at the brigade level.

7. Henri Laporte, *Journal d'un Poilu* (Paris: Editions Mille et Une Nuits, 1998), 26.
8. 'Cambronne's word' is a polite euphemism for the word *merde*. Campana, *Treize de Saint-Cyr*, 103.
9. Laporte, *Journal d'un Poilu*, 25–6.
10. *Ibid.*, 28.
11. *Ibid.*, 30.
12. *Ibid.*, 45.
13. *Ibid.*, 46–8.
14. Christian Frogé, *La grande guerre vécue, racontée, illustrée par les Combattants* (Paris: Libraire Aristide Quillet, 1922), 228.
15. Campana, *Treize de Saint-Cyr*, 113.
16. *Ibid.*, 114.
17. Frogé, *La grande guerre vécue*, 228.
18. Basteau, 'Carnet de route du lieutenant Roger Basteau', 4.
19. Jubert, *Verdun*, 147–8.
20. Basteau would receive the first of many citations, this one in the Order of the Division, for his actions over the course of the three days of intense combat. After recovering from his wounds and judged fit enough to return to service, Basteau would return to the regiment on 15 October 1915.
21. Lieutenant Colonel Moisson had left on furlough on 29 June, handing command over to Commandant Dô, who himself had been transferred from the 6 *Régiment d'Infanterie Coloniale* in May to take command of 1 Battalion.
22. L'Huillier abandoned his greatcoat, which contained in one of the pockets his sixth war notebook, covering his departure to the front and his period in the Argonne. L'Huillier had considered it forever lost in the fierce fighting on 1 July 1915. Until one day in 1919 when his mother received it in the mail out of the blue. A German officer recovered it immediately after the fighting and had then handed it to the medic treating him. The medic, a French soldier captured in 1914 and pressed into the German army medical service, found the 'return to sender' inscribed on the inside cover. Out of fear that her son was dead and not wishing to cause the mother anymore pain, he had hesitated returning it. With the war finally over, the repatriated medic decided the

best course was to post it back. L'Huillier's mother was deeply touched by the gesture and replied thanking the man and assuring him her son was very much alive.
23. Divisional records differ, with one citing this figure while another claiming there were only 59 officers and 2,316 men present.
24. André L'Huillier, '1914–1917 – Carnets et souvenirs de guerre de André L'Huillier, 1KT 48 – Fonds L'Huillier, Service historique de la Défense de l'Armée de Terre, Vincennes.
25. In a matter of minutes, the 94 IR lost 1,200 men. The 8 and 16 LIBs, each of which went in with more than 1,000 men, were annihilated. After the fighting, barely 150 chasseurs could be mustered in either unit.
26. L'Huillier, 'Carnets et souvenirs de guerre de André L'Huillier'.
27. Campana, *Treize de Saint-Cyr*, 117–18.
28. *Ibid.*, 125–7.
29. *Ibid.*, 127.
30. *Ibid.*, 136.
31. Laporte, *Journal d'un Poilu*, 66–7.
32. Campana, *Treize de Saint-Cyr*, 145.
33. *Ibid.*, 158–9.
34. *Ibid.*, 159.
35. *Ibid.*

Chapter 5: Opening Operations at Verdun

1. Michelin Guide, *The Battle of Verdun (1914–1918)* (Clermont Ferrand: Michelin & Cie, 1920), 7–8.
2. Guy Le Hallé, *Verdun, les Forts de la Victoire* (Paris: Citédis, 1998), 15.
3. David Mason, *Verdun* (Moreton-in-Marsh: The Windrush Press, 2000), 110–11.

Chapter 6: Into the Furnace

1. Campana, *Treize de Saint-Cyr*, 165.
2. Romains, *Verdun*, 344.
3. Campana, *Treize de Saint-Cyr*, 166–7.
4. *Ibid.*, 170–1.
5. *Ibid.*, 170.
6. *Ibid.*, 170–1.
7. *Ibid.*, 171.
8. Laporte, *Journal d'un Poilu*, 69.
9. *Ibid.*, 70.
10. Jubert, 35–6.
11. Basteau, 'Carnet de route du lieutenant Roger Basteau', IV.
12. Jubert, *Verdun*, 41–2.
13. Campana, *Treize de Saint-Cyr*, 176.

14. *Ibid.*, 177.
15. The names of the four casualties of 11 Company are recorded in the regimental 151 JMO: Adjutant Roger Folliart, Sergeant Oscar van Walleghem, Private Paul Daniault, and Private Eugene Arquillère. Jubert, *Verdun*, 50–1.
16. *Ibid.*, 64–5.
17. Laporte, *Journal d'un Poilu*, 72–4.
18. Campana, *Treize de Saint-Cyr*, 183.
19. Jubert, *Verdun*, 55–6.
20. *Ibid.*, 57. Private Gustave Maronne, class of 1911, was born in Paris and recruited in Aurillac. He was killed on 9 April 1916 at the age of 24 during the regiment's second rotation at Verdun.
21. *Ibid.*, 61.
22. *Ibid.*, 64–5.
23. *Ibid.*, 70.
24. *Ibid.*, 70–1.
25. Laporte, *Journal d'un Poilu*, 74.
26. *Ibid.*, 72–3.
27. *Ibid.*, 75.
28. *Ibid.*, 85–6
29. It was at Verdun where a process of disinfecting water through chlorination was first developed. The persistent presence of human and animal corpses in rivers and water points required the French army had to find a way to distribute potable water to its troops. The process was appropriately enough called 'Verdunization'.
30. Campana, *Treize de Saint-Cyr*, 195–6.
31. Laporte, *Journal d'un Poilu*, 76–8.
32. *Ibid.*, 78.
33. Campana, *Treize de Saint-Cyr*, 200–1.
34. *Ibid.*, 204–5.
35. *Ibid.*, 207.
36. *Ibid.*, 208–9.
37. *Ibid.*, 209.
38. Jubert, *Verdun*, 91–2.
39. *Ibid.*, 221.
40. Journal des Marches et Opérations – 151e RI – 26 N 697/9, Service historique de La Défense de L'Armée de Terre, Vincennes.

Chapter 7: Shellography

1. https://en.wikipedia.org/wiki/Canon_de_75_mod%C3%A8le_1897.

2. In the French army, the calibres of the cannon are referred to in millimetres, corresponding to the diameter of the bore. By extension, the shells they fired are referred to by the same unit of measure.
3. Lieutenant Colonel Lazard, *Ecole d'application de l'artillerie et du génie. Cours de fortification. 2me partie. Fortification permanente. 3me section, la fortification permanente pendant la guerre 1914–1918* (Vincennes: Lithographie de l'École, 1931).
4. https://en.wikipedia.org/wiki/Canon_de_75_mod%C3%A8le_1897.
5. Henry Beston, *A Volunteer Poilu* (New York: Houghton Mifflin Company, 1916), 84.
6. https://en.wikipedia.org/wiki/Skoda_305_mm_Model_1911.
7. Edward D. Toland, *The Aftermath of Battle: With the Red Cross in France* (New York: The MacMillan Company, 1916), 96–8.
8. Dubrulle, *Mon régiment dans la Fournaise*, 25.
9. Stéphane Audoin-Rouzeau, *Men at War 1914–1918: National Sentiment and Trench Journalism in France During the First World War* (Oxford: Berg Publishers, 1995), 73.
10. An additional consideration with incoming shells was the distance travelled. The American medic Edward Toland included a footnote to his description featured above that stated: 'When shells come from a long distance, as these did, they lose some of their spin and steadiness of flight and begin to turn on their long axis. The result is a very curious sound, wow–wow–wow–wow, which increases in intensity as the shell comes nearer. At short ranges, the shell travels faster than sound; but at long ranges, when it has lost its initial velocity, the noise of an approaching shell is audible for several seconds before it arrives. This has enabled many men to save their lives. The force of these big shells is tremendous; there are several instances of death caused by concussion alone.'
11. Beston, *A Volunteer Poilu*, 70.
12. G.J. Meyer, *A World Undone: The Story of the Great War 1914 to 1918* (New York: Random House Publishing Group, 2007), 361.

Chapter 8: A Life of Battle

1. Christina Holstein, *Verdun: The Left Bank* (Havertown: Pen & Sword, 2016), 31–47.
2. Alistair Horne, *The Price of Glory: Verdun 1916* (New York: Penguin, 1991), 162.
3. Jubert, *Verdun*, 102–3.
4. *Ibid.*, 104.
5. Laporte, *Journal d'un Poilu*, 80.
6. Campana, *Treize de Saint-Cyr*, 212.
7. *Ibid.*, 212.
8. *Ibid.*
9. Laporte, *Journal d'un Poilu*, 80.

10. Campana, *Treize de Saint-Cyr*, 213.
11. Laporte, *Journal d'un Poilu*, 80.
12. Jubert, *Verdun*, 107–8.
13. Laporte, *Journal d'un Poilu*, 81–3.
14. Campana, *Treize de Saint-Cyr*, 215.
15. Another version of the German-Polish prisoner incident comes from Campana, who asserted that the deserter was in fact first caught by Lieutenant Olivier's patrol and was brought directly to Captain Carrère's CP for an initial interrogation. The language in the the JMO implies that the German found his own way to the French first line and was allowed to approach. Moreover, while Campana would have likely heard the story second-hand, L'Huillier was there in person. Laporte's telling seems to corroborate the fact that the prisoner came over to 2 Battalion's first line, which was quite close to the German one, with the distance between advanced listening posts no more than 10 to 20m. It should be noted that Laporte also claimed to have accompanied both prisoners to the 2 Battalion CP.
16. Campana, *Treize de Saint-Cyr*, 218.
17. Jubert, *Verdun*, 115.
18. L'Huillier, 'Carnets et souvenirs de guerre de André L'Huillier'.
19. Campana, *Treize de Saint-Cyr*, 219.
20. Laporte, *Journal d'un Poilu*, 86.
21. L'Huillier, 'Carnets et souvenirs de guerre de André L'Huillier'.
22. Campana, *Treize de Saint-Cyr*, 219.
23. Laporte, *Journal d'un Poilu*, 87.
24. Campana, *Treize de Saint-Cyr*, 221.
25. *Ibid.*, 221–2.
26. *Ibid.*, 223.
27. *Ibid.*, 224–5.
28. Faglain had already proven himself in the Argonne where he was cited for his exemplary conduct and valour during the attacks of July 1915. He would be the recipient of the Croix de Guerre with bronze star and would again go above and beyond the call of duty at Mort Homme in May, where he would meet his end. Laporte, *Journal d'un Poilu*, 87.
29. L'Huillier, 'Carnets et souvenirs de guerre de André L'Huillier'.
30. *Ibid.*
31. Jubert, *Verdun*, 116–17.
31. *Ibid.*
33. *Ibid.*, 117–18.
34. *Ibid.*, 119–20.
35. *Ibid.*, 123.
36. *Ibid.*, 141.

37. *Ibid.*, 124.
38. Laporte, *Journal d'un Poilu*, 88–90.
39. Jubert, *Verdun*, 131–3.
40. *Ibid.*, 142–3.
41. Campana, *Treize de Saint-Cyr*, 27–8.
42. *Ibid.*, 228.
43. *Ibid.*, 238–9.
44. Jubert, *Verdun*, 180.
45. *Ibid.*, 158.

Chapter 9: The Infernal Machine

1. Charles Auguste Bordinat, 'Grande Guerre Européene 1914–1918 – Mémoires et souvenirs des Episodes, Passages, Etc. – Vecus Pendant Cette Grande Guerre', Bordinat family.
2. *Ibid.*
3. Horne, *The Price of Glory*, 170.
4. The first line comprised Tranchée Poutres, Garçon, and the northwest portion of Chapeau Chinois. The covering line a couple dozen metres behind included Tranchée Couplet and Zouaves.
5. Campana, *Treize de Saint-Cyr*, 241–3.
6. *Ibid.*, 246–7.
7. Jubert, *Verdun*, 163.
8. *Ibid.*, 165–6.
9. *Ibid.*, 180.
10. *Ibid.*, 183.
11. Occupying Tranchée Poutres, Garçon, Zouaves, and the northwest portion of Chapeau Chinois.
12. Jubert, *Verdun*, 185.
13. *Ibid.*, 187–8.
14. *Ibid.*, 188.
15. *Ibid.*, 192.
16. *Ibid.*, 194.
17. Chevallier, *Fear*, 219.
18. Private Albert Faglain's actions were cited in the official regimental history: '[T]he sole survivor of his machine-gun platoon and with an extraordinary calm, he set his gun up on the parapet and coolly mowed down the enemy columns which, after several attempts, fled back in disorder, holding them off for two hours until a bullet arrived felling him across his gun.'
19. This wasn't simply a sentiment inserted after the fact. Jubert mentioned his admiration in his official after action report written on 23 May.

20. Second Lieutenant Erkens would be killed on 23 August 1917 at Bezonvaux during the Second Battle of Verdun.
21. An inquiry into De la Ferrière's actions on the afternoon of 20 May appears in the after action reports. Questions were asked as to why he left his platoon in Tranchée de Foix without orders. In his defence, De la Ferrière claimed he had been told by an unknown liaison agent that their left had been turned and they were in danger of being encircled. With his own runner wounded, he left for the battalion command post to get his orders directly from Commandant Oblet. De la Ferrière descended down Boyau de Chattancourt, which was packed with the dead and wounded of 1 Battalion, arresting his progress. When the *boyau* came under enfilade fire from above, he fled with others down the *boyau* to the bottom of the ravine. The enemy's enfilade fire which swept the ravine and the *boyau* made it impossible for him to rejoin his unit, a claim which was indeed true. Once darkness arrived, he made his way back up to the battalion command post and reported to Oblet. In his report, the battalion commander attested to the bravery and devotion the second lieutenant had shown in the Argonne but lamented the fact that he had effectively abandoned his post under dubious circumstances.
22. Killed: Le Gallo, Bouchard, and Lartigue. Wounded: Sellier, Hue, Salmon, Hugon, Perrault, and Savary mortally. Missing: Castet-Baron, Boisson, Jubien, Lemereier, Bonfiglio, Collin, Dievart, and Ritter.
23. The 2 Battalion was now under the command of De la Ruelle, newly arrived from the 64 IR.
24. The dates recorded by Bordinat in his account do not align precisely with the events as recorded in the regimental JMO of the 151. At the same time, there are discrepancies in the JMO of the 151 in the period of time covered. For example, the JMO of the 151 states that the entire regiment was at rest by 23 May following its relief by the 254 IR. However, not all units had made it back yet. Bordinat states that the remains of his company (6 Co./2 Bat.) was belatedly relieved by the 150 IR early in the morning hours of 24 May. Bordinat's record is backed up by the *JMO*s of the 150 IR, which notes that two of its battalions would relieve elements of the 151 IR (along with the 332 IR) on the night of 23–4 May, with the relief not being completed until 1.00 am on the morning of 24 May.
25. Bordinat, 'Grande Guerre Européene 1914–1918'.
26. *Ibid.*
27. *Ibid.*
28. Jubert, *Verdun*, 206.
29. *Ibid.*, 207–8.
30. The regiment reported another 112 casualties on 21 May. A regimental roll taken on 22 May listed the following effectives as present for duty:

1. Battalion – 42 total: 1 Co. (12), 2 Co. (22), 3 Co. (3), 4 Co. (5).
2. Battalion – 624 total: 5 Co. (161), 6 Co. (161), 7 Co. (145), 8 Co. (157).
3. Battalion – 339 total: 9 Co. (99), 10 Co. (46), 11 Co. (45), 12 Co. (109).
MG Companies: 1 MG Co. (29), 2 MG Co. (2), 3 MG Co. (2).
Total effectives: 1,038.
31. By the night of 21 May, the mix of units recorded as being present in the Second Position included (from left to right) a company of the 332 IR at Ouvrage Gers, 12 Company/151 at Ouvrage Macker, then two companies of the 251 RI, 9 Company/151 at Ouvrage Laborderie, Territorial Engineers Co. 6/3, and finally the 11 Company (151).
32. Bordinat, 'Grande Guerre Européene 1914–1918'.
33. http://le-meruvingien.over-blog.com/2016/02/les-enfants-de-meru-au-front-de-14-18.html. Pierre Rouquet would return to the regiment, going on to fight on the Somme in 1916 and other battles in 1917, being wounded several times. This included being gassed at the Bois de Chaumes during the Second Battle of Verdun in 1917. Rouquet survived the war and resumed his work as a metre verifier in the regions impacted by the war. He eventually married and had a son. In the years following the war, he dedicated himself to volunteer service in many local associations, including his local veterans society, the Red Cross, the League Against Cancer, and the fire brigade. Rouquet would go on to participate in numerous French national radio and television programmes on the subject of the war. It was from one of these radio interviews that his testimony about Mort Homme was recorded.
34. Bordinat, 'Grande Guerre Européene 1914–1918'.
35. *Ibid.*
36. Basteau, 'Carnet de route du lieutenant Roger Basteau', VIII.
37. The *JMO* of the 332 IR confirms the time and date of this attack as 7.00 pm on 23 May. Journal des Marches et Opérations – 332e RI – 26 N 753/16, Service historique de La Défense de L'Armée de Terre, Vincennes.
38. Bordinat, 'Grande Guerre Européene 1914–1918'.
39. A partial number can be seen in the records of the Divisional Stretcher Bearers Group of the 42 ID Between 5–23 May, it evacuated 534 dead, 2,364 wounded, 457 sick cases (primarily typhoid and dysentery), totalling 3,331.
40. Bordinat, 'Grande Guerre Européene 1914–1918'.

Chapter 10: Closing Operations at Verdun (May–December 1916)

1. Horne, *The Price of Glory*, 215.
2. Christina Holstein, *Fort Douaumont* (Havertown: Pen & Sword, 2010), 76–87, 91.
3. Desagneaux, *A French Soldier's War Diary*, 27.
4. Horne, *The Price of Glory*, 271–2.

256   *The Verdun Regiment*

5. Robert A. Doughty, *Pyrrhic Victory: French Strategy and Operations in the Great War* (Cambridge: Belknap Press, 2005), 306.
6. Service historique, Ministère de la Guerre, *Les Armées Françaises dans la grande guerre*, Vol. 4: Verdun et la Somme (Paris: Imprimerie Nationale, 1926), 509.
7. According to the United States Department of Veterans Affairs, the US suffered 53,000 combat deaths and 63,000 non-combat deaths.

Chapter 11: From the Somme to the Armistice

1. Several organizational changes took place in the summer of 1916, which had a direct impact on the 151. On 4 July 1916, the fourth company (i.e. the 4, 8, and 12 Companies) of each of the regiment's battalions was detached. This was presumably done in order to form a separate depot battalion. The larger context is that in the face of unsustainable losses, French command was reducing the regiment level formation. The end state is that the regiment would now consist of battalions of three companies (from twelve down to nine in total). Changes were made at the company level as well. The effectives of each company were reduced to 195 divided into 4 platoons, with each platoon organized into 2 half-platoons. The first half-platoon consisted of a squad of hand grenadiers and a squad of automatic-rifle gunners. The second half-platoon consisted of two squads of skirmishers with two VB rifle grenadiers each. On a larger level, but for the same reasons, the French army reorganized at the division level by dissolving the infantry brigade formation, with a reduction of the standard four regiments per division to three. In addition, fifty reserve regiments – many having suffered heavy losses fighting at Verdun – were disbanded with the battalions mostly transferred en masse to other regiments to bring all the reserve infantry regiments up to the three-battalion composition, though others were turned into divisional infantry units.
2. Laporte, *Journal d'un Poilu*, 104–5.
3. Colonel E.L. Bourgoin, '1914–1918 – Extraits des mémoires d'un officier du 151e RI. 1KT 85 – Papiers Bourgoin', Service historique de la Défense de l'Armée de Terre, Vincennes.
4. Laporte, *Journal d'un Poilu*, 106.
5. Citation in the Orders of the 6th Army, no. 436, 11 January 1917. The regimental colours would also be decorated in January 1917 with the Croix de Guerre 'with palm'.
6. Bordinat, 'Grande Guerre Européene 1914–1918'.
7. *Ibid.*
8. L'Huillier, 'Carnets et souvenirs de guerre de André L'Huillier'.
9. *Ibid.*
10. Laporte, *Journal d'un Poilu*, 107.
11. Bordinat, 'Grande Guerre Européene 1914–1918'.

12. *Ibid.*
13. *Ibid.*
14. Within the 69th Division, the original regiments – 251, 287, and 332 IRs – were themselves reassigned, the exception being the 267 IR. This last would remain until September 1917 when it was dissolved, eventually to be replaced with 129 IR in January 1918.
15. Bordinat, 'Grande Guerre Européene 1914–1918'.
16. David Murphy, *Breaking Point of the French Army: The Nivelle Offensive of 1917* (Barnsley: Pen & Sword, 2015), 55–68.
17. *Ibid.*
18. *Ibid.*
19. One of the officers counted among the dead was Captain Carrère (adjudant major of the 1 Battalion), who was killed by a fragment from one of his men's grenades, which accidentally detonated after being struck by a shell fragment. Carrère was a highly decorated officer (a recipient of the Chevalier de la Légion d'honneur and two Médailles Militaires) who had served with the 151 since October 1915. In Champagne he had once forbidden Second Lieutenant Campana from continuing to venture out to find the body of his friend among the countless bodies of the dead in the wake of the bloodbath of the 6 October attack. He was there on Mort Homme in April, commanding 1 Company, where he directed his company in repelling waves of German assault troops. He had also won commendations while fighting on the Somme. Now he lay dead on the mournful plains of the Aisne. It was while recuperating from his gunshot wound at a hospital in Mailly that Jubert completed his autobiography about his experiences at Verdun. It was the first installment of what Jubert envisioned would be a series of works covering the Argonne, the Somme, and the Nivelle Offensive.
20. In one of the only uplifting episodes to occur during this battle a lone stretcher-bearer from 10 Company captured an entire German company. Private Charles Léon Henon (class of 1908) had been with the 151 since 1914 and had received several citations and the Croix de Guerre in his role as stretcher-bearer. During the attack on 16 April, Henon got word that some of their wounded were sheltering in an abandoned German dugout. Taking along two other stretcher-bearers, Henon went out in search of them. Coming upon a German dugout, the small party descended into the expansive subterranean shelter. Henon eventually pressed on alone into an adjoining tunnel, only to stumble into an entire company of German infantry. Henon decided on an audacious course. Providing false intelligence to the German officer, he fabricated a tale that a strong French attack was about to be launched to wipe out any still surviving enemy troops. The story was convincing enough and the German officer requested that Henon serve as a mediator for their surrender. Henon hustled back up to inform his commanders and then returned

to escort the officer and all 180 German soldiers back as prisoners. For his actions, Henon received the Medaille Militaire presented by General Pétain himself and a special mention in the regiment's official history. But the devoted stretcher-bearer would not survive the war. The 29-year-old Henon would be reported as missing after the fighting on 21 July 1918 at Saconin and at last pronounced killed in action in 1919. Like so many thousands of others, his grave will likely never be known.

21. Citation in the Orders of the 5th Army, No. 237, 16 April 1917.
22. Lawrence Sondhaus, *World War One: The Global Revolution* (Cambridge: Cambridge University Press, 2011), 255.
23. Murphy, *Breaking Point of the French Army*, 122–4.
24. *Ibid.*, 121.
25. Bordinat, 'Grande Guerre Européene 1914–1918'.
26. For his bravery and strong leadership, Lieutenant Colonel Moisson was promoted to full colonel on 6 July 1917.
27. L'Huillier, 'Carnets et souvenirs de guerre de André L'Huillier'.
28. Bordinat, 'Grande Guerre Européene 1914 -1918'.
29. According to divisional records: 9 Co. had 43 men, 10 Co. 48, 11 Co. 65, and 3 MG Co. 74.
30. Jubert, *Verdun*, 155.
31. L'Huillier, 'Carnets et souvenirs de guerre de André L'Huillier'.
32. Citation in the Orders of the XXXII Army Corps, No. 654, 3 November 1917. This would subsequently be changed to a Citation in the Orders of the Army.
33. Bourgoin, '1914–1918'.
34. By 9 September, 5 Company counted only 20 men in the ranks, while 10 and 11 Companies had a combined strength of 70.
35. *Historique du 151ème régiment d'infanterie et du 351ème régiment d'infanterie – 1914–1918* (Paris: Imprimerie Berger-Levrault, 1919), 15.
36. L'Huillier, 'Carnets et souvenirs de guerre de André L'Huillier'.
37. Bordinat, 'Grande Guerre Européene 1914–1918'.
38. *Ibid.*
39. *Ibid.*
40. Citation in the Orders of the 10th Army, No. 344, 12 November 1918.
41. In yet another testament to the losses suffered and the inability to replace these, on 1 October one company from each battalion (the 3, 7, and 9 Companies) was dissolved and the men transferred into the other companies. Consequently, for the last two months of the war, each battalion consisted of only two specialist companies and one machine-gun company, around 600 men in total. At the same time, a company of Senegalese Tirailleurs from the 103rd Battalion was assigned to each battalion to help guard the lines.

42. Referred to as *groupe francs* or *corps francs* ('free groups' or 'free corps'), these special platoons were started in 1917 at the regimental level using all volunteers placed under the command of a motivated lieutenant or captain sharing the same spirit of adventure and daring. For all intents and purposes, they acted as a permanent raiding group within the larger unit. Those who chose to join them were exempted from the normal menial chores. And though their special missions were highly dangerous and intensely violent, they were also provided with the opportunity to earn greater distinction and compensations in the form of supplemental food, liquor, and furloughs. The men of the free groups formed small, closed units highly jealous of their prerogatives and a little often too imbued with their own exploits.
43. Bordinat, 'Grande Guerre Européene 1914–1918'.
44. Demobilizing the millions of Frenchmen under arms had not been anticipated or planned for by French authorities. The operation was largely done in two phases. The first was between December 1918 and April 1919, when 2.5 million men mustered out of service. The second was between July and September 1919, with a further 2 million sent home. Demobilization was organized with the principle of egalitarianism in mind, with the order of release determined by the time spent in the army. The number of dependent children was also taken into account.

Conclusion

1. Stéphane Audoin-Rouzeau and Annette Becker, *14–18: Understanding the Great War* (New York: Hill and Wang, 2002), 21–4.
2. *Historique du 151ème régiment d'infanterie et du 351ème régiment d'infanterie – 1914–1918* (Paris: Imprimerie Berger-Levrault, 1919), 25.
3. Jubert, *Verdun*, 156.
4. *Ibid.*, 170–1.
5. *Ibid.*
6. *Ibid.*, 214.
7. Campana, *Treize de Saint-Cyr*, 260.
8. Horne, *The Price of Glory*, 337.
9. *Ibid.*, 270.
10. Bordinat, 'Grande Guerre Européene 1914–1918'.
11. Horne, *The Price of Glory*, 340.
12. Gordon Wright, *France in Modern Times: 1760 to the Present* (Chicago: Rand McNally, 1960), 394.
13. Ousby, *Road to Verdun*, 14.

Select Bibliography

Audoin-Rouzeau, Stéphane. *Men at War 1914–1918: National Sentiment and Trench Journalism in France During the First World War* (Oxford: Berg Publishers, 1995).
Audoin-Rouzeau, Stéphane and Annette Becker. *14–18: Understanding the Great War* (New York: Hill and Wang, 2002).
Audoin-Rouzeau, Stéphane, Annette Becker, Leonard V. Smith, and William Beik. *France and the Great War* (London: Cambridge University Press, 2003).
Barthas, Louis. *Poilu: The World War I Notebooks of Corporal Louis Barthas, Barrelmaker, 1914–1918*, trans. Edward M. Strauss (New Haven: Yale University Press, 2014).
Basteau, Roger. 'Carnet de route du lieutenant Roger Basteau du 151e RI (Jan. 1915–Nov. 1918)', 1KT 187 – Fonds Basteau, Service historique de la Défense de l'Armée de Terre, Vincennes.
Bertaud, Jean-Paul and William Serman. *Nouvelle histoire militaire de la France, 1789–1919* (Lille: Fayard, 1998).
Beston, Henry. *A Volunteer Poilu* (New York: Houghton Mifflin Company, 1916).
Bordinat, Charles Auguste. 'Grande Guerre Européene 1914–1918 – Mémoires et souvenirs des Episodes, Passages, Etc. – Vecus Pendant Cette Grande Guerre', Bordinat family.
Bourgoin, Colonel E.L. '1914–1918 – Extraits des mémoires d'un officier du 151e RI, 1KT 85 – Papiers Bourgoin', Service historique de la Défense de l'Armée de Terre, Vincennes.
British General Staff. *Handbook of the French Army, 1914 edn* (Nashville: Battery Press, 1995).
British General Staff. *Trench Fortifications, 1914–1918: A Reference Manual* (Nashville: Battery Press, 1998).
British General Staff. *Handbook of the French Army*, 1914 edn (Nashville: Battery Press, 2002).
Campana, Roger. *1914–1964: Treize de Saint-Cyr dans la Grande guerre de 1914–1918* (Paris: Debresse, 1964).
Chevallier, Gabriel. *Fear*, trans. Malcolm Imrie (London: Serpent's Tail, 2011).
Clayton, Anthony. *Paths of Glory – The French Army 1914–18* (London: Cassel, 2007).

Delvert, Charles. *From the Marne to Verdun: The War Diary of Captain Charles Delvert, 101st Infantry, 1914–1916*, trans. Ian Sumner (Barnsley: Pen & Sword Books, 2016).

Desagneaux, Henri. *A French Soldier's War Diary, 1914–1918*, trans. Godfrey Adams (Barnsley: Pen & Sword, 2014).

Doughty, Robert A. *Pyrrhic Victory: French Strategy and Operations in the Great War* (Cambridge: Belknap Press, 2005).

Dubrulle, Paul. *Mon régiment dans la Fournaise de Verdun et dans la Bataille de la Somme, impressions de guerre d'un prêtre soldat* (Paris: Plon-Nourrit, 1917).

Ellis, John. *Eye Deep in Hell: Trench Warfare in World War I* (Baltimore: The John Hopkins University Press, 1989).

Horne, Alistair. *The Price of Glory: Verdun 1916*. (New York: Penguin, 1991).

French General Staff. *French Trench Warfare, 1917–1918: A Reference Manual*, ed. British General Staff (Battery Press: Nashville, 2002).

Frogé, Christian. *La grande guerre vécue, racontée, illustrée par les Combattants* (Paris: Libraire Aristide Quillet, 1922).

Holstein, Christina. *Fort Douaumont* (Havertown: Pen & Sword, 2010).

Holstein, Christina. *Verdun: The Left Bank* (Barnsley: Pen & Sword, 2016).

Horne, Alistair. *The Price of Glory: Verdun 1916* (New York: Penguin, 1991).

Jubert, Raymond. *Verdun, mars-avril-mai 1916* (Paris: Payot, 1918).

Laporte, Henri. *Journal d'un poilu* (Paris: Editions Mille et Une Nuits, 1998).

Le Hallé, Guy. *Verdun, les Forts de la Victoire* (Paris: Citédis, 1998).

L'Huillier, André. '1914–1917 – Carnets et souvenirs de guerre de André L'Huillier', 1KT 48 – Fonds L'Huillier, Service historique de la Défense de l'Armée de Terre, Vincennes.

Mason, David. *Verdun* (Moreton-in-Marsh: The Windrush Press, 2000).

Meyer, Jacques. *La Vie Quotidienne des Soldats Pendant la Grande Guerre* (Paris: Hachette, 1966).

Michelin Guide. *The Battle of Verdun (1914–1918)*, Clermont Ferrand: Michelin & Cie, 1920.

Ministre de la Guerre. *Administration et comptabilité intérieures des corps de troupe. Ordinaires. Livre de cuisine militaire aux manoeuvres et en campagne* (Paris: H. Charles-Lavauzelle, 1915).

Murphy, David. *Breaking Point of the French Army: The Nivelle Offensive of 1917* (Barnsley: Pen & Sword, 2015).

Neiberg, Michael S. *The Second Battle of the Marne* (Bloomington: Indiana University Press, 2008).

Ousby, Ian. *The Road to Verdun: World War I's Most Momentous Battle and the Folly of Nationalism* (New York: Anchor, 2003).

Smith, Leonard V. *The Embattled Self: French Soldiers' Testimony of the Great War* (Ithaca: Cornell University Press, 2007).

Sondhaus, Lawrence. *World War One: The Global Revolution* (Cambridge: Cambridge University Press, 2011).
Sumner, Ian. *French Poilu, 1914–18* (Oxford: Osprey Publishing, 2009).
Sumner, Ian. *They Shall Not Pass: The French Army on the Western Front 1914–1918* (Barnsley: Pen & Sword Books, 2012).
Smith, Leonard V. *Between Mutiny and Obedience: The Case of the French Fifth Infantry Division During World War I* (Princeton: Princeton University Press, 1994).
Tyng, Sewell. *The Campaign of the Marne* (Yardley: Westholme Publishing, 2007).
Watt, Richard M. *Dare Call It Treason* (New York, Simon and Schuster, 1963).
Young, Peter. 'Battle of the Frontiers: The Ardennes', in B. Pitt (ed.), *Purnell's history of the First World War, Volume I* (London: Purnell and Sons Ltd, 1969–70).
Zuber, Terence. *The Battle of the Frontiers, Ardennes 1914* (London: The History Press, 2008).

Military Records

Journal des Marches et Opérations – 151e RI – 26 N 697/6 – 26 N 697/12, Service historique de la Défense de l'Armée de Terre, Vincennes.

Journal des Marches et Opérations – 332e RI – 26 N 753/16, Service historique de la Défense de l'Armée de Terre, Vincennes.

Journal des Marches et Opérations – 84e BI – 26 N 520/1 – 26 N 520/8, Service historique de la Défense de l'Armée de Terre, Vincennes.

Journal des Marches et Opérations – 42e DI – 26 N 342/1 – 26 N 342/7, Service historique de la Défense de l'Armée de Terre, Vincennes.

151e Régiment d'Infanterie août 1914 – août 1918, 25 N 155 – Carnets d'ordres, 25 N 156-159 – Operations, Service historique de la Défense de l'Armée de Terre, Vincennes.

42e Division d'Infanterie – 1e Bureau – 24 N 975-977 – Situations, pertes, Service historique de la Défense de l'Armée de Terre, Vincennes.

84e Brigade d'Infanterie – 24 N 1006-1011 – Opérations, 1009-1010 – Argonne, Champagne, Verdun, Service historique de la Défense de l'Armée de Terre, Vincennes.

Index

11 November 1918, 229
22 August 1914, xxiv, 9, 11–12
37mm cannon, 160
58mm mortar, 42, 221

aeroplanes, iv, 39, 98–9, 110–11, 114, 132, 140, 175, 182, 191, 199, 209, 211–12, 225–6
alcohol, 59, 109, 114, 124, 189, 193, 204, 218, 230, 259
American army, xxvi, 215
  formations
    5th US Marines Regiment, 224
    104th US Infantry Regiment, 224
    326th US Infantry Regiment, 228
American troops, 224
Argonne Forest, xxiii, 34–56, 145, 160, 181, 219, 248, 252
artillery, vii, xix, xxii, xxiv, 7–13, 15, 18–19, 21–3, 28, 35, 38, 40, 42, 46, 50–1, 58–61, 63, 65, 67, 74, 76–82, 90, 92–4, 98–101, 103, 106, 108–13, 116–20, 122–3, 125, 128–30, 133, 135–6, 138–40, 142, 147, 155, 165, 167–8, 170–1, 173–4, 176, 179–80, 182, 185, 194, 197, 199, 202, 205, 210–13, 215, 218, 220–1, 223–9, 235
atrocities, 39, 97
Aubérive-sur-Suippes, 19, 56–8, 62, 74
Audoin-Rouzeau, Stéphane 124, 251
automatic rifles, 144, 220, 224, 256
Autrécourt, 110, 114, 125
Ayon, Private, xxiv

Bagatelle, 50, 53–5
Baillat, Second Lieutenant, 216
Baleycourt, 86, 110, 114, 125, 165, 195
Bar-le-Duc, 5–6, 77, 80, 160, 164, 233
barbed wire, 23, 28, 60, 68, 70, 89, 122, 126, 139
Barthas, Louis, 32, 247, 260
Basteau, Second Lieutenant, xviii, 7, 35, 44, 52, 54, 89, 146, 184, 193, 205, 207, 220, 229–30, 232, 243, 247–9, 255, 260

Bastille Day, 55, 216
battle honours (of the 151 RI), 25, 161, 203, 216, 228
battles
  Aisne, xxiii, 20, 210
  Aisne (Second), xxvi, 208–14, 216; *see also* Nivelle Offensive
  Ardennes, 9
  Champagne (Second), 57–69
  Frontiers, xxiii–xxiv, 3, 8–9, 56
  Marne, xxiii, 14–18, 77
  Matz, 224–6
  Pierrepont, 9
  Soissons, xxi, 223, 226–8
  Somme, xxvi, 80, 196–9, 201, 203, 207–8, 215, 227
  Yser, xxiii, 20–3
  Verdun (Second), 216–23
Bauzée-sur-Aire, 85
Belgian army, 21–2
Berry-au-Bac, 208
Beston, Henry, 119, 251, 260
Bikschote, 22
Blanleuil, 37, 42, 48, 50–2, 54
Blercourt, 86, 125, 159, 165
Boasson, Marc, 238
Bois, 65
Bois Bourrus, 126, 157, 194–5
Bois Claque-Dents, 210
Bois d'Haudraumont, x, 79, 89, 91–2, 95, 98, 101, 111–12, 199; *see also* Carrières d'Haudraumont
Bois de Caillette, 196
Bois de Doncourt, 9–11
Bois de Goëmont, 10–11
Bois de Grand Champ, 11
Bois de l'Homme-Blanc, 18
Bois de la Branle, 14–15
Bois de la Caillette, 199
Bois de la Gruerie, xx, 34, 44, 46, 51; *see also* Slaughter Wood
Bois de Nawé, 111–13

Bois de Tappe, 9–10
Bois de Warphemont, 12
Bois des Caures, 78–9
Bois des Caurettes, 172
Bois des Caurières, 79, 217–18
Bois des Clairs Chênes, 165
Bois des Corbeaux, 122, 136, 172
Bois des Fosses, 79, 220, 223
Bois du Bout-de-la-Ville, 14–15
Bois le Chaume, 220
Bois Saint-Médard, 12
Bois Saint-Pierre-Vaast, 203–4
bombardment, artillery shelling, xxiv, 21–3, 28, 31–2, 35, 40–2, 45, 50–2, 54, 57–61, 63–5, 78–80, 92–5, 98, 100–4, 106–8, 110–13, 117–20, 122–3, 126–7, 129–33, 135–8, 142–3, 148, 151, 155–8, 165–8, 170–6, 178–80, 184–5, 187, 189–93, 197–9, 201–2, 204–7, 210–13, 215, 217–18, 220–1, 224, 226, 228, 234
Booitshoeke, 22
Bordeaux, 3–5, 35, 49, 62, 207, 246
Bordinat, Private, xviii, xx, 4–6, 164–5, 174, 184–6, 188–9, 191–6, 204, 206, 208–9, 211–12, 214–15, 220, 223, 225, 231, 238, 253–6, 258–60
Bossut, Commander, 210, 212
Bourgoin, Lieutenant, then Captain, 202–3, 216, 220, 256, 258, 260
Bouxières-aux-Chênes, 229
Boyau/Avenue No. 3, 185, 193
Boyau de Chattancourt, 127–8, 133, 136, 144, 152, 180–1, 190, 191
Boyau des Zouaves, 127, 136, 148
Bras, 12, 90–1, 99–100, 107, 110
Brillon-en-Barrois, 159, 163, 165, 195
British army, 12, 14, 20, 77, 80, 120, 201, 224, 244
Brugère, Commandant, 66
Buisson, Second Lieutenant, 148–9, 154

Caillet, Corporal, 221
Camp Chalons, 56, 59, 73
Camp Mailly, 215–16, 220
Campana, Second Lieutenant, xviii, xxv, 3–4, 7, 29, 35–40, 44–5, 48–9, 55, 63–8, 70, 72–3, 81–2, 85–7, 90, 92, 96–7, 99, 104–6, 109–14, 126–8, 132–6, 138–42, 145, 149, 152, 159–63, 166–70, 226, 232, 236–7, 246, 252, 257
Carrières d'Haudraumont, 197, 199, 223; *see also* Bois d'Haudraumont

casualties, xvii, xxiv, 4, 12, 14, 18, 20–5, 38, 41–2, 44, 50, 54–7, 62–3, 67, 71, 79, 103, 114, 123, 144, 150, 153–5, 159, 163, 170, 173, 177–8, 181, 184, 195–201, 203, 208, 213, 219, 223, 226, 228–9, 232, 245, 249–50, 253–5, 257–8
  of the 151 IR, xxiv, 12, 14, 18, 20–5, 38, 41–2, 44, 50, 54–7, 62–3, 67, 71, 103, 114, 144, 150, 153–5, 159, 163, 170, 173, 177–8, 181, 184, 195, 203, 205, 208, 213, 219, 223, 228–9, 232, 245, 249–50, 253–4, 257–8
Cavallier, Lieutenant, 74, 89, 154
Chamousset, Commandant, 160, 163
Champagne, 27, 29, 56, 65, 68–9, 71–2, 76, 92, 134, 140, 201, 236, 257
Charleville, 2–3
Chattancourt, 124, 126–31, 133, 136, 144, 146–7, 151–2, 157–8, 169, 181, 183, 188, 190–2, 254
Chattancourt Ravine, 128, 136, 144, 146–7, 157, 181, 188, 190
Chedal-Bornu, Second Lieutenant, 4, 60, 68
Chemin-des-Dames, 214–15; *see also* Nivelle Offensive
Chevallier, Gabriel, 31, 119, 179, 247
Choléra (Ferme de), 208, 212, 216, 226
Christmas, 3–4, 24–5, 160
citations, 145, 161, 163, 216, 219, 248, 257
class of
  1914, 4, 20, 24, 26, 34
  1915, 7, 34, 43, 245
  1916, 6, 115, 145, 150, 160, 186, 191
  1917, 205
Clémendot, Captain, 22–3
Coltat, Commandant, 147
Compiègne, 223, 225–7
Coppier, Private, 228
Corfélix, 15
Côte 259, 129, 147
Côte 265, 122–3, 127, 135, 140–3, 165
Côte 285.9, 123–4, 127, 144, 180–2, 190; *see also* Mort Homme
Côte 286.4, 123–4, 165; *see also* Mort Homme
Côte 287, 183, 189–90, 228, 256
Côte 295, xx, 91, 123, 127, 129, 135–6, 138, 149, 161, 165–6, 171, 178, 182; *see also* Mort Homme
Côte 304, 122, 128–9, 132, 135–6, 165, 168, 196–7, 199, 216, 218
Côte 329, 9–10

Côte de Froide-Terre, 90, 93, 98, 100, 110, 127
Côte du Poivre, 100, 110
Couplet, Second Lieutenant, then Lieutenant, 23, 43, 133, 154
Courreaux, Second Lieutenant, 152
Covering Corps, 8, 244
Croix de Guerre, 42, 62, 72, 114, 145, 150, 161, 216, 219, 223, 236, 252, 256–7
Croix-Gentin, 41, 52
Crouy, 227–8
Crusnes, 9
Cumières, 122, 136, 168, 196, 216, 218
Cyrard, 4, 7; *see also* Saint-Cyrien

'D' System, 30–1, 41
Dalidet, Doctor-Major, 51–2
De Bontin, Commandant, 22–4
De Castelnau, General, 57, 77, 79
De la Ferrière, Second Lieutenant, 4, 52, 95, 183, 202, 226–7, 253–4
De Riancey, Second Lieutenant, 4, 54, 111, 113, 145–6, 154
Death Ravine, 79, 91, 107, 111, 113, 127; *see also* Ravin de la Mort
depots, 3, 6–7, 13, 20, 24, 32, 34, 43, 63–4, 74, 83, 102, 160, 164, 166, 170, 188, 205, 207–9, 244, 256
Desagneaux, Henri, 27, 197, 247, 255
desertion, 83, 159–60, 214
Detrais, Captain, 187
Deville, General, xxii, 10, 19–20, 56, 72, 82, 88–9, 91, 115, 123, 152, 161, 203, 243
Dijon, 6, 164
Diksmuide, 22
Dillemann, Colonel, then General, 24, 43
disease, 71, 103; *see also* dysentery; influenza; Spanish flu; typhoid
Dombasle, 86
Doncourt, 9–11, 56
Douarnenez, 64
Dreux, 5
Dubondieu, Corporal, 162, 168
Dubot, Second Lieutenant, 148
Dubrulle, Sergeant, xxiv, 9, 117, 243, 247, 251, 261
Dudot, Adjudant, 149–51
Dufour, Gunner-Sergeant, 139, 141
Dunkirk, 20
dysentery, 255

effectives, 12–13, 18–20, 25, 35, 41, 43, 55–6, 59, 63, 109, 114, 131, 147, 164, 205, 213, 219, 228, 243, 247, 254, 256
Enfants-Perdus, 37, 44
engineers, 9, 21, 24, 42, 47–8, 50, 62, 78, 86, 91, 132, 153, 165, 171, 174, 227–8, 255
Erkens, Second Lieutenant, 154, 173, 178, 182, 253
Étréaupont, 7
executions, 25, 124, 198, 217, 247

Faglain, Private, 143, 180–1, 252–3
Falkenhayn, von General, 77, 79–80, 122, 134, 199
Faubourg-Pavé, xxiii
Fayolle, General, 216, 231
Ferme des Chambrettes, 199, 217
first-aid posts, 39, 48, 51–2, 55, 62, 102, 112, 137, 146, 168–9, 190, 193, 204–5, 207, 222–3
flamethrowers, 39, 51, 78, 133, 139, 166, 168, 180–1, 194, 197, 206
Flanders, 20, 26–7, 35, 161
Fleury (devant-Douaumont), 98–9, 198–9
Fleury-sur-Aire, 114, 125
Florent-en-Argonne, 36, 41, 43, 48–9, 55
Fond des Rousses, 221
Fontaine-aux-Charmes, 37
Fontaine de la Madame, 36–7
Forges stream, 122
Forges-sur-Meuse, xxiii, 122, 132
Fortified Region of Verdun, 76, 79
Fortin '413', 58
Fortin '414', 58, 61, 63
forts
  Belleville, 90
  Chaume, 86
  Douaumont, 79, 82, 90, 95, 98, 196–7, 199, 217, 221, 255, 261
  Froide-Terre, 90, 94, 111–12
  Saint-Michel, 111, 113
  Sartelles, 86
  Souville, 98, 198–9
  Vaux, 80, 197–9
fourragère, 161, 216, 231
French army formations
  armies
    2nd Army, 79
    5th Army, 14, 18, 57
  army corps
    II Army Corps, 14
    VII Army Corps, 122
    X Army Corps, 18

divisions
  40th Infantry Division, 183, 196
  42nd Infantry Division, xix, xxiii, 8–9, 13, 15, 18–20, 22, 24–5, 34, 37, 53, 56, 61–2, 67, 69, 73, 81–2, 86, 89, 103, 114, 136, 154, 160, 183, 195–6, 201, 203–4, 208, 218, 229, 243, 247, 253–5, 258
  51st Infantry Division, 78–9
  69th Infantry Division, 157, 166, 180, 182–3, 195–6, 208, 225, 226–8, 230, 256
  72nd Infantry Division, 78, 122, 227
brigades
  84th Infantry Brigade, xxiii, 15, 19, 21; see also Verdun Brigade
regiments and battalions
  8th Light Infantry Battalion, 42, 54, 130, 136, 139, 144–7, 153
  16th Light Infantry Battalion, xx, 15, 42, 58–9, 62, 86, 249
  19th Light Infantry Battalion, 8
  25th Light Infantry Battalion, 11
  27th Infantry Regiment, 6
  58th Infantry Regiment, 5
  61st Field Artillery Regiment, 82, 86, 135
  94th Infantry Regiment, 58–9, 86, 91, 94, 101, 153, 157, 164, 183, 189, 203, 247, 249
  106th Infantry Regiment, 15, 24
  116th Infantry Regiment, 111–13
  134th Infantry Regiment, 5
  144th Infantry Regiment, 4
  147th Infantry Regiment, 24, 36–7
  148th Infantry Regiment, 24, 148
  150th Infantry Regiment, 64, 91, 124, 158, 166, 194, 254
  162nd Infantry Regiment, xxiii, 11, 15, 24, 36, 42–3, 50, 52, 59, 65, 78, 86, 91, 101, 103, 110, 130, 135, 153, 156–7, 174, 176, 180–1, 189, 203, 205, 208, 229, 243
  251st Infantry Regiment, 183, 188–9, 255–6
  254th Infantry Regiment, 157
  351st Infantry Regiment, xx, 13, 26, 64, 78–9
  359th Infantry Regiment, 27–8
  6/3 Engineers Company (9th Engineers Regiment), 86, 91, 153, 165, 171, 174, 255
Fromeréville, 170, 184–5

frostbite, 41–2, 69–71, 114, 208; see also trench foot

Ganot, Lieutenant, 102, 147
Genevoix, Maurice, xxv, 16, 17, 119, 246–7
German army formations
  2nd Army, 14
  5th Army, 8–9, 51, 77–8
  III Army Corps, 78
  VII Army Corps, 78
  XII Reserve Corps, 19
  XVIII Army Corps, 78
  2nd Guard Reserve Division, 15
  12th Reserve Division, 87, 122, 146
  22nd Reserve Division, 122
  203rd Infantry Regiment, 180
  204th Infantry Regiment, 180
German spring offensive, 224
Germonville, 125–6, 128
Goose Foot, 35
Goulette Ravine, 91, 100–1, 111
Gournay-sur-Aronde, 225–6
Grandes-Loges, 72
Grasset, Captain, 11
Great Retreat, xxiii, 7, 12
'Green Cross', 178, 198; see also poison gas
grenades, 40, 44–6, 51–2, 55, 58, 63, 78, 97, 108, 128, 134, 136, 139, 143, 148, 155, 160, 166, 175, 179, 181, 197, 207, 212, 215, 220–2, 257
Grenadiers, 50, 57, 72, 143, 150, 155, 206, 224, 256

Han-devant-Pierrepont, 11
Haudraumont, x, xxiv–xxvi, 79–115, 133, 181, 197, 199, 223, 240
Hayette Ravine, 124, 129, 180; see also Ravin de la Hayette
Henon, Private, 216, 257
Horne, Alistair, xviii, 251, 253, 255, 259, 261
Hotchkiss machine gun, 139, 141, 181, 224, 248; see also machine gun

influenza, 114

Joffre, General, 14, 27, 69, 73, 77–9, 196, 223
Jouy-en-Argonne, xiv, 125, 146, 165–6, 170–1, 174, 184, 188–9, 195
Jubert, Second Lieutenant, xviii, 2–3, 6, 44, 53–5, 88, 90, 93–5, 98–103, 113–14, 125,

129, 132, 134–6, 147–54, 157–8, 162–3, 171–3, 175–8, 180–2, 186–8, 195, 213, 216, 219, 226, 232–5, 238, 243, 245, 248–54, 257–9, 261
Juvigny, 19

L'Huillier, Sergeant, then Second Lieutenant, xviii, 6–7, 49–50, 52–4, 59–62, 68, 74, 84–5, 128–9, 133–5, 137–9, 143–4, 146, 161, 205, 207–8, 216–17, 219–20, 222–3, 232–3, 236–7, 246, 248–9, 252, 256, 258, 261
La Harazée, 36, 41, 43, 48–50, 53
Laporte, Corporal, then Quarter-Master Corporal, xviii, 7, 43, 45–8, 51–2, 55, 69, 87–8, 95–6, 100, 104, 106, 108, 119, 126–7, 129–30, 132, 134, 138, 140, 143, 155–6, 201–2, 206–8, 226, 248–52, 256, 261
latrines, 19, 29, 104
Le Balle, Second Lieutenant, 12
Le Boulanger, Captain, then Commandant, 66, 128, 133, 144, 146, 148, 161
Le Gallo, Second Lieutenant, 146, 182, 254
Le Guével, Corporal, 228
Le Hallé, Guy, 249, 261
Le Moing, Captain, then Commandant, 7, 74
Légion d'honneur, 42–3, 72, 146, 161, 219, 221, 223, 236, 246, 257
Les Culots, 15, 18
lice, 33, 41
Line 1A, 124, 129, 174, 182, 188, 190
Linthes, 18
Lizerne–Bernardplaats sector, 24
Ludendorff, von General, 199

machine gun, 11, 15, 22, 51, 53, 58–61, 63, 65–6, 77, 93, 108, 110, 129, 134, 138–43, 149–52, 154–5, 172–3, 175, 179–82, 187, 190, 194, 202, 206, 211–13, 215, 218, 221–2, 224–9; *see also* Hotchkiss machine gun
Malochet, Commandant, 160, 180
Mangin, General, 196
Manhoué, 230
Marathel, Lieutenant Colonel, 176–7, 208
Marraines de guerre, 70, 105
Médaille Militaire, 161, 213, 236
Mérel, Corporal, 227
Mesté, Second Lieutenant, 152, 154
Mézières-en-Drouais, 5, 238
minenwerfers, 40–1, 47, 51, 121, 133, 137, 175, 179, 221

mines, 17, 35, 40, 42, 46–8, 58, 97, 121, 141
Miribel Barracks, xxiii, 8, 217
Moisson, Lieutenant Colonel, xxii, 7, 24, 42–3, 55, 65, 71–2, 74, 86, 89, 106, 108, 111, 114, 124, 134, 144, 150, 153, 161, 170, 184, 213, 222, 225, 248, 258
Mollet, Second Lieutenant, 148
Monphous, Commandant, 13, 20, 21–2
Montfaucon, 128–9, 135
Mort Homme, xi–xvi, xviii–xix, xxiv, 115–16, 122–4, 126–9, 131–2, 134–6, 138, 144–7, 151, 153, 155, 157–8, 160–6, 168–74, 178–84, 187–9, 193, 195–7, 202, 216, 218, 220, 226, 233–5, 238, 246, 252, 255, 257
Mourmelon-le-Grand, 19, 56, 72
mud, ii, xviii, xxii, 26, 32, 35, 37–8, 40, 58, 62, 69–70, 79, 85, 107, 111, 113, 127, 130, 157–9, 163, 171–2, 205–6, 208, 210, 219–20, 234
mustard gas, 218, 224, 227–8; *see also* poison gas
mutinies, 214–15

Netter shelters, 157, 174, 188, 190
Neufchâteau, 224
Nieuwpoort, 21
Nivelle Offensive, xxvi, 208–14, 216; *see also* Chemin-des-Dames
Nivelle, General, xxvi, 154–5, 195–6, 198–9, 210, 213, 215
Noël, Second Lieutenant, 148–9, 151–2, 154

Oblet, Commandant, 181, 183–4, 187, 254
Olivier, Lieutenant, then Captain, 7, 132–3, 135, 142, 165, 190, 203, 252
Orders of the Army, Army Corps, Division, 62, 114, 154, 161–2, 203, 207, 213, 216, 219–20, 226, 228, 256, 258
Orders of the Day, 14, 154, 195, 220
Ousby, Ian, xxv, 240, 243
ouvrages
  de Lama, 218, 220
  Gers, 124, 182, 255
  Laborderie, xx, 124, 129, 136, 147, 166, 171, 174, 178, 180–2, 255
  Macker, 124, 255
  Mollandin, 124, 136, 166, 171

Paris, 1, 3, 5–6, 43, 51, 53, 76, 82–3, 86, 132, 147, 216, 243, 245–50, 255, 258–61

Pascal, Commandant, 15, 18, 22
patrols, 12, 24, 28, 39, 95, 97, 103, 115, 133, 154, 180, 182, 229–30, 252
Pershing, General, 223
Pétain, General, 79, 154, 196, 215–16, 222–3, 237, 257
Petit Sillery, 20
Pierrepont, 9, 11, 56, 71
Pig Tail, 35
pinard, 89, 97, 104, 108, 163, 188
Place d'Armes, 124, 129, 134, 136, 145, 166, 174–5, 180, 182, 186, 188–9
Pogny, 73–4, 81–2
poilu, xviii–xix, 31–2, 41, 59, 70, 72, 75, 79, 88, 97, 104, 107, 110, 115, 120–1, 128, 130–1, 139, 149, 151, 155–6, 159–60, 177, 194, 202, 205, 213–15, 229–33, 238, 244, 247–52, 256, 260–2
poison gas, ii, 42, 50–1, 53, 58, 65, 91, 97, 110, 116, 120–1, 132, 134, 156, 178–9, 197–8, 206, 211, 218, 224, 227–8, 255; *see also* 'Green Cross'; mustard gas; tear gas
Ponchon, Aspirant, 222
Possesse, 81–2, 84
prisoners, 19, 143, 153, 162, 199, 202–3, 207, 213, 220, 228, 252, 257

Quimper, 3, 7, 34, 43, 49, 74, 160, 170, 207

raids, 24, 35, 39–40, 42, 46, 49, 83, 206, 221, 224, 228–9
Ramskapelle, 21–2
Rancourt, 201–3
rats, 69
Ravin d'Hassoule, 220
Ravin de Chattancourt, 183
Ravin de la Caillette, 197
Ravin de la Couleuvre, 197
Ravin de la Dame, 79
Ravin de la Fausse-Côte, 197
Ravin de la Hayette, 136, 182–3; *see also* Hayette Ravine
Ravin de la Mort, 79, 197; *see also* Death Ravine
Ravin du Helly, 218
Ravin l'Hermitage, 218
Ravin Sec, xx, 51–2, 54
recruitment, 1, 6, 244–5
Red Cross, 55, 84, 117, 223, 246, 251, 255
Reims, 3, 13, 19–20, 208
reinforcements, 7, 13–14, 18, 20–2, 24, 26, 34–5, 41, 43, 49, 56, 63, 74, 77, 80, 88, 106, 115, 123, 132, 134, 144, 151–3, 155, 157, 160, 164–5, 182–4, 186, 188, 202, 205, 208, 219, 224, 226, 239
Remy, Commandant, 54–5, 111
resupply parties, 19, 69, 80, 91, 100, 102, 104, 106–8, 130–2, 180, 187, 191–2, 203, 206–7, 215, 218, 227
revetments, 31, 70
Richard, Second Lieutenant, 4, 49, 53, 262
rivers
  Aisne, xxi, xxiii, 20, 208, 210, 227, 257
  Meuse, xxii, xxiv, 12, 76, 78–80, 90, 93, 122, 143, 196, 216–17, 232
  Miette, 208, 210–11
  Moselle, 228
  Ourcq, 14
  Petit Morin, 14–15
  Retourne, 13
  Saar, 231
  Seille, 230
  Somme, 17, 77
  Yser, 21
Romains, Jules, xxv, 81, 240, 243
Rouquet, Private, 189, 238, 255

Saconin-Breuil, 227, 257
Saint-Cyr, 3–4, 35, 42–4, 49, 145, 161, 236, 246
Saint-Cyrien, 4, 12, 35, 226; *see also* Cyrard
Saint-Gond Marshes, 14, 17
Saint-Idesbald, 21
Saint-Médard, 12, 228
Saint-Waast, 228
Sainte-Catherine Hospital, 88
Sainte-Menehould, 6, 8, 49, 55–6, 84
Sainte Croix, 35, 39
Sainte Geneviève, 228
Salomon, Corporal, 13, 17–18
Saudrupt, 159, 163, 195
Second Position, 124, 129–30, 132, 136, 145, 158, 166, 171, 174, 177, 179–80, 183, 188–9, 211, 213, 255
Second World War, 236–7
Segonne, Commandant, 42
shell-shock, 71, 103, 114, 232
Sivry-la-Perche, 86, 125
Slaughter Wood, 34, 41, 46, 55–6, 226; *see also* Bois de la Gruerie
Smith, Leonard, 124
snipers, 28, 97, 104–6

Somme-Py, 6, 59, 62, 236
Spanish flu, 225
Steenstraet, 22–3, 43

tactics, 50–1, 72, 160, 202, 209–10, 224
tanks, 210, 212, 225–6
tear gas, 42; *see also* poison gas
territorials, 20, 22, 80, 164, 245
Thiaumont, 197–9
Tirailleurs
  Moroccan, 22, 59, 91
  Senegalese 258
Toland, Edward, 251
training, 3–4, 6–8, 11, 20, 34, 43, 49, 57, 72–4, 149, 160–1, 163, 195, 202, 209, 215, 220
  American troops, 224
Tranchée Couplet, 181, 183, 253
Tranchée de Foix, 146, 166, 174, 181, 183, 191, 253
Tranchée de Mésopotamie, 220
Tranchée des Zouaves, 127, 136, 148, 172
Tranchée du Chaume, 218
Tranchée du Ruisseau, 211
Tranchée Garçon, 127, 136, 166, 172, 181, 253
Tranchée Gilbert, 127, 135
Tranchée Guilbert, xx, 127, 135, 152
Tranchée Molina, 127, 135
Tranchée Perchenet, 220, 225, 228
Tranchée Perrenet, 127, 135–6, 152
trench foot, 23, 42, 71

trucks, 36, 80, 82, 86, 100, 110, 114, 124–5, 159, 165, 170, 195, 225
typhoid, 55, 69, 114, 164, 255

Valmy Quarter, 84
Verdun Brigade, xxii–xxiii, 88, 243; *see also* 84th Infantry Brigade
Verdun Hôtel de Ville, xxii, 88
Vésigneul, 73–4, 81
Vienne-le-Château, 36
Ville-sur-Cousances, 86
Villeneuve-lès-Charleville, 15, 18, 227
Villeseneux, 19
Voie Sacréev, 80, 125, 238

War Council, 25, 83, 160
water, lack of, 100, 104, 106, 186, 188–9, 191–2, 197, 204–5, 221, 227, 250
Westende, 21
Wilhelm, Crown Prince, 77
Wright, Gordon, 239, 259

Yser Canal, xxi, xxiii, 20–3, 25, 56, 203

Zeepanne, 21
Zeppelin, 39, 75
Zillebeke–Verbrande Molen area, 24
Zouaves, 22, 59, 91, 150